# Courtyard Housing

Courtyard housing is one of the oldest forms of domestic development spanning at least 5,000 years and occurring in distinctive form in many regions of the world. Traditionally associated with the Middle East where climate and culture have given shape to a particular type of courtyard housing, other examples exist in Latin America, China and in Europe where the model has been reinterpreted.

The book has four themes: history and theory of courtyard housing; climatic and environmental factors; social and cultural dimensions; and finally contemporary examples. The book argues that sustainable courtyard housing is possible and desirable; it offers technical, planning and design solutions that allow the courtyard house to meet a variety of social and commercial needs in the future. Areas addressed by experts include gender issues and courtyard housing, the culture of cities in the Middle East, the cosmology of the courtyard house, Islamic practice in the area of domestic construction and climatic imperatives.

This book demonstrates through discussions on sustainability and regional identity and via a series of case studies, that courtyard housing has a future as well as a past.

**Brian Edwards** is the Professor of Architecture at Edinburgh College of Art, Heriot-Watt University. He has a PhD from the Mackintosh School of Architecture at Glasgow University. With more than 16 books to his name, he has considerable expertise and experience in the area of sustainable housing urban design and architecture.

**Magda Sibley** is the Director of the Architecture undergraduate course at Liverpool University and the Departmental international links coordinator. She obtained her PhD in Architecture from the School of Architecture at the University of Sheffield. Dr Sibley has conducted various design workshops in cities such as Cairo, Amman and Fez, and has recently completed research projects (funded by the UK Arts and Humanities Research Board) on housing and public baths in the world heritage cities of Fez, Aleppo and Damascus.

**Mohamad Hakmi** is Dean of Architecture at Al-Baath University in Homs, Syria. With a PhD from Sofia University he has held several senior academic positions in the Middle East and is the author of a number of books and journal articles on architecture, urban design and heritage conservation. His research interests include high-density courtyard housing, an area of academic concern which flowed in part from his election a few years earlier as Mayor of the City of Homs.

**Peter Land** is Professor of Architecture at the Illinois Institute of Technology, Chicago. Educated at the Architectural Association in London, Yale University and Carnegie Mellon University, his research interests include high-density housing, low-energy design and courtyard typologies. He was the UN Chief Architect for the Lima Experimental Housing Project in Peru which features a neighbourhood of 450 courtyard houses.

# Courtyard Housing

## Past, Present and Future

Edited by Brian Edwards, Magda Sibley,
Mohamad Hakmi and Peter Land

Taylor & Francis
Taylor & Francis Group

First published 2006 by Taylor & Francis
2 Park Square, Milton Park, Abingdon, Oxon, OX14 4RN

Simultaneously published in the USA and Canada
by Taylor & Francis
270 Madison Avenue, New York, NY10016

*Taylor & Francis is an imprint of the Taylor & Francis Group*

Designed and typeset in Optima by Alex Lazarou, Surbiton, Surrey
Printed and bound in Great Britain by The Cromwell Press, Trowbridge, Wiltshire

*British Library Cataloguing in Publication Data*
A catalogue record for this book is available from the British Library

*Library of Congress Cataloging in Publication Data*
A catalog record has been requested

ISBN 0-415-26272-0

# Contents

Acknowledgements                                                                                      ix

Illustration credits                                                                                  xi

Contributors                                                                                          xiii

Foreword – Courtyard: a typology that symbolises a culture                                            xv

Preface                                                                                               xvii


**Part 1      History and theory**                                                                    **1**


1      The courtyard house: typological variations over space and time                                3
       *Attilio Petruccioli*


2      The shared characteristics of Iranian and Arab courtyard houses                                 21
       *Gholamhossein Memarian and Frank Brown*


3      The courtyard houses of Syria                                                                   31
       *E. Mahmoud Zien Al Abidin*


4      The courtyard houses of Southern Algeria                                                        39
       *Arrouf Abdelmalek*


5      The courtyard houses of North African medinas, past, present and future                        49
       *Magda Sibley*


**Part 2      Social and cultural dimensions**                                                        **63**


6      The power of the veil: gender inequality in the domestic setting of traditional courtyard houses   65
       *Reem Zako*

Contents

7   The role of privacy in the design of the Saudi Arabian courtyard house          77
    *Omar S. BaHammam*

8   The traditional courtyard house of Kuwait and the influence of Islam            83
    *M. Anwarul Islam and Nawal H. Al-Sanafi*

9   The cosmological genesis of the courtyard house                                95
    *Faozi Ujam*

10  The deconstructed courtyard: dwellings of central Oman                         109
    *Soumyen Bandyopadhyay*

11  The European perimeter block: the Scottish experience of courtyard housing     123
    *Brian Edwards*


**Part 3    Environmental dimensions**                                            **133**

12  Courtyards: a bioclimatic form?                                                135
    *Dana Raydan, Carlo Ratti and Koen Steemers*

13  The courtyard garden in the traditional Arab house                            147
    *Maher Laffah*

14  Climatic aspects and their effect on the dimensions of courtyards in Arab buildings    155
    *Hani Wadah*

15  The thermal performance of the internal courtyard in the hot-dry environment in Saudi Arabia    163
    *Khalid A. Megren Al-Saud and Nasser A. M. Al-Hemiddi*


**Part 4    The contemporary dimension**                                          **171**

16  Type as a tool: courtyard housing and the notion of continuity                173
    *Kevin Mitchell*

17  The geometry of single and multi-family courtyard housing                     187
    *Mohamad Hakmi*

18  Courtyard housing in Saudi Arabia: in search of a contemporary typology       203
    *Tarek Abdelsalam*

19  New design thinking for contemporary courtyard housing                        211
    *Yassine Bada*

20    Conclusions                                                                     219

21    Courtyard housing: an 'afterthought'                                            233
      *Peter Land*


      Bibliography                                                                    239
      Glossary                                                                        241
      Index                                                                           243

# Acknowledgements

The editors and authors wish to thank in the first instance the universities which have provided the infrastructure of support essential for the production of this book, in particular Edinburgh College of Art, Liverpool and Huddersfield Universities in the UK, along with Al-Baath University, Homs, Syria and the Illinois Institute of Technology in the USA. Many other academic institutions have through their staff provided papers and furnished research material on different aspects of the courtyard house. In this regard the editors wish to thank the many contributors who have persevered in this publication over a long gestation period for their patience.

Special thanks are due also to the British Council, the Arts and Humanities Research Board and the Aga Khan Foundation for the financial support provided for both the Syrian conference which forms the backbone of the book and associated areas of research. Without the partnership of academic institutions, cultural organisations and research councils, the ideas in this book would not have seen the light of day.

Finally, the editors wish to record their appreciation of the efficiency and professionalism of Spon Press in steering this project to fruition.

*Dr Magda Sibley*
*Professor Brian Edwards*
*Professor Mohamad Hakmi*
*Professor Peter Land*

# Illustration credits

M. Z. El Abidin   3.1, 3.2, 3.3, 3.4, 3.5, 3.6, 3.7, 3.8, 3.9, 3.10, 3.11, 3.12, 3.13, 3.14

Arrouf Abdelmalek   4.1, 4.2, 4.3, 4.4, 4.5, 4.6, 4.7, 4.8

T. Abdelsalam   18.1, 18.2, 18.3, 18.4, 18.5, 18.6, 18.7, 18.8, 18.9, 20.19

Agha Khan Trust for Culture   colour plates 1, 2, 3, 5, 6, 9, 10, 11, 12, 13, 14, 15, 16, 17

N. H. Al-Sanafi   8.1, 8.2, 8.3, 8.4, 8.5, 8.6, 8.8, 8.9

Yacine Bada   19.1, 19.2, 19.3, 19.4, 19.5, 19.6

O. S. BaHammam   7.1, 7.2, 7.3, 7.4, 7.5, 7.6

V. Ballampanos   11.7

S. Bandyopadhay   10.1, 10.4, 10.5, 10.6, 10.7, 10.8, 10.9

B. Edwards   1, 2.3, 2.5, 2.6, 9.1, 9.2, 9.3, 9.4, 9.5, 9.6, 9.7, 9.8, 9.9, 9.10, 9.11, 1.02, 10.3, 11.3, 11.4, 11.5, 11.6, 11.8, 20.1, 20.2, 20.4, 20.6, 20.7, 20.8, 20.9, 20.10, 20.11, 20.12, 20.13, 20.14

M Hakmi   17.1, 17.2, 17.3, 17.4, 17.5, 17.6, 17.7, 17.8, 17.9, 17.10, 17.11, 17.12, 17.13, 17.14, 17.15, 17.16, 20.18

Libya Air Survey   20.6

G. Memarian   2.2, 2.4, 2.7, 2.8, 2.10, 2.11

K. Mitchell   16.1, 15.2, 16.3, 16.4, 16.5, 16.6, 16.7, 16.8, 16.9, 16.10, 16.11, 16.12, 16.13, 16.14

Mitchell Library   11.9

A. Petruccioli   1.1, 1.2, 1.3, 1.3, 1.4, 1.5, 1.6, 1.7, 1.8, 1.9, 1.10, 1.11, 1.12, 1.13

D. Raydan   12.1, 12.2, 12.3, 12.4, 12.5, 12.6, 12.7

S. Santelli   colour plate 5

M. Sibley   2, 5.1, 5.4, 5.6, 5.7, 5.8, 8.7, 20.3, 20.15, colour plates 3, 4, 7, 8

*RIBA Journal*   11.1, 11.2

K. A. Al-Saud   15.1, 15.2, 15.3, 15.4, 15.5, 15.6, 15.7, 15.8

Skidmore, Owings and Merrill   3, 20.16, 20.17

R. Zako   6.1, 6.2, 6.3, 6.4, 6.5, 6.6, 6.7, 6.8, 6.9

H. Waddah   14.1, 14.2, 14.3, 14.4, 14.5, 14.6, 14.7, 14.8, 14.9, 14.10, 14.11, 14.12

# Contributors

**Arrouf Abdelmalek** teaches in the Department of Architecture at the University of Batna in Algeria. He has an M.Phil in housing design for arid zones and particular interest in the re-use of vernacular knowledge in contemporary design.

**Tarek Abdelsalam** trained as an architect in Egypt, has a PhD from the University of Huddersfield, and is currently in practice in Riyadh. His research interests include identity, cultural continuity and modernism subjects on which he has published several journal articles.

**Nasser Al-Hemiddi** is on the academic staff in the Department of Architecture and Building Sciences at King Saud University. Dr Al-Hemiddi has a particular interest in climatic aspects of courtyard housing.

**Nawal Al-Sanafi** was educated at the University of Kuwait and at Manchester Metropolitan University where she obtained her MA and PhD. She has a particular interest in the heritage of Kuwait, especially the conservation of traditional architecture.

**Yassine Bada** teaches at the Department of Architecture, University of Biskra, in Algeria. He has an M.Arch from Washington University in St Louis and a particular interest in visual perception and adaptation of public space in the settlements of southern Algeria.

**Omar BaHammam** is Associate Professor and Chairman of the Department of Urban Planning in the College of Architecture at King Saud Univerity in Riyadh. A Fulbright Scholar, Professor BaHammam has a PhD from the University of Edinburgh. He has a particular interest in sustainable and behavioural aspects of Saudi Arabian courtyard houses.

**Soumyen Bandyopadhyay** teaches in the School of Architecture at Liverpool University where he also received his PhD. His research interests include oasis settlements and the architecture of central Oman from historical, social and cultural perspectives.

**Frank Brown** is an architect and senior lecturer at the Manchester School of Architecture. Dr Brown has a particular interest in traditional building types and the morphology of cities, subjects on which he has published widely.

**M. Anwarul Islam** works at the Manchester School of Architecture and the Manchester Institute of Research and Innovation in Art and Design. His research interests include aspects of Islamic architecture, especially the evolution of house design in Arab countries.

**Mahar Laffah** teaches in the School of Architecture at Tishreen University, Syria. Dr Laffah has a particular interest in the environmental aspects of the courtyard garden.

**Khalid A. Megren Al-Saud** is Associate Professor in the Department of Architecture and Building Sciences at King Saud University. Dr Megren Al-Saud has a particular interest in climatic aspects of courtyard housing.

**Gholamhossein Memarian** is Assistant Professor of Architecture at Iran University of Science and Technology, Tehran. He is a Doctor of Architecture of the University of Genova and has a PhD from Manchester University.

**Kevin Mitchell** holds degrees in architecture and philosophy. He is currently a member of academic staff at the American University of Sharjah where he was Chair of the Design Foundations Programme and served as Interim Dean.

**Attilio Petruccioli** is Professor of Landscape Architecture and Dean of the School of Architecture at the Polytechnical University of Bari, Italy. From 1994–98 he was the Aga Khan Professor of Architecture at Harvard University and the Massachusetts Institute of Technology.

**Carlo Ratti** is an architect and engineer, and is presently on the academic staff of the Massachusetts Institute of Technology where he directs the SENSeable City research project. He is also active in practice and exhibited at the Venice Biennale in 2004.

**Dana Raydan** trained as an architect in the Lebanon and the UK. Her research at the University of Cambridge was into the potential of renewable energy in urban environments, a subject on which she has published widely. Dana combines architectural practice in London with teaching and research.

**Koen Steemers** is Director of the Martin Centre for Architectural and Urban Studies at Cambridge University. His research interests include aspects of environmental design in architecture, a subject on which he has published widely in book and journal form.

**Faozi Ujam** co-ordinates the PhD programme at Edinburgh College of Art/Heriot-Watt University. Trained as an architect and urban designer in Baghdad and Edinburgh, Dr Ujam's research interests span from cultural ecology to aesthetics and environmental psychology.

**Hani Wadah** is Assistant Professor at the Department of Architectural Design, Tishreen University, Syria, and is Visiting Professor at the University of Yemen. With a PhD from Poznyn University, he has a particular interest in the creative tension between tradition and modernity in Islamic architecture.

**Reem Zako** is a Research Fellow at the Bartlett School of Graduate Studies, University College London. Her research interests are in housing and social inclusion, especially the social dimensions of spatial configurations.

**Mahmoud Zein Al-Abidin** studied architecture at Yildiz University, Istanbul. His research interests include Turkish domestic architecture and Ottoman mosques, both the subject of recent books. He is currently working in Saudi Arabia on the restoration of traditional mosques.

# Foreword – Courtyard: a typology that symbolises a culture

## SUHA ÖZKAN

The idea of courtyards as a plan configuration goes back thousands of years to Neolithic settlements. In the beginning, the logic behind this type plan was mainly to provide a protective area from outside forces, such as invasion by human and wild animals. Over time, it has developed into a solid, logical configuration that maximises the built-up area in the urban context and allows controlled sunlight, especially in regions where it is abundant.

The courtyard as a house plan type exists extensively from China to Morocco. However, it becomes a generic typology in hot, arid, climatic landscapes and forms the basis of the urban pattern in the *madinas* of the Islamic World. Apart from the climatic and functional efficiencies of this plan typology, its cultural relevance is of equal importance.

In Islam, the house and residence are very private realms. Guests are welcome, but in many cases with a separation of genders. Guest access is well defined to designated areas in order to ensure genders do not mix. The courtyard is an exclusively private part of the house and is used only by members of the family. The courtyard, having been defined by the house itself and by high walls, is an 'open to sky' space and is used primarily as an extension of the living quarters.

This generic type of planning offers the possibility of very dense urbanisation and the maximum use of urban land. The compact nature of planning around a courtyard offers efficient use of the streetscape, as it is primarily used for accessibility and circulation. Therefore, by its nature in the historical districts of hot, arid regions, very high densities are achieved by low-rise architecture and an urban pattern that is humane. Substantial built-up areas and a high population density are the two basic aspects for the efficient use of the urban land. High population density creates intensely strong social interaction, and the low-rise architecture offers possibilities for the people to relate directly to earth and nature.

In a well-defined courtyard the two natural elements – earth beneath and sky above – ensure direct contact with nature. It has always been an important aspect of the comfort of a courtyard to include a monumental tree or a calm and cool pond. In many house types, the kitchen also opens to this space with an oven or a *tandoor* where the fuel is kept, and smoke is let out of the house immediately. Cooking is a major household activity for the women, and the preparation of food, cooking and, according to the season, food processing, like drying, pickling or other activities of food preservation, all

**Courtyard houses in Agadir, Morocco, by François Zevaco**

**Residence Andalous in Sousse, Tunisia, by Serge Sautelli**

take place in the courtyard. The courtyard has become a multi-purpose room where most of the activities of the family take place. The courtyard also provides a climatically controlled space from many of nature's unwanted forces, such as winds and storms.

In the Aga Khan Award for Architecture, three distinct types of courtyards have been interpreted in contemporary design vocabulary, and each of their generic values have had substantial influence on the contemporary design vocabulary.

In the first cycle of the awards in 1980, 10 of the 15 winning projects had various types of courtyards. Among these, Jean François Zevaco's courtyard houses for earthquake victims in Agadir, Morocco, is a generic type. The direct use of the forecourts as 'open to sky spaces' offers each and every house a small, manageable and pleasant open space, while also referring to the urban structure of the *medina* architect which accomplishes rather high building density in this housing.

In the 1983 awards, Serge Santelli's Residence Andalous in Souse, Tunisia, brought back from the Islamic era of Andalusia the richness of courtyard planning as a new planning discipline. His courtyards have most of the historical elements of the old palaces; water and well-groomed greenery, with well-treated hard surfaces which are the most important architectural elements of this project.

In Tuwaig Palace, Riyadh, Saudi Arabia, architects Basem Shihabi and Nabil Fanous of Omrania developed an idea of a courtyard that responds to the harsh desert climate of the country. The sinusoidal wall-like building defines and protects a courtyard which has lush, green intense landscaping that reminds us of another natural element in the region: the oasis. Tuwaiq Palace is not an interpretation of multiples of courtyards forming an urban pattern, but rather a big courtyard that embraces an oasis in the middle of the sandy Saudi desert scape.

Courtyard planning will remain a major design tool for architects and designers that enables them to link the present with history in uninterrupted continuity.

**Tuwaig Palace in Riyadh, Saudi Arabia, by Basem Shihabi and Nabil Fanous**

# Preface

The idea of a book on courtyard housing stemmed from academic collaboration between Al-Baath University in Syria and Huddersfield University in the UK. Cooperation in the area of architectural education and research between the two respective Departments of Architecture had existed for a number of years before the decision was made in 1999 to jointly host an international conference on courtyard housing. Studies suggested that the scholarship surrounding courtyard housing was not fully explored: neither was there sufficient systematic research into the contemporary application of the courtyard typology as a means of solving the problems faced today by rapid urbanism in the Middle East and elsewhere. Recent conflicts in the region and a greater regard for the concept of sustainable development also fuelled an appetite for re-establishing the importance of courtyard housing as a means of solving contemporary problems.

The conference on courtyard housing was well attended by academics and practitioners from the Middle East and beyond. Over a hundred research papers were presented over a three day period by academics and practising architects drawn from nearly forty universities from around the world. The conference held in Homs, Syria enjoyed the support of the Aga Khan Trust for Culture and the British Council in Damascus. Besides the papers there were visits to historic courtyard houses and to recent developments around Homs which, with the support of the Syrian government, had sought to revive the application of the courtyard form in both building and urban plans.

Although the papers presented at the conference were made available during the conference, it was felt necessary to disseminate a selection of them for wider use as essays in an edited book on courtyard housing. Four editors took on the task of choosing the papers to publish in book format and in guiding the project forward. These were Dr Magda Sibley from the University of Liverpool but formerly employed at the University of Huddersfield, Professor Mohamad Hakmi from Al-Baath University, Syria, Professor Peter Land from the Illinois Institute of Technology and Professor Brian Edwards at Edinburgh College of Art, Heriot-Watt University (also formerly employed by the University of Huddersfield).

The editors successfully attracted the UK publisher Spon Press to take on publishing the book. In this regard they are indebted to Caroline Mallinder, Publisher, for guiding the book to fruition with characteristic thoroughness and charm.

The aim of the book is simple: to make available recent scholarship on courtyard housing to a wider community of academics and practitioners than those who were able to attend the conference. In so doing, the editors and various chapter authors have sought to influence planners and designers to reconsider the benefits of courtyard housing in the context of modern day city building.

## Introduction

Courtyard housing is widely considered to be a responsive typology to low rise high-density urban housing and is an appropriate form of housing within contemporary mixed use sustainable urban developments. Too often Western models

1    **Traditional urban fabric based upon courtyard housing**

Although the subject of the book has a deep sense of historical legitimacy, the hope is to influence the present, and by implication, the future. The final part of the book, with chapters by Professor Mohamad Hakmi and Kevin Mitchell in particular, seeks to test the courtyard model in the context of contemporary housing in Syria and the United Arab Emirates. Hakmi's modification and hybridization of housing types shows that the courtyard model is inherently more flexible at an urban level than high-rise apartment solutions currently in vogue, and Mitchell's redesign of the detached courtyard house suggests that it is equally suitable as a replacement for the suburban villa. With this flexibility to different scales and types of site goes a better response to the harsh Middle Eastern climate and a more sympathetic accommodation of complex cultural and family needs.

Implicit in a book on courtyard housing is a concern for non-Western values and the pursuit of multiculturalism in

of urban housing are applied indiscriminately in locations where the climate, building methods and cultural traditions require something quite different. Not only are Western typologies such as tower blocks, linear apartment buildings and suburban villas built with scant regard to the social and cultural context, but the building regulations and planning law adopted by countries such as Egypt, Libya and Saudi Arabia are modelled on European practice. Hence traditional courtyard housing, which may have existed as the prime urban building type for perhaps two thousand years, finds itself contravening modern regulations.

This book seeks to challenge the basis upon which these regulations and practices gain their supremacy. It does so by taking three main perspectives on the courtyard house – the social and cultural context, analysis of historical models, and environmental and climatic response. By addressing in detail themes such as gender, privacy, environmental performance, energy and water conservation, the editors hope to present a case whereby the courtyard house is seen as representing a better model for sustainable development in the Middle East than imported housing typologies. As such the intention is to revive the courtyard house as a model and bring it up to date in terms of current legislation so that it can assume greater importance in the rebuilding and expansion of cities throughout the world.

2    **Courtyard house at Bastion 23, Algiers. Notice the fine craftsmanship**

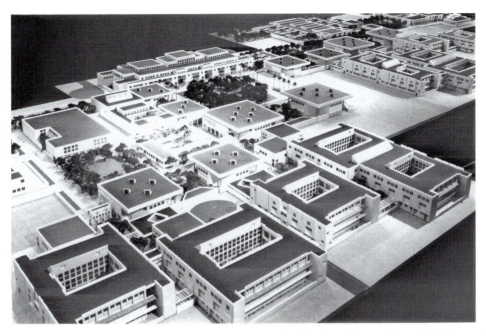

3  **The use of courtyards in modern architecture as here at Helwan University in Saudi Arabia allows climate to be modified by natural means (Architects Skidmore Owings and Merrill)**

architecture. The diverse background of scholars involved in this book confirms the internationalism of architectural discourse and the striving for the realization of what Hassam Fathy calls the 'alternative tradition'. The various perspectives brought to bear necessarily reflect local or regional agendas, but collectively they demonstrate the rich and complex panorama of ideas surrounding the topic of courtyard housing.

Although the chapters are brought together into themes which mirror current social and technological concerns, there remains an important aesthetic dimension to the book. Many of the examples of courtyard houses described are excellent specimens of craftsmanship and design. With their integration of gardens, fountains and buildings into a coherent whole, the traditional courtyard house is a work of architecture of considerable quality. Collectively, the ancient cities which contained these houses could be seen as works of art. In his book *The City as a Work of Art* the urban historian Donald J. Olsen suggests that certain cities are works of collective art expressed through architecture, landscape and civic design. This is certainly the case with Damascus, Tripoli, Fez and Aleppo. The courtyard house together with the mosque, dome and minaret are the main architectural elements of these cities.

The various authors in the book present arguments which generally support Olsen's thesis. It is the visual, spatial and aesthetic components that are the thrust of this book, although these themes often have their roots in social, cultural, climatic and environmental interests. In other books, buildings and the cities they create are normally discussed in the context of changing economic, technological and demographic conditions. The approach here is slightly different: this book gives equal weight to exploring the courtyard house from cultural and phenomenological angles as to technological and social ones. In this context light and space carry meanings which are at least the equal of material concerns such as construction and building services.

Cities are arguably man's greatest collective artefacts. They represent the society that created them but also embody the higher values to which their people subscribed. Their ideas and values fashioned the courtyard house just as comparable ones elsewhere shaped the detached villa or terraced (row) house. It is the interface between cultural values, climate and building design which is the core discourse in this book.

## Bibliography

D. J. Olsen (1984) *The City as a Work of Art: London, Paris and Vienna.* Cambridge, MA: Yale University Press.

Part 1

# History and theory

# 1 The courtyard house: typological variations over space and time

ATILLIO PETRUCCIOLI

## Introduction

Studies of the courtyard house rest on an ever-present ambiguity that tends to perpetuate the image of a generic and universal type, indifferent to the site and immutable over time. However, the work of Orientalists and Arabists, celebrating the courtyard as the heart of the *dar*, the extended family, have confused matters in architectural terms. Satisfied with generic symbolic and functional virtues, they have omitted structural and typological components that are essential to the full appreciation of the courtyard house. They have failed to recognize the historical phases which mark the change of the type and its various translations in different geographical locations.

In the following passage Vittorio Gregotti underscores the tectonic importance of the courtyard as an architectural act par excellence:

> The enclosure not only establishes a specific relationship with a specific place but is the principle by which a human group states its very relationship with nature and the cosmos. In addition, the enclosure is the form of the thing; how it presents itself to the outside world; how it reveals itself.[1]

Given the fact that the archetype courtyard house represents a primordial act of enclosure and construction, it is senseless to establish a primogeniture for something that is as essential to mankind as the wheel. Nevertheless, it is necessary to consider that every cultural region developed shelter and enclosure along different lines, through the choice of a specific elementary cell or by addressing the typological process in a specific direction.

This chapter seeks to describe the typological processes inherent in the evolution of the Mediterranean 'Islamic' courtyard house with reference to the forces intrinsic to the building plot. It will also discuss the complex problems found at the level of the aggregation of building types and the accumulation of the courtyard house into the characteristic Middle Eastern city.

## The courtyard house

In the typological history of the courtyard house there was a critical moment when a precursor marked off an area around a monocellular unit by an enclosing wall. After that the enclosing wall became a reference point, with an aggregation of more cells around a central space. Unlike the side by side placement of serial cells, the enclosure simultaneously suggests the final form of the courtyard house and emphasizes its inward looking content.

Much has been written about the sacred significance of the courtyard house. For example, it has been suggested that the courtyard of an Arab house evokes the Garden of Eden.[2] Gottfried Semper[3] associated the enclosure with a southern Mediterranean agricultural society that must struggle to coax a harvest from grudging soil and protect it from the elements; G. Buti used linguistics to tie it to Indo-European nomadic people. The type is, however, a generic domestic form of residence which independently evolved in various places from the Egyptian–Sumerian civilization to the Mediterranean, Asia Minor, and right up to the Indus Valley.[4] The closed and reinforced courtyard house is thus a product of cultural polygenesis dating from the Bronze Age, and it has endured in the Mediterranean basin in the form of the classical Roman *atrium* and Greek *pastas* house.

The kernel of the type is the concept of the organism or better, the specific balance between a serial and/or organic attitude of putting together forms that is the genetic patrimony of every culture. A courtyard house in Jilin, China, a courtyard house in Fez and a *domus* in Italica, Spain, are, however, deeply different in spite of a generic similarity. The Chinese house disposes its pavilions inside the enclosure in a scattered manner, scarcely related to the wall of the perimeter. The house in Fez lays out the elementary cells enmeshed along the border of the plot, while double symmetry controls the regularity of the patio, but without influencing the whole building. The *domus* in Italica disposes the cells around the peristyle in an organic way, ordered by a biaxial symmetry that crosses the whole building from the entrance to the exedra. Spaces have different sizes and are hierarchically composed in

a variety of ways, in spite of their superficial similarity as courtyard houses.

In order to better understand the courtyard model in all of its guises it is useful to introduce the fundamental typological differences between the courtyard house and the row (or terraced) house. The row house always lies on a road, faces onto it, and is directly accessible to it from the outside. Its pertinent area is behind, to be covered in subsequent stages as the area is filled in. The pre-eminence of the building site and the high property value attached to its facing front determine the dimensions of the lot, the front of which is equivalent to the size of the elementary cell, usually around 5 metres. The courtyard on the contrary has a superior sense of the familial territory, so that the form coincides with borders of the same territory. The same strict relationship to the road does not apply in the courtyard type, so any side of the lot can face the street without interfering with the internal organization of the house. A first building is even conceivable in which the courtyard is some distance from the road. The unbuilt area dominates the built area because the former must mediate between the inside and the outside of the enclosure as well as distribute the organism from within. Furthermore, the courtyard-house type lacks external openings: they appeared only recently in both East and West following a lengthy process and exclusively in urban areas. The fact that a room has only one source of light, that is, from the courtyard, limits its depth to 6 metres or less, depending on the size of the elementary cell used by a society. This depth can be extended by adding a ground-floor portico into the courtyard with a loggia on the upper level. The building bay can be doubled only by making an opening in the wall that faces the street, which then allows the portico to be enclosed.

Guy Petherbridge offers an overall explanation for the dispersal of the courtyard house type by distinguishing two varieties:

> The interior courtyard house, where the house encloses a courtyard, characteristic of urban areas; and the exterior courtyard house, where the courtyard borders the house, providing a protected area contiguous with the dwelling units but not enclosed by them.[5]

Andre Bazzana finds that this distinction holds for the Iberian peninsula; he calls the first 'block-like' and the second 'attached'. According to Bazzana the difference between the two is a result of a difference in economies: the exterior court-

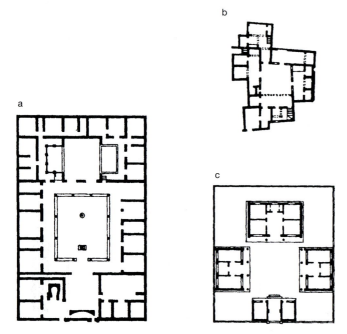

**1.1  Three examples of courtyard houses which appear identical but feature different uses of seriality: (a) house in Italica, Spain, (b) house in Fez, Morocco, (c) house in Jilin, China**

yard was used by semi-nomads; the interior courtyard, pat-terned after the ksar of the Sahara, was originally inhabited by sedentary farmers.[6] Such a schematic analysis is doubtful since it is conducted at too low a level of typological speci-ficity. Petherbridge's contrast between the two models assumes a stereotyped dichotomy between urban mercantile and rural society which does not allow for a plethora of inter-mediate positions. The contrast is artificial, and is less the result of an Orientalist mentality than the mindset of geogra-phers, who focus on territory, and historians, such as Torres Balbas, who concentrate on exceptions, such as the opulent and lavishly decorated homes of merchants and city officials.

Furthermore, if we look closely at local typological processes in the Maghreb and Andalusia, we not only discover the inappropriateness of the closed and open models of the courtyard house as an explanation, but also discover that the Arab–Islamic city, whose fabric gives the impression of being frozen in time between the thirteenth and eighteenth cen-turies, is not monotypological at all. On the contrary, it is based on a wealth of variants which in no way jeopardize the fundamentals of the courtyard type. Misconceptions like Bazzana's result from the fact that the idea of an elementary courtyard lingers in the cultural memory long after its physical demise, and is replicated and reused in the same area even after a substantial lapse of time.

## General nomenclature and typological process

The approach here is to begin the analysis of typological processes with the study of the rural version of the courtyard house. The limited changes it undergoes allows for a clearer reading of the matrix type and early diachronic phases. Generally there are two types of rural buildings in the same enclosure: the residence and the annexes, which include sta-bles and a shed for tools and farming equipment. Annexes are usually located on the side opposite the house. When the res-idential part of a structure in an enclosure is located on the side in front of the entrance, they either line up parallel to the entrance or on the perpendicular side. In North African Arab–Islamic urban houses, traces of these annexes coincide with the kitchen or *metbah*, the pantry area or *bayt el-hazim*, and the bathroom, and are grouped together on the side opposite the main bayt.[7] The dimensions of the enclosure are

in no way restricted by the built area: such interdependence is a feature mainly of urban planning. In the Mediterranean, one finds it in both the ancient Greek *pastas* house, whose frontage varies between 9 and 18 metres[8] and the Roman *domus*, whose frontage measures between 12 and 18 meters.[9]

Two key factors in the first phase determine the whole growth of the house: orientation and access. The building unit is oriented to take the greatest advantage of direct sun, which in the Mediterranean basin corresponds to a south south-western exposure. Because choice of orientation relates more to production needs than to the building itself, this rule is rigid in rural areas but not so strictly adhered to in towns, although it is still prevalent in the majority of the town houses. Given the prevalence of a southern orientation, the built part within the enclosure is either parallel or perpendicular to the road. There are then only three possible access variants for the courtyard house: in the first case, when the building is parallel and adjacent to the route, entry is through the building unit, where in order not to limit the distributive possibilities of the building, it is pushed to a far end. In the other two cases, the building is either opposite or perpendicular to the road, and the entry lies in the centre of the free side.

Figures 1.2–1.6 demonstrate situations that produce differ-ent diachronic variations, their relative processes, and the most interesting transitions in these processes. These transi-tions, in turn, are capable of generating parallel processes of synchronic variants which for reasons of space are not repre-sented in the various diagrams.

In the A 1-2-3 (Figure 1.2) series the elementary courtyard is gradually transformed as more and more of its area is covered, so that activities that once took place outdoors begin to take place indoors. This is achieved through the addition of rooms on the opposite side of the initial cell; these new rooms are then consolidated with a portico, after which the two parts are unified by a covered passage, and the process ends by form-ing a courtyard in the centre. Because the example in this series is single family, mezzanines and other possible vertical additions typical of different processes are not included, although it is common to reserve at least one cell with an inde-pendent external entry for newly-wed couples or house guests.[10]

In this first series, the house has a rather low level of spe-cialization. The plot size, even in an urban area, is large enough to allow division of function on a single level. Further hierarchies occur when an addition is made on the upper level or by acquiring adjacent courtyards to form a larger building

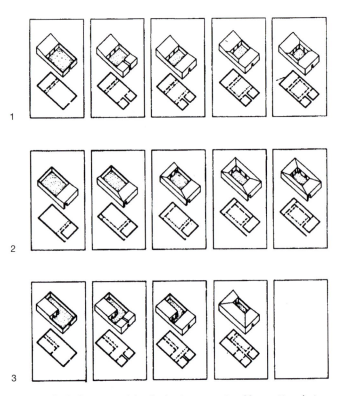

unit. This choice will not be an arbitrary one, but determined by cultural, political and economic factors. An important step in the process of making a house more complex and specialized occurs when functions other than residential ones are introduced. This can take place whenever a residential area comes into contact with a strongly commercial outlying area. The B 1-2-3 series (Figure 1.3) describes this development, which we shall refer to as a *taberna* process (from the Latin *taberna* meaning shop), a term first used by the Muratori school to refer to the commercialization of residential property. The appeal of commerce leads to the transformation of the front part of the courtyard house into shops, which is achieved simply by creating a new and direct access from the outside to the existing cells of the house. The *taberna* develops independently to the point that it becomes a row house on the edge of the road, where it behaves like an independent elementary cell: it is doubled in height by introducing a staircase and is elongated on the sides to form the embryo of a row-type tissue, which recalls the evolution of the monocellular unit as in the diagram in Figure 1.2. Where possible, the façade is doubled at the expense of the public road by adding a front portico.

1.2  **Typological process of the single-storey courtyard house (A series)**

1.3  **Typological process of the development of the courtyard house and shop into a multi-storey arrangement (B series)**

This process determined the formation of bicellular rows that, once codified, became the basis in medieval Europe for all the expansions in extra-moenia villages. The phenomenon occurred at Ostia Antica, Rome's trade centre, and was identified and described in detail by Alessandro Giannini.[11] Further additions occur as public space is occupied, a universal and elementary anthropic behaviour.

This phenomenon was widespread in the Middle Ages, especially in those Arab cities where the classical foundations – the forum and agora – had been swallowed up, leaving a bare minimum of road. In the linear souk of Islamic cities a strip of tiny shops provides the background for a residential tissue of patio houses. In the case of spontaneous first settlement, if the tissue cannot accommodate bicellular shops on the street front, it will allow demolition and substitution inside the house, ultimately resulting in a change in use.[12]

This process of progressively filling in a courtyard, which we might call the 'insula process,' coincides with the transition into multi-family residences of the earlier domus.[13] The C 1-2-3 series (Figure 1.4) describes this process: it begins at a side of the courtyard with a row of cells that doubles in height served by a balcony. The stairwell is strategically located in the portico of the original cell; by doubling the row on the side opposite, a single

stairwell can efficiently serve another balcony.[14] In another version, the stairs are provided for every single unit. If the open courtyard is eventually fully utilized, then it is reduced to a linear passageway. However, if the process begins on the side opposite courtyard C1 and C2, the tendency is to maintain a small square enclosure. The two processes do not take place independently of one another. On the contrary, commercialization of residential space (the *taberna* process) and the apartment-block phenomenon (the insula process) often occurred concurrently.

The insula process was triggered by two opposing tendencies. In a period of political or economic crisis, social upheaval causes a decrease in specialization; as the rich move out, their houses are occupied and subdivided by poor families. In a period of rapid economic growth, the city attracts new inhabitants, leading to land pressures and the need for major housing stock, which must be created by occupying the interior of existing houses. It should be made clear that building increment is a normal phenomenon that a society is able to control under normal conditions, but moments of marked social imbalance could generate pathological phenomena like wild encroachment or speculative phenomena like demolition and substitution of the courtyard house with denser apartment houses.[15]

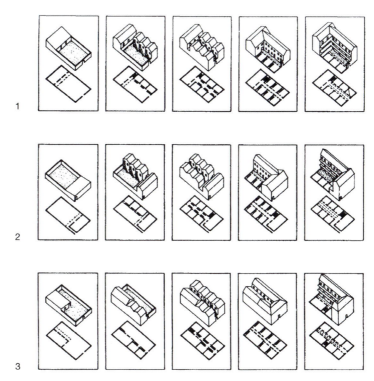

1.4 **An example of the growth of multi-storey, multi-occupancy courtyard housing with the incorporation of interior balconies (C series)**

1

2

3

In the Arab or Ottoman pre-industrial city the insula process occurred mainly in the limited cases of great metropolises, such as Cairo during the Ottoman period, because it was connected to proletarization, which is much less frequent in a medina of merchants and artisans, leaving light marks in the urban fabric.[16] The deep changes that occurred in Muslim society in the second half of the last century have mined the roots of the patriarchal structure of the family, and therefore constitute the main reason for the survival of the monofamilial courtyard house. The process of subdivision has assumed an exponential progression and no one medina is exempted.

Series D1, in which a whole module doubles, and D2 (see Figure 1.5), in which there is an increase of half a module, describe the fusion of two neighbouring units. The process is subject to any of five basic outcomes. First, an unhierarchized aggregation of heterogeneous courtyards; second, a simple joining of two plots by eliminating the dividing wall and making no further modifications; third, an unhierarchized aggregation of homogeneous courtyards; fourth, a union of two pre-existing organisms; and, finally, fifth, a closing of the courtyard on all four sides.

This overall process happens differently in cities in the Maghreb, where the expansion of a house is achieved through the serial addition of another autonomous organism. For instance, a very large house may have three courtyards, but they would never be rehierarchized as they were in the Italian Renaissance case of serial courtyard buildings being turned into a palace. Instead the resolution of the whole is achieved by making an opening in one of the walls of the acquired unit, which if it is smaller becomes a service unit, or by adding an elevated passage (sabat).

The E1-E2-E3-E4 (Figure 1.6) series describes processes relating to the subdivision of a lot. Each new portion, if uniform in

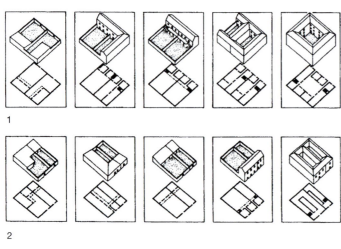

1.5 **The development of courtyard housing over additional modules in plan (D series)**

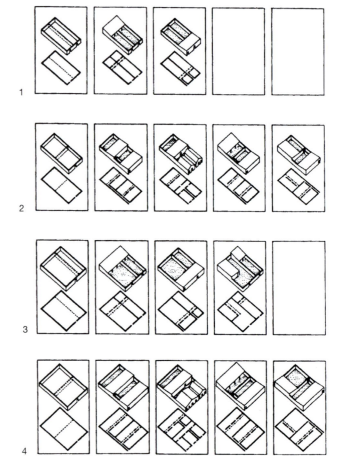

1.6 **Synchronic variations of the courtyard house as adaptations of earlier types (E series)**

size, will behave like an autonomous type, taking into consideration the presence of a corridor that must serve the innermost dwelling without being disruptive.

The purpose of Figures 1.2–1.6 is to reconstruct the principle phenomena tied to the typological processes of the courtyard house. The diagrams are not intended to serve as a universal model, and are therefore subject to adjustment. It should be kept in mind that every building culture behaves differently and privileges its own itineraries within the universal scheme. For instance, the elementary cell may vary in shape and size with the aggregation of cells depending on the level of organicity of the culture.[17]

## The courtyard house: structural organization

The Islamic house displays structural complexity in the organization of the building. The composition of the building can be analysed through examples taken from the same cultural area. The 'bourgeois' houses of Fez of the seventeenth and eighteenth centuries and their typological variants are the point of arrival of a long experimental route of the typological, technological and functional components that are the result of a profound artisanal know-how. With reference to construction these houses are built of wood and masonry materials, utilized in a fashion which simultaneously exploits structural and thermal properties.

For the purposes of the organizational analysis it is necessary to leave out the accessory spaces that are not essential to our discourse like minor partitions of rooms, encroachments that may close the courtyard, rooms acquired outside of the original plot, and hangings (tahal) or suspended passages (sabat). For a detailed description of all domestic parts the reader should consult the exhaustive work of Jacques Revault.[18] The typical courtyard house at Fez is a two-storey building with a patio closed on four sides with a double porch or external gallery. It is constituted of modular rooms called bayt or byt of elongated rectangular form and arranged along the edges of the plot. Secondary rooms like the kitchen, toilet facilities and pantry are in the corners, sometimes served by a corridor. The stair is located in the corner opposite the entrance. In more wealthy dwellings the vertical arrangement is doubled: a stair leads to the quarters of the guests, another to the harem and the terrace. The arrangement of the bayts at

the ground floor is replicated at the upper floor, where the spaces are served through an external balcony or through the rooms in succession.

The terrace, usually reserved for women and children, is closed by a high wall along the perimeter of the house, while a short parapet protects people from the void of the patio. In the mutual collaboration of the rooms, the plan of each bayt deforms itself in trapezoid forms in order to absorb the external irregularities of the urban fabric, but it maintains the walls at 90° along the courtyard in order to preserve the geometric regularity of the central courtyard or patio. The footprint of the patio tends to be rectangular or square and contains one or two axes of symmetry, marked by the position of the doors of the bayt facing themselves in the centre of the side of the courtyard. Sometimes a small fountain at the centre reinforces the virtual intersection of the two axes. The patio's symmetry does not involve the whole building (unlike the Roman domus or the Renaissance palace): the doors facing the courtyard are in asymmetrical relation to the single bayt.

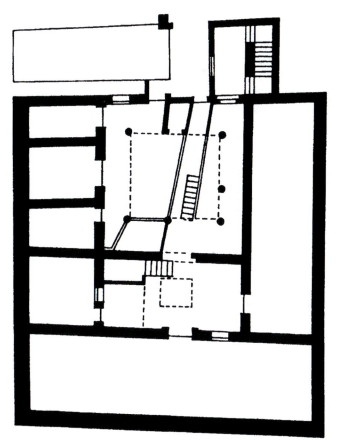

1.7   **A subdivided courtyard house in Essaouira, Morocco**

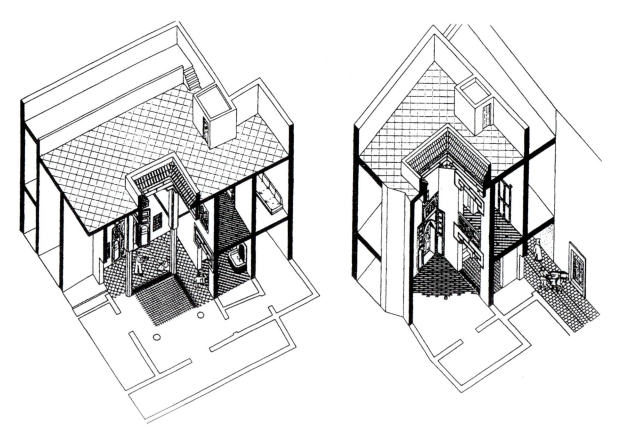

1.8 **Axonometric sections of courtyard houses in Meknes, Morocco**

The relation of the house to the urban fabric is accommodated the adaptation of the peripherical cells. On the contrary the patio or *wast ad dar*, with its elementary stereometry, its arrangement of the openings controlled by symmetry, is the centre of the composition and gives the essential light and air to the house. Moreover, the transition from the well of the patio to the sky, the special treatment of the overhanging attic with green-painted tiles and the wood decoration bestow to the patio the value of an autonomous sub-organism with its own rules of arrangement and construction.[19]

In the courtyard house types of Fez a system of structures, closed and heterogeneous, uses the elementary cell *bayt*, a tridimensional module of 220 cm max width – equivalent to a *kama* or a double arm of 165 cm plus a *dra* or cubit of 55 cm – whose length extends itself up to 7–8 metres. According to some scholars the width is determined by the ancient use of palm wood beams. Functionally the *bayt* has the highest flexibility and autonomy: it contains either the master bedroom or the living-room couches, and is separated from the patio by a monumental door. It can be easily transformed into an independent dwelling unit for a nucleus of the extended family.

The gallery on pillars or columns is an open structure that architecturally enriches the houses of the wealthier families as at the Abu Helal house. The inferior order sits on posts of masonry that define a porch of minimal width, which filters air

and light to the more internal spaces. A dense decorative pattern of stucco covers the surface, reducing its weight and making it vibrant under the sun. The upper balcony has the same function as the patio and porch of arranging the routes avoiding the passage in succession in the rooms. Rarely the gallery runs along the entire perimeter of the patio: more frequently it is a loggia in front of the main entrance.

The structural members are aggregates of elements that contribute to the formation of a system. The timber structure is constructed as a frame, i.e. an open discontinuous structure that works with interlapsed supports; the masonry structure is closed and continuous and it stands as a permanent element. The system of mixed structures in the Fez houses reached a high level of integration that required the alternate presence of the mason and the carpenter on the site. The foundations of the houses are in continuous masonry made of bricks and stone laid in mortar. Three sides of the house are normally shared with the neighbouring houses, the fourth, the façade, has no relevant openings apart from the main entrance. The unitarian treatment of the surface of the façade with a plaster of lime and sand reinforces the sense of continuity of the masonry involucre. In the interior the wall is permeable to light via small high-level openings and the façade is articulated by balconies. Normally the door is realized with an arch, more rarely all the wall is cut away revealing the ceiling.

Of all the combinations of elements the ceiling received particular attention, because it was the most visible manifestation of the building tradition in different cultural arenas. Conceptually the ceiling is the projection of the roof on a horizontal plane, therefore in those cultures that use gable roofs the ridge purlin will be transformed into a master beam.[20]

Timber horizontal structures in Fez have different levels of complexity. The simple ceiling of a *bayt* is made with joists – *ga'iza* – ranged with a span of 15–20 cm and encased at both extremes. On this structure sit floorboards of 1 cm thickness on which is spread a bed of mortar. Above sits a stratum of rubble materials (50 cm for the ceiling and 30 for the roof), on which are fixed the ceramics or the waterproof mantle. This type of structure guarantees the uniform distribution of weights on both main bearing walls, but can span only 220 cm

in width. To increase the span of the ceilings brackets were a common feature.

Galleries built on pilasters required a more complex structure of the ceiling in order to create a passage of 60–120 cm in width. In this case the joists are laid on a continuous beam that goes along the perimeter of the courtyard. The latter usually sits on two overlapping beams supported by the columns and cantilevered towards the centre to reduce the span. The beams are coupled with elements of the same section and assembled in the form of a box. The timber structure is faced with a cedarwood strip with floral motifs – *turi* – or cufic lettering – *qufi* – to improve its appearance.

In an alternative system the carpentry of the *halqa* touches the highest constructive level with a stratum of several overlapped beams and brackets. The stratum of joists then supports the parapet and the crown of tiles. The first system

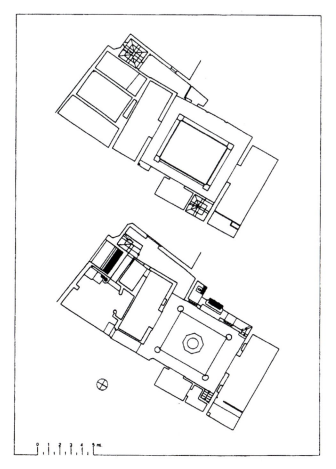

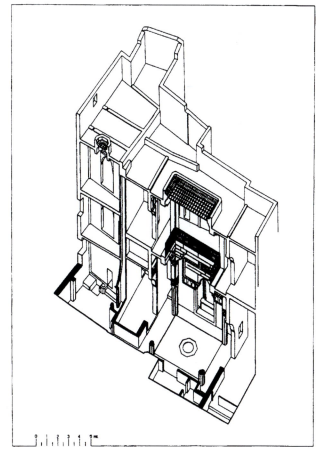

1.9  **Dar Bouhellal in Fez, Morocco, is an example of a double unit courtyard house**

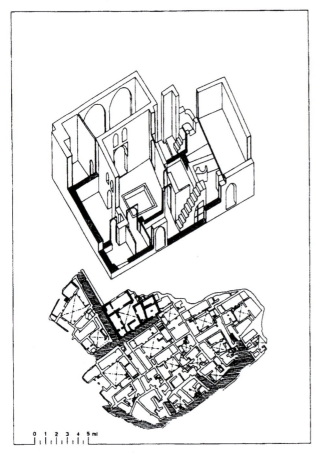

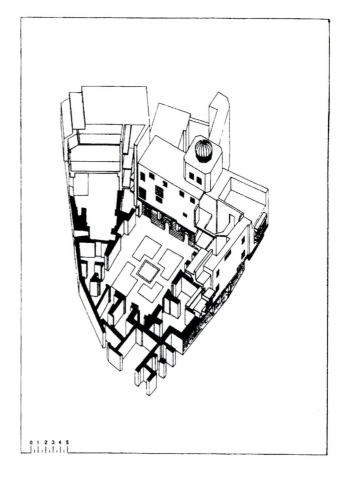

1.10　**Courtyard house in Sisaya, Murcia, Spain**

through repetition of supports has no theoretical limits of width, save those codified by the type of wood employed, and in Fez is about 18 metres. The second system is restricted to courtyards no larger than 5 metres.

In spite of the fact that the contrast between the light colour of the masonry and the dark of the cedar timber produces tones of great visual effect, the attractive appearance of the traditional courtyard house should not hide the strict functionality of the structural methods employed. The sequence of masonry–timber–masonry is a defining feature of the house type.

With regard to the masonry construction, the method of building usually gives priority to decorative bricks laid with various types of textures: double-header course, oblique, herringbone or toothcomb type, and built and with courses of stones and wood to produce façade patterns. The three main textures – horizontal, oblique and herringbone – could appear in the same wall with alternate sequence. Externally the wall is covered with plaster, internally with stucco, ceramics or plaster.[21]

The timber structures are composed of components always readable as separate entities by the tectonic deconstruction of the junctions. The openings within the arch are closed with a rectangular door 350 cm high which rotates on cylindrical pivots inserted in a hole in the floor and in the wooden frame (*rtej*).

## Is the courtyard house a universal archetype?

The discussion so far has been of typological processes in more or less synchronic terms. The next question is whether or not the courtyard house is a universal archetype. A number of scholars have observed that while the courtyard house is the leading type in many regions, such as Padania (the Po Valley), the Maghrebs and the rest of the Middle East, it is not uniformly dispersed throughout the Mediterranean and north Africa. While it is reasonable to assume that the territories of the Roman Empire were influenced by the *domus* up to at least the fifth century, no trace of it can be found in parts of central Italy (including Rome), southern Italy (excluding the Naples area), and Provence. Climate is not the underlying reason for the courtyard house – for instance, Milan and Aleppo share the same building type but not climate.[22]

Perhaps the reason for the dispersed presence of the courtyard house lies in the continuity of Byzantine culture; in areas that had been abandoned by the empire, the revival of

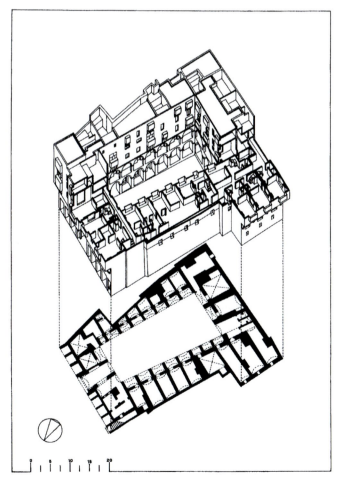

**1.11    Courtyard house in Kairouan, Tunisia**

building was based on a relatively retrogressive type almost consistent with the elementary cell. Within the Islamic world the courtyard type, inherited from Byzantium, also responded effectively to the essential Muslim requirements of secluding and protecting women. This explains the easy transition at the Umayyads from earlier Yemenite models to the courtyard type when they reached the shores of the Mediterranean.

In Europe the transformation of the *domus* led directly to the codification of the row-house type, while in precolonial Arab Islam this happened only sporadically. Thus in the Maghreb the insula type was reproduced imprecisely, and it was also always strongly resisted in North Africa whenever the core of the house, the *wast ad dar*, was threatened by population pressure. Even when faced with a population density of 500 inhabitants per hectare, the house responds by growing in height and subdividing in an effort to preserve the integrity of the courtyard.[23] Although the courtyard itself lost its 'cosmic' value (as Hasan Fathy called it) long ago in the transition from single-family to multi-family dwelling, it continues to represent in the mind of society an idea of unity that goes beyond its distributive function. The status of the row-house type provides the additional proof for Islamic resistance to the insula development in the Mediterranean. In the Islamic city the row house was generally considered a lower-class house, while in medieval Europe it was the house of the urban middle class. The row-house type nevertheless has a local history along the Arab Mediterranean coast, as the excavation of small bicellular row houses at Fustat attests, and is found in the form of the small cells built on top of shop fronts and lying in a protective screen on the border of a residential neighbourhood. Even today the row or terraced house is as alien in the region as the modern detached villa of Western origin.

A type cannot be stretched beyond the limits of spatial and cultural geography. The metamorphosis of the courtyard house has, therefore, limits which are social rather than spatial. Recent surveying of some densely populated medinas of North African urban centres (such as Casablanca where more than 1,000 residents were squeezed into a single hectare) has revealed that the subdivision of courtyard space is common. The tendency is to divide up the courtyard into thin access strips that can be covered when necessary. It has been suggested that as these are the seeds of future row or apartment houses, the changes will bring with them subsequent modification in the Islamic idea of the house and the city itself.[24]

In order to navigate in the archipelago of the typological processes involved in the evolution of the courtyard house, it is useful to deepen the concept of cultural area. A residential type is an expression of a culture, anchored in a territory, where a society has built its identity. To say that the residential type does not travel is a partial truth, that cannot hide the osmosis and interactions between cultures. Linguistic disciplines demonstrate that the more the frontiers are impenetrable, the more arduous are contacts and hence design transitions. Relationships are never linear but hierarchically ordered: in a region there are sub-areas economically and socially dominant, like the county town in the plains. It may happen that the 'bourgeois' families of the latter form their building types based upon the models in the main city. The concept is relative, since it is enough to enlarge the scale from the region to a larger geographical area. Inevitably, the county towns will be cultural debtors of the superior area – the State capital. If in the eighteenth century the plateau of Medea, the piedmont of Blida and the coast of Tipasa were dependent from Algiers, the regional capitals of Algiers, Damascus, Tripoli and Baghdad were acutely aware of the fashions of Istanbul, the capital of the Ottoman Empire. First discourses on the Mediterranean typological processes confirm a division between Levant and the areas west of the Mare Nostrum. In Southern Spain and Maghreb the patio house prevails, well represented by the houses of Fez we have just analysed. What makes them recognizable, as members of the same family is the *taddart*, the elementary cell that is permanent in time and space all over the west Mediterranean. Recent ethno-archaeological studies such as E. Laoust's work on central Morocco[25] have allowed us to isolate the *taddart*, a long narrow cell that is fairly consistent from tribe to tribe. It could be argued that the *taddart* is the elementary type that in the Maghreb becomes a component of spatial structure, the *bayt* – on a par with the Eastern-imported T-shaped room – of both rural and urban homes. As the dwelling of transients, the *taddart* is nothing more than the stone version of a tent, placed along the perimeter of a courtyard, just as nomads would place their tents around the douar leaving room in the middle for their animals.

Conversely, the fact that the western Muslim areas have abandoned the quadratic 5 × 5 metres cell has cut them off from the continuity of the Roman world. Houses in Venice, Lebanon, Turkey and Cairo will be used to trace typological processes because their evolution, taking up the thread of the discourses of centrality and tripartition of the rooms, can be reconstructed reasonably well from the beginning using archaeological evidence. Aside from its historic relationship with the eastern Mediterranean, Venice is a key area because it offers a clear reading of typologies and urban morphology. The work of Saverio Muratori, Paolo Maretto and Gianfranco Caniggia[26] brings an unparalleled wealth of information to the subject, from a systematic survey of the city's tissues and buildings to a refined theoretical analysis of the data.

1.12  **The sequence of separation in traditional courtyard housing**

## The Venetian courtyard house

A peculiarity germane to the layout of a Venetian house is that it tended to remain unchanged over time due to the special building techniques required by its unique foundations. The high cost of a foundation on wooden piles discouraged variations that involved moving the supporting walls. This and the natural resistance of property lines are the reasons why the so-called Byzantine layout has remained almost intact in spite of stylistic trends over time.[27] The first building type in Venice, the elementary *domus*, is identified in a room set against the northern wall of the enclosure and joined to a distributive element, the portico (*portego*). Planimetric location favoured this solution over two others, for these were houses belonging to fishermen, and the courtyards served as a transit point between water along one side of the plot and street along the other. The concern to connect the two sides of the plot determined the character and the peculiar typological solution in the Venetian house.

The type was at its most developed when a second storey and a *squero* (a service space used to store and repair boats) were added on, and the front of the building was closed up. At this point, the portego lost its original function and was transformed into the sala veneta, open at either end: it then served a distributive function rather than providing light. The placement of street access was symptomatic and can still be read today in either the zone of the portego or the courtyard, which was later covered by successive building bays that were often open loggias. The original bay, however, always remained solid and can be easily recognized even from the outside elevation. This would explain the recurring asymmetry of many Venetian façades such as those in Campo Nazario Sauro, Lista di Spagna and the San Stae area.

An early development in the insula process established the mercantile type, a combination house–warehouse with a front loggia; its systematic occurrence led to the important development of the street-courtyard type. When considered as an independent type, its use is evident in all of the city's major planned projects: the Rialto, the Cannaregio waterfront area, and the working-class housing financed by the Republic in the fifteenth and sixteenth century. This type is an extremely functional combination consisting of a street segment running from the water to the main overland route flanked on both sides by row houses. Once codified, it was used in all Venetian-influenced Mediterranean settlements, including Dubrovnik. The similarities between this tripartite layout with

a central crossing hall and both the Venetian plan and the Byzantine triklinium are striking.

## The Lebanese courtyard house

F. Ragette conducted important parallel research on the Lebanese house[28] in the 1960s that allows us to reconstruct a typological process in that area. This work is important for its breadth – it covers numerous mid-nineteenth-century examples, the layouts of which betray an archaic substratum. In Lebanon an elementary type with a vaulted square or elongated plan can be identified in many rural examples. Changes in the type are generated either by doubling the width or height. The first case can lead to a serial aggregation of up to five cells, with the addition of an optional front gallery.[29] The crucial point is where, even in rural houses, the intermediate cell became specialized and gave rise to the *iwan*, locally know as *liwan*. This is a room closed on three sides, and located either on the main level or an upper story. It is an architectural element known throughout the Middle East and is possibly of Persian origin.[30] The iwan played a central role in the formation of the Lebanese courtyard house because access to the house did not depend on it. Instead an external or side staircase fulfilled that function, allowing the iwan to became the ordering element for the whole house.

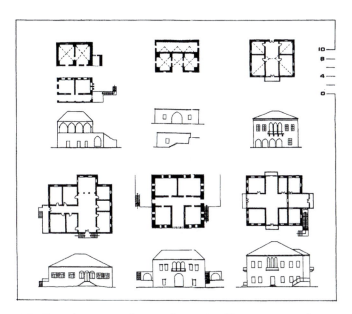

**1.13** **From elementary cell to complex courtyard house – an example from Lebanon**

There are two basic categories of liwan and cell combination: the first involves the association of elementary groups around the liwan arranged as a courtyard. As the point of departure for the geometrical axis, the liwan establishes hierarchy and scale: some variants have one, two, or three liwans, or two liwans and a portico. This category includes the Mamluk house in Aleppo studied by J. C. David, in which the iwan reaches monumental proportions.[31]

The second type involves the extension and modification of the iwan into a crossing hall. The iwan protrudes from the façade supported by a series of cantilevered and embedded arches. The room can be reached from either the front through a gallery or from the side by a corridor. This pattern of access results in two important variants – a T- or cross-plan – both of which were common in the late nineteenth century. The front access creates a main room and liwan separated by a series of arches, up to 20 metres long in large residences. Side access allows the two free sides to accommodate the liwan and a loggia or bow window. The similarity with the Ottoman sofa house is noteworthy, but it is not the goal here to discover a comprehensive system of relations,[32] or to answer the age-old question of the origins of the Turkish house. However, by referring to Sadat Eldem's research,[33] we can reach a limited conclusion with regard to the Ottoman Turkish house of what he calls the sofa type.

## The Turkish courtyard house

The Turkish house differs from other Middle Eastern houses in one important and determining way: the elementary cell or *oda* is consistently the ordering element and is formally and functionally autonomous. It establishes an extremely articulated planimetry in buildings which breaks up the envelope of the house by playing freely with the spaces. The sofa, a product of the predetermined disposition of the oda, is always expressed by a strong topological or geometric centrality and reinforced by symmetrical references. Given this, Eldem identifies the essence of the sofa type in its multifunctional mechanism and introduces an evolving classification. He begins with a hayat matrix type, and then follows with an exterior sofa type with the idea that an iwan can be placed between two odas to form a T-shaped sofa. Next a *kosk* (kiosk) is built opposite the sofa, with the latter becoming interiorized over time, and in the final phase there is both an interior and a central sofa. In these variants Eldem argues

that the courtyard continues to play a crucial role in house planning.[34]

The similarities between the tripartite layout with a central crossing hall of the mature Lebanese house, of the Venetian portego, and the Turkish sofa house are striking. Excluding important cultural migrations in one direction or the other, it is reasonable to say that the three parallel typological processes have been elaborated autonomously from a common fundamental type, the Byzantine *domus*.

## The Egyptian courtyard house

Cairo provides another important case study, for the complexity of its urban structures results from the long stratification of the tissues and the specialization of the types. With the exception of some aristocratic houses and grand residential complexes, the fabric of the city has been totally replaced. Although a reconstruction of the processes will inevitably be incomplete and in need of adjustment, the history of the Egyptian courtyard house can be traced back using the archaeological and documentary evidence of the *waqf*. The relatively recent excavations at Fustat[35] led by Scanlon reveal a wide array of types that incorporate earlier discoveries made by Gabriel.[36] Gabriel offers the following description of ninth-century courtyard houses that appear to be based on a model from Samarra in Iraq.

> Most early houses are based on a composition of two perpendicular axes radiating from a central courtyard. A portico with three recesses lines one side of the courtyard: on the other three sides lie several iwans of varying depths; at times they constitute real rooms but in general are simply modest recesses or even flat niches. The triple-bay portico that leads to the main living quarters is usually oriented east; it never faces due south or north.[37]

Little evidence exists to help us shed light on the transition from the early courtyard houses of Fustat to the Mamluk qa'a: no archaeological remains of Fatimid-era houses exist, with the exception of the schematic plan Pauty published of the four-iwan courtyard of the Sayyidat al-Mulk palace. Although the proportions are grander, the same elements are present: a composition on two axes; portico and salon on one side; open iwan on the other three.

A relief on the reception hall of the Ayyubid palace (dated c. 1240) on Rawda Island provides the plan of a house of two T-shaped rooms joined to a courtyard. The dimensions of the room are relatively close to those of Fustat courtyards, and correspond to the durqa'a of fourteenth-century Mamluk houses. The qa'a of the palace at Dardir described by Creswell[38] as a closed rectangular hall illuminated from above by a cupola on the central axis could be interpreted as a later phase in which the courtyard was covered. The hypothesis is plausible and analogous to similar processes: for example, the derivation of the 3–6–3 metres religious structure from the covering of the atrium of the *domus*, once thought to be an imitation of the model for the 6–12–6 proto-Christian basilica, the first to be codified.[39]

In the reconstruction of the maq'ad, we do not consider the north-facing upper-storey loggia as an independent type because it is incapable of formal autonomy from the Mamluk dar with which it combines to make up a system. A combination of two qa'as and a maq'ad can be found on the uppermost story of the Manzil Zaynab Hatun, an affluent dar from the reign of Qaytbay (1468–96).[40] The structure has two entrances: they lead to two separate apartments of unequal size which face the same courtyard. If the reading of the plan is correct, this example represents an important stage in the rise of the bourgeois house. The annexes were intended as rental property.[41] As the durqa'a becomes more important to family life the courtyard's importance decreases. Eventually it becomes little more than a passageway, along which various activities took place and different forms were imposed. During the Ottoman period in particular the dar was reduced to an informal composition of volumes centred on a void.[42]

The fact that there is a qa'a in every building confirms that the courtyard type was the leading model in the typological processes of Cairo. It is especially distinctive in a certain type of collective residence known in Cairo as a *rab*. There were two types of collective residence in Ottoman Cairo: the *hawsh* and the *rab*.[43] The first was a large enclosure, sometimes as large as an entire block, given over to the poor where they can put up some sort of shelter. More a shanty town than anything else, the building tissue was easily reabsorbed in more recent times and reapportioned without leaving any obvious traces.[44] The second type was closer to the modern version of a middle-class residential apartment complex. It was formally structured and consisted of a series of apartments derived from the qa'a, distributed around a courtyard in duplexes or sometimes triplexes. Each apartment included a portion of the terrace,

the only external outlet for the residence. Often a rab was next door to a wakala caravanserai, in which case the ground floor and mezzanine of the complex were used for storage and business transactions and the upper stories were purely residential. The apartments opened onto the landings of a series of stairways that led to the outside. In this way the autonomy of both areas was maintained. This layout is legible on the outside of the building through the surface punctured with windows and mashrabiyyas; it rested on a solid rustic stone base with a full-height monumental entrance cut into it.

Despite differences in nomenclature, the ritual and sequences of use of the traditional qa'a were largely the same, whether located in palaces or more modest houses. The meeting of Ottoman culture and local customs at the time of Muhammad Ali (around 610 AD), however, produced a new type, the fasha.[45] A combination of a central hall and grand staircase, it was used in large buildings and condominiums. The distributive hierarchy of the building began with a large courtyard from which a number of different stairways led to various fasha. These in turn acted as internal covered courtyards, onto which the individual apartments open, and in which the common service areas were located. The layout of the apartment was similar to that of the rab: an elongated living room was divided into a vestibule, reminiscent of the durqa'a, and an iwan with a projecting balcony. The niches of the qa'a were large enough to function as secondary rooms.

Perhaps the most important lesson of the typological process in Cairo is that it elaborates the parallels in the progressive specialization and hierarchization of the urban tissue and the complex growth and changes in the courtyard house. In the modern history of Cairo, the passage from the first Fatimid settlement to the Mamluk city and then the Ottoman metropolis is mirrored by the changes in the courtyard house. Adaptation based on variations of the courtyard house in the qa'a (a more compact residential type subject to insertion either in a house, or a palace, or a rab, or even a modern condominium), joined to make Cairo a special place.

## Conclusion

As a synthesis it might be useful to begin by emphasizing that the terms 'serial and organic' represent the premise behind any rigorous reading of the built environment. Every civilization has as part of its own cultural expression a different way of putting together objects or components of a set, which ranges from a maximum of casual seriality to a maximum of organicity. For this reason, while an archetypal form like the courtyard house, the product of polygenesis, is different in plan in the Maghreb and in the Roman atrium house, this should not disguise the universal nature of the type.

The domestic cell, the initial matrix in the evolution of the courtyard house, exists as a largely standard dimensional element irrespective of cultural origins. The basic cell can evolve through successive duplications to form a row house, apartment house or courtyard dwelling. The courtyard house, however, requires attention because it is the residential type which responds simultaneously to cosmic, cultural and climatic forces. As such it is the main residential type of the Arab region, although it enjoyed a form of parallel evolution beyond the Middle East. Of particular significance are the two processes of commercial specialization (the *taberna* process) and subdivision and fragmentation (*insula* process), which are at the root of any phenomenon of the metabolization into the dynamic cities of the Arab world.

With regard to different cultures, the similarity in the courtyard houses of Syria, Lebanon, Turkey and Venice does not represent, as some suppose, a phenomenon of cultural osmosis, but the sharing of a common taproot in the Levant. Hence these houses share in the basic genetic type or *substratum* of the *domus*. On the other hand courtyard houses of Cairo display different characteristics where the qa'a slowly evolves into the vestibule of the modern apartment. In the case of Algiers, an alien European culture violently combines with a local one to produce a radical change in favour of imported building types (the apartment) and aggregations (blocks) based on open streets as opposed to closed courts.

From both Cairo and Algiers we can learn the important lesson that it is not the basic domestic cell that produces the courtyard house but how the cell is put together. The resolution of the public realm (street) and the private realm (cell) in designs which exploit both plan and section to produce shelter and privacy is the essence of the courtyard house.

## Notes

1   V. Gregotti, 'Editoriale', *Rassegna*, 1 December 1979, 6.

2   J. E. Campo, *The Other Sides of Paradise: Explorations into the Religious Meanings of Domestic Space in Islam,* Columbia: University of South Carolina Press, 1991; P. Oliver, *Dwellings: The House Across the World*, Austin: University of Texas, 1987; G. T. Petherbridge, 'The house and society', in *Architecture of the Islamic World: Its History and Social Meaning*, ed. G. Michell, London, 1978, Thames and Hudson, pp. 193–204.

3   G. Semper, *The Four Elements of Architecture and Other Writings*, Cambridge, Cambridge University Press, 1989.

4   G. Buti, *La casa degli Indo-europei. Tradizione e archeologia*, Florence, Sansoni, 1962.

5   G. Petherbridge, 'The house and society', p. 176.

6   A. Bazzana, *Maisons d'al-Andalus. Habitat medievale et structures du peuplement dans l'Espagne orientale*, Madrid, Espasa Calpe, 1992, p. 169. For a more general discussion, see C. Flores, *Arquitectura espagnola popular*, 5 vols, Madrid, Espasa Calpe, 1973.

7   J. Revault, *Palais et demeures de Tunis XVIIIe et XIXe siecles*, Paris, Sindbad, 1971.

8   More precisely, 9 m and 18 m façades are found at Priene in two different quarters; 15 m at Olinto and Kassope; 18 m at Dura Europos, and even 21 m at Abdera. The oversized façade of the last example can be explained by the fact that the courtyards there line up with the predominant side parallel to the route onto which the entrances open. W. Hoepfner and E. L. Schwandner, *Haus und Stadt im Klassichen Griechland*, Munich, Deutsche Kunstuerlag, 1994.

9   On Roman metrology, see A. Martini, *Manuale di metrologia*, Turin, 1883.

10  A non-commercial use derived from the taberna process is found in the Maghreb in the annex to the dar – called an *ali* in Tunisia and Algeria and a *masriya* in Morocco.

11  A. Giannini, 'Ostia', *Quaderno dell'Istituto di Elementi di Architettura e Rilievo dei Monumenti* vol. 4, p. 36 ff.

12  Alexandre Lezine notes that in a Tunisian block on rue de Tamis, three courtyard houses were transformed in this way after the seventeenth century. *Deux villes d'Ifriqiya*, Paris, Editions Ceres Productions, 1970, p. 160.

13  Some classical archaeologists call any tall building an insula in order to distinguish it from the *domus*; others use the term to mean a block.

14  The balcony in a courtyard that has undergone the insula process gives the maximum result in so far as it allows a single staircase to provide access to many residences.

15  On typological substitutions and their corresponding social features in old Cairo, see L. Christians, O. Greger, F. Steinberg, *Architektur und Stadtgestalt in Kairo*, Berlin, 1987, especially the section on the Husayniyya quarter, 84 ff.

16  A question that arises is that of family structure. The dar, especially in old cities, was associated with the extended family – a structure closer to the Latin idea of *gens* than to the modern nuclear family. The growth of a family generates new units, often producing building complexes.

It is not unusual to find that over time an extended family grew so numerous as to generate its own neighbourhood.

17 A more organic area will tend to organize along a central or dividing axis; the corner cell can be part of a larger rectangular cell (as in the Maghreb) or part of a unitary composition (as in Pompeii).

18 A detailed description of the domestic architecture of Fez can be found in the exhaustive work of Jacques Revault: J. Revault, L. Golvin, A. Amahan, *Palais et demeures de Fes: 1. Epoques merinide et saadienne (XIVe–XVIIe siecles)*, Paris, 1985.

19 The archetype for the skifa is found in the so-called Door of the Spirits in the Chinese house; a wall recessed with respect to the external wall and perpendicular to the access axis of the courtyard. In addition to this example, the distributive element is also apparently found in Semitic regions.

20 The ceilings in Essaouira are very different from those in Fez. The beams are of thuja rather than rare wood, and are no bigger than 3.2 metres. They support a secondary structure covered with a layer of tassuit branches. The floor is made by covering a layer of dry leaves with a mixture of mortar and earth.

21 Some of the different patterns found in bricklaying include curtain, cross, oblique, herringbone, double herringbone, and stone and wood inlays. 'Schema directeur d'urbanisme de la ville de Fes', dossier technique IV, 2, in *Les techniques traditionnelles de l'architecture et du decor a Fes*, Paris, 1980.

22 Theorists of sustainable technology claim that the courtyard is capable of thermo-regulation. G. Scudo, 'Climatic design in the Arab courtyard house', Technology. From tradition to innovation, ed. A. Petruccioli, special issue of *Environmental Design*, 1988, no. 1, 82–91.

23 In Algiers a metal screen is ingeniously placed over the courtyard to act as both a surface to be walked on and a covering in case of rain. This creates two insulae, one on top of the other, while still keeping the courtyard as a global space inside the house.

24 A. Petruccioli, *Dor-es-Islam: Architecture du territoire dans les pays islamique*, London, Brill Academic/Routledge, 1998.

25 E. Laoust, *L'habitation chez les transhumants du Maroc central*, Paris, 1955. See also R. Riche, 'La maison de l'Aures', *Cahiers des arts et techniques d'Afrique du nord*, vol. 5, 30–6.

26 S. Muratori, *Per una operante storia urbana di Venezia*, Rome, 1959; P. Maretto, *La casa veneziana nella storia della città dalle origini all'ottocento*, Venice, 1986.

27 P. Maretto, *L'edilizia gotica veneziana*, Rome, 1961.

28 F. Ragette, *Architecture in Lebanon*, London, Chalto and Windus, pp. 25–27.

29 H. De Beyle, *L'habitation byzantine*, Paris, 1903; A. Deroko, 'Quelques reflections sur l'aspect de la maison byzantine,' *Actes du Congres international d'etudes byzantines, 1955*, Istanbul, 1955, 124-5.

30 There is considerable debate over whether the iwan is the product of an autonomous evolutionary process – a local interpretation of a pre-Islamic idea familiar throughout the Orient – or simply an imported model. A Persian term, iwan (liwan in Arabic), describes a space – dependent or independent – closed on three sides by walls and completely open on the fourth. It is usually vaulted. The form can be applied to a platform or an entire building. For a detailed discussion of the monumental iwan, see Iwan in the *Encyclopaedia of Islam*, 2nd edn, London, Brill.

31 J.C. David, *Le waafirp, as a Alep* (1063–1653) Paris, Institute Francais de Parras 1982.

32 M. M. Cerasi, *La città del Levante*, Milan, 1986, 176 ff.

33 S. H. Eldem, *Turkish House: Ottoman Period*, vol. 1, Istanbul, Eserlerin, 1984.

34 Ibid., pp. 26–31, for the planimetric drawings, in part reproduced in figure 68. Eldem vehemently rejects the idea of a marked Byzantine influence, arguing that no trace of the Byzantine house exists in Istanbul. Nevertheless the similarity with the Byzantine type called triklinium is striking.

35 G. T. Scanlon, 'Fustat expedition: Preliminary Report 1965', *Journal of the American Research Center in Egypt* **5**, 1966.

36 A. B. Bey and A. Gabriel, *Les fouilles d'al Foustat et les origines de la maison arabe en Egypte*, Paris, E. De Boccard, 1921.

37 Ibid. pp. 276–9.

38 K. A. C. Creswell, *The Muslim Architecture of Egypt*, 2 vols, Oxford, Oxford University Press, 1959, p. 208.

39 That Santa Maria in Antiqua (located in the Roman Forum) is directly derived from a *domus* is evident when comparing the planimetry of the church with that of the so-called Surgeon's House in Pompeii. Similar analogies exist throughout the Mediterranean culture area, particularly in Syria.

40 J. Revault, 'L'architecture domestique du Caire a l'epoque mamelouke XIII-XVI siecles,' *Palais et maisons du Caire, 1. L'epoque mamelouke*, ed. J. C. Garcin, B. Maury, J. Revault and M. Zakariya, Paris, 1982, pp. 108–9.

41 Both Andre Raymond and Nelly Hanna discuss the important consequences this has for the urban whole. N. Hanna, 'La maison Waqf Radwan au Caire', *L'habitat traditionnel* **1**, 61–77.

42 D. Behrens-Abouseif, 'Alternatives to Cadaster maps for the study of Islamic Cities,' Urban Morphogenesis, a special volume of *Environmental Design*, ed. A. Petruccioli, 1993, nos 1-2: 92-5; and idem, 'Notes sur la function de la cour dans la maison moyenne du Caire ottoman,' *L'habitat traditionnel* **2**: 411–18.

43 In *Great Arab Cities in the 16th–18th Centuries* (New York, New York University Press), 1984, pp. 323–6, Raymond describes the hawsh and its presence throughout the Ottoman Empire. According to Clerget

(op. cit., 1, 312) each hawsh in Cairo was village-like and housed thirty or forty families. There were many hawsh in the city and suburbs of Aleppo according to the traveller A. Russell, who describes them as 'a wide space surrounded by a certain number of low, mediocre dwellings of two or three rooms each. The common area is haphazardly paved, with the exception of the space in front of each house . . . There are no fountains but there are numerous wells'. A. Russell, *The Natural History of Aleppo*, vol. 2, London, G. G and J. Robinson, p. 1794, 36.

44  Jean Claude David located what is probably of series of Ottoman-period hawsh in the Qarleq quarter of north-eastern Aleppo; J. C. David, 'La formation du tissu de la ville arabo-islamique: apporte de l'etude des plans cadastraux d'Alep,' *Urban Morphogenesis*, 138–55.

45  Olivier Blin, 'Le Caire XIX-XXe siecles. De la fasaha a la sala comme modeles,' *Les cahiers de la recherche architecturale 20–21*, 1987, pp. 96.

# 2 The shared characteristics of Iranian and Arab courtyard houses

GHOLAMHOSSEIN MEMARIAN AND FRANK BROWN

## Introduction

A comparative study of Iranian and Arab courtyard houses can be undertaken from many different points of view – religious, social, cultural, climatic, technological, economic – all of which provide useful insights. The traditional courtyard house was the product of many diverse influences, but to deal with these adequately would take us well beyond the space available. To make the study manageable, we concentrate on the two determinants of built form: the architectural–climatic and the cultural–religious.

As a starting point it is instructive to note the similarities in architectural terminology throughout the Middle East. Persian words such as *ivan* (a semi-open space or veranda), *talar* (large veranda) *sardab* (full basement) and *badghir* (wind-catcher) have been adopted by the Arabic language (Shooshtari 1969). Conversely, Arabic terms such as *shenashil* (latticed and supported balconies), *tarme* (veranda), *majlis* and *mozif* (men's reception rooms) have become absorbed into Persian usage, particularly in the south and south-west of Iran, where there is a strong relationship with the neighbouring Arab countries. As will be shown, a strong cultural relationship has existed between Iran and its Arab neighbours over the centuries. Some of the architectural terms noted here will appear in the discussion later in this paper and are indicative of the transcultural language employed.

This chapter is divided into two main sections, the first of which provides a background to the use of the courtyard in Iranian architecture. The second section focuses on the shared characteristics of Arab and Iranian courtyard houses in

terms of response to climate and patterns of family privacy and hospitality, which are customary in both traditional Iranian and Arab cultures. These two insights are necessary to ensure that function and meaning are dealt with in an integrated fashion.

## The courtyard: background

There is evidence that houses with courtyards existed in Iran around 8000 years ago. These have been excavated in the Ghazvin region (to the north-west of Tehran). Here the rooms were positioned on one side of the courtyard, and included living spaces, stores and barns (Malek-i Shahmirzadi 1986). The courtyard was also an important architectural feature in the later Mesopotamian civilisation. There are a number of surviving buildings with courtyards from both the pre-Islamic and the Islamic period. These include the original building of the Chogha Zanbil from 1250 BC (Ghodar 1978); the 'Suhkte' building in 'Tepe Hesar', Damghan, from 1000–800 BC (Malek-I Shahmirzadi 1988); the 'Susa' palace of Dario of the Achaemenid dynasty from 550 BC; the 'Asur Palace' from the Parthian period; the 'Firuz Abad' Fire Place (third century AD); the Palace at Sarvistan (fifth century AD); the Jami Fahraj Mosque (eighth century AD); the Jami Mosque at Shiraz (ninth century AD); the Nuo Mosque at Shiraz (thirteenth century AD) and the Khan Madresseh at Shiraz (seventeenth century AD). These examples confirm the longevity of the symbiotic relationship between courtyard and house in Middle Eastern society.

2.1 **Nineteenth-century view of Baghdad showing a house with shenashil (after J. Dieulafoy)**

courtyard is a fenced plot within which the buildings are placed: its primary function is to define the boundary of the property. The dwelling consists of a number of structures, such as the house, barns and stores, which are effectively surrounded by the courtyard. The fence separates the yard from other houses and allows the inhabitants of these houses to directly observe their farms, which were usually close at hand. For this reason, massive climatic modifying walls are unnecessary. In the hot-humid zones of southern Iran and parts of Iraq and Saudi Arabia, on the other hand, the courtyard has an important role to play in air circulation and cooling. Cool winds are channelled through several openings in the house and then through the courtyard and out through other openings on the opposite side. This helps to keep the house comfortable in summer, not only by enhancing ventilation by the thermal capacity of the walls themselves.

In typical Iranian and Arab courtyard houses, the courtyard performs a number of these functions but rarely all at once. Suites of habitable rooms and other spaces (e.g. stores) commonly surround the courtyard and, in the compact urban texture of historic towns such as Shiraz, Yazd and Isfahan, the house is usually bounded either by neighbouring dwellings or by narrow streets. Access could be circuitous and, for reasons of privacy, openings on to the external spaces were avoided. The house was therefore entirely inward-looking and the courtyard became a small garden, which, with its pool, provided a cool space in the spring and summer. As we shall see, seasonal rooms, private and reception areas are organised around different parts of the courtyard, which serve to relate

The courtyard, however, does not always perform the same function in domestic architecture. Its role differs from one region to another in both Iran and in neighbouring Arab countries. By reference to variations of types, it is possible to identify the following functions of the courtyard:

- the demarcation of limits of the property
- the definition of a place of privacy for the family
- the unification of spaces and elements in a house
- the provision of a circulation element
- the creation of a garden or cool place
- the promotion of ventilation (Memarian 1993).

These functions are sometimes treated separately and sometimes work in combination. For example, in the rural houses of the Ghilan region, in the cooler north of Iran, the

2.2 **Detail of shenashil at courtyard house in Bushire, Iran**

2.3 **Shenashil at a house in Hama, Syria**

these different spaces one to another. Climatic and organisational functions can be seen in other Iranian cities, e.g. Kashan, Kerman and Bushehr, and in the cities of Kuwait. The difference from one city to another lay in the particular character and disposition of the interior elements, such as the main winter room, the *talar* and the pool, and the design of the garden. Differences also exist in the techniques employed to moderate the harsh climate, but generally these are minor compared to the organisational role the courtyard plays in domestic life.

## Architectural–climatic patterns

Climate has had a great influence on Iranian and Arab architecture for at least 8000 years. This is not, however, meant to imply a unitary response to climatic conditions throughout these countries. An architectural–climatic pattern denotes the commonly-shared architectural characteristics that have developed in a given locality in response to the prevailing conditions. In various Arab countries, as in Iran, variation in climate led to variation in architectural response, altering the role of the courtyard and its design features.

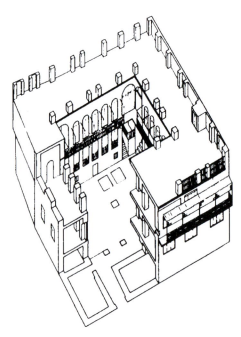

2.4 **Axonometric drawing of an Iranian courtyard showing both interior and exterior shenashil**

In a broad classification Iran, Iraq, Kuwait and Saudi Arabia all lie in the hot-arid zone, where relative humidity is low, winters are cold or mild, and daytime summer temperatures may in places rise to 50°C or even higher (see Olgyay 1963). The diurnal temperature range (i.e. the difference between day and night temperatures) is also very large. Under these extreme conditions, a number of methods were employed to maintain comfort. These include the use of building materials of high thermal insulation, the construction of basements, the provision of verandas and other semi-open spaces and the use of *badghir* (wind-catchers) and subtle changes in the sectional profile of the courtyard.

One of the features of domestic life in Iran and in the neighbouring Arab countries is the seasonal movement that occurred between rooms, or suites of rooms, on different sides of the courtyard. In winter the inhabitants would stay mostly in rooms with few openings, e.g. a corner room or (in Iran) *pastoo*. During the daytime, however, they might also make use of larger, more open rooms, where these faced south on to the courtyard. These might take the form of an *otagh orsi* (sash-window room) or some type of colonnaded gallery or veranda, such as the *tarme* or *talar*. The dominant orientation of traditional houses in Iran is north-east/south-

west. This allowed winter quarters to be located where they would receive sunlight (on the north-east side) and summer quarters to be in shade (on the south-west side). In cities such as Shiraz and Yazd this orientation also coincides with the direction of Mecca, which is important in Moslem daily life.

The north-east/south-west orientation may be found also in Iraq, Kuwait and Saudi Arabia, although a north-west/south-

2.5 **Interior view of a shenashil showing the effect of timber latticework on reducing sunlight penetration**

east axis is also common. Habitable rooms may be grouped on two, three or even four sides of the courtyard, but the main family accommodation is commonly divided between the north and south sides. In the traditional courtyard houses of Iraq the family may spend much of their time in a semi-open space at the south-eastern end of the courtyard. Below this is the basement *sardab* or *sirdab*, where they take their summer afternoon siesta. The flanking south-western wall may be blank and left unused (see Al-Azzawi 1969) because of the high temperature.

A sample of 45 houses in Shiraz in Iran (Memarian 1998) revealed various patterns of occupation and movement within the house. The main winter rooms might be on the north-east or north-west sides, and the summer rooms could be on the south-west or the south-east sides. As in many other places in the hot-arid regions, a general shift took place around the end of May from the winter rooms to the summer rooms on the south of the courtyard. In some cases, however, the house was without distinct winter accommodation; in others there were no summer rooms on the south side. In the Qavam-al-Molk, a large traditional house with two courtyards, each court was organised on a different axis. The reception courtyard, with its entrance direct from the main street, is oriented north-east/south-west, while the private courtyard, accessed separately from a side street, is oriented north-west/south-east. In the former the main winter rooms are on the north-western end of the courtyard; in the latter they are at the north-eastern end. This shows the important role climate played in the planning of the courtyard house, a role in which the occupants played a key part by their own seasonal movement.

While the seasonal migration from northern to southern quarters in the house was a widespread practice throughout the Middle East, residents might also choose to move back and forth between the northern sitting rooms and the basement – a vertical rather than a horizontal movement. In those houses that were not provided with rooms on the southern side of the courtyard, we can infer that vertical migration was the usual pattern of movement. As with the *Sirdab* in Iraq, the basement would often be preferred in any case during the afternoon, as it offered a cool retreat in the hottest part of the day. From late afternoon, the inhabitants of Shiraz would return to the courtyard or, where there was one, to the *talar* or *ivan* (veranda) on the south side. The final vertical movement occurred at night, from the courtyard to the roof.

The largest room in the houses of Shiraz is generally the so-called 'central room', a large sash-windowed space *otagh orsi*, which is centrally positioned along one or other of the plan axes. The great majority (40, i.e. 89 per cent) of houses in the Shiraz sample had a central room of one kind or another, and this was most often on the north side of the courtyard, i.e. at the heart of the winter quarters. It is interesting, however, to note that the room could occur on any one of the four sides of the courtyard. Thus it would appear predominantly to be a winter room, but might also be used at other times of the year. This flexibility is a mark of traditional courtyard housing in Shiraz, and can be attributed to the comparatively benign climate of this city. High in the plateaux of the Fars region, conditions are more equable than in much of central Iran, and impose fewer restrictions on spatial arrangement. This analysis allows a distinction to be drawn between the flexible occupation of the courtyard house where residents move according to season or time of day, and the fixed occupation of the Western house.

This pattern is, however, in sharp contrast to the city of Yazd to the east. Located on the edge of the great central

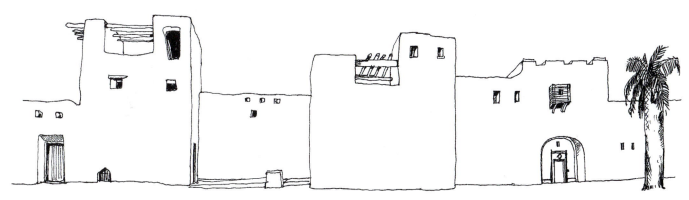

2.6  **A street view of courtyard housing showing the high-level ventilation grilles and open roof balconies**

desert – the 'sand-sea' – this historic city experiences some of the most extreme climatic conditions in the whole of Iran, with a fierce summer sun, cold winters and frequent sand storms. As a result room positions tend to be less variable and room-uses more prescribed than in Shiraz. Basements are common and the *talar* figures as a much more important space. Of a sample of 24 single-courtyard houses in Yazd, 23 had a *talar* (veranda), and this was normally on the south side of the courtyard, where it provided summer shade. (In the Shiraz sample only five houses had a *talar* and this could be on the north or south side of the courtyard.) Yazd is also noted for the widespread use of *badghir* (wind-catchers), which help to reduce internal air temperatures by 'catching' the prevailing wind and forcing it through the *talar* or into the basement. *Badghir* were also employed in a similar way to ventilate the basements (the *sirdab*) of Iraqi houses, as shown by Al-Azzawi (1969), and are a striking feature of traditional housing in the hot-humid regions of Iran and the other Arab states bordering the Persian Gulf.

## Cultural–religious patterns

The nature of private life in the Islamic countries is similar irrespective of climatic or geographical differences. This is rooted in a shared Islamic culture, which demands that sexual and emotional activities should be centred on the family nucleus to consolidate family life and reduce social stress (Mottahari 1973). This is to be achieved in two ways: first, a man must not look on any woman to enjoy her beauty. Second, a woman must cover her body (except her face and hands) to avoid the attention of men. Furthermore, Islam prescribes the roles of men and women in ways, which have a direct impact on architectural design. For example, Qur'anic verses underline the importance of family privacy by emphasising the importance of knocking at the door before entering a house:

> O you who believe! Do not enter houses other than your houses, until you have asked permission and saluted their inmates; this is better, for you may be mindful.
>
> *Qur'ān*, 24:27

But if you do not find anyone therein, then do not enter until permission is given to you; and if it is said to you:

> Go back, then go back; this is purer for you; and Allah is Cognizant of what you do.
>
> *Qur'ān*, 24:28

Hospitality and privacy has its roots in the relation of friendship and kinship that exists among all members of Islamic society. Islam emphasises that all Moslems are brothers and sisters:

> Believers are surely brothers. So restore friendship among your brothers. Have fear of Allah so that you may attain mercy.
>
> *Qur'ān*, 49:10

Religious leaders have sought to consolidate the relationship between the members of Islamic society in practical ways. One of these is by visiting one another at home (Koleini 1983). Here the reception of friends becomes a work sacred to Allah: 'The guest is the beloved of God' is a common expression among Moslems. The guest should always be welcomed very warmly. It is advised that the best part of the room or house should be offered to the guest, though he may, for reasons of humility, decline to sit there. Ghazali, the great Persian scientist of the eleventh century, advises that the guest should not sit in the best place, but also that his sitting place should not be near the women's area (Ghazali 1976).

Visual privacy is of great importance in the Iranian house and, as in the Arab–Islamic house, great care was taken to protect female members of the household from the eyes of male strangers. Spatially the house might be divided into two distinct areas, the *birooni* and the *anderooni*. *Birooni*, which literally means 'outside', referred to those quarters that were situated close to the main entrance. This was traditionally a male area, where *na-mahram* male visitors (those with whom marriage was not disallowed) would be entertained by the men of the household. *Anderooni*, literally 'inside', denoted the family quarters, which would be predominantly female. While female visitors might on occasion be entertained in the reception rooms within the *birooni*, they were more likely to be taken to the *anderooni*. In large houses there might be separate retinues of servants for the two areas – female for the *anderooni* and male for the *birooni*.

Similar domestic arrangements are found in many Arab countries. In Kuwait the men's reception court is called *Hoash al-Diwaniyya*. This area is characterised by a large courtyard, a liwan or loggia and a men's reception room or *majlis*. The private area of the house also has large courtyard, a loggia, and a number of rooms. These characteristics can be seen in *Beit al-Ghanim* in Kuwait (Lewcock and Freeth 1978). According to Al-Azzawi (Al-Azzawi 1986) the courtyards of traditional courtyard houses in Baghdad houses can be grouped under four categories, viz. *Hoash al-Haram* or courtyard of the family quarters, *Hoash al-Diwan-Khana*, the courtyard of the business or guests' quarters, *Hoash al-Matbakh*, or the kitchen courtyard, and *Hoash al-Tola*, the courtyard of the stable. The territorial zoning of the traditional courtyard house reflects a socio-spatial pattern whose roots are cultural as well as religious.

In Iran, the *birooni-anderooni* division was fully developed only in wealthy households, since it necessitated the building of least two separate courtyards, i.e. one for the private quarters, the other for the reception area. In our survey of houses in Shiraz and Yazd, there were many examples of multi-courtyard houses, some dating from the early Safavid period, i.e. 1491–1722. The majority of houses, however, had one courtyard only. In such cases it would have been very difficult to achieve complete sexual segregation, especially where there was seasonal and diurnal movement between rooms. Private and reception rooms had to be deployed around the one courtyard and a special reception room would be provided as far as possible away from the private spaces. This was usually close to the main entrance, while the private area occupied the back of the courtyard, well away from the entrance and not visible to prying eyes.

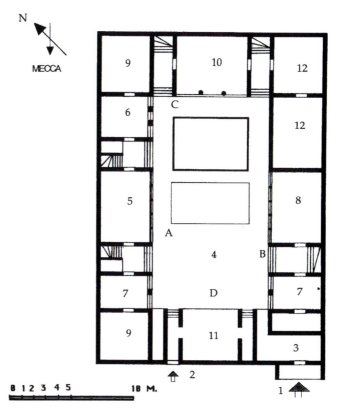

2.7 **Plan of Moadel House, Shiraz, Iran**

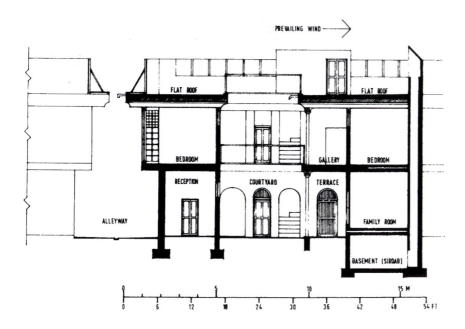

2.8 **Section through a typical courtyard house in Iraq. Notice how the Badghir to the left faces the prevailing wind (after Al-Azzawi)**

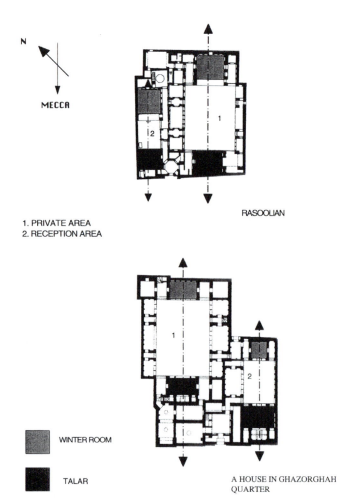

N

MECCA

1. PRIVATE AREA
2. RECEPTION AREA

RASOOLIAN

WINTER ROOM

TALAR

A HOUSE IN GHAZORGHAH
QUARTER

N

MECCA

A

B

0 1 2 5    10 M.

**2.9  Comparison between plans of two courtyard houses in Baghdad showing (a) the orientation on Mecca and (b) the zoning into public and private areas**

**2.10  Monsoori House in Shiraz, Iran with (a) private and (b) public courtyards**

In both the Iranian and the Arab house, the entrance arrangements were also of great importance. Iranian houses were seldom more than single-storey, but the surrounding walls were high, thick and mostly blank. Openings, where necessary, were small and placed above eye level to prevent passers-by from looking in. Often the presence of a single heavy door was the only indication of the habitation within. But the entrance did not, under any circumstances, allow a direct view of the private quarters of the house. Its position is therefore precisely calculated, and in some cases it was located away from the courtyard altogether. The selection of private quarters may be determined, or reinforced, by the shape of the passageway that leads from the entrance to the courtyard. This may be a straight line, an 'L-shape', or have

some form of chicane. The intention is always to prevent direct sight of the interior. If a linear form of passageway is adopted, this usually leads to a corner of the courtyard, where there are no household activities. The planning of the entrance was as carefully considered as that of the courtyard itself.

Other authors have drawn attention to the widespread use of the 'bent' entrance in traditional courtyard housing in the Arab countries. This type of entrance was a pronounced architectural feature of the main gates of the Round City of al-Mansour in Iraq, built in AD 762 (Al-Azzawi 1969). In the early days the function of the bent entrance was wholly defensive. Later it was employed, as in Iran, to ensure the privacy of the courtyard and the related internal spaces. Privacy was further

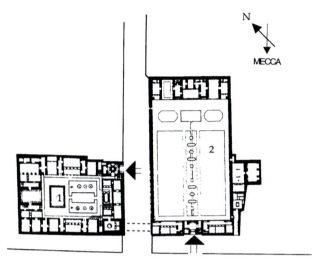

N

MECCA

Lotf-Ali Khan Zand Street

**2.11  Qavam-al-Molk House in Shiraz, Iran, showing the transition from the public street to the private courtyards of the house**

enhanced by the use of double doors. Thus what started as a defensive measure became, over time, a perceptual one.

In the case of Iranian houses, the vestibule or *hashti* was also an important part of the entry sequence. This was designed as a stopping point and could be used as a temporary reception room for those persons who did not need to enter the guest room. In plan the *hashti* was commonly octagonal, but it could also be square, rectangular, or of various other polygonal shapes. It normally contained the main entrance and gave access to the roof and to the corridor leading to the courtyard. In double courtyard houses, the vestibule would give access to both courtyards and there were usually two or three niches, which provided a place for people to sit.

Where the entranceway – the passage or corridor – opened directly onto the courtyard, a reception or guest room might be provided close by. This is the kind of arrangement we find, for example, in single-courtyard houses in the plains of southern Iran. As noted above, examples are also recorded in Kuwait of houses where a reception room, known as the *majlis*, is set aside for male guests. This is positioned close to the *dehliz* or entrance hall, and the living room is on the opposite side of the courtyard (Lewcock and Freeth 1978). In some of the rural houses of Saudi Arabia, a reception room is located close to the vestibule and passageway, and entered

without entering the courtyard: the private and reception areas are completely separated (Kaizer 1984). The pattern is by no means casual but a carefully considered response to the balance needed between hospitality and privacy.

## Conclusion

In this chapter we have identified a number of spatial and physical characteristics that are shared by traditional court-yard houses in Iran and those in neighbouring Arab countries. These stem in part from the harsh climatic conditions that prevail in these countries, and in part from the shared Islamic faith, which teaches the virtues and importance of hospitality and of privacy. Various spatial mechanisms have been employed to secure the privacy of the family, especially the female members of the household, whilst providing convivial surroundings for all. These measures include the division of the living quarters into distinct areas – the *birooni* and the *anderooni* – and the creation of complex, chicane-like entrance arrangements. Both are subject to variation according to the size of the house, local traditions and the number of courtyards it contains. A more detailed study would undoubtedly reveal further similarities, but probably also subtle but important differences between the rich traditions of Iranian and Arab–Islamic architecture. The main factor that alters the underlying spatial-religious structure of the courtyard house is that of climate and particularly how its impact can be modified by architectural means.

## Bibliography

Al-Azzawi, S. (1969) 'Oriental houses in Iraq'. In Oliver, P. (ed.) *Shelter and Society*, London, Barrie and Jenkins Ltd, pp. 91–102.

Al-Azzawi, S. (1986), 'The courtyards of Oriental houses in Baghdad, non-functional aspects'. In Hyland, A. and Al-Shahi, Ahmed (eds) *The Arab House, Proceedings of Colloquium held in the University of Newcastle-upon-Tyne*, University of Newcastle-upon-Tyne, CARDO (1984) pp. 53–60.

Ghazali, Tusi A. I. M. (1976) *Kimiya-ye Sa'adat*, Tehran, Ketabhaye Jibi, p. 298.

Ghodar, A. (1978) *Honar-i Iran (Art of Iran)*, Tehran, Melli University, pp. 182–7.

Kaizer, T. (1984) *Shelter in Saudi Arabia*, New York, Academy Edition, p. 57.

Koleini, M. (1983) *Kafi*, Tehran, Amiri, p. 107.

Lewcock, R. and Freeth, Z. (1978) *Traditional Architecture in Kuwait and the Northern Gulf*, Kuwait, aarp, p 23.

Malek-i Shahmirzadi, S. (1986/1366) 'Shahrneshini va Shahrsazi dar Hezareh Panjom Ghabl az Milad', in M. Kiani (ed.) *Nazari Ijmali bar Shahrsazi va Shahr Neshini dar Iran*, Tehran, Jahad–ndash i Daneshgahi, pp. 5–12.

Malek-i Shahmirzadi, S. (1988/1368) 'Esharehi be Pish az Tarikh Damghan' (A view on pre-historic Damghan), in *Banaha va Shahr-i Damghan*, Tehran, Nashr-i Faza, pp. 85–100.

Memarian, G. (1993/1373), *Ashnaii ba Memari Maskooni Irani: Ghuneh Shenasi Darunghara (Courtyard Houses)*, Tehran, Iran University of Science and Technology, pp. 13–26.

Memarian, G. and Brown, F. E. (1996) 'Patterns of privacy and hospitality in the traditional Persian house', *Proceedings of the IASTE Fifth International Conference: Identity, tradition and built form*, Vol. 100, Berkeley, University of California, pp. 42–82.

Memarian, G. (1998) *House typology in Iran with special reference to Shiraz*, Ph.D. dissertation, Manchester, UK: University of Manchester, Faculty of Arts.

Mottahari, M. (1973/1353), *Hejab*, Tehran, pp. 68–83.

Olgyay, V. (1963) *Design with Climate: bioclimatic approach to architectural regionalism*, Princeton, NJ, Princeton University Press.

Shalaby, T. (1986) 'Behavioural patterns and the Arab house'. In Hyland, A. and Al-Shahi, Ahmed (eds) *The Arab House, Proceedings of Colloquium held in the University of Newcastle upon Tyne*, University of Newcastle-upon-Tyne, CARDO (1984) pp. 73–82.

Shooshtari, I. A. (1969) 'Barresi Nofooze Shiveh Memari Irani dar Memari Islami', *Bastanshenasu va Honar* **2**, pp. 18–23.

# 3 The courtyard houses of Syria

E. MAHMOUD ZEIN AL ABIDIN

## Introduction

Courtyard housing dates back to the beginning of the third millennium before Christianity when it appeared in the buildings of al-Sham and those of between the two rivers: the Tigris and Euphrates. Arab nomads made use of the concept of a courtyard during their movement and stay in desert. They set up their tents around a central space, which provided shelter and security to their cattle. With the development of Arab–Islamic architecture, the courtyard became an essential typological element. It is likely that the previous nomadic desert lifestyle of Arabs had a strong influence on their desire to have an open space or spaces within their permanent houses. The courtyard therefore fulfils a deep-rooted need for an open area of living.

This chapter describes the courtyard house typology in Syria, and presents a number of examples of courtyard houses in Aleppo.

The traditional courtyard house in Syria is composed of three parts:

- a basement floor
- a ground floor comprising the main living areas called 'Al Salamlek'
- a first floor comprising the private areas called 'Al Haramlek'.

The basement floor enjoys an even temperature throughout the year. It is therefore an attractive living space in periods of extreme winter or summer temperatures. The basement acts as

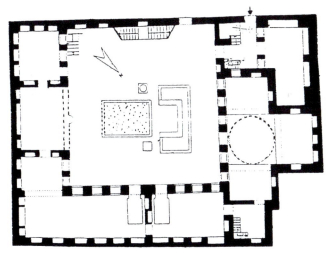

3.1 **Plan of Wakil House, Aleppo, Syria**

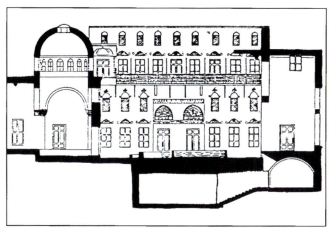

3.2 **Section of Wakil House, Aleppo, Syria**

3.3 **View looking into a courtyard of Wakil house**

a thermal moderator during the hot dry season, as it allows the hot air collected by the wind-catchers to be cooled and humidified before it is released to the courtyard space. It is also used for the yearly storage of food supplies as is the case in many courtyard houses of Aleppo, a city that endured many wars.

The houses are usually accessed through a humble space leading into a spacious and beautifully landscaped courtyard. The entrance door consists of one or two wooden door-leafs, reinforced with lead plates fixed with steel nails. The small size of the external door represents humbleness, which is also portrayed in the lack of decorations of the external windows. It is very difficult, therefore, to judge the level of wealth or poverty of the houses from their external appearance. The entrance door usually leads to a narrow passageway at the end of which another door or curtain filters the entrance to the courtyard, allowing this latter to be totally private and visually inaccessible from the outside, even if the entrance door is left open, which was frequently the case as the old city neighbourhoods used to enjoy a high level of security.

The transition from the outside to the inside is marked by a contrasting spatial experience, from a modest and sometimes austere entrance to a highly decorated internal open courtyard with a central fountain (and sometimes a well) and beautiful façades.

Landscaping also plays an important role in the courtyard of the traditional Syrian courtyard. It consists mainly of two categories: decorative planting such as climbing jasmine and rose bushes, which add colour and scent to the courtyard atmosphere, and citrus trees such as orange and lemon.

The façades of the internal courtyard are highly decorated with intricately woven geometric patterns and shapes.

3.4 **High- and low-level windows facing the courtyard at Wakil house**

3.5 **A typical bedroom in Wakil house**

The *iwan* is an important covered open space from which the aesthetic qualities of the courtyard can be enjoyed. It provides a raised platform (by one or two steps), used as a pleasant and comfortable open-air reception and seating area and a venue for evening events such as playing of traditional music. The *iwan* is usually located on the north façade of the courtyard to catch the cool breeze during the summer. The *iwan* comprises two symmetrical rooms facing each other and has

3.6 **The dome in the main hall of Wakil house**

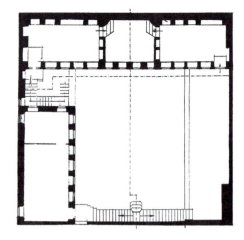

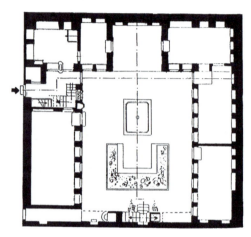

3.7 **Ground and first floor plan of Baleet house, Aleppo, Syria**

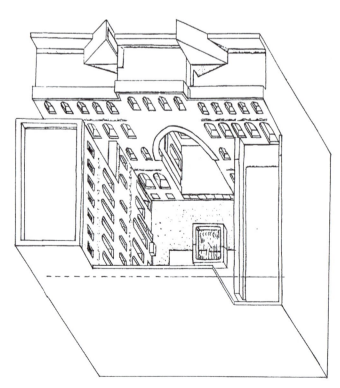

3.9 **Axonometric view of Baleet house**

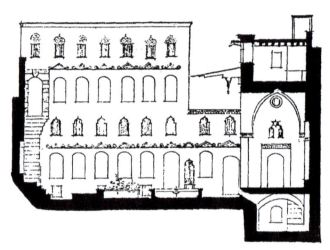

3.8 **Cross-sections of Baleet house**

an ornamental front stone arch facing the courtyard. The transition from the courtyard to the *iwan* space is marked by a multicoloured marble patterned floor, which resembles an oriental carpet.

Facing the *iwan* is the main guests' reception hall used for special ceremonies and festivities such as Eid. This hall is the most decorated space in the house (Figure 3.6) and contains the best furniture items. In some houses, such as the Wakil, Basil and Ghazali houses in Aleppo, the main guests' hall is covered with a dome

In addition to the *iwan* and the reception areas, the ground floor also contains the kitchen and toilets.

The first floor is called the *Haramlek*. It is a word of Turkish origin meaning a women's section in the house. The living and sleeping areas are totally segregated.

The accessibility from the ground floor to the first floor is through a staircase located in the courtyard (Figure 3.7). Small apartments can sometimes be found on the first floor, particularly in the case of extended families. The first floor can also contain some terraces, allowing the sun's rays to penetrate the courtyard. These provide useful open spaces used for sleeping or seating during the evenings of the hot season. The roof spaces are usually well protected by high parapet walls, providing adequate privacy.

## The architectural elements of the Syrian courtyard house

The *Mushrabiya* is a wooden balcony located on the outer façade of the house. It provides a cool screened space for women, allowing them to view public spaces without being

3.11   **Main hall of Acikbas house**

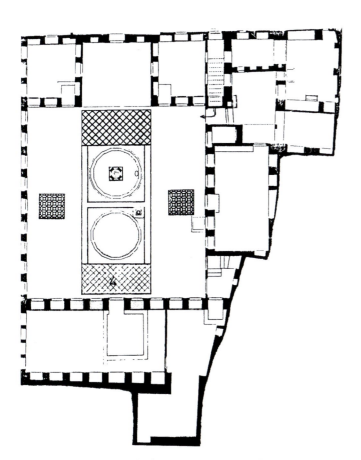

3.10   **Ground floor plan of Acikbas house, Aleppo, Syria**

seen. It is usually supported by two cantilevered wooden beams, which are anchored in the external wall.

The windows are divided into two types: those located on the external façade of the house and those located on the courtyard façades. Because the house is inward looking, the external façade windows are small, plain and located from the first floor onwards in order to avoid overlooking from pedestrians in the narrow public streets (Figure 3.8).

The courtyard windows are much larger and are more decorated, providing light and ventilation to the rooms (Figure 3.4). The ground floor windows facing the courtyard comprise a glass window located to the inside of the thickness of the wall and a wooden shutter, located to the outside of the wall thickness. Other types of windows can be found at the base of the courtyard. They are small, arched with no decorations and provide light and ventilation to basement floor. The doors of the ground floor rooms are two-leaf wooden doors with a

3.12 **Ceiling decoration of intersecting slats at Acikbas house**

minimum of ornamental carvings, the first floor doors are, however, relatively undecorated.

In the main reception hall, built-in wall cabinets are used within the thickness of the walls to display ornaments such as intricate wooden ornamental carving. The walls around the cabinets are sometimes covered with wooden panels with calligraphy carvings matching the cabinet design. The ceilings are also highly decorated, with wooden panels displaying intricately woven ornamental geometrical shapes. This is particularly the case in the main reception hall, where the ceiling is the highest in the house and consists of intersecting wooden panels with rich carving and gold-plated designs. Symmetry plays an important role in the composition of the ceiling's decorations.

The internal decorations are based on the following four types of patterns:

- calligraphy based on verses of the holy Qur'ān or verses of poetry
- floral patterns derived from stems and leaves of various plants
- patterns derived from animal forms such as birds

- geometric patterns derived from the combination of circles, squares, rectangles and triangles.

Geometric patterns are formed by multicoloured stone inlays and intersecting timber slats and form floor and ceiling decorations (Figure 3.12). They are most evident in the floors of the main reception hall, the iwan and the courtyard area in front of the iwan.

## Courtyard organization and climatic factors

The courtyard organization is appropriate to hot dry climates because it maximizes shading and allows for the creation of a pleasant microclimate. The availability of plants and a water feature within the courtyard helps in cooling and humidifying the internal atmosphere.

The construction technique, which is based on thick load-bearing stone masonry, provides adequate thermal mass. The existence of cooling towers allows for a good summer ventilation as hot air is funnelled down into the basement where it is cooled and let out into to the courtyard space. The narrowness of the external streets and passageways leading to the houses also helps in creating a cool and shaded outdoor environment.

## Economic factors

As previously discussed, all Syrian courtyard houses share a humble external appearance. However, their size and level of internal decorations depends on how wealthy the families who occupied them were. Three categories can be identified: the large courtyard houses of the rich families, the medium-

3.13 **Views of the courtyard at Acikbas house**

sized houses of traders and craftsmen and the small and humble houses of the workers.

## Building material and construction techniques

The building materials locally available have greatly influenced the construction and shape of the Syrian courtyard house. The abundance of stone in the area made it the main building

3.14 **View of the basement kitchen at Acikbas house**

material in the construction of the courtyard houses of Aleppo. Walls are frequently formed by layers of white and black stones called *Al Ablaq* which forms a distinctive characteristic of the courtyard houses of Syria.

## Social factors

Social, cultural and religious factors have played an important role in the shaping of the courtyard house in Syria. The need for privacy has had a paramount influence on the inward organization of spaces and the treatment of the entrance, the external windows and the separation between family and guest areas within the house. Furthermore, the extended family structure has meant that the Syrian courtyard house was organized with the possibility of semi-independent subunits functioning independently but still maintaining strong family ties.

Entertaining guests and relatives was and is still important in the lives of Syrian families. Thursday weekly courtyard parties were very common. Guests were invited for dinner and were entertained in the courtyard with folkloric music bands. Female parties were also very common and took place on a weekly basis, strengthening both family and neighbourly ties.

## Conclusion

Having considered the traditional Syrian courtyard house and its characteristics, it is evident that the courtyard house form presents a number of qualities that are still relevant to contemporary domestic life in Syria.

However, two major changes have occurred in the in the social structure of Syria which affect to some extent the viability of the traditional courtyard house for contemporary family living. These are:

- the decrease in family size with more women working outside the home
- the change from the extended family structure to the nuclear household type.

Furthermore, most families rely on multi-storey apartments as an affordable housing solution and cannot afford large courtyard houses. The Arabic house with its internal courtyard has become rare and has almost completely disappeared in contemporary architecture. So how are we to live in a rapidly-changing world where all meanings of family tradition and culture have changed dramatically?

Is there a scope for a new affordable housing typology based on maximizing the benefits of a courtyard organization and responding to the needs of contemporary small nuclear households?

# 4 The courtyard houses of southern Algeria

## ARROUF ABDELMALEK

## Introduction

The present chapter discusses the historical development of courtyard housing in Algeria, and attempts to highlight the main factors that have contributed to the geographical spread of the courtyard typology. Architects, sociologists, social anthropologists, psychologists and historians have employed many theoretical approaches for developing an understanding of the factors that have influenced the formation of courtyard architecture.

There is a wide range of recurrent ideas and assumptions that are accepted as credible. To think, however, about the future of courtyard housing, itself an ill-defined and undervalued architectonic concept, we must be careful about simplistic and stereotyped explanations and generalisations.

Asking the question about the relevance and the responsiveness of courtyard housing to contemporary situations cannot be answered without a deep understanding of the reasons for the emergence of the courtyard organisation, with its specific typology in various geographical areas. The study of the evolution of courtyard housing within a given limited geographical area could help in providing such an understanding.

The present chapter is based on a longitudinal survey and observation of courtyard housing in different parts of Biskra, a city at the edge of the Algerian Sahara. The survey was aimed at understanding the process of formation and transformation through time of the courtyard housing typology in this region from social, cultural and climatic perspectives.

## Three key factors

Three factors have helped shape the courtyard house of southern Algeria: social, climatic and cultural. Although each made a distinct contribution, they are interlinked into a network of evolutionary forces.

### Social factors

As with all southern Algerian towns, Biskra started as an oasis settlement. It is a vernacular settlement based on the repetition of housing models developed through centuries of trial and error. The courtyard model common to all social groups, presents a series of limited choices among various alternatives[1] and is transmitted through non-verbal communication until it produces an implicit schemata that becomes characteristic of the group. Since a great amount of the actual dwelling is still vernacular, the actual occurrence of the courtyard type is possibly the result of social diffusion through time of the original model. The spread of the courtyard house in the vernacular settlement is based on the repetition of unconsciously inherited mental images of the house. In order to test this hypothesis, it is important to compare ancient courtyard forms with more recent ones to find possible permanent elements and traces of subsequent transformation.

## Climatic factors

It has been common for scholars to explain the design and subsequent development of courtyard housing as a response to extreme climatic conditions. In fact, one of the most accepted explanations of the emergence of courtyard as an architectonic housing element is the climatic one. It is widely accepted that the courtyard is a climatic moderator in hot and dry climates. Many case studies have identified the different ways in which a centrally-enclosed courtyard open only to the sky can reduce daytime temperatures within the building, and, with the introduction of a fountain, add to the humidity levels.

## Cultural factors

There is no doubt that the climatic context had its impact on numerous architectural and construction elements. But many elements that characterise architecture could be explained by sociocultural conditions too. In fact, design is all about giving meaning to form, and the activity of architecture is engaged when man identifies himself with what he builds, using it as a means of expression, and making the building imbued with symbolic or social meaning. Indeed, in a region where traditional practices and religious beliefs are strongly and deeply rooted, there are good reasons to believe that sociocultural variables such as religion, culture and customs might be strong parameters when it comes to assessing the significance of these forces in determining architectural and spatial arrangements.

This point of view leads one to examine the extent to which sociocultural factors shape the mental image that a social group might have of a courtyard housing and how its members participate in the formation, development and spread of the type. This chapter seeks to understand the social role of the courtyard house, its possible significance on built form in the past and its potential to fashion the future.

## A study of Biskra: a southern-Algerian courtyard town

Biskra is a town in southern Algeria. It is situated five hundred kilometres south of the capital Algiers. Its development was the result of three rings of growth, each characterised by a dif-

ferent form of architectural expression. Their stratification along time has produced the town's distinctive urban form, based largely on courtyard housing.

## The pre-colonial stage: The Ksour settlements

This stage is the most important of Biskra's foundations. The built and plural form of the *Ksour* corresponds to what is known in North Africa as *Ksar*. The Ksar is certainly the oldest, the best-elaborated and most adapted planning form for the climatic and ecological constraints of the Sahara region of southern Algeria. It forms the backbone of the modern town of Biskra. Erected through a process of trial and error, the Ksours have become, with little variation, models of what human settlements can achieve using courtyard housing in arid zones. Even in its smallest detail Ksourian architecture from the fifteenth century onwards is a lesson in both ecological and climatic architecture.

Ksourian logic is simply the antithesis of aridity and desert. The Ksar tries to be, at all scales, what the desert is not. The town is both a desert landmark and offers, through the use of courtyards, a high level of climatic comfort. This is achieved mainly through the employment of local sources of construction material and local cultural emblems used to decorate the buildings.

Because the desert is seen as empty it is synonymous with loss, danger and the unknown. In order to live in desert regions man has learnt that he has to 'belong' and situate himself in a specific place. That is why the Ksours felt it necessary to create towns as landmarks based on the logic of a centrality with a sacred essence. At the scale of the region, the organisation of the Ksours tribes, together with their location in the desert, is made in relation to other centres. There is usually either the shrine of a saint belonging to the group,[2] or another *Ksar* which has been developed one from the other, forming a network of embryonic settlements.

The Sahara is only space and sand: it is the eternal outside where time passes by but remains always the same. Situated in these huge spaces, without any proportion to man, the Ksours are really little 'places' in the perception of desert nomads. As such the Ksour settlements are particular points and locations in space and time which carry community meaning. Their organisation, often radio-concentric, their scale, the manner of the grouping of dwellings, the layout of main and secondary streets, as well as the scale of architecture have made

Ksours places worthy of continuous habitation since the middle ages. Built at an average density of 485 inhabitants per hectare, desert settlements like Ghardaia provide shade, shelter and potential productivity in places once exposed to the continuous glare of the sun.

## The creation of microclimates

Built out of a great knowledge of water engineering systems, whether underground or pluvial, and exploiting the oasis effect created by the planting of palm trees, the Ksours were able to develop the art of microclimate design. In addition, the clever use of the spatial configuration of the settlements allowed the Ksours to integrate their approach to the design of buildings with that of the engineering of the town as a whole. In particular the use of narrow streets,[3] and covered passages leading to dense urban groupings of courtyard houses which were themselves equipped with terraces for summertime sleeping, allowed the Ksours to modify the severe climatic constraints of Saharan life.

The Ksours were established accordingly to a consistent spatial hierarchy where the main and secondary streets, together with blind alleyways, form the main urban components. The climatic protection starts at the urban scale. Although often radio-concentric, the Ksar's layout tends to favour an east–west orientation for the main streets. This arrangement of the urban layout allows for the reduction of exposed surfaces to the sun. Concepts like centrality and linearity, spatial hierarchy, compactness and closeness were retained at this stage and influenced subsequent desert developments.

The main streets are the ones that link the Ksar's centre to its fortifications and to its gates whereas the secondary streets provide the links to the different groupings of buildings. This hierarchy whose traces we find at the toponymic level (Zekak, Zenka, Derb, Zenika...) is characterised by intermediate levels formed by covered passages. This network forms the ancient heart of Biskra. The main urban elements play the role of quasi city gates. They facilitate the transition from the obscure to the lit and from the covered to the uncovered. They also highlight for the user the passage from a public socio-spatial entity to an altogether more private one. In the process they also create climatically comfortable places which are shaded and ventilated, thereby encouraging people to sit down and talk. As such these spaces are

seen as belonging to the community within each portion of the Ksar.

In opposition to today's trends, the streets are rarely wide and rectilinear with parallel sides. The sinuosity of the streets and their other attributes, such as their general dimensions and width to height ratio, reflect the role of the street as an ecological regulator. It breaks the sandstorms and hot winds that are frequent in the Sahara region: thus the fresh air which accumulated during night-time is not rapidly dispersed by the winds. It also creates an important shadowing of the adjacent façades, thereby reducing their luminosity. In the Ksar, the façade is conceived as a street entity, and possesses its own identity. It does not belong only to the building, to which it serves as an enclosure, but to the street as well. To the latter, it serves as a shading enclosure, a shelter from desert winds and as an important aesthetic signifier of collective values.

In addition to the multiplicity of cantilevered features and overhangs, there are a number of other small overhangs and salient features. Even the wall surfaces are rough to absorb and soften the harsh desert light. Thus, shading strategy is omnipresent. It goes from macro to micro-level, from the rooms crossing the street, to the multiple overhangs and jettied out balconies. Concepts such as the inwardness of the external space (the urban space) and the façade conceived as a street entity are elements that give these Saharan settlements their character.

The urban block in conventional terms does not exist in the Ksar. The morphological units constituting the Ksar, be they Kasbet[4] or blocks of built parcels, form largely self-contained urban entities. Their proximity to other similar entities gives rise to the compact layout of the Ksar. However, since these entities are generally close to each other, there is a high volume to space ratio which makes the town vibrant socially and rich culturally.

The isolated entities, on the other hand, have a lower surface to volume ratio, which are, in thermal terms, also relatively efficient. These blocks may be further divided into plots of land. The plot is normally associated with the dwelling, which means that it has a large number of sides and an increase in opportunity for interior courtyards. The built plot may also be easily associated with other plots, providing flexibility of layout without climatic disadvantage. The court type of the built parcels facilitates this and is itself the product of the system of land development. Hence the concept of associativity may be derived from that of the courtyard house.

## The courtyard house design

The courtyard house is the main building unit of the settlement and constitutes the principal socio-economic asset of the community. It is generally part of a block common to the same family: its form is often irregular and corresponds to the first land ownership acquired by each family member. The typical house is inward-looking, that is, the main rooms are arranged surrounding a special central courtyard with very little in the way of external openings. The whole design adopts a tripartite hierarchy system where there is first, a public reception space composed of the entrance called a *skifa*, then a semi-private area and finally the intimate family part of the house.

The access of the house is usually through a relatively small front door which leads directly to the skifa. Off the skifa is a reception room for male guests called *bit diaf* or guest room, followed by an offset way into the courtyard. This scenario of displacement from one part of the house to another is usually a delightful aesthetic experience involving the appreciation of open and covered spaces, a succession of light and shade, and a continuity of scale evoking a deepening sense of interior.

The house is generally developed on one or two storeys with a terrace reserved for female activities and a further area used for sleeping during the summer nights.

## The courtyard

The courtyard is the centre of the house and equally the centre of the family life. It is the most liveable part of the house. Here, the women carry most of their domestic activities and the children play: it is also where the family gathers to conduct its social life. A typical courtyard is a central private space, totally separated from the outside. Its main exterior opening is its large upper vista to the sky, called *rozna*. This opening does not correspond to the whole area of the court: it is an opening in the roof partly closed by means of crossed metal pieces which support shading mechanisms. This special form of courtyard incorporates an ingenious system which allows fresh air into the house whilst keeping it shaded during long periods of the day in order to reduce heat gains and solar radiation.

## The colonial stage

This urban development stage is one corresponding to the French colonisation during the nineteenth century. It has the main characteristics of the French town, based upon wide boulevards and formal urban planning. Completely isolated from the indigenous[5] agglomeration of the Ksours town, the French plan was designed with chess-like precision. Here everything is different to the previous occupation, with blocks which are regular geometric forms and dense blocks of vegetation grouped into well-defined separate entities called squares. The streets are now wide orthogonal corridors which favour sun penetration and dissipate the cooling effect of breezes. The houses have a new relationship to the street and are built with tiled pitched roofs, large outdoor windows and prominent doorways. The French houses were built around a new kind of courtyard, which often incorporated an underground cellar used as a granary and area for sleeping in the summer.

## The French courtyard

The courtyard of the colonial era is closer to what is currently called a patio in Mediterranean environments. It is a larger space than in the earlier vernacular examples and is totally open to the sky. It often contains a water source, is surfaced in coloured ceramic tiles and is usually planted with luxurious vegetation. This type of court is the exact opposite of the traditional ones in terms of environmental understanding. Where the traditional courtyard uses closeness and fabric awnings to mask the sun and bring freshness and shade, the French one uses vegetation and water to produce the same effects.

The important difference lies not in the climatic response but in the social use of the courtyard space. The French courtyard is not a place for domestic activities or social life, but rather a space to receive guests for coffee drinking and enjoying the fresh perfumed garden atmosphere. Even if it participates in the climatic regulation of the house, the French courtyard is more the expression of a particular mental image imported from another culture to the fringes of the Sahara desert.

*The post-colonial stage: the self-constructed courtyard*

This period has known numerous housing forms, but courtyard housing still survives in a form known in Algeria as 'self-built housing'. This form of dwelling, designed, managed and constructed by the inhabitants themselves without the help of architects and planners, today constitutes the biggest provider of housing in the country. Most of the houses constructed are based on the French system of land parcels known as *lotissement*, a kind of new city or suburb evolved on French planning concepts. The houses built are mainly of multi-storey construction with regular geometric forms, horizontal roofs, limited exterior openings and, importantly, interior courtyards. New architectonic elements such as balconies and verandas appear and the terrace is re-adopted as a nocturnal summer sleeping space. The general organization of the house is centred on an open interior space called *wast dar* which is simply a new form of courtyard. Clearly, the modern vernacular tradition continues to support the supremacy, socially, climatically and culturally, of the courtyard house.

This last courtyard type is simply a new version of the traditional model. There is, a central space, without outside openings, except the roof's hole, which is also called *rozna*. In some cases this opening is absent and the *wast dar* becomes a sort of large interior hall. On the social level, this court is still a very important space. It is highly valued for family gatherings, children's play and a variety of domestic activities such as food preparation. This new form of courtyard house corresponds closely, even in toponymic terms, to vernacular models. Not only has it a similar physical appearance, although constructed out of modern materials, but its social and climatic role, as well as its symbolic significance, seem to share a common meaning.

## Biskra's climate and courtyard housing

In order to assess the continued relevance of courtyard housing for such a region, a climatic study was felt necessary. The first step was to determine the climatic chart of Biskra using data based on fifteen years of statistics gathered by the local meteorological services. The second step was to elaborate the temperature matrices and to calculate the solar radiation intensity during the different months of the year. Finally the last step was to study the shade profiles during different periods of the year in courtyards of different shapes.

By combining the results of this last step (summarized in Table 4.1) with the other cited results we find that an open courtyard is a horizontal surface which is protected during the overheated periods, especially those between midday and mid-afternoon. Based on these results it seems that there is little need for an open courtyard space for climatic comfort

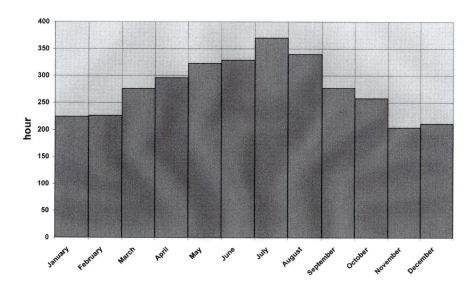

4.1 **The monthly average of sunny hours in southern Algeria**

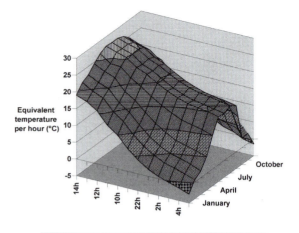

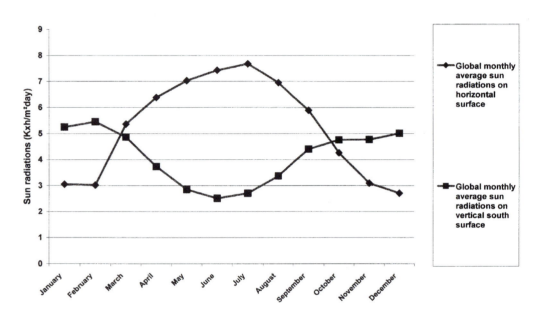

4.2   Typical matrix of annual temperatures in southern Algeria

■ -5-0   ■ 0-5   ■ 5-10   ▨ 10-15   ▨ 15-20   ■ 20-25   ▥ 25-30

— Global monthly average sun radiations on horizontal surface

— Global monthly average sun radiations on vertical south surface

4.3   The monthly average of horizontal and vertical radiation in Southern Algeria

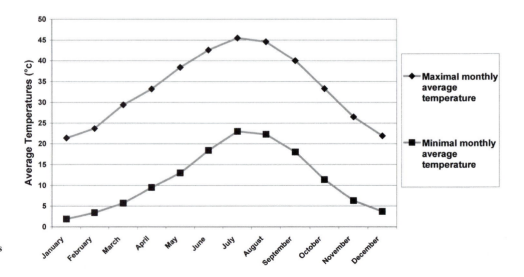

— Maximal monthly average temperature

— Minimal monthly average temperature

4.4   The monthly average temperatures in southern Algeria

4.5  The monthly average relative humidities in southern Algeria

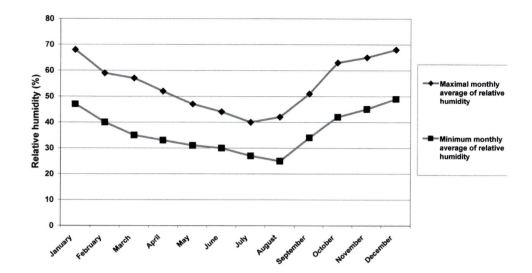

4.6  Intensity of solar radiation on horizontal surfaces in Biskra, Algeria

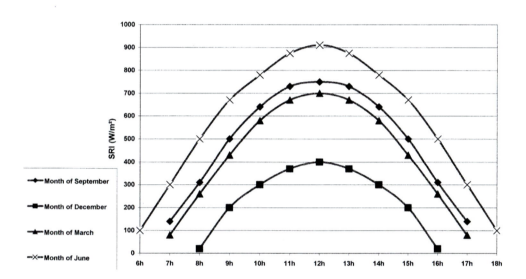

Table 4.1  **The percentage of shaded courtyard surface at different times of the day and at different times of the year for different courtyard forms**

| Period | Summer solstice | | | Equinox | | | Winter solstice | | |
|---|---|---|---|---|---|---|---|---|---|
| Form | 9h | 12h | 16h | 9h | 12h | 16h | 9h | 12h | 16h |
| | 37 | 6.15 | 66.5 | 66.2 | 19.23 | 100 | 95.69 | 43 | 100 |
| | 26.19 | 10 | 42.3 | 52.86 | 28.75 | 73.02 | 97.77 | 70 | 100 |
| | 31.84 | 8 | 51.5 | 57.44 | 24 | 85 | 93.28 | 55 | 100 |

45

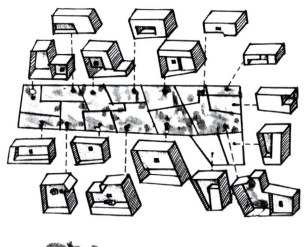

4.7 **Diagrammatic layout of courtyard housing in Biskra, Algeria**

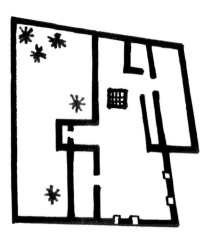

4.8 **Ground and first floor plan of a typical courtyard house in Biskra, Algeria**

conditions alone. On the other hand, one could be more ingenious and flexibly cover the courtyard space to bring practically the same protection conditions as with a fully covered roof with the possibility of ventilation and of light gain, especially during summer days. This is exactly what has been done in both the traditional and self-constructed housing settings.

The model adopted is climatically extremely efficient, but this is not the important issue. The real and intriguing question is why this model and not the solution of a completely closed central space was adopted as has occurred elsewhere. The climatic explanation does not appear to be the determinant one in this case.

## Courtyard social study

In order to establish the significance of social forces in shaping the courtyard forms, it was decided to undertake a comparative study of its social roles for each type. The obtained results summarised on Table 4.2 show the important weight of sociocultural factors in defining not only the form of courtyard selected in each case, but also its existence as a domestic space.

## Conclusion: directions for the future

The climatic study suggests that the best solution for Biskra's climate is that of closeness, self-shading and use of interior

Table 4.2  **Comparative study of social definition of each courtyard type**

| Courtyard type | Activities | Occupation frequency | Privacy level | Symbolic position | Possibility of reference |
|---|---|---|---|---|---|
| Pre-colonial courtyard | Female domestic activities<br>Family gathering<br>Eating<br>Female guests are received<br>Children playing | All liveable diurnal and nocturne time | | Private familial space open only to the family members | Centre of the house Important symbolic position |
| Colonial courtyard | Having coffee<br>Receiving guests | Specific moments of the day and night | Social space, open to all guests and family friends | No specific position No symbolic importance | Mediterranean patio |
| Post-colonial courtyard | Family gathering<br>Eating<br>Female guests are received<br>Children playing | All liveable diurnal and nocturne time | Private familial space open only to the family members | Centre of the house Important symbolic position | Traditional model |

Table 4.3  **Directions for future courtyard housing in hot arid regions**

| Courtyard type | Pre-colonial courtyard | Colonial courtyard | Post-colonial courtyard | Future directions |
|---|---|---|---|---|
| Symbolic position | Centre of the house Important symbolic position | No specific position No symbolic importance | Centre of the house Important symbolic position | Select important symbolic position<br>Giving courtyard a more cultural signification as a cultural identifier |
| Climatic efficiency | High | Average | High | High |
| Activity | Female domestic activities<br>Family gathering<br>Eating<br>Female guests are received<br>Children playing | Having coffee<br>Receiving guests | Family gathering<br>Eating<br>Female guests are received<br>Children playing | Family gathering<br>Eating, especially traditional meals and during traditional feasts<br>Children playing: preview necessary equipment for new kind of toys and plays<br>Guests received<br>Reading space<br>Watching TV |
| Form | Central space covered with an opened roof | Open planted space with water cell<br>Aesthetically well made | Central space covered with an opened roof | Space covered with an opened roof<br>Insert water elements and vegetation<br>Giving more and more importance to aesthetic aspects (ceramics, arabesque...) |

courtyards. The three historic settings studied have each adopted a specific form of courtyard, although not always for the same reason. In fact, even if the traditional courtyard form readopted in the self-constructed housing is climatically efficient, it is still best explained and understood in the light of sociocultural factors.

It has been argued in this chapter that the courtyard, by its position in the house, its organisation, its configuration and its social role suggest more a sociocultural need than a physical one. If we have to imagine future directions for it, it is important to base them on this ground rather than the climatic argument. Indeed, for courtyard housing to continue to exist, it is important to imagine courtyards not as a climatic regulator on their own but as a social space able to adapt to the changing conditions of modern life in north Africa in an environmentally responsive fashion (Table 4.3).

## Notes

1   See Amos Rapoport (1980) 'Vernacular architecture and the cultural determinants of Form' in *London, Building and Society, essays on the social development of the built environment*, Routledge & Kegan Paul.

2   The *Zaouia* is an institution, generally established by a man of religion, where he gives his teaching, often his *Tarika*, and offers shelter to his students and to travellers and people passing by. The social groups influenced by such teaching end up identifying themselves with the *Zaouia*, which acquires sacrament through the years.

3   The streets' width has a mean value of 2.40 m. They are wide enough to allow a loaded donkey to pass through.

4   Plural of *Kasba*, which means fortress.

5   Indigenous is the term usually used by the French to signify local inhabitants.

## Bibliography

Abdelmalek, A. *et al*. (1997), 'A methodology for upgrading Algerian legislation for Saharan settlements, based on traditional models of Ksours', *Proceedings of the Third International Conference on Saharan Towns*, Assiout, Faculty of Architecture, Assiout University.

Abdelmalek, A. (1999), 'The re-use of vernacular urban space concepts to achieve an architectural continuity', *Proceedings of the Fifth Iraqi Conference*. Baghdad, Baghdad Technology University.

Abdelmalek, A. (1997) 'Pour une épistémologie de l'architecture. Cas de l'architecture vernaculaire', *Proceedings of First National Architecture Conference: Town and Architecture in the Algerian Context*. Biskra, School of Architecture, Biskra University.

# 5 The courtyard houses of north African medinas, past, present and future

## MAGDA SIBLEY

## Introduction

The courtyard house represents a constant feature of domestic architecture in most Muslim regions: it was, however, developed in different ways as influenced by existing local traditions, construction materials and environmental factors. The courtyard houses of north African medinas display different characteristics than those of Egypt, Syria and Iraq as they feature the most formalised configuration with an absolute centrality of the courtyard.

Entire clusters of traditional courtyard houses are still lived in today by poor families, as north African medinas have managed to survive into the twenty-first century, with varying degrees of transformations and disrepair.

The aim of this chapter is to present the distinctive characteristics of traditional courtyard houses in north Africa through examples from three capital cities: Tunis, Algiers and Fez. It highlights the generic architectural and spatial qualities of such houses and discusses why and how these have failed to influence most contemporary north African housing projects.

Courtyard houses were part of north African settlements well before the arrival of Islam in the region. The Berbers (the original north African inhabitants) had their houses organised around courtyards and this is still the case in various mountain villages. Courtyard houses were also widely spread in north African Roman settlements such as Volubilis in Morocco, Carthage and El Djem in Tunisia; Timgad, Djemila and others in Algeria.

The expansion of Islam beyond Egypt around 670 AD meant that Arabs controlled the north coast of Africa including Tunisia, Algeria, Morocco and Andalusia. Arabs called this conquered territory *Maghreb*, meaning the West.

Clusters of courtyard houses form the main component of the urban fabric of major Islamic cities in the Maghreb. These clusters form small neighbourhood units within which basic neighbourhood facilities were provided such as a bakery, a public bath, a small mosque and a Qur'ānic school.

The early courtyard houses of Egypt of the eighth and ninth century AD (as revealed by the excavations of Fustat) show regular central square courtyards, with symmetric rooms and T-shaped reception rooms. It is very likely that this early house form has influenced the Maghrebi courtyard house organisation. The T-shaped rooms are evident in the courtyard houses of Tunis (Tunisia) and Algiers and could be reminiscent of the early Fustat courtyard houses. However, this is less evident as we move further west to Morocco. The courtyard houses in Tunis, Algiers and Fez present some regional variations as well as some permanent organisational principles. These are examined in the following section.

## The courtyard house in the medina of Tunis

The spatial characteristics of the traditional Tunisian courtyard houses have remained unchanged from the sixteenth to the nineteenth century (Revault 1967). The courtyard is surrounded by a series of long and narrow rectangular rooms or *bayts*. Their length is defined by the dimensions of

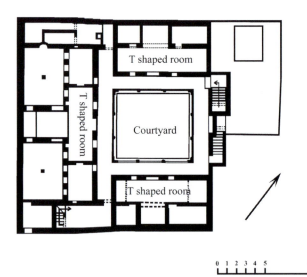

The courtyard or *wast ed dar* (meaning the centre of the house) is the focus of various domestic activities such as food preparation, laundry, children's play and outdoor living space. The access to the courtyard houses of Tunis is no different from any other courtyard houses of the Muslim world. It presents a bent circulation space which prevents any visual intrusion (from the semipublic spaces of the alleyways) into the private central space of the house.

Most of the courtyard houses that have survived in the medina of Tunis date from the eighteenth century. *Dar Sfar* illustrates a typical example of a 'bourgeois' residence with an architecture that is almost identical with early Al-Fustat residences in Egypt (see Figure 5.2).

the courtyard, varying between 6 to 10 metres, while their depth rarely exceeds 3 metres, possibly because of the limits of beams length. Their T shape is in fact an ingenious way to balance the long and narrow proportions of the rooms. The central area of the room (referred to locally as *Kbu*) opens onto the courtyard and balances the two lateral sitting bays (see Figure 5.1). Each room constitutes an autonomous spatial unit with a multi-purpose use and has its own entrance and courtyard façade.

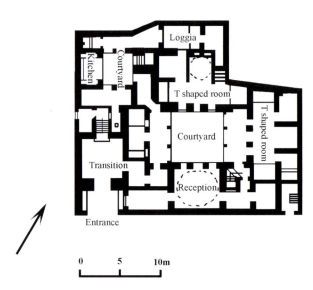

5.2  *Dar Sfar* in Tunis

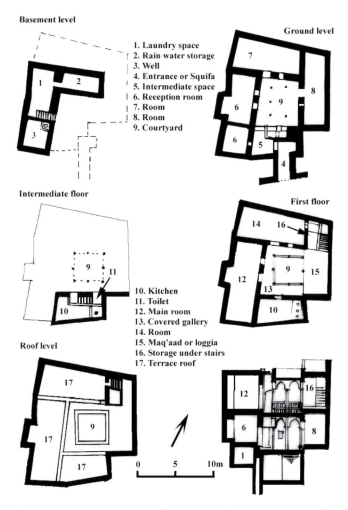

1. Laundry space
2. Rain water storage
3. Well
4. Entrance or Squifa
5. Intermediate space
6. Reception room
7. Room
8. Room
9. Courtyard

10. Kitchen
11. Toilet
12. Main room
13. Covered gallery
14. Room
15. Maq'aad or loggia
16. Storage under stairs
17. Terrace roof

5.3  **A modest courtyard house in the Casbah in Algiers (after Galvin 1988)**

## The courtyard house in the Kasbah of Algiers

The modest urban courtyard house in the Kasbah of Algiers presents a number of unique characteristics (Golvin, 1988). The basic house type consists of a three-floor structure organised around a deep square courtyard or *wast ed dar* (Figure 5.3). The individual rooms are long and shallow and occupy a full side of the square court. The courtyard is surrounded by three-arched galleries on the four sides (Figure 5.4), providing a covered circulation and a transitional space between the rooms and the open courtyard space.

The courtyard houses of the medina of Algiers usually comprise a ground floor and two storeys (Figure 5.5). The courtyard is accessed through a *sqifa*, a small bent space acting as a buffer zone between the semi-public spaces of the alleyway (*driba*) and the private space of the house, *west ed-dar*. Secondary spaces such as kitchen(s), toilets, stairs and storage are relegated to the irregular-shaped corners of the house. The kitchen or kitchens(s) are usually located on the

**5.4  Three arched galleries surrounding the courtyard in the houses of the Casbah in Algiers**

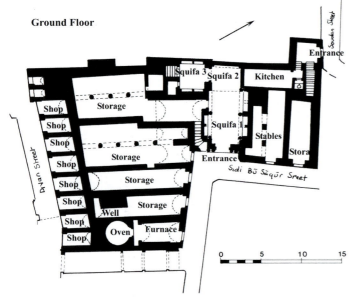

**Ground Floor**

Entrance

Squifa 3 · Squifa 2 · Kitchen

Shop

Storage

Shop

Shop

Squifa 1

Shop

Storage

Stables

Shop

Entrance

Stora

Shop

Storage

Shop

Well

Storage

Shop

Oven

Furnace

Shop

Dylan Street

Sidi Bū Sāqūr Sreet

Soudan Street

0   5   10   15

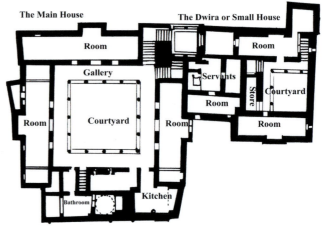

**First Floor**

The Main House

The Dwira or Small House

Room

Room

Gallery

Servants

Room

Courtyard

Courtyard

Store

Room

Room

Room

Room

Bathroom

Kitchen

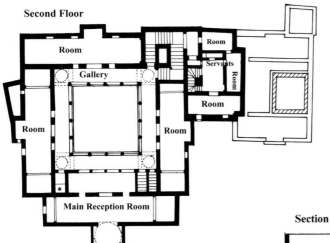

**Second Floor**

Room

Room

Gallery

Servants

Room

Room

Room

Room

Main Reception Room

5.5   **Dar Aziza: an example of a large courtyard house in Algiers**

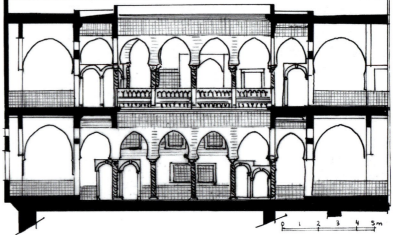

**Section**

0  1  2  3  4  5m

first floor. This indicates local residents' preference to be closer to the roof terrace where different activities take place such as laundry and the preparation of cous-cous (a traditional North African dish).

The courtyard and the roof space provide completely different spatial experiences which complement each other. The shaded, enclosed and highly private courtyard space is in complete contrast with that of the roof terraces. This latter re-establishes a strong visual relationship between the house and the city and allows female neighbours to socialise on a different layer of urban space: the flat roof spaces.

Internal decorations consist of beautifully tiled walls with tiles imported from Delft or Italy. Specific decorative features also include the 'twisted' columns surrounding the courtyard which are unique to the courtyard houses of Algiers (Figure 5.6)

5.7 **One of the main streets in the Casbah, Algiers. The overhanging corbelled volumes allow the house to gain extra floor area whilst providing side views along the street**

5.6 **Twisted columns and internal decoration in a large courtyard house in Algiers**

Other specific features can be found in the corbelled overhanging volumes on the external façades (Figure 5.7), allowing discreet side views from the house to the public streets. Compared to the houses in Tunis, the courtyard houses of Algiers have higher vertical proportions. This can be explained by the nature of the site (steep slopes) and the need to increase density as the city expanded in the sixteenth century.

## The courtyard house in the medina of Fez

Unlike the medinas of Tunis and Algiers, the medina of Fez has managed to survive in its integrity and entire large residential quarters are still lived in today. It still presents entire clusters of modest courtyard houses as well as fine examples of wealthy families' large courtyard houses.

The work of Jacques Revault on the courtyard houses of Fez in *Palais et Demeures de Fes* presents a thorough analysis

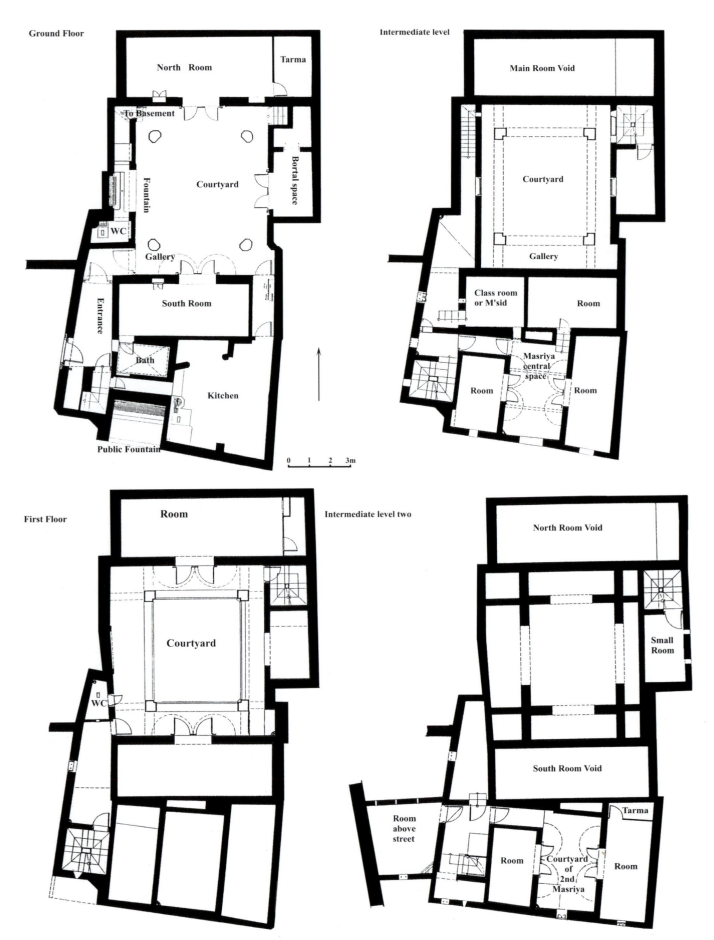

**Ground Floor**

North Room

Tarma

To Basement

Fountain

Courtyard

Bortal space

WC

Gallery

Entrance

South Room

Bath

Kitchen

Public Fountain

0 1 2 3m

**Intermediate level**

Main Room Void

Courtyard

Gallery

Class room or M'sid

Room

Masriya central space

Room

Room

**First Floor**

Room

Courtyard

WC

**Intermediate level two**

North Room Void

Small Room

South Room Void

Room above street

Room

Tarma

Courtyard of 2nd Masriya

Room

5.8 **Dar Bouhellal: an example of a large courtyard house in the Medina of Fez, Morocco (after Revault 1985)**

54

of a sample of 32 carefully selected courtyard houses. Unlike previous studies carried out by Revault on the courtyard houses of Tunis and Algiers, the study in Fez includes a larger number of modest courtyard houses. The sample is qualitatively representative and includes a variety of houses varying in size, period and location (Revault, 1985).

Revault's studies reveal that the typology of the courtyard house in Fez has remained unchanged from the fourteenth century until the nineteenth century and that the organisational principles are the same whether for a large palace or a modest courtyard house. Size and level of decorations are the only indicators of differences in wealth between courtyard houses' owners and occupants.

Courtyard houses in Fez are characterised by their verticality and their deep courtyards. Most of them are built on rectangular-shaped plots with a width to height ratio varying between 1.5 and 2. The rooms are organised along the longitudinal axis which frequently presents a north–south orientation (as is the case in two-thirds of the houses surveyed by Revault). The main rooms face each other and have large double-winged portals. The staircases are placed in strategic corners of the building without being exposed to the courtyard. Only one staircase leads to the roof terrace which, in the case of wealthy houses, may have an extra room or *bhu* used as a living and sitting area during the summer season.

Adjacent houses are occasionally joined to form one large house. In that case one of the houses becomes the private domain of the family. Some large houses have an independent residential unit called *masriya* or *dwiriya* which is organised around a light well and provides a private living area for a married son or for guests (Figure 5.8).

The houses are usually three-storey structures with intermediate levels and the courtyard has a height varying between 9 and 18 metres, with an average height of 11.5 metres. The majority of the houses in Fez show courtyard walls of 6 to 10 metres length. The oldest type of houses date from the Merinid period (fourteenth–fifteenth century) present either continuous columns up to the projecting roof or two layers of columns interrupted by a first floor gallery around the courtyard (Figure 5.9.)

The houses are highly decorated with beautiful patterns of floor and wall tiling (locally called *zellidge*) and intricate stucco and wood carvings (Figure 5.10). As mentioned previously, the typology of the courtyard houses of Fez has remained largely the same until the middle of the nineteenth century, when new quarters of the aristocratic class appear in

5.9 **An example of a courtyard in a Merinide house**

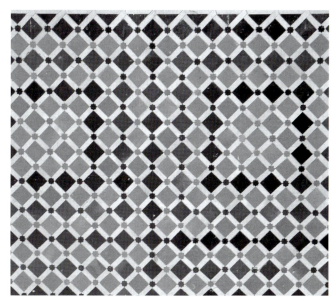

5.10 **Patterns of *zellidge***

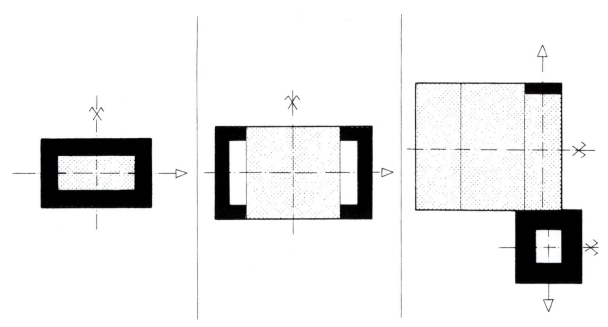

**5.11   The Riyadh, a house organised around a large garden rather than a courtyard**

the periphery of the medina. The development of these quarters has witnessed the introduction of some typology variations of the wealthy families' courtyard houses. The houses are built on much larger plots and are organised around a garden or *Riyadh* rather than around a courtyard, with variations according to the following three scenarios of relationship between house and garden:

- the garden is within the house (see Figure 5.11)
- the house is in the garden
- the house is next to the garden.

Such changes have altered the relationship between built form and outside space in the traditional domestic architecture: the open space was initially contained in the built form and then became the container of the built form.

## Comparison of the courtyard houses in Tunis, Algiers and Fez

The dominant formal characteristics of the courtyard house in the three cities are the absolute centrality of the courtyard

with its perfect geometric form and ingenious adaptation to the irregular contours of the plot.

> Symbolically speaking, the symmetrical and totally balanced order of the courtyard can be interpreted as the timeless centre of gravity of the house, while the periphery responds to the given circumstances and pressures of the earthly environment.
>
> Bianca 200, p. 82

The plan of the *dar* may vary in detail, but its basic characteristics are always the same. The hierarchy of the spaces and the general organisation of the houses are very similar. The relationship of the house to the outside world follows the same logic: the entrance is bent and is followed by a transitional space creating a buffer zone. The courtyard is deep and the stairs and service areas are located in the corners of the house. The reception room is the most decorated room and is usually near the house entrance. However, the size and character of the houses and their courtyards in the three cities do vary. The courtyard houses of Fez are the most intricately decorated, with variations of patterns in wall and floor tiling as well as stucco and cedar wood carvings. Ceramic tiles in both Fez and Tunis' courtyard houses are locally produced, whereas

5.12 **Dense urban fabric in the Medina of Fez, Morocco**

5.13 **General view of Fez, Morocco**

they tend to be imported from Italy and/or the Netherlands for the Algiers houses.

The presence of water is particularly dominant in Fez, with fountains located on one side of the courtyard and/or in the centre and is enjoyed by the presence of a covered open sitting area facing the fountain named the *bortal*.

The courtyards in Tunis' medina are rather wide and open, whereas they tend to be narrow and deep in most of the houses of Fez and Algiers, possibly because of the higher densities required as both cities rapidly expanded (Figure 5.12).

In all three cities the terrace roofs are accessible. The inward-looking buildings do not isolate the house from the outside world; however, they do create a peaceful, private environment, shutting off noise and intrusion from public spaces. Furthermore, the courtyard typology allows constant contact with the natural world – sun, sky, fresh air and water – on the ground floor, and re-establishes the relationship to the outside world with the accessible terrace roof space level. These roof spaces provide spectacular views of the city and its surrounding environment (see Figure 5.13) particularly when the city is built on a sloping site as is the case in Algiers and Fez.

The widespread assumption that the courtyard houses provide women with a secluded environment, cutting them off the external world, is therefore to be questioned.

The houses were usually occupied by extended families and provided a well-adapted and comfortable living environment. There was no spatial segregation between poor and rich families, as both lived next door to each other with no outside signs of differences of wealth between the houses.

## Impact of French colonisation/ protectorate on the perception of the courtyard house

During the French colonisation, housing built for the Europeans in Algeria, Tunisia and Morocco conformed to European standards. Apartment blocks formed a major part of the colonial city as did the development of villa neighbourhoods.

French colonial urban developments have resulted in the juxtaposition of two clearly contrasting urban forms and architectural typologies. The position taken by the French in relation to the medina of Fez was rather different from the one taken in relation to the medinas of Tunis, and Algiers. The new French colonial city established itself away from the medina of Fez, leaving the Islamic city in its entirety. This was not the case in Algiers or Tunis, where important parts of the historic fabric where demolished to make way for the new urban developments.

Rural migration to cities and the proliferation of large squatter settlements (or *bidonvilles*) around the European colonial cities has forced the French authorities to tackle the issue of housing for the local population. In 1923, the French colonial authorities of Casablanca built a new medina, El-Habous, to provide dwellings for families living in squatter set-

tlements. The new medina was designed by Albert Laprade an Ecole des Beaux Arts-trained French architect and reflected the local traditions of courtyard houses clusters, public baths, mosques and schools.

In 1948, a housing development for the rapidly expanding population of Tunis was designed by B. H. Zehrfuss, J. Drieu and J. Kyriakopoulos. This also reproduced the traditional typology of courtyard houses.

There was a clear shift of attitude of the colonial authorities in the provision of housing in the 1950s. Attempts were made to house the local population in blocks of flats. Le Corbusier's former followers Georges Candilis, Shadrach Woods and Vladimir Bodiansky began working for the African office of ATBAT (Atelier des Batisseurs) in Casablanca. Five-storey apartment blocks were introduced with a two-storey balcony, called a 'suspended courtyard', reminiscent of Le Corbusier's 1922 Immeubles-Villas. The plan de Constantine in Algeria was also established in the 1950s to provide mass housing to the local population in the form of walk-up apartment blocks with minimal floor areas and a small balcony allocated to each flat in order to compensate for the lack of a courtyard.

French occupation in Algeria, Tunisia and Morocco has played an important role in the introduction of different housing typologies: apartment blocks and villas, which were associated with a higher standard of living.

The independence from French occupation in all of Algiers, Tunis and Fez was followed by the shift of the population from the medina to the colonial city.

The well-off population left the courtyard houses in the medina to occupy flats or houses: leaving the courtyard house and acquiring a flat or a villa in the colonial city was perceived by the local population as a sign of social promotion. The medinas became a magnet, attracting the rural population who were migrating to the cities in search of work and better living conditions. This has resulted in severe overcrowding as the courtyard houses were occupied by various families of rural origins, each family occupying a room within a house.

## Courtyard houses in historic centres today

Courtyard houses in north Africa are today associated with appalling living conditions, poverty and lack of progress. Multi-family occupation, lack of building maintenance and

5.14 **The transformation of the courtyard in Dar Msafer in the Guerniz neighbourhood of Fez**

insensitive internal alterations have all resulted in a very rapid degradation of the traditional urban fabric and the collapse of a significant number of courtyard houses.

Recent field work on a cluster of eight courtyard houses in the Guerniz neighbourhood of the medina of Fez was carried out by the author in February 2004 as part of a research project funded by the UK Arts and Humanities Research Board (AHRB). The study revealed that traditional courtyard houses continue to sustain a high level of multi-family occupation and that transformations are taking place inside these houses to provide independent living units.

The case of one large house (*Dar El Msafer*) is particularly intriguing as walls were built around the courtyard to visually separate the ground floor units on the four sides of the court-

yard in order to provide more visual privacy to each family unit (see Figure 5.14).

Families interviewed in this house were of different opinions as to whether they would prefer to live in an independent flat. Most expressed a strong wish to move out in order to live in a flat and be completely independent of neighbours, but some were of the opinion that the courtyard was an important space, safe for the play of young children and useful for special occasions such as wedding parties.

The widespread use of apartment buildings and villas in the European city are symbolically associated with social promotion, better living conditions, progress and modernity. Post-independence housing projects were therefore heavily influenced by French planning regulations which remained unchanged and the courtyard organisation was totally abandoned. There has been a complete rejection and devaluation of the traditional framework that was perceived as ill-adapted to the new lifestyles and progress.

floor. The rooms were still organised around a central space, however; their function was becoming more specific, particularly with the introduction of modern commodities such as the television and the fridge.

## Low-income informal housing: a transitional typology?

A significant proportion of the population who can afford to move out from the medina or the Kasbah will do so. Some of these families end up in self-built informal settlements where land was subdivided and plots sold off more or less legally by private land speculators. A research project carried out in the 1980s on low-income self-built urban housing in Morocco and Tunisia shows clearly that the self-built houses of lower working class north African urban families illustrate continuing reference to the traditional courtyard houses (Santelli 1985). The self-produced houses are invariably of the courtyard type. In the case of the Ettadhamen neighbourhood near Tunis, the houses are organised around a real courtyard whereas in the El Hajja neighbourhood (on the periphery of Rabat), the courtyard is a more or less covered central space.

In the El Hajja settlement (Morocco) plots are of 70 to 80 square metres. The first floor of the dwelling projects over the street and the courtyard of the lower floors is covered with glass bricks to allow light to filter down. Stairs are placed in a corner of the street façade to ensure the privacy of each level, particularly when the owner rents out lower floors to non-family. In the case of the Ettadhamen settlement in Tunisia, the land plots range from 150 to 200 square metres, and the houses are single-storey with a larger courtyard. This is because the housing crisis in Tunisia is less acute than in Morocco.

In both of these informal settlements, self-built houses display a modern façade similar to that of a villa. The façade becomes the focus for symbolic investment claiming progress and modernity. Yet the space configuration of the houses remains traditional, with the organisation of rooms around a central space.

The study of Santelli provides evidence that low income self-built houses were still making a strong reference to the traditional house model but were evolving towards a more contemporary model. These houses were occupied by various unrelated households, each household having a separate

## Persistence of traditional space use patterns

Research carried out by the author at the end of the 1980s on the way low and middle income families inhabited mass housing flats in Algiers revealed interesting results. A survey of 128 flats was carried out in four mass housing estates in Algiers. Records of how the flats were furnished and occupied were made systematically (Behloul 1999).

There was a strong tendency amongst the vast majority of the sample (128 households) to separate the guests' reception room from the living room, despite the acute shortage of space within the dwelling units. The guests' reception room was furnished in a 'modern' way and sometimes contained a dining table which was rarely used, whereas one of the bedrooms was used as a traditional living space with flexible arrangement (bunk beds and a moveable tray) similar to that of the spaces in courtyard houses. There was a strong tendency amongst middle income households to display a modern way of living in the guest's reception room and to maintain a more traditional, multi-purpose and flexible use of space in one of the bedrooms. It is important to point out that this was also the case for nuclear families where both parents are highly educated and both work. When asked about their housing aspirations, most respondents mentioned that they would like to build a modern villa.

The occupancy of modern apartments shows a tendency towards exhibiting modernity through the furnishing of the guests' room and the daily use of traditional furnishing in the living room. The symbolic importance of exhibiting a modern façade, whether in the guest room or in the treatment of the house façade, combined with the persistence of traditional space use patterns illustrates a clear conflict.

The persistence until today of traditional space-use, patterns among the medium to high-income households living in modern apartments illustrates how cultural factors are resistant to change over time.

## Courtyard housing today

North African cities have witnessed the wide spread of four- to five-storey apartment blocks (provided by both formal and informal sectors) with three-roomed apartments as the average size. The number of contemporary courtyard housing projects built in north African cities is low.

One of these rare projects can be illustrated in the case of the Hafsia neighbourhood in Tunis. The neighbourhood is located in the lower part of the medina of Tunis. In 1933 the quarter was declared unsanitary and the first demolitions took place. Half the vacated site was then built up between 1973 and 1978 with new housing and commercial facilities. This first phase of this project received an Aga Khan Award for Architecture in 1983. The second phase was conceived in 1981–2 by the Tunisian Association for the Safeguard of the Medina.

A variety of house types were developed to satisfy the needs of different socio-economic groups. The majority of the houses were organised around a courtyard and most could be divided into two dwellings: one on the upper level and lit from the street, the other opening into the courtyard on the ground floor. The traditional typology of courtyard houses was respected and the integration of this new project within the existing traditional urban fabric was to some extent successful.

The dwellings built in the second phase of the project consist of terraced courtyard houses formed by two apartments: one on the ground floor and the other on the first floor. The privacy of the ground floor flat is then affected as the first floor dwelling overlooks the courtyard. Clearly the use of the courtyard typology to create independent apartments on ground- and first-floor levels requires careful consideration and planning of the openings. The roof space could form the outdoor space for the upper flat and could be a source of light.

It is interesting to note that surveys conducted among the population concerned with this project revealed that the majority of the respondents aspired to a villa with a front garden, and not a courtyard house (Santelli 1995).

## Conclusion

Several research projects have been carried out in the past on the traditional courtyard house in the historic core of Arab cities (Noor 1991). Most of these studies highlight the high level of responsiveness of this typology to the social, economic, cultural, religious and environmental factors at play when they were built. These studies also recommend the use of the internal courtyard typology in contemporary housing architecture in the Arab world because of its environmental qualities and the high level of privacy that such an organisation provides. However, most clients who have the opportunity to hire an architect to design their house insist on the use of spatial configurations that do not allow for an internal courtyard organisation. Planning regulations, which are not sympathetic to the exploration of the internal courtyard configuration, further aggravate this.

Courtyard housing is a sustainable form of housing that has existed for thousands of years and in various geographical regions. It is particularly responsive to the development of contemporary low-rise high-density urban housing. There is, therefore, a strong need to increase public and decision-makers' awareness of the unexplored potential of such a house form through experimental and innovative contemporary projects.

## Bibliography

Behloul, M. (1999) Post-occupancy evaluation of five-storey walk-up dwellings: The case of four mass housing estates in Algiers. In A. Awotona (ed.) *Housing Provision and Bottom-up Approaches, family Case Studies from Africa, Asia and South America*. Ashgate Publishing Ltd

Bianca, S. (2000) *Urban Form in the Arab World, Past and Present*. London, Thames & Hudson.

Giovenetti, F. (1992) De la Kasbah D'Alger. *Journal of the Islamic Environmental Design Research Centre* Vols 1–2, pp. 66–77.

Golvin, L. (1988) *Palais et Demeures d'Alger a la Periode Ottomane*. Aix en Provence, France, Edisud.

Mitchell, G. (1978) *Architecture of the Islamic World: Its history and social meaning with a complete survey of key monuments*, London, Thames and Hudson.

Noor, M. (1991) The Function and Form of the Courtyard House. *The Arab House*, University of Newcastle upon Tyne, School of Architecture, CARDO, pp 61–72.

Raverau, A. (1989) La *Casbah d' Alger et le site crea la ville*, Paris, Editions Sinbad.

Revault, J. (1967) *Palais et demeures de Tunis*, Paris, Editions du Centre national de la Recherche Scientifique

Revault, J. (1985) *Palais et demeures de Fes*, Paris, Editions du Centre national de la Recherche Scientifique.

Santelli, S. (1995) *La Ville le Creuset Mediterraneen: Tunis*, Paris, Editions du Demi-Cercle. CNRS.

Santelli, S. (1992) *Medinas: traditional architecture of Tunisia*, Tunis, Dar Ashra Editions.

Santelli, S. (1985) Self-built urban housing, Rabat and Tunis. *Mimar* No. 17, Jul–Sep. pp. 41–8.

Spigai, V. (1992) Semiotique d'une architecture urbaine, la maison a patio sd'Alger. *Journal of the Islamic Environmental Design Research Centre*, Vols 1–2, pp. 54–65.

# Part 2

# Social and cultural dimensions

# 6 The power of the veil: gender inequality in the domestic setting of traditional courtyard houses

REEM ZAKO

## Introduction

The courtyard house was the most widespread house form in traditional Arab and Islamic cities. While modern house building in the region has moved away from this form, the courtyard house continues to be the focus of numerous studies, ranging from those that deal with external environmental issues to those that address the suitability of courtyard housing to meet the social agendas of prevailing governments (Azzawi 1969; Noor 1986; Warren and Fethi 1982).

On one hand, the traditional need to entertain male guests while at the same time barring their access and contact with females of the household has given rise to additional complexities of design particular to Islamic domestic architecture (Al-Shahi 1986). On the other hand, religious demands require privacy and calm. In other words, the social agendas and requirements that influence the design of the house are numerous and in some instances can seem contradictory. Studies that have dealt with these social agendas focused on the need for separation between the private and public lives, and the segregation of women to maintain their privacy. A large number of the studies about the courtyard house dealt with, and paid special attention to, the detailing and fine-tuning of architecture of the house to deal with the various constraints. The concern for privacy was reflected in the physical forms in several ways. Among these are the placement of doors within the street, the avoidance of or the architectural treatment of windows on the street where any openings in the ground floor are small, grilled and above the line of vision of passers-by. In house architecture, the screened balcony allowed the female occupants to view the outside world without being seen and it also performed the important function of modifying the climate in hot regions. In the interiors of houses, screens may be built opening from the harem onto the reception rooms so that male gatherings and festivities can be observed from safety. Another important detail was the design of the entrance by placing a wall to ensure the visual privacy of the interior, resulting in the 'bent-entrance' principle (Warren and Fethi 1982).

The focus of this study is the spatial organisation of the courtyard house as a whole in an attempt to assess the underlying spatial structure that makes it possible for a centrally open house form to accommodate the contradicting requirements of the daily life of its inhabitants. A centrally open space through which movement and activities take place could lead to the convergence of the various categories of people in the house, thus violating privacy and segregation requirements. Specific attention will be paid to the way this spatial organisation differentiates between the requirements for the women and the men in the household and maintains the privacy of the women in their own homes and their status within.

## Methodology

Space syntax originated through the work of Hillier and Hanson in an effort to understand the relation between space and social life (Hillier and Hanson 1984; Hillier et al. 1984, 1987; Hanson 1998).

The theory of space syntax focuses on the study of the space within the built form or the settlement. A building achieves its function mainly within its spaces and not through its built form. Accordingly, buildings create and order the empty spaces in which their purpose and function take place. Social meanings in buildings take place within the spaces of the buildings, and the ordering of spaces in buildings is really about the ordering of relations between people.

According to space syntax, a certain structure underlies any spatial arrangement, linking the social and spatial orders, would be localised in the syntax of space itself and can be called a genotype. The genotype is an abstract form that describes the features of the spatial organisation, which represent the arrangement of individuals within a space and the organisation of space itself. It also shows how things may be put together and how others may be kept apart. The genotype gives to space its social meanings in the relations and interface between different categories of people.

A set of techniques has been developed within University College London (UCL) for the representation, quantification, and interpretation of spatial configuration in buildings and settlements, and to demonstrate the social logic of space. Configuration is defined as the minimum relation between two spaces taking into account a third, or the maximum relations among spaces in a complex taking into account all other spaces. Spatial configuration is thus a more complex idea than spatial relation, which need invoke no more than a pair of related spaces. The theory of 'space syntax' is that it is primarily – though not only – through spatial configuration that social relations and processes express themselves in space.

Figure (6.1a) is a divided cell in which space (a) is linked to space (b) through a gap. The gap creates a 'relation' that is called 'permeability' between the two spaces. But it means little until we know the relation of each to at least one further space – that is, until we know the position of each with respect to a configuration. For example, (6.1b) and (6.1c) show two possible relations of the spaces (a) and (b) to the outside, space (c). In (6.1b) both spaces are directly connected to (c) but in (6.1c) only space (a) is so connected, so that it is necessary to pass through space (a) to get to space (b) from space (c). This means that the relation between (a) and (b) is changed when (c) is considered. In one case, (a) controls the path from (c) to (b); in the other it does not.

This difference may be graphically clarified by a useful technique for representing spatial configuration: the justified graph. This is a graph in which a particular space is selected as

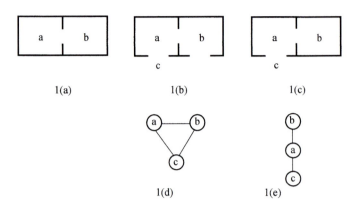

6.1 **Configurational relationships in the distribution of domestic spaces (after Hillier et al. 1987 and Hanson 1998)**

the 'root', and the spaces in the graph are then aligned above it in levels according to how many spaces one must pass through to arrive at each space from the root. Thus (6.1d) and (6.1e) are justified graphs of (6.1b) and (6.1c) respectively. A space is at depth 1 from another if it is directly accessible to it, at depth 2 if it is necessary to pass through one intervening space in order to move from one to the other, at depth 3 if a minimum of two spaces must be passed through, and so on.

Depth will be used in a more developed and quantitative form, which is called integration. The integration value of a space expresses the relative depth of that space from all others in the graph through the following formula and its transformations in order to unify and be able to compare the results across a sample:

$$\frac{2(md - 1)}{k - 2}$$

where (md) is the mean depth of spaces from the space and (k) is the total number of spaces in the graph. Lower values indicate maximum integration, that is, least depth from that space, and higher values maximum segregation, that is, maximum possible depth. The integration value of a space thus expresses numerically a key aspect of the shape of the justified graph from that space.

In most spatial complexes, integration values will be different for different spaces: such variations are one of the keys to the way in which cultural and social relations express themselves through space. For example, different functions or activities in a dwelling are usually assigned to spaces that integrate the complex to differing degrees. Function thus acquires a spatial expression that can be assigned a numerical value. If these numerical differences in functions are in a consistent order across a sample, then a cultural pattern exists, one that can be detected in *things*, rather than just in the way it is interpreted by minds. This particular type of consistency in spatial patterning is the inequality genotype, which is one of the most general means by which culture is built into spatial layout. How strong or weak these inequalities are in a complex or in a sample is therefore also of importance. To measure this, an entropy-based measure called difference factor was developed to quantify the degree of difference between the integration values of any three (or more with a modified formula) spaces or functions. This is essentially an adaptation of Shannon's H-measure (Shannon and Weaver 1948) for transition probabilities, in which the integration value of a space over the total integration for the three spaces is substituted for the transition probabilities in Shannon's equation:

$$H = -\left[\frac{a}{t}\ln\left(\frac{a}{t}\right)\right] + \left[\frac{b}{t}\ln\left(\frac{b}{t}\right)\right] + \left[\frac{c}{t}\ln\left(\frac{c}{t}\right)\right]$$

where (H) is the unrelativised difference factor for three spaces; (a), (b) and (c) are the integration values of the spaces; and (t) is their sum.

This (H) can then be 'relativised' between ln 2 and ln 3 to give a 'relative difference factor', (H*), between 0 (the maximum difference, or minimum entropy) and 1 (the minimum difference, or maximum entropy, that is, all values are equal):

$$H^* = \frac{H - \ln 2}{\ln 3 - \ln 2}$$

An 'inequality genotype' with a low entropy value will therefore be 'strong' genotype, whereas one that exists, but tends to have a high entropy, will be a 'weak' genotype.

These simple measures are able to express culturally significant typological differences among plans because the concepts on which they are based have in themselves a kind of intrinsic 'social logic'. Depth among a set of spaces always expresses how directly the functions of those spaces are integrated with or separated from each other, and thus how easy and natural it is to generate relations among them, whereas the control (of the actual movement) that a space has over another depends on the availability of alternative routes of movement.

## Case study

Studies that trace the development of house form have highlighted that the courtyard house, or the inward-looking oriental urban house, has been the dominant house form shared by the four ancient civilizations in Mesopotamia, the Nile Valley, India and China. It developed and became more sophisticated during the Islamic era. With the expansion of the realm of Islam, the concept of the courtyard house followed the path of the conquerors and has survived to the present day (in various degrees) as the prototypical urban dwelling in the region (Schoenauer 1981).

The principle identifiable spaces and rooms of the house are: the *mejaz* (the entrance passageway), *dolan* (the entrance vestibule in the larger house), *salamlik* (the reception room), *tarma* (the balcony that overlooks the courtyard), *iwan* and *talar* (open rooms which widen the balcony into a usable space), the *iwanchas* (smaller opening off the tarma), the *ursi* (this is the great room of the house), the *shenashil* (protruding sections from the first floor rooms), the *kafshakan* (a room suspended halfway between the upper and lower floors, which is a retreat for the elders) and the *takhatabush* (a raised ground floor room). These spaces are not necessarily present in all houses, but any combination of them could be present at any one time (Warren and Fethi 1982).

For the purposes of this study, two medium-sized courtyard houses have been chosen to test the theory of space syntax and its applicability in various cultures and backgrounds.

### Courtyard house A

This house has two courtyards, within an irregular-shaped plot and a single entrance. The first courtyard acts as an entrance courtyard (Figure 6.2). The entrance space is square and comparatively large: it leads to the first (entrance) courtyard from which there is a staircase to parts of the first floor. While the first courtyard leads to the central courtyard on the ground floor, the rooms around each courtyard on the first floor are not linked together. The link between the two courtyards is designed on the 'bent-entrance' principle, where visibility from one courtyard into the other is restricted.

The main reception rooms (for male visitors) are situated off the entrance courtyard, while the women of the household and their female visitors will be using the spaces adjoining the main courtyard and the first floors spaces.

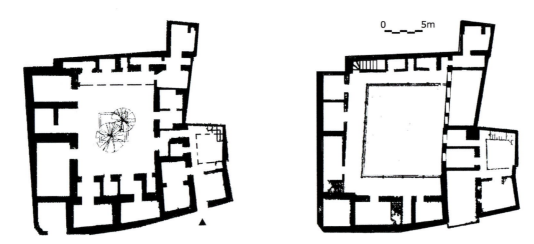

6.2   **Ground (left) and first floor plan (right) of house A. Notice how the house entrance is via the secondary courtyard B (after J. Warren and I. Fathy 1982)**

## Courtyard house B

This house is built around two courtyards, both of which are perfectly square-shaped but result in an irregularly shaped house (Figure 6.3). Each courtyard is linked to the outside and they are also linked together by a space very similar in its design to the bent-entrance principle, thus restricting the view in between the two courtyards to the minimum. The entrance to the first courtyard is almost direct from the exterior, while the entrance to the second, larger courtyard is through a long entrance space followed by a corridor. Another dominant feature of this household is the full linking of upper floor spaces overlooking both courtyards.

The main reception rooms (for male visitors) are situated off the first courtyard, while the women of the household and their female visitors will be using the spaces adjoining the main courtyard and the upper floors spaces.

In formal and geometric terms these two houses vary. In house B, geometric symmetry has been carried out to the finest detailing in the design and placement of the rooms opposite each other, *ursis* facing each other, the *kabishkans* occupying the four corners and both courtyards being perfect squares. This is not the case in house A, where geometric rules were not followed either in the design or placement of the main rooms, not even in the *ursis*, which are the showpiece of the house and in which symmetry is usually carried to the highest point.

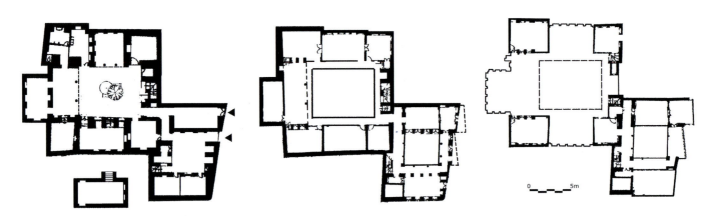

6.3   **Ground (left) and first floor plan (right) of house B (after J. Warren and I. Fathy 1982)**

## Analysis and findings

The first task undertaken was to provide a convex analysis of each of the two houses, by breaking their spaces into the largest and least number of convex spaces, translating this convex analysis into a permeability graph, and identifying the most integrated and segregated spaces in each case.

Figure 6.4a shows the permeability graph of the convex analysis justified from the exterior of house A. Figure 6.4b shows the same permeability graph with the spaces coded according to their integration sequence (from a being the most integrated, through to b, c, d, e1, e2 and f being the most segregated). Figure 6.5 illustrates the convex spaces in house A, coded according to this sequence.

This reveals that the most integrated spaces are the main courtyard and circulation spaces connected to it, following in the sequence are the entrance courtyard and more of circulation spaces. The *ursis* vary in their integration values while the men's reception room is quite segregated (but is not the most segregated).

Figure 6.6a shows the permeability graph of the convex analysis justified from the exterior of house B. Figure 6.6b

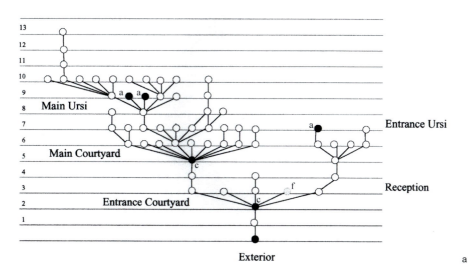

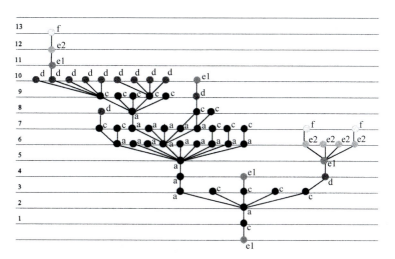

6.4 **Permeability graph of house A justified from the exterior (a) and coded according to the integration sequence (b) – a, b, c, d, e1, e2 and f represent the integration sequence, with 'a' being the most integrated and 'f' being the most segregated**

 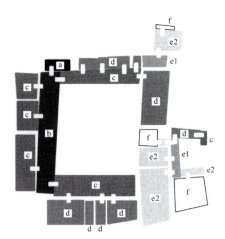

6.5  **Integrated convex analysis of house A. Ground floor (left) and first floor (right)**

shows the same permeability graph with the spaces coded according to their integration sequence, and Figure 6.7 illustrates the convex spaces in house B coded according to this sequence. A similar pattern to that of house A appears in that the most integrated spaces are those concentrated in the circulation areas. Once again the *ursis* vary in their integration values. Finally, as one might suspect, the most segregated spaces in this house are the *kabishkans* on the upper floor.

In order to understand the space syntax characteristics of these courtyard houses, the next task was to identify the key function or activity spaces in each house and put them in a sequence according to their integration values. At this stage, it is worth noting that in the courtyard house the rooms and spaces are not necessarily function-specific as is the case in Western houses. Reuther noted that:

He (the Oriental) divides his house into two; the diwankhana, reserved for guests and the haram, which is used by the family. Individual rooms, however, he prefers to distinguish according to whether they are more pleasant to live in during the summer or winter, at morning, noon or night ... Thus the idea of bedroom is as meaningless as a dining room.

Warren and Fethi 1982

Therefore, a range of functions and activities can take place in any one space what is of more importance is the way the person (or persons) who occupy the space in order to carry out an activity make the spaces 'user-labelled'. The fluidity of the space/function relationship make the type of analysis undertaken here necessary in order to understand the deeper meanings associated with the courtyard house.

The integration sequence for house A is:

**Main courtyard** > *mejaz* > entrance court > **main *ursi*** > **reception** > **Exterior** > Entrance *ursi*
**0.803** > 0.988 (mean) > 1.193 > **1.342** > **1.467** > **1.751** > 2.400

The integration sequence for house B is:

**Main courtyard** > *mejaz* > entrance court > **main *ursi*** > **reception** > **Exterior** > Entrance *ursi*
**1.037** > 1.213 (mean) > 1.239 > **1.443** > **1.451** > **1.510** > 1.546

We can notice that in both houses, the main courtyard is most integrated, followed by the *mejaz* (its link to the entrance courtyard), then the entrance courtyard. These spaces provide the 'hub' of the movement and activity in the house, and their integration values (which is a quantification of the relationship of every space in the system to every other space) are a clear manifestation of this. While the reception room and the *ursis* are quite segregated. The spaces that are 'static–activity' and 'user-labelled' spaces are most segregated as opposed to movement spaces or the spaces in which multitudes of activities take place or converge in them. In this sense, the men's reception room and the *ursis* have the same relation within the spatial configuration. The integration values of the exterior have also been calculated and are included

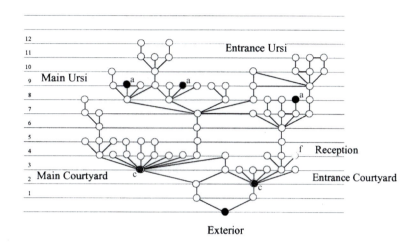

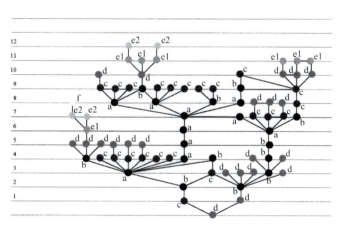

6.6  **Permeability graph of house B justified from the exterior (a) and coded according to the integration sequence (b) – a, b, c, d, e1, e2 and f represent the integration sequence, with 'a' being the most integrated and 'f' being the most segregated**

in the sequence because of its potential role in providing alternative routes in and out of both houses.

Comparing the above integration sequences for the identified key spaces in the two houses, a striking resemblance appears, in that both sequences are identical. This means that the spatial configurations of these houses are very similar to each other, especially in the way that these specific spaces are placed in relation to each other to create the overall spatial pattern. Considering that the spaces identified consist of both the user-labelled spaces (reception room and *ursi*) and the 'convergence of activity' spaces (both of the courtyards), the relation of these spaces and therefore the activities that take

place in them, and their users are consistent. In other words, both these houses belong to the same genotype.

Previous studies that have been carried out using the space syntax methodology on houses in other parts of the world have identified genotypes with only a three-space sequence. In this case a seven-space sequence is evident, which suggests a much stronger genotype in which the relation between these spaces within the whole configuration is much more defined and structured (Hillier *et al.* 1987; Hanson 1998).

As our focus in this study is the differentiation between the use of space by the various categories of people and the relations between them, the difference factor has been calculated

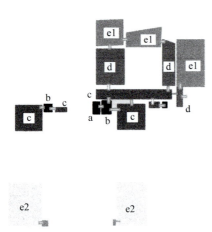

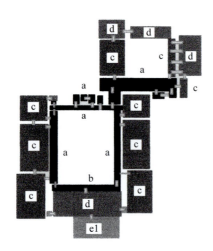

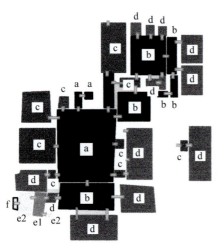

**6.7  Integration convex analysis for house B**

for each between the main courtyard, exterior and the reception (and *ursi*) to determine the variations or similarities. We have also calculated the difference factor for the minimum, mean and maximum integration values for each house.

The relativised difference factor is a figure that ranges between 0 and 1, with figures close to 1 having most entropy or 'similarity', and lower figures more structure. An inequality genotype with a low entropy value will therefore be a 'strong' genotype.

When comparing these values for each house separately in Table 6.1, we find more differentiation between the (mean/minimum/maximum) than that between labelled spaces. In house A, H* all = 0.777 which is lower than both H* male/ H* female, as is the case in house B. On the other hand we notice that the difference factor between the two sets of labelled spaces (H* male and H* female) in each house is very similar. So, the configurational position of the reception (or main *ursi*), between the main courtyard (as the hub of the internal movement and activity in the house) at one end and the exterior of the house on the other is similar to one another. In this sense, the spatial configuration of the courtyard house and its labelling of spaces according to the user do not discriminate or differentiate between the inhabitants of the house and their locations internally. Comparing the difference factors for the two houses, we can notice more differentiation in house A and more similarity in house B, especially when comparing the differentiation between the labelled spaces. This could be explained by the existence of a single entrance to house A – as opposed to two entrances to house B – which makes the relation of the exterior of the house to its interior much more differentiated than in house B, in which alternative movement routes exist.

In trying to further investigate the issue of accessibility or movement within the two houses, axial analyses have been carried out by drawing the longest and fewest lines that go through all the convex spaces in each of the two houses. We then used the same procedure as for the convex analysis to establish the most integrated and segregated lines of movement.

Figures 6.8 and 6.9 show the axial lines coded according to their integration values from most to least, integrated for houses A and B respectively. In both houses a high degree of correspondence exists between the convex spaces and the axial lines, in that the most integrated lines go through the most integrated spaces and the least integrated (i.e. the segregated) lines go through the segregated spaces.

Table 6.1 **Summary of relativised difference factor for houses A and B**

|  | Relativised difference factor (H*) | House A | House B |
|---|---|---|---|
| H* male | Main courtyard / reception / exterior |  |  |
|  | 0.803 / 1.467 / 1.751 | 0.884 |  |
|  | 1.037 / 1.451 / 1.510 | . | 0.968 |
| H* female | Main courtyard / main *ursi* / exterior |  |  |
|  | 0.803 / 1.342 / 1.751 | 0.885 |  |
|  | 1.037 / 1.295 / 1.510 |  | 0.972 |
| H* all | Mean / minimum / maximum |  |  |
|  | 1.454 / 0.803 / 2.400 | 0.777 |  |
|  | 1.400 / 0.860 / 2.238 |  | 0.823 |

If the convex space is the static domain for the location of a specific category of people or the activity/function they carry out in the space, then the axial line that goes through the space or led to it is its dynamic manifestation. In this sense, the axial line analysis confirms the findings of the convex space analysis regarding the relations of the spaces within the configuration as a whole and the movement within these spaces, but the spatial configuration of these houses is not only about the movement or accessibility within them.

The next issue to investigate would be more of a local issue of the relationship of each space with its neighbouring spaces but within the configuration as a whole. This will be carried out by looking at specific spaces (namely the reception room and *ursis*).

In both houses, the reception room is only three spaces deep (four in the case of house B from the exterior (i.e. one needs to pass only two spaces) and in any case cannot see much further into the house than that. Also, their locations are moved away from the integration core of the house (or its

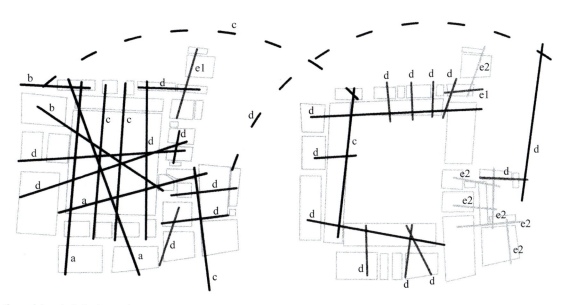

6.8 **Integration axial analysis for house A**

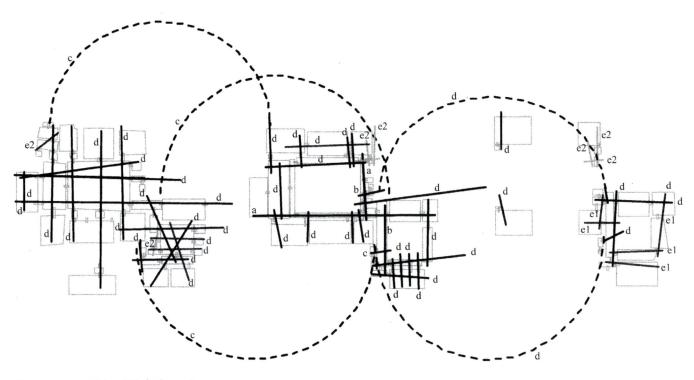

6.9 **Integration axial analysis for house B**

hub). There is a combination of a limited permeability into the house combined with an equally limited visibility, and in any case the only (slightly) integrated space a visitor will see or go through is the entrance courtyard.

Conversely, the location of the *ursi* offers a greater variety in terms of accessibility and visibility. In house A, the *ursi* (located off the main courtyard) is quite deep from the exterior of the house (eight steps away), but is directly connected to the integration core. In addition, the entire movement spaces of the first floor and most of the courtyard could be seen from it, so it dominates these visually. It also overlooks the connecting space with the entrance courtyard, so anyone entering the main courtyard could be seen from the *ursi*. The same happens in house B, where the *ursi*, (located off the main courtyard) although deeper from the exterior, also enjoys direct connection to the integration core and visual control of the movement spaces and the main courtyard. Additionally, anyone entering the main courtyard would be visible from the *ursi*.

The *ursis* overlooking the entrance courtyard are slightly different in the two houses. In house A, where there is no con-

nection between the upper floors surrounding the two courtyards, the *ursi* is quite deep, segregated and overlooks only the minimum spaces required to reach it. On the other hand, its counterpart in house B enjoys a much more central location within the main integration core of the house, both in terms of the accessibility and visibility to the core.

The 'male' spaces – or the spaces that male visitors are invited into – are spaces that are very shallow from the outside and are not integrated in the household. This corresponds with and reflects the literature concerning this attribute, male guests are invited into rooms close to the main entrance of the house and usually through a 'bent' vestibule. These do not lead to further/deeper spaces in the household. Moreover, they do not have any visual control on other parts of the household.

Women of the household and their female guests use the spaces that are deeper in the house from the outside – especially in the case of the single entrance house. While these spaces are deeper than the male-dominated spaces, they enjoy further characteristics. First, their control over the other spaces of the household, either by being parts of rings within the household or by being distribution spaces to other in the house, and second, by having visual control over the other spaces of the household, even over the 'male' spaces.

As the house gets larger (which indicates mostly a higher economic status), its spatial configuration tends to provide the women with much greater flexibility of movement and control within the house: they can observe whatever is happening in any part of it without being noticed or observed. With the introduction of the second entrance they can even venture to the outside world without passing through the entrance courtyard, as is the case in house B.

## Conclusion

This chapter has investigated an alternative method for the classification of space that goes beyond the formal and geometric analysis and tries to link the structure and use of the domestic spaces with the underlying social orders.

In summary, although the women in these houses were subject to the constraints of a male-dominated society with strict codes and rules of behaviour, they are not completely subject to forces outside their control, and they have a variety of strategies enabling them to mitigate the effects of male control. To the female belonged the domestic domain and the tasks she performs there are by right exclusive to her. In controlling much of this domain, she partially controls its inhabitants, including men, thereby giving an element of order to the whole house. So, in the courtyard house there is a reversal of roles and within it, the men (and specifically the visitors or the non-kin) are segregated and excluded from core activities.

While this chapter is based on the analysis and comparison of two houses only, further research using the same methodology on a much larger sample could give more conclusive results. It will also be beneficial if examples from various locations can be studied independently and then compared as a whole, in order to establish any regional differences within them.

## Acknowledgements

I would like to express my thanks to Mr John Warren for granting me his kind permission to use the illustrations of the two houses from his book *Traditional Houses in Baghdad*.

## Bibliography

Al-Shahi, A. (1986) 'Welcome my house is yours'. In A. D. C. Hyland and A. Al. Shahi (eds) *Proceedings of the Colloquium held in the University of Newcastle upon Tyne on the Arab House*. Newcastle upon Tyne, University of Newcastle upon Tyne.

Azzawi, S. (1969) 'Oriental Houses in Iraq'. In P. Oliver (ed.) *Shelter and Society*, London, Barrie and Rockliffe Press.

Hanson, J. (1998) *Decoding Homes and Houses*. Cambridge, Cambridge University Press.

Hillier, B. and Hanson, J. (1984) *The Social Logic of Space*. Cambridge, Cambridge University Press.

Hillier, B., Hanson, J. and Peponis, J. (1984) 'What do we mean by building function?' In J. Powell (ed.) *Designing for Building Utilisation*. London, Spon, pp. 61–72.

Hillier, B., Hanson, J. and Graham, H. (1987). 'Ideas are in things: an application of the Space Syntax method to discovering housing genotypes'. *Environment and Planning B: Planning and Design* **14**, 363–85.

Noor, M. (1986) 'The function and form of the courtyard house'. In A. D. C. Hyland and A. Al. Shahi (eds) *Proceedings of the Colloquium held in the University of Newcastle upon Tyne on the Arab House*. Newcastle upon Tyne, University of Newcastle upon Tyne.

Schoenauer, N. (1981) *6000 years of Housing, Volume 2: The Oriental Urban House*. New York, Garland STPM Press.

Shannon, C. and Weaver, W. (1948). *The Mathematical Theory of Communication* Chicago, University of Illinois Press.

Warren, J. and Fethi, I. (1982) *Traditional Houses in Baghdad*. London, Coach Publishing Houses Ltd.

# 7 The role of privacy in the design of the Saudi Arabian courtyard house

OMAR S. BAHAMMAM

This chapter explores the evolution of the traditional courtyard house in Saudi Arabia. The main focus is upon behavioural and cultural factors, especially the importance of privacy and how its imperatives have found expression in building layout. The question of privacy is related to Islamic teachings, and through an examination of religious texts an argument is constructed for the conceptualization and physical form of the courtyard house.

## Introduction

Man's first environmental problem was the search for shelter in order to protect himself physically. He solved that problem in two ways: either by finding a ready-made shelter or by constructing shelters to his own design. The first constructed shelters were built out of available materials and different societies in different geographical locations developed their own type of shelters. They were all intended to solve the same need and to express the same idea: that of providing physical protection in the simplest possible way.

Many things have changed greatly since primitive man began establishing rudimentary shelters. The most important change is the ability to consider other factors over and above the simple need for a physical shelter. Of these factors, the behavioural ones emerge as a significant element affecting the design and the spiritual values and religious ideas that help to form people's cultures.

The interaction of complex forces influences the layout and design chosen by various societies for their houses. People with differing attitudes and ideas react with their environments differently. The variety in architectural form can be seen as a result of a host of social, cultural, economic, physical and technological variables (Rapaport, 1969). Open architectural spaces such as courtyards take different shapes and sizes from one environment to another according to the existing physical and behavioural factors, yet different forms of architectural open spaces exist in different parts of the world despite similar physical conditions. This variety in forms is a reflection of the different behavioural factors in each society which influence not only the design of buildings but of the open spaces surrounding or within them.

The social and cultural life of the people is a key factor in giving architecture its identity and character. This argument is as true in Saudi Arabia as in any other society. The interaction of cultural and religious values, together with physical considerations, has had a significant influence in giving Saudi architecture its own distinctive style. Behavioural factors related to architecture include a wide range of human concerns, responses and attitudes. Privacy is one of these factors and, because of its strong role in Saudi society, it has become the determining behavioural factor in shaping the design of Saudi dwellings. This chapter will illustrate the influence of privacy on the design of the Saudi courtyard, and will discuss how people have translated the need for privacy into architectural spaces and forms and at the same time made their architecture express fundamental cultural ideas.

## Behavioural factors and architectural identity

The study of any society's traditional architecture should include the social and cultural aspects of that particular society. The purpose of such a study would be to arrive at an understanding of the real interaction between social and spatial orders. A full understanding of this complex interaction, however, cannot be reached without an examination of both intellectual and subconscious patterns of thought. The distinction between what a form is and what it means to a particular social group is the key to understanding courtyard architecture. The distinction between form and meaning, awareness of the difference, its acceptance and its recognition are the four steps leading from a naive to a mature view of architecture (Bonta 1979). The rationale behind the composition of built elements depends on our understanding of the forces that shape it. In the case of the behavioural element, rationality is dependent upon our understanding of the factors and aspirations that underlie the behaviour. Knowing what these factors might be is the key to being able to make proper design judgments.

The design of spaces of the Saudi house, in addition to being physically functional, is also a response to the behavioural values of the society. The courtyard, as one of those architectural elements, is a result of physical and behavioural factors. In many places in the world where the same climatic

7.2 **Sketch of Matmala in Tunisia showing the use of circular courtyards**

forces exist, several types of courtyard solution have resulted in vernacular structures (see Figures 7.1 and 7.2). In his book *Privacy and Freedom* Westin expressed this idea by saying:

> Indeed, people in different cultures experience the world differently not only in terms of language but also with their senses. They inhabit a different sensory world, affecting the way they relate to one another in space.
>
> Westin 1970, p. 15

It is clear that the values people had led to patterns of behaviour which in turn gave shape to built forms. Ultimately, values are the root of architectural meaning and give validity to functional solutions.

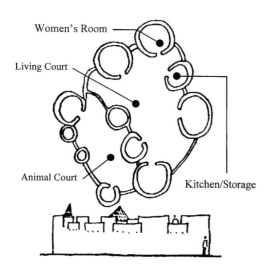

7.1 **Traditional Somba village house showing the use of two courtyards – one for people, the other for animals**

## Privacy in Saudi architecture

The desire for privacy is a significant sociocultural factor influencing housing design in almost every society. A wide range of solutions has evolved in various cultures to accommodate peoples' need for privacy as one of the basic demands on form. Architectural layouts achieve privacy through physical means by planning, arranging and creating an order of spaces which work together to provide privacy. Gottlieb (1965) expressed the need for privacy as a basic demand for almost all humans:

A glass house could be made to satisfy all of one's needs for physical shelter, but there are very few people who would feel sheltered in one; shelter must satisfy the need for a physiological feeling of protection, a feeling that there is something solid around one.

Gottlieb 1965, p. 155

Different forms of privacy are demanded by different cultures around the world. Saudi society's forms of privacy are the result of deeply held religious teachings. As an Islamic society, the hierarchy of privacy in Saudi Arabia is arranged according to the teaching of Islam. Two forms of privacy that affect the shape and the design of the Saudi traditional dwelling – female privacy and family privacy.

## Female privacy

According to Islamic teaching, a Muslim woman is expected to seek protection for her own body from being seen when she is in public. The Muslim woman is not allowed to reveal her figure to anybody other than her husband, family members, and/or close women friends. At the same time, Muslim men are expected to lower their gaze and not stare at women. To maintain this privacy, houses have a protective role, Allah says in the Qur'ān (Surah 33: Part 22: Verse 59):

O Prophet! Tell your wives and your daughters and the believing women that they should cast their outer garments over their persons (when out of doors): that is most convenient, that they should be known (as such and not molested).

*Holy Qur'ān*, pp. 1264–5

This Qur'anic verse and many other references in Islamic law explicitly dictate a special form of privacy for women to protect them against visual intrusion from the eyes of an unrelated male.

This form of privacy is translated into reality in many built forms and public actions. It is clearly visible in the daily dress of Saudi women, in the form of the *hejab*[1] which provides total privacy for the female form (see Figure 7.3a). This behaviour is also reflected in the Saudi traditional built environment. The architectural form of the house is totally veiled from the outside, giving complete privacy to its components and spaces whilst also providing protection to its inhabitants against outsiders (see Figure 7.3b).

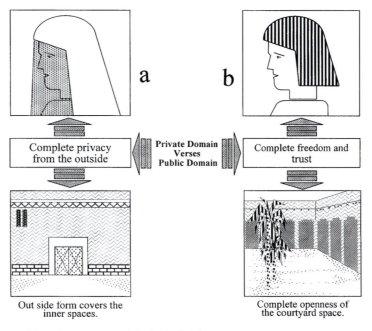

7.3 **The courtyard house reflects the need for privacy, expressed also in the *hejab***

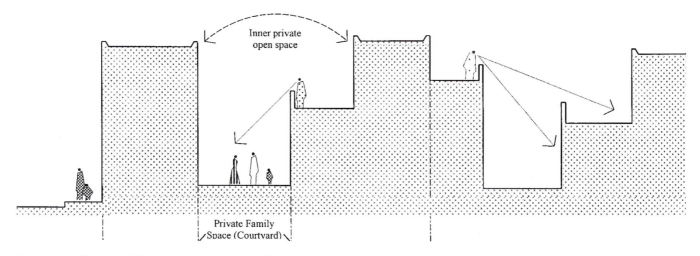

Inner private
open space

Private Family
Space (Courtyard)

7.4  **A section through adjoining houses showing how setbacks are used to maintain privacy between neighbours**

## Family privacy

Islam also protects and regulates family privacy between family members and other people. This form exists mainly in dwelling units, where there would be a distinction between the family's private domain and the outdoor domain. In the Qur'an (Surah 24: Part 18: Verse 27) Allah says:

> O ye who believe! Enter not houses other than your own, until ye have asked permission and saluted those in them: that is best for you, in order that ye may heed (what is seemly).
>
> *Holy Qur'an*, p. 1011

The verse reveals an important principle of family privacy by asking respectful permission before entering. In a further explanation of this principle, the Prophet said:

> It is not lawful for a Muslim person to peep into the house of another person until he has asked permission. Otherwise, if he peeps into the house before asking permission, verily [it is as if] he had entered.
>
> Al-Bukari 1955, p. 281

This insistence on privacy is intended to give the family of the house its protection against outside visual intrusion (Figure 7.4). The design of the traditional dwelling responds to this by sealing the architectural form of the dwelling from the outside and opening the entire spaces to the inside (see Figure 7.5). Subtle planning arrangements are also adopted at the entrance to further safeguard privacy. The courtyard is placed in the centre of the house to provide total protection and freedom for the family members. It acts as a general space between the elements of the house and is designed to be the

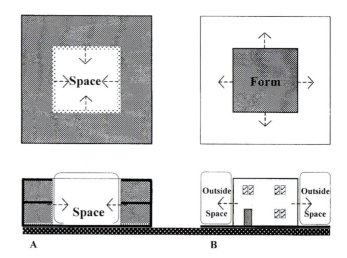

7.5  **The different concepts of space in a courtyard house (A) and a Western house (B)**

7.6  **A sketch showing the relationship between openings and the courtyard**

focal point, drawing various activities from the rooms to its central open space (see Figure 7.6). It is an active architectural space for sitting, eating, gathering, celebrating, playing, and even sleeping during hot summer nights. It performs many of the functions of the living room of the Western house.

These demands explain the main sociocultural ideas behind the evolution of the courtyard. It is designed to be a multifunctional family space in the house; it has the quality of drawing the family members from their individualities in the surrounding rooms to the shared space in the centre. The courtyard holds the family together while providing the proper atmosphere for social interaction within a single protective and secluded space. As such the courtyard reinforces family values, just as the Qur'an intended.

## The layout of the courtyard house

The layout of the traditional Saudi house consists of a composite structure built around one or more rectangular-shaped courtyards. The main courtyard is usually located in the middle of the house, the exterior courtyards are on the periphery and have different functions to the central one. These courtyards are usually found in the houses of wealthy families who have male servants and domestic animals.

The central courtyard is the family space. Main rooms and service areas such as the kitchen, storage and staircases surround the courtyard. The central courtyard is the only link between the family living spaces and the male, guest and the servants' sections (see Figure 7.6).

On the second floor, a gallery that overlooks and usually surrounds the central court on three sides connects the rooms. A terrace is usually located on the fourth side of the court allowing light and air to penetrate to the inner ground courtyard. This terrace also acts as an extension of the courtyard space on the second floor.

## Access to the courtyard

Access to the inner space of the house from outside is through an intermediate area (an entrance) which emphasizes the distinction between the external public and internal private spaces. At the same time, this area constitutes a filter which establishes a sequence of penetration and control through changes in direction. It is designed to obstruct any view of the inside, and hence does not give immediate access to the inner courtyard.

The entrance is usually located at the furthest point of the house, which is normally the corner, to provide maximum privacy. In other types of buildings such as schools, mosques and other public buildings where courtyards are a climatic necessity and there is no demand on privacy, the entrance is located in the middle point and opens directly into the courtyard.

The enclosed sanctuary of the house is designed to protect the privacy of the family. Means of access and filters are multiplied in order to create different degrees of intimacy as one proceeds from the external public spaces to the internal private ones. These degrees of access establish a hierarchical order in plan which is a characteristic of the courtyard house in Saudi Arabia. As such the primary role of the courtyard and the secondary role of the entrance establish architectural parameters which define the type.

## Openings to the inner courtyard

The Saudi house is an introverted form conceived from the inside outwards. External walls are very high to ensure that the domestic interior cannot be overlooked. The openings in the ground floor are small, grilled and above the vision line of passers-by (see Figure 7.3b). Windows on upper floors are generally larger to bring in light and air: as they are usually designed to prevent violating the privacy of neighbouring courtyards and terraces, some ingenuity in design is usually required.

Most of the openings of the house are oriented to the private inner spaces (i.e. the courtyard). The demand for privacy expressed by the opening to the inside leads to an emphasis on embellishing the interior elements: the courtyard terrace and the courtyard façades. The courtyard may contain small corner plants, paved ground and decorated features. All these elements are used in order to create an attractive space within the shell of the house – a courtyard which contains all the elements of the exterior landscape: the plants, the sun and the sky. The courtyard can therefore be seen as an idealized parcel of the outside world, one where the family can exist in a kind of self-contained earthly paradise.

# Conclusion

The study of courtyard houses in Saudi society reveals the role behavioural factors play in shaping human built environments. Each society throughout history has created an architecture that fits its own specific needs. Saudi society has developed its own manifestation of the courtyard house in order to satisfy functional and climate demands and also as an expression of wider cultural values. As a result, the traditional courtyard house has meaning and significance for the Saudi people, in spite of a reluctance to revitalize the form for modern needs.

The traditional courtyard house was built to accommodate complex climatic dictates and to serve equally complex human needs. Its form in plan and section was fashioned by the need to provide protection from the harsh heat of summer and to meet the need for privacy. The courtyard house is therefore veiled climatically and culturally. Its form mirrors closely the two agendas and hence the house and *hejab* are metaphorically connected. The design of components and spaces provide further protection to its inhabitants against outsiders, especially in the layout of the entrance and the positioning of the upper floor windows.

In order to provide privacy for the family, the courtyard is placed in the centre of the house as a focal point to accommodate the various activities of the family members in complete freedom and privacy. The entrance of the house follows a sequential pattern that allows the entry through changes in direction to obstruct any view of the inside, thus protecting the privacy of the occupants. Means of access and filters are multiplied in order to create different degrees of intimacy as one proceeds from the external public spaces to the internal private ones.

Although the house is a complete perimeter enclosed from the outside, it is entirely open to the inside: the opening of the rooms and the spaces are oriented to the private inner courtyard space. This places emphasis on decorating the interior elements of the courtyard with arches, terraces and panelling. The courtyard may contain a small garden, a well or a small pool and stands in marked contrast to the austere and unembellished external realm of the house. Although climate is a factor in the design of these houses, it is the need for privacy and the maintenance of family life which is the main generator of architectural form.

# Note

1   *Hejab*: the complete veil worn by women when out of their homes (see Figure 7.3a).

# Bibliography

Al-Bukari, (1955) *Al-Adab Al-Mufrad*. Cairo, Al-Maktbah Al-Salafea.

Al-Bukari, (1976) *Sahih Al-Bukari*, (trans. Dr Muhammad Muhsin Khan). Islamabad, Seth1 Straw Board Mills.

Alexander, C. (1977) *A Pattern Language*. New York, Oxford University Press.

Alexander, C. (1973) *Notes on the Synthesis*. Cambridge, MA, Harvard University.

Bahammam, A. (1986) *Architectural Patterns of Privacy in Saudi Arabia*. Masters Thesis. Montreal, Canada, School of Architecture.

BaHammam, O. (1995) *The Social Needs of the Users in Public Open Space: The Involvement of Socio-Cultural Aspects in Landscape Design of the Outdoor Urban Environment in Ar-Riyadh, Saudi Arabia*. A Ph.D. Thesis. Edinburgh, Scotland, Department of Architecture, University of Edinburgh.

Belkacem, Y. (1981) *Bioclimatic patterns and human aspects of urban form in the Islamic city: The Arab City*. Proceedings of a Symposium held in Medina, Kingdom of Saudi Arabia, The Arab Town Organization, King Saud University Press.

Bonta, J. P. (1979) *Architecture and its Interpretation*. London, Lund Humphries.

Gottlieb, L. D. (1965) *Environment and Design in Housing*. New York, Macmillan.

Grange, J. (1989) Place, body and situation. In D. Seamon and R. Mugerauer (eds) *Dwelling, Place and Environment*. New York, Columbia University Press, a Morningside Book.

Hall, T. E. (1966) *The Hidden Dimension*. Garden City, New York, Doubleday & Company Inc.

Kaplan, S. (1983) A model of person-environment compatibility. *Environment and Behavior* **15**, 3, 311–33.

Newman, O. (1972) *Defensible Space*. New York, Macmillan Company.

Rapaport, A. (1969) *House Form and Culture*. Englewood Cliffs, New Jersey, Prentice-Hall.

Rapoport, A. (1990) *The Meaning of the Built Environment: A nonverbal communication approach*. Tucson, Arizona, The University of Arizona Press.

Westin, A. F. (1970) *Privacy and Freedom*. New York, Atheneum.

# 8 The traditional courtyard house of Kuwait and the influence of Islam

## M. ANWARUL ISLAM AND NAWAL H. AL-SANAFI

## Introduction

The principle of building a house with rooms surrounding a courtyard has been in use since the beginning of human civilisation. In ancient Egypt, temples were built with courtyards and most houses included one or more courtyards. In the east, the Mesopotamian civilisations over the years – the Sumarians, the Babylonians and the Assyrians, whose empires included the area around the modern state of Kuwait – have also used courtyards in their houses, temples and palaces. Later, in the Greek and Roman architectures, courtyards were usually surrounded by a row of columns in public buildings, and by rooms and stores in private houses.

It is in the Arab lands of the seventh and eighth century, however, that the courtyard house has been adopted as the basic form of house design and remained as the predominant style until modern times. Recently, however, technological innovations leading to environmental control by mechanical means have generated compact form of housing units without courtyards, either in single storey or in multi-storey buildings.

The first known example of Islamic architecture, i.e., the house-cum-mosque of the Prophet Muhammad (peace be upon him) in Madinah built in 622 AD is basically a courtyard house. But unlike the elaborate multi-storey courtyard houses of the contemporary Jewish families in the neighbouring lands, it was a simple and unostentatious building to serve the basic functions of a dwelling house for his family and a covered area for congregational prayer. This house-cum-mosque set the pattern of mosque design for the next several centuries. The typical Arab mosque (Figure 8.1), which evolved from the Prophet's building, is likely to have influenced the development of low-rise courtyard houses over succeeding centuries.

## Courtyard houses of Kuwait

Before discussing the various factors that have influenced the choice of courtyard type and its continued use in this region since the beginning of Islam, it is necessary to look at the

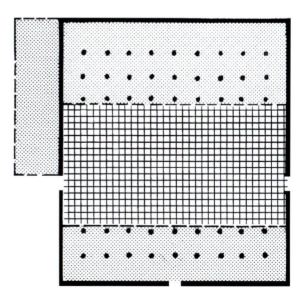

8.1a **Plan of a typical Arab mosque of the Middle Ages**

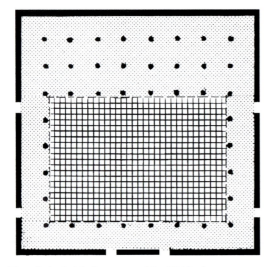

**8.1b   Plan of a typical Arab mosque of the Middle Ages**

tinually in front of them. The high roof of the rooms is made of mangrove and bamboo frames and the *liwan* columns are made of hard wood. The total area enclosed by the outer walls is 870 m$^2$ of which the courtyard is 357 m$^2$ or 40% of the total area. It has 10 sleeping rooms and 10 other rooms, thus making it a relatively big house with a large courtyard. However, if further rooms were added on the fourth side of the courtyard, which may have been the original design intention, the courtyard would have been reduced to a more standard size (i.e. 25–30% of the house area).

The plan of an earlier single-courtyard house built in the late nineteenthth century AD (Figure 8.4), shows the following main differences when compared to the house in Figure 8.3:

1   The courtyard in this house is surrounded by rooms on all four sides although the loggia runs on three sides only.
2   The walls are made of mud bricks and mud.
3   Both the house and the courtyard are smaller, i.e., 690 m$^2$ and 180 m$^2$ respectively.

An even earlier example of a courtyard house in Kuwait (Figure 8.5) illustrates a smaller size house compared to the other two.

In all three houses, the courtyard provides the occupants, especially the women, with a private external environment within the house. On hot sunny days, it provides a fully or partially shaded area from awnings fixed to the walls and the use of trees. In other cases, a sheltered open gallery, the *liwan*, provides a shaded buffer area between the hot open spaces of the courtyard and the cool rooms surrounding it.

In Kuwait, many of the courtyard houses would also have water pools or wells. These act to soften the effects of the hot and dry climate of the courtyard and provide a more pleasant environment where outdoor activities can be carried out with

characteristics of a courtyard house, particularly that in Kuwait. As we know, the court of a courtyard house is the enclosed space, open to the sky, usually surrounded by rooms on all four sides. In Kuwait there are houses which started with rooms only on one side of the enclosed courtyard. As families got bigger and needed more and more accommodation, the houses grew by adding rooms on other sides of the courtyard. Figure 8.2 illustrates the sequence of growth of such a building, the information having been obtained through an interview with a retired master builder who is aware of this building's phased development. This house, first built in 1937, ended with rooms surrounding the three sides of its courtyard as illustrated in Figure 8.3.

This is a single storey construction with internal and external walls made of sea rock and mud. The rooms are entered from the courtyard through the loggia (*liwan*) which runs con-

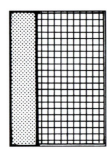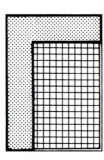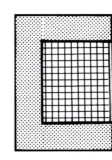

**8.2   The sequence of growth of a traditional courtyard house**

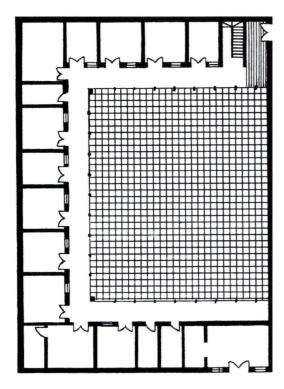

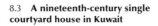

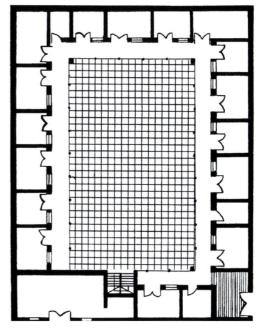

8.4 **A single-courtyard house built in the late nineteenth century**

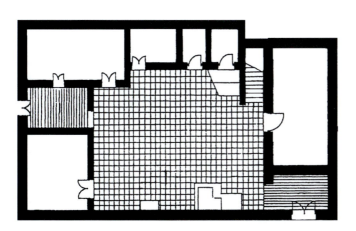

8.5 **Example of a small courtyard house in Kuwait (after Lewcock 1978)**

protection from sun, wind and dust (sand). As the external walls of the house have few or no openings, the courtyard also acts as the source of light and ventilation. For the latter, wind towers with an opening in the roof (*badgir*) are sometimes used to trap wind and circulate it through the rooms into the courtyard.

## Double-courtyard houses

In a single-courtyard house women have to vacate the courtyard to enable a male visitor or guest to reach the men's reception room (*diwaniya*) from the main entrance if the access happens to be through the courtyard. This problem is avoided in a double-courtyard house (Figure 8.6) where one of the courtyards is likely to be exclusively for the use of women and other close members of the family amongst whom no privacy is required. Sleeping rooms, the kitchen and other rooms which are used by the family members usually surround this courtyard, commonly known as the 'family courtyard'. This arrangement allows the other courtyard, next to the main entrance, to be used by the men of the house and their male guests and visitors.

Large houses in Kuwait usually have more than two courtyards. Compared with the large courtyard houses in other Arab countries, Kuwait seems to have a much larger percentage of multi-courtyard houses where each courtyard serves a particular household function. Apart from the family courtyard and the men's courtyard there may be a courtyard exclusively for the services: the kitchen, the stores, the toilets, etc. The kitchen courtyard may have provision for washing, cleaning (ablution) and bathing. There may also be an animal courtyard or stable having either a separate entrance from the outside or entered through the men's courtyard. Some or all the rooms surrounding this courtyard will be used to accommodate animals owned by the family. In some houses, e.g., a

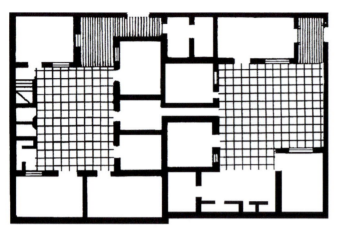

merchant's house, in addition to the men's courtyard there may be a business courtyard, used by the owner for business meetings and trading, which could also include storage rooms for the merchandise. The famous Bayt al-Badr, built in 1840 AD, which is now maintained by the government as a museum, is an example of a house where five courtyards exist, each with a separate function (Figure 8.7). The plan of another multi-courtyard house, Bayt al-Ghanim, which has four courts, is illustrated in Figure 8.8.

8.6 **Plan of a double courtyard house in Kuwait**

## Seafront courtyard houses

The city of Kuwait lies on the shore of the Bay of Kuwait, the shoreline being on the north of the city – slightly inclined

8.7 **Plan of Bayt al-Badr: a large multi-courtyard house in Kuwait**

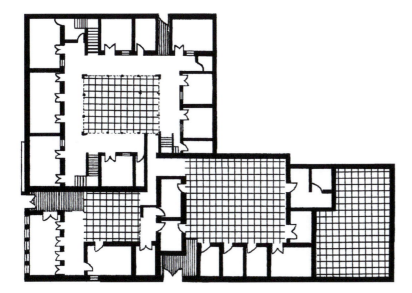

8.8 **Plan of Bayt al-Ghanim: a medium-sized multi-courtyard house in Kuwait**

towards the west. The two multi-courtyard houses shown in Figures 8.7 and 8.8 are on this shoreline and belong to rich merchants. Their alignment, particularly that of the courtyard, appears to be influenced by their proximity to the shore. Although many of the other seafront houses are large in size, there are also some which are smaller in size, and some have only one courtyard. Despite the variation in size and number of courtyards, most of the design characteristics of traditional courtyard houses in Kuwait are common. The external walls are essentially plain with few or no openings except in the front wall facing the road which, in the shoreline houses, is usually on the north side, i.e., towards the sea. The main entrance is in this wall, usually a large door of wooden panels with a wicket door of convenient size within it (see Figure 8.9). Compared to the stark simplicity of the wall façades, the door panels are either carved and/or decorated. In the shoreline houses, the main entrance is located on the north side and is therefore always in the shade. Masonry benches are frequently provided along the entrance wall and provide visitors with a relatively cool place to sit. The external walls of the houses have high and narrow external openings for light and ventilation. The only external windows are those found in the men's reception room.

Access to the men's reception room from the main entrance is as discrete as possible in order to maintain women's privacy. In multi-courtyard houses this access is usually through the men's courtyard. It is also a common practice to provide a passage between the main door and entrance to the courtyard so

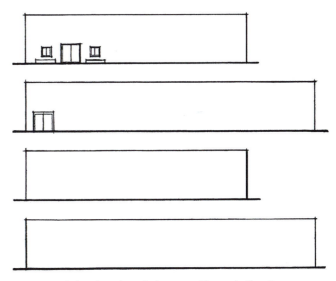

8.9 **External elevation of a typical courtyard house in Kuwait**

that there is no direct view of the interior of the house from the outside, even when the door is open. In some houses, the men's reception room may be entered directly from this passage without going through the courtyard (Figure 8.5) while in others the main entrance leads directly to the men's reception room (Figure 8.3). In the latter case, there is a separate entrance for the family members.

In addition to having a multi-courtyard organisation, the traditional large houses of Kuwait tend to be single-storey buildings. While a high proportion of large courtyard houses in Iraq are more than one-storey high, even the very large houses in Kuwait were built as single-storey buildings, although in some of them rooms have been added to the roof subsequently. The roof space is made usable by building perimeter parapets of adequate height. Access to such roofs is through one or more staircases leading from the courtyards. In smaller houses, rooms are sometimes built upstairs either with the same materials as in the ground floor or, more commonly, with a light roofing structure. Such a room is oriented in such a way to gain maximum ventilation from cooling breezes and would be used for sleeping, especially during the hot summer nights. In the house where the roof is not being used, parapets will be of lower height and the access to the roof may be by a ladder.

A large number of the seafront houses on the shoreline of the city of Kuwait, most of which were built during the last 150 years, still exist. Very few of the traditional buildings can be seen today within the city itself, as there has been large-scale demolition of old properties in order to build the modern city of Kuwait. The redevelopment of Kuwait following the oil boom of the 1970s necessitated the creation of purpose-built shopping areas, commercial and residential zones linked by wide roads and highways. However, we know that a large proportion of the demolished buildings were houses, built on similar principles to those of the shoreline houses. These were courtyard houses built close together, separated by narrow, winding lanes and alleyways wide enough to allow the passage of animal-drawn carts and designed to offer shade, trap air currents and minimise the build-up of heat.

## Town courtyard houses

Like the shoreline houses, the town houses varied considerably in size, although the building units had a degree of uniformity in width caused by the restricted length of available mangrove trunks used for roof joists. Difference in the size of the houses was usually due to the number of courtyards in the house: very large houses may have had a series of courtyards interlinked by passageways. As mentioned earlier, each courtyard would serve a particular function. Like the shoreline houses, the façades of these houses were bare apart from the main entrance door with its wicket, flanked by benches fixed against the front wall. Again, there would have been a few high-level window slits to admit light and act as ventilators.

Rooms had high ceilings, specially the sleeping rooms, to maximise the circulation of air and the beds would have been placed on plinths well above the floor to offset the effects of heat.

Town houses were also the ones where the practice of phased growth within the compound, as mentioned earlier, happened, i.e., initially with rooms on one or two sides of the courtyard, followed by subsequent developments on the other sides and ending up with a courtyard fully enclosed by rooms. One of the reasons for this type of extension would be that, unlike the shoreline houses, town houses would usually have little or no scope for expansion beyond the original compound because additional land was not available. As the population grew, the roof was also used extensively to create additional enclosed space for rest and relaxation, covered space for storage and even by adding first floor sleeping rooms in part or whole of the roof. Air circulation and ventilation are of paramount importance in town houses and extensive use was made of *badgirs*. A stone-covered storage well or chamber in the courtyard was also a typical feature of town houses.

## Common characteristics

The characteristics of a traditional courtyard house of Kuwait may be summarised as follows:

- There is an enclosed space or spaces open to the sky surrounded by rooms accommodating the various activities of the dwelling house.
- With hardly any opening in the external walls, the houses are inward-looking towards the courtyard, on which it has almost total dependence for light and air circulation, sometimes in conjunction with high level slit-like openings and a badgir (wind-catcher).
- The façade of the external walls is usually plain, devoid of any decoration with the elevations expressing a play of rectangles, squares and straight lines (Figure 8.9 shows external elevations of a house).
- Before subsequent expansion, the houses are usually built as one-storey structures with raised parapets in the roof which is accessed by a stair from the courtyard so that the roof space can be used for various purposes.
- The courtyards may have trees, water pools and/or wells, awnings, etc. to soften the effects of heat and glare.

- There are covered loggias (*liwans*) surrounding one or more sides of the courtyard which provide further protection from the sun.
- The number of courtyards varies, usually from one to five.
- The main entrance door is usually decorated as opposed to the austere treatment of the façade and exterior walls.
- The entrance is usually at the end of a passage which maintains the privacy of the house.

## Factors of influence in the design of Kuwaiti courtyard houses

### General

Several factors are likely to have influenced the use of the courtyard house as the basic form of housing in the Arabian peninsula and its surrounding countries. For the people of the desert, the environment created by a courtyard house seems to offer the ideal conditions they desire in an abode.

The natural environments, the desert, in which the Arabs lived for many generations before settling in cities has also been a major influence on them, i.e., the scarcity of water, lack of plants, high glare and endless open space. As a result when they settled they used to close their houses to the outside and turn them into courtyards. These courtyards often embodied most of the missing aspects of the desert such as water, plants, shade, reference points and a sense of enclosure.

Noor, 1991

As such, the courtyard was an idealised world around which family life revolved.

### Climatic

As mentioned earlier, the origin of courtyard houses in the areas surrounding Kuwait has a long taproot in history, and climatic considerations were one of the main factors for the adoption of the type. The extremely hot climate makes it necessary to close the living areas from the external atmosphere and the solid outer walls provide insulation against the intensity of heat outside. To make up for the absence of any opening in the exterior walls, the inner walls were required to provide adequate openings towards the courtyard to allow light to come in and, with its shaded areas and water sources, the courtyard offers a relatively comfortable outdoor space within the house. Although the courtyard may be fully or partly exposed to the sun, the *liwans* (loggias) which run between the courtyard and rooms shield the latter from exposure to the direct glare of the sun while allowing the entry of light. Apart from acting as a light well for the rooms the courtyard also acts as an air well into which the cool dense air sinks. It also protects the rooms from sandstorms that are occasionally experienced in Kuwait. Adjustable flaps have been developed for the *badgirs* (wind-catchers) which can be closed when a sandstorm is brewing.

The principle of a courtyard house is an effective way of building a dwelling house to create an agreeable internal environment which counteracts the climatic conditions of Kuwait. It acts as a modifier of the climate in hot and dry regions and allows the occupants to carry on outdoor activities with protection from the sun, wind and dust.

### Building materials

Apart from the coral stones extracted along the coastline and mud and straw to make sun-dried bricks, few other building materials are available locally in Kuwait. Mud has also been used to bond the coral stones or bricks as well as for plastering along with gypsum which is extracted locally. Some houses were built entirely of mud bricks; some with coral stones in the foundation with mud brick superstructure and others entirely of coral stones.

Unlike further north in Iraq, where burnt bricks have been used by the Muslims since the seventh century AD, the mud bricks that were available in Kuwait would not permit large scale construction of multi-storey buildings, neither would the available stones, which 'do not make very good building materials, and unless protected with plaster will quickly weather' (Lewcock 1978).

Timber is not available locally except as date palm trunks, large quantities of which were obtained from the nearby areas of Iraq. Roofing timbers are usually imported from India and the east coast of Africa, i.e., the mangrove trees which produce roof joists of up to 4 m long. Teak and other hardwoods are usually imported from India. The restricted length of the mangrove poles used for roof joists puts a constraint on the span and as such, on the width of the buildings.

The two factors discussed above – i.e., the restrictions on the vertical and horizontal sizes of the building – may have influenced the choice of a courtyard-type solution which allows a number of rooms, compatible to each other, to be grouped together around a central space within easy reach of one another. These constraints have also given the traditional courtyard houses of Kuwait a sense of uniformity in their widths and heights. Typically a courtyard house is a building with a relatively large central space surrounded by narrow rooms of even depth.

## The importance of privacy

Although the basic function of a courtyard house is to provide an acceptable internal environment for usual household activities, its adoption has also been influenced by the sociocultural needs of the people, who have been following the religion of Islam for fourteen centuries. Throughout the world Muslims have developed different types of design for their houses satisfying local climatic conditions, economic structures and the available building materials and construction technology. However, there has always been a large area of commonality based upon the courtyard in this design due to the customs and practices originating from the principles of Islam. Design criteria for a house generated by these practices played as important a role as the physical needs of human comfort in the evolution of the traditional courtyard house of Kuwait. The courtyard, therefore, ideally suits both climatic and religious imperatives.

As stated earlier, the courtyard provides an external environment within the privacy of the house, which enables women to enjoy the outdoor atmosphere without being seen by unknown men. This practice of privacy for women has been followed by the Muslims since the beginning of their religion, although in the modern era of global socio-economic transformation such practices have seen significant modification.

Guidelines for the maintenance of women's privacy are given both in the Qu'rān and the Hadith and there are also recommendations about the actions of a visitor to a house in relation to the privacy of the female inmates. A verse in the Qu'rān states, 'And when you ask of them (the wives of the Prophet) anything, ask it of them from behind a curtain' (33.52). Although the passage relates to the Prophet's wives, all

Muslims are supposed to follow this example. This passage also provides one of the strongest indications in the Qu'rān about the need for the separation of women from men, especially from unknown visitors. Several Hadith also deal with the subject of visitors to a house and the privacy of the inmates.

If any one of you asks permission three times to enter (a house), and permission is not given, then he should return.

Sahih al-Bukhari: 8.262

If anyone removes a curtain and looks into a house before receiving permission and sees anything in these which should not be seen, he has committed an offence which it is not lawful for him to commit. ... But if a man passes a door which has no curtain and is not shut and looks in, he has committed no sin, for the sin pertains only to the people inside.

Mishkat al-Masabih: 3526

From the above passages, the following guidelines, which directly and indirectly affects the design of a Muslim's dwelling house, emerge:

1   privacy of women should be respected in all circumstances
2   the entrance of a house should have a door, curtain or some kind of screen so that the passer-by cannot look in, and
3   a visitor should wait for permission to be given before entering a house.

All these requirements are satisfied by the design of the traditional courtyard house in Kuwait. In a single-courtyard house, when there is a male visitor the women may have to retreat to one of the surrounding rooms to avoid being seen by him during his passage from the main entrance to the men's reception room (diwaniya). As mentioned earlier, intelligent planning may make it possible for the visitors to enter the diwaniya without disturbing the female members of the family in the courtyard. In a multi-courtyard house, the second courtyard is likely to be the family courtyard, which may always be used, in complete privacy from the male visitors.

The guidelines mentioned above also emphasise the importance of the door at the main entrance, and create an opportunity to treat it differently than other parts of the external façade. In the courtyard houses of Kuwait, where the façade of the walls is absolutely plain and all the four elevations depict austerity, the main door, in contrast, is usually decorated as if to emphasise the point of separation between the private interior and the public exterior of the house.

> Invasion of domestic privacy in Islam is discouraged by a formidable system of religious, legal and social prohibition so that the house entrance – the vulnerable threshold between the household and the public – is accorded particular symbolic importance.
>
> Petherbridge, 1978

The importance of privacy is one of the primary considerations in the design of a Muslim's house. Yet, according to the interpretation of other guidelines, the male guest visiting the house, from whom this privacy is intended, is to be accorded as much hospitality as possible and treated like a member of the family. In the Qurān, a Muslim has been asked to consider another Muslim as his brother and treat him accordingly, 'The believers are but a single brotherhood'(49.10) and 'Merrily, this brotherhood of yours is a single brotherhood …'(21.91).

There are numerous quotations in the Hadith where the Prophet asked people to treat their guests generously. In one of them he said, 'Whosoever believes in Allah and the Last Day should not harm his neighbour and entertain his guest generously.' (Sahih al-Bukhari: 8.47). In another, he said 'Anybody who believes in Allah and the Last Day, should serve his neighbours generously, … should serve his guests generously by giving him his reward' and the reward is '(to be entertained generously) for a day and a night with high quality food, and the guest has the right to be entertained for three days (with ordinary food)' (Sahih al-Bukhari: 8.48).

In keeping with the above guidelines, it is an age-old custom in Kuwait that all the guests – near and distant relatives as well as close acquaintances, people of the same village, etc. – will be offered lodging by a city dweller in his house. The way the courtyard houses have been designed indicates that this particular aspect of the religion, i.e., the entertainment of guests, has had some influence. In a multi-courtyard house, the courtyard next to the main entrance will be the one used by men and, as such, will be available for the male visitors to use without disturbing the women using the family courtyard at the same time. Among the rooms surrounding the men's courtyard will be the men's reception room and at least one sleeping room, which will be used by the guest. In a single-

courtyard house, if the access to the men's reception room is not made directly from the main entrance or exclusively through a passage, the women will withdraw from the courtyard to allow the male guests to reach their destination. By similar arrangement the guest may also be allowed to use the courtyard along with other male members of the house. Thus the guest will be offered most of the conveniences enjoyed by other members of the house.

## Neighbour issues

In the two quotations from the Hadith stated above 'neighbours' have also been mentioned along with the guests. Similar guidelines regarding a Muslim's duties towards neighbours, which influence design characteristics, are found in the Hadith. Prophet Muhammad is reported as saying that nobody can be a true Believer unless his neighbours feel secure and safe at his side: 'do not block his air by raising your building high without his permission' (Abdalati 1978).

The fact that the traditional Kuwaiti courtyard houses are generally single-storey buildings, thus precluding the possibility of overlooking into a neighbour's house from an upper floor, is likely to have been partly due to the influence of sociocultural customs and practices generated by the religion. Moreover, the absence of windows in the exterior walls avoids the viewing out of the room as much as looking in by outsiders. The provision of raised parapets in the roof which is used by the occupants as a living space is as much for the privacy of the neighbours as it is for their own protection, as advised by the Prophet: 'If anyone spends the night on the roof of a house with no stone palisade, Allah's responsibility to guard him no longer applies' (Abu Dawud: 5023).

At the same time, the parapet should not be too high to block the wind flow and natural ventilation of the neighbour's house.

Some codes of the modern building regulations in Kuwait are manifestations of some of these principles:

1  If the ground floor of the house extends up to the boundary of neighbour's land, then the maximum permissible height of the house is 4 m.
2  Buildings higher than that, i.e., those more than one storey high, should have an offset of 2.5 m from the boundary.
3  Maximum permissible height is up to three floors.
4  Maximum height of roof parapet is 2 m.

The final group of religious edicts which is likely to have affected the design of Muslims' houses concerns the practice of modesty in life. In the religion of Islam, the existence of eternal life after the short life in this world is one of the requirements for the follower to believe. The practice of modesty in every aspect of life in this world is one of the guidelines strongly recommended to all the believers. In several places in the Qu'rān a follower of the religion is forbidden to spend money in vanity or in showing off one's wealth: 'Allah loveth not ... those who spend of their substance to be seen of men ...' (4.38). 'Exult not, for Allah loveth not those who exult (in riches). But seek with the (wealth) which Allah bestowed on thee, the Home Hereafter' (28.76–7).

In the Hadith we find some guidelines more specific to the subject of spending on buildings and the practice of modesty is again the main recommendation, e.g., 'Every building is a misfortune for its owner, except what cannot' – "except what cannot" meaning except what is essential' (Abu Dawud: 5218). 'All spending is in Allah's cause except that on building, for there is no good in it' (Mishkat al-Masabih: 5183).

The visual austerity of the traditional Kuwaiti courtyard houses seems to reflect the implementation of these guidelines. The stark, plain outside of these buildings, devoid of any decoration or embellishment, represents the simplicity and modesty of the owner. Along with the low height of the buildings, usually not taller than one storey, these external characteristics depict the owner's humbleness in their short life in this world. The Prophet seems to have associated the height of a building with an expression of vanity and extravagance by the owner. In answer to a question about when the Hour of doom will come, he said: 'The Hour (of doom) will not be established till ... the people compete with one another in constructing high buildings ...' (Sahih al-Bukhari: 9.237).

## Conclusion

The basic aim in the design of a living environment is to fulfil the functional needs of its users and to satisfy climatic and spiritual requirements. As the courtyard type has been used as the basic form of traditional housing in the Arab world – where Islam is the predominant religion – since the seventh century AD, it must be compatible with the customs and practices of its people. Unlike many other religions, Islam offers guidelines to its believers for all aspects of their life. In the dis-

cussions above, the link between the practices the adoption of a courtyard type house and the religious guidelines relevant to these practices has been established. Although the climatic conditions as well as the available building materials and technology vary in the different countries of the Middle East, the Arab world has adopted the courtyard house as the basic type of dwelling house because of its ability to satisfy the practices and living habits prescribed in the Qu'rān and the Hadith. The specific guidelines that have influenced the design of traditional courtyard houses of Kuwait are:

1   privacy of the occupants, especially women, in relation to outsiders and male visitors
2   the treatment of guests
3   responsibility to the neighbour, and
4   modesty in life.

These, added to climatic factors and the available building materials, are the prime factors in forming the shape and size of the traditional courtyard house in Kuwait. Unfortunately, the large-scale redevelopment of Kuwait following the oil boom has necessitated the building of multi-storey housing as opposed to the courtyard type. In spite of its popularity and the link between domestic design and Islamic principles, the courtyard house has been rejected, largely as a result of material and technological considerations. System building, cost and speed of construction have undermined a tradition extending back over a thousand years. With its new-found wealth, Kuwait should reflect upon the suitability of its housing and building regulations for the twenty-first century.

## Bibliography

Abdalati, H. (1978) *Islam in Focus*, International Islamic Federation of Student Organizations, Kuwait, p. 136.

Hadith (1992) Compiled by *Abu Dawood, Winhadith Version 0.1b*, Islamic Computing Centre, London.

Hadith (1992) *Mishkat al-Masabih, Winhadith Version 0.1b*, Islamic Computing Centre, London.

Hadith (1990) *Sahih al-Bukhari*, Translated by Khan, M. M., Kazi Publications, Karachi, 1990.

Noor, M. (1991) 'The function and form of the courtyard house', *The Arab House*, University of Newcastle upon Tyne, School of Architecture, Centre for Architectural Research and Department Overseas, pp. 61–72.

Lewcock, L. (1978) *Traditional Architecture in Kuwait and the Northern Gulf*, Art & Archaeology Research Papers, London, p 11.

Petherbridge, G. T. (1978) 'Vernacular architecture: the house and society'. In Michell (ed.) *Architecture of the Islamic World*, p. 76. London, Thames and Hudson.

Quotations from the Qu'rān are as translated by Abdullah Yusuf Ali in *The Meaning of the Holy Qu'rān*, Brentwood, MO, Amana Corporation, 1991.

# 9 The cosmological genesis of the courtyard house

FAOZI UJAM

## Introduction

The courtyard house, one of the most enduring architectural achievements made in the history of urbanism, was created in Mesopotamia by the Sumerians during the third millennium BC. Although there is substantial literature on the origins of the courtyard house (mainly conference proceedings and journal papers), the author's interest is in the mystical quality of the courtyard house. This is a difficult area to explain by attempting objective analysis, historical review or epistemological speculations. The author is also aware that personal reflections do not do justice to the intellectual and ontological motivations

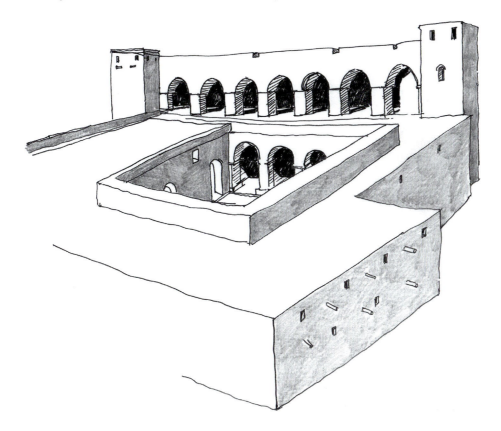

9.1 **A fifteenth-century courtyard house for a wealthy merchant, Baghdad**

behind the evolution of the courtyard house itself. Of all building types, however, the courtyard house allows the spectator to be simultaneously connected to the land and the sky through their emotions. These indigenous buildings are part of the reality of everyday places and therefore require little further justification beyond their existential role in many Middle Eastern cities. As Karl Popper notes, such vernacular buildings are part of 'objective knowledge' and exist as social and cultural icons requiring little rational explanation (Popper 1992, pp. 64–80).

At the outset we should ask whether the mystical quality of the courtyard house is something inherent in the design of the house. Perhaps we should qualify the word mystical, which the author considers to be a quality that evokes a spiritual experience; an experience which belongs to the metaphysical world. From the author's own childhood recollection, much of the experience of living in the courtyard house was dominated by the sky with all that it means or contains; moon, sun, breeze, clouds and shooting stars. Most importantly, memories of the family were engraved in and guarded by the sky. According to Sumerian cosmology, the universe consisted of heaven and earth (An-Ki) which were united until *Enlil*, god of air, separated them. Since then, heaven and earth have become driven by a great passion for each other and by longing to reunite. The Sumerians response to this was the creation of a courtyard architecture, which realised this unification. Therefore the court's spiritual quality, to which the

people of Iraq and elsewhere relate, can be attributed to the embodiment of the longing for reunification between earth (the court) and heaven (the sky). This chapter explores this dimension of the courtyard housing tradition.

It would not have been possible to put forward these seemingly poetic notions, to address a concrete architectural phenomenon like the courtyard house, without having many texts in support of the author's 'hypothesis' on the impact of Sumerian cosmology on the evolution of the house. Scholars of Mesopotamia and, in particular, Sumer, provide confirmation of the impact of cosmology on built form. Archaeologists such as Kramer, Woolley, Childe, Giedion, Oates, Oppenheim and Lloyd have deciphered scripts from numerous clay tablets, stelae and cylinder seals suggesting a direct link between religious or spiritual beliefs and secular ideas of town planning and building design.

The various themes that this chapter discusses are mainly inspired by the writings of these scholars. They are used to shed light on the implications of Sumerian values and religion on the genesis of the courtyard house. According to these historians, such spatial organisation was not the result of an elaborate design philosophy but the consequence of centuries of evolutionary processes in which Sumerian cosmology played a crucial role in the development of building design.

a  b

9.2 **Nature symbolised in household artefacts. (a) A ninth–tenth century Iranian dish and (b) a tenth century ceramic bowl**

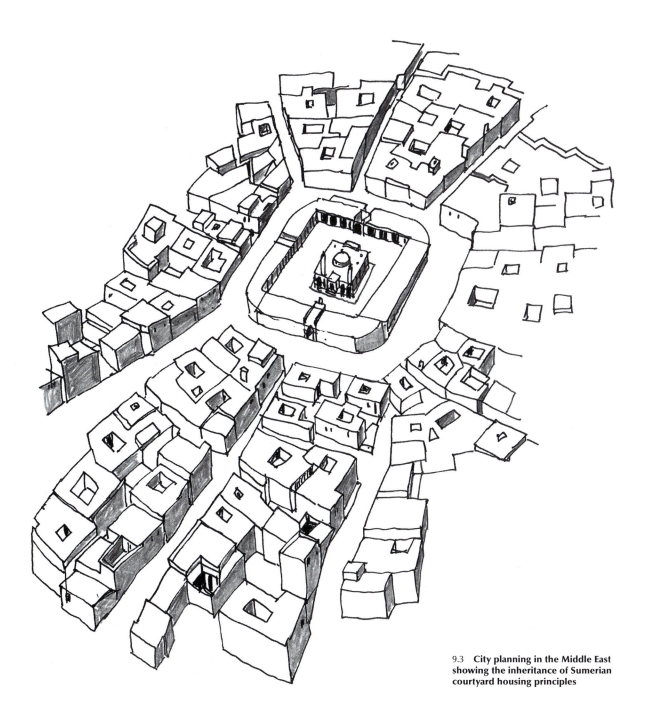

9.3 **City planning in the Middle East showing the inheritance of Sumerian courtyard housing principles**

## The real and the spiritual

A fundamental attribute of Islamic culture is its inherent tendency towards the abstraction of nature. It transforms the physicality of the 'real' world into ideas, ideals, images and symbols. The processes of transformation and abstraction crystallise across various scales, leading to further maturation in abstraction until buildings and artefacts reach the ultimate status of holism and spirituality. These ideals become embedded in the mind of the individual and are shared by society. Built form becomes a symbol and the means for unification of man and the natural world, whose boundaries begin to disap-

pear. In the case of Iraq and adjoining countries such as Syria, the ancient Sumerians embedded their ideals of cosmos in the organisation of the earthly dwellings they created. By this means the gods were brought down to earth and given earthly responsibilities for looking after water, land, houses, and ultimately the people who occupied them.

The historian Gordon Childe (Childe 1964, p. 22) believes that ancient Middle Eastern societies behaved as if they were reacting to a spiritual environment as well as to a material one. He argues that social ideology – its superstitions, religious beliefs, loyalties and artistic ideals – were used to control and transform nature. This argument may explain why, in much

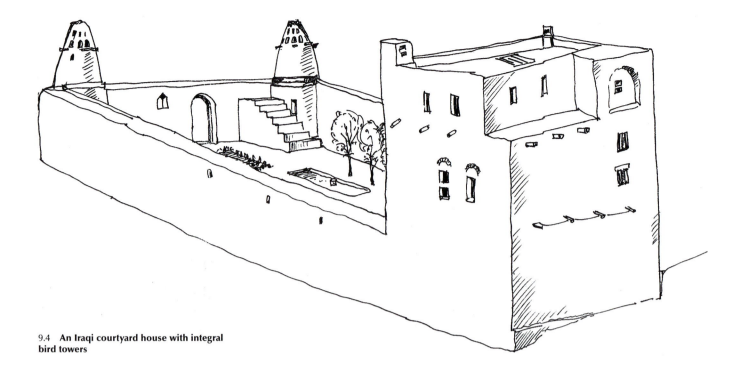

9.4 **An Iraqi courtyard house with integral bird towers**

indigenous Arabic architecture, features intended for utilitarian purposes are fashioned with great care, delicacy and artistic appeal. It seems as if their creators want to make implements that are not only functional but also beautiful and hence imbued with spiritual value.

If Childe introduces us to the value of the spiritual in domestic architecture, Kramer establishes the importance of ideas to Sumerian culture. He asserts that the Sumerians were remarkable not only for their material and technological achievements but also for their 'ideas, ideals and values'. Spiritually and psychologically they laid great stress on ambition, prestige and recognition. On the material side, they

invented the brick mould for shaping and baking the ubiquitous river clay. They devised such useful tools, skills and techniques as the potters wheel, wagon wheel, plough, sail boat, building in arch, vault and dome. They also invented casting in copper and bronze, as well as riveting, brazing and soldering. The Sumerians also originated a system of writing on clay, which was used all over the Near East for some two thousand years. They also organised their cities and buildings to house their social and religious beliefs, basing their design upon the ubiquitous courtyard. As such the courtyard house owes its origin to Sumerian invention around 3,000 BC.

9.5 **A typical mountain landscape with vernacular courtyard houses**

## Writing and religion

The invention of writing by the Sumerians happened in parallel to the creation of the first monumental architecture. This shows that in Sumer, like most of the ancient world, religion had a pervasive role in shaping every aspect of life; politics, social relations, architecture, art and literature. Writing was used by the Sumerians to preserve the divine knowledge and cultural traditions, handing on to future generations techniques of building construction and plan organisation.

Writing, like architecture, was initiated to serve religious purposes in the first instance. The priests found themselves in charge of the administration of wealth, which belonged to the Sumerian deities. This involved the administration of the temple revenues on behalf of the divine master by keeping accurate records of receipts and expenditures. These records had to be intelligible not only to the official who made them, but to his successors and other partners. Because, according to the Sumerian religion, cities, farms, animals and trees were the property of the deities, records had to be kept in both graphic and written form.

Oppenheim mentions that in Mesopotamia around 2,500 BC the use of writing for administrative purposes developed rapidly to keep records of incoming taxes, tributes and the yields of the year. This type of recording, strictly formalised and astutely coordinated, led to the establishment of rules for the design of artefacts such as the courtyard house. The effect was to put a freeze on tradition, or at least to encourage the perpetuation of a consistent pattern of building (Oppenheim 1977, p. 232). As such, once the rules of urban organisation were written down, the conditions existed for its perpetuity.

## Architecture and religion

The argument that is being promulgated that architecture specifically expresses the unity of man-nature through religious and cosmological beliefs supports Giedion's thesis that 'in the earliest high civilisations, as in prehistory, the separation of belief from reality, the sacred from the profane, was not yet accentuated' (Giedion 1981, p. 2). Giedion, along with other historians, has suggested that the impact of religion on architecture can be explained by man's longing to make contact with supernatural forces through building design in order that mankind may gain knowledge of the future. The longing

for a prolongation of life and for a continuation of existence after death also finds expression in ancient Middle Eastern architecture. The optimistic Egyptian belief in life after death led the ordinary dead to be accorded the grace to live like gods. Contrary to this was the Sumerian's vision of death. 'It was in Sumer that the expression was given for the first time to the tragedy of human existence and the fateful destiny that all must endure' (Giedion 1981, p. 9). The Sumerian saw the nether world as a place hostile to life, a place of misery and darkness. The dead had to rest beneath the earth. There was nothing for them in heaven. It would thus be meaningless to build permanent dwellings for the dead and Mesopotamian graves were simply covered with earth.

In contrast to their view of death, the Sumerians attitude to life is that of joy and optimism. They developed many colourful, variegated and complex rituals and ceremonies, most revolving around the courtyard house and the courtyard temple. It was almost inevitable that the Sumerians should develop an architecture which expressed their optimistic approach to life and which sustained a strong contact with natural phenomena. The court, which acknowledges and enhances contact with nature, accommodated the numerous ceremonies and cultural traditions that can still be observed in many Iraqi, Syrian and Iranian towns.

The joy of celebrating under the sky but within the enclosure of a house evokes a sense of continuity and eternal existence (Giedion 1981, p. 138). This is part of a universal concept that in Sumerian society there is nothing more reassuring than living under the benevolence of the sky. It may also be the result of prolonged and precise observations of the stars and their movements, which reflect a longing to establish the interdependence between stars and earth, stars and man. In ancient Mesopotamia, and some neighbouring countries, celebrations of the seasons are important traditions which take place in the courtyard. For centuries the Iraqi people produced a rich tradition of folkloric fairy tales, literature, popular songs and poetry which was often relayed within the closed domestic community of the courtyard. On the more objective side, the stars were seen as the cosmic ceiling of the courtyard house – the courtyard was not open to the sky but roofed by the sky.

9.6 **A courtyard house from Aleppo, Syria**

## Sumerian cosmology

Architectural forms like the Sumerian ziggurat, temple and courtyard dwelling, came to be regarded as symbols of the divine order of nature. At this time the contrast between symbol and meaning was not yet sharply defined (Childe 1964). The Sumerians saw value in creating ideals (gods) which symbolised what had practical significance for their culture and at the same time answered the question of the origin of their universe. Although it seemed to Childe that such an approach would make the Sumerian religion more materialistic, it could be argued that the cult of the gods was created to impose social order and harmony. Therefore, in the process of pleasing the gods, people devoted themselves to achieving good harvests. The task of Sumerian clerks was not to test experimentally or criticise this 'magico-theological' view of the world, rather it was to systemise the complex and often incoherent beliefs that they had inherited. So they created not what we would call 'philosophy', but a 'theology' or 'mythology' which bound all things together. This view is supported by Kramer, who argues that:

The Sumerians failed to develop a systematic philosophy in the accepted sense of the word. It never occurred to them to raise any questions concerning the fundamental nature of reality and knowledge and they therefore evolved practically nothing corresponding to the philosophical subdivision which is commonly known today as epistemology.

Kramer 1981, p. 75

But they did create a theology of enormous architectural potential whose chief manifestation is the courtyard house and the courtyard cities of the region.

Since its historical beginning in the fourth millennium BC, Mesopotamian architecture has rarely been the result of rational enterprise. Kramer asserts that the Sumerians had their own speculations on the nature and origin of the universe. In their quest for satisfactory answers, they evolved a cosmology carrying a high intellectual conviction. Influenced by this world view they accepted as axiomatic truth that cultural phenomena and historical events came ready-made, 'fully grown and fully blown' (Kramer 1963, p. 76). On the intellectual level Sumerians did, however, develop religious

9.7 **Dumma Goulia courtyard house, Homs, Syria**

ideas and spiritual concepts which have left a deep imprint on the modern world, especially by way of Judaism, Christianity and Islam. At an aesthetic level, the Sumerians also created what was probably the richest mythology of the ancient world, a mythology which cut the gods down to human size but did so with reverence and, above all, originality and imagination.

Kramer (1963, 1972, 1981) unravelled the Sumerian cosmology and religion by deciphering thousands of scripts in his forty years of scholarly work. Kramer states that for the Sumerians the major components of the universe were heaven and earth; indeed, their term for universe was An-Ki, a compound word meaning 'heaven–earth.' Between heaven and earth they recognised a substance which they called *lil*, a word whose approximate meaning is wind (air, breath, spirit) and whose most significant characteristics are understood to be movement. The sun, moon and stars were taken to be made of the same substance as the atmosphere but endowed with the additional quality of luminosity. Surrounding the heaven–earth on all sides and on the top and bottom was a boundless sea, in which the universe somehow remained fixed and immovable. This structure of the universe seemed to the Sumerian thinkers an obvious and indisputable fact, from which they evolved a cosmogony to fit. To keep this universe operating the Sumerians assumed the existence of a pantheon consisting of a group of living beings, man-like in form but also superhuman and immortal.

This pantheon of living beings guided and controlled the entire cosmos. The great realms of earth, sea and air; the major astral bodies, sun, moon and planets; atmospheric forces such as wind, storm and tempest; elements of landscape such as river, mountain and plain found expression in Sumerian artefacts. Cultural entities such as city and house, ditch, field and farm, and even implements like the pickaxe, brick mould and plough were deemed to be under the charge of one or another of these superhuman beings. Their role was to express the cosmological order in the human condition, not to suppress it.

Of all these hundreds of deities fashioning the ancient world, the four most important were the heaven god, *An*, the air god, *Enlil*, the water god, *Enki*, and the great mother goddess, *Ninhursag*. By far the most important deity, one who played a dominant role throughout Sumer in rite, myth and prayer was the air god, *Enlil*, who is also known to be king of heaven and earth. *Enki*, another leading Sumerian deity, was known to be the god of wisdom and who organised the earth in accordance with the decisions of *Enlil*. The fourth among the creating deities was the mother goddess, *Ninhursag*, who was also known to be *Ki* (mother earth). In addition to these four leading deities there were three important astral deities: the moon god, *Nanna*, who is also known as *Sin*; *Nanna's* son, the sun god, *Utu*, and *Nanna's* daughter, the goddess *Inanna*, known later as *Ishtar* (the planet Venus). It is this group of seven deities – *An*, *Enlil*, *Enki*, *Ninhursag*, *Nanna-Sin*, *Utu*, and *Inanna* (*Ishtar*) – that is referred to as the seven deities who decree the fates. Thus the Sumerians awarded much significance to the main cosmological phenomena as guiding forces in building design. Their belief in the heaven–earth unity was reflected in the organisation of their buildings, particularly the temple and the courtyard house.

## The house and the temple

'Mesopotamia is the birthplace of architecture' (Giedion 1981, p. 176). This statement by Giedion refers to the remarkable event of the emergence of temples, cities and dwellings as evidence of the first monumental architecture in the history of mankind. In this Giedion makes an important distinction between the design of buildings and the creation of architecture. He suggests that 'at the opening of history in Mesopotamia around 3000 BC, the form of the temple was already fully developed. It represents the first monumental type of architecture' (Giedion 1981, p. 189). Giedion argues that the earliest temples provide information about a society's cultural values at the time of their building. The temple took the form of a human habitation in which invisible forces and later the deity were presumed to dwell. From the ground plan of Sumerian temples it is clear that in this early period the faithful had direct access to the alter and to the entire interior, similar to the arrangement in the courtyard house for the fam-

ily members. The architectural typological model for the earliest temples was the newly developed block-like dwelling house, rectangular in plan and open in the centre. This regular rectangular house, which has remained even to this day as the standard form for a dwelling, evolved under the influence of the temple and in parallel with it.

Both temple and house consisted of a long rectangular room with small chambers on either side. In the beginning, according to Giedion, the ground plans were so similar that it is difficult to distinguish one from the other. However, whilst the temple retained its long rectangular form up to the late centuries of Babylonian culture, the dwelling tended towards a square ground plan with rooms surrounding an open inner court. It was Sir Leonard Woolley who first discovered the ancient courtyard house during his excavations in Ur south of Iraq, cited later by Morris (1994). Woolley discovered a whole new urban quarter of highly developed town houses dating from around 2,000 BC. The essential feature of the ground plan of these houses is the central courtyard, a rectangle, often with a central well or pool, surrounded by chambers opening on to it.

As described by Woolley (1965) the ordinary private house conformed to a recognised type modified merely by the means of the owner and the exigencies of ground space. The general idea was that of a quadrangle facing inwards on to a court which served as a light well for all the rooms. The front door opened onto a small lobby, sometimes provided with a water jar and a drain, from which one passed directly into the central court. This was paved with brick and in the middle had a drain or well made of terracotta rings set one above the other. The house was two storeys high and was built of brick throughout. The ground floor rooms had no windows at all, but derived their light through their high arched doorways. A staircase led from the court to a wooden gallery running round the inside of the house and giving access to the first floor rooms which were the living quarters for the family.

Of the ground floor rooms, generally the largest and facing the entrance from the street was the reception room. The kitchen, with its brick fireplace, was in a separate room, and below the stairs was a lavatory with a drain in its paved floor. In some of the houses there was also a private chapel in the form of a small and rather narrow chamber, with the pavement at one end slightly raised and on it, against the back wall, a brick altar. Either behind the altar or in the side-wall close to it there was a niche or recess intended to receive the cult figure, painting or clay statuette and close to the altar again, a square pillar of brick set against the wall. A normal house might therefore contain 12 to 14 rooms and often as many people. There were also smaller houses than this, and there were others with a second courtyard and surrounding chambers (Woolley 1965).

## House organisation and space conception

Man has always expressed a desire to create space in which to belong both functionally and spiritually. Factors that help to induce a sense of 'place', therefore, are given particular consideration. One of the most effective of these factors is light, to the extent that light and space are inseparable and that when light is eliminated from a space the emotional content of space disappears. The essence of architectural space lies in the interaction of the elements that define it. We can observe the relevance of the indivisible interplay of space and light in the case of the courtyard house. Throughout the year the sun sends its glaring light during the long hours of the Middle Eastern day. Even in the dark nights of Mesopotamia, light sent by the moon's brightness or even by the distant stars is sufficient for the creation of a sense of space, although one imbued with mystery. The natural response made by the Sumerians, therefore, was the development of an instinctive space conception tied to natural light – which led to the organisation of the inner court as a way of harnessing the light without the climatic disadvantage of heat gain.

The space conception of a period can give insight into man's attitude towards the cosmos, towards nature and towards eternity. As so often in high civilisations space has manifold meanings. On the one hand the symbolic background to architectural space was bound up with a grandiose cosmic outlook based on the movements of the stars and the natural cycles of the day; on the other it was tied to a rigid social hierarchy. According to Giedion (1981, p. 176), the elements whose combinations build up our first conception of space are: abstraction; the supremacy of the vertical; the plane surface; and volumes in space. These things, susceptible to vision and touch, also carry symbolic meanings. The realisation of these elements in the courtyard house is an expression of Sumerian cosmology. Accordingly, the first element, abstraction, is represented by man's longing for contact with supernatural forces. Verticality is represented by the link

between heaven and earth and the different storeys of the house. The third element of the plane surface relates to the Sumerian religious belief in a flat earth provided by the paved ground of the court. Finally the fourth element, volumes in space, relates to space as interior domain, best demonstrated by the surrounding chambers.

Interestingly, Giedion's thoughts on the Sumerian conception of space as hollowed-out volume are contested by a rather different conception put forward by Winter, which is not less intellectually engaging. In her article 'Reading concepts of space from ancient Mesopotamian monuments' (Winter 1991) the author draws attention to the idea of direction, rather than volume, as an underlying element in Sumerian space conception. Accordingly, the court as a space is formulated to encompass movements within, that is, to facilitate passing through to the various chambers open to the court. The notion of a vertical link, coming from connecting the ground floor to the upper levels, relates to the link between heaven (sky) and earth. By including her thoughts I seek to widen the understanding of the cosmological influences on the formation of the courtyard house.

Winter argues that the ziggurat can be reduced to a linear measure, a place between heaven and earth. At the same time via the great staircases, priests and the king (if not the general populace) would ascend to the temple in ritual procession. Hence, we have movement both down from the heavens and up from the land. That the emphasis was upon and limited to the vertical is apparent from the concentration of the staircases on a single façade. The thrust of the ziggurat seems to have been wholly along the lines of the vertical. Winter links this to the Mesopotamian conception of space as predicated upon linear one-dimensional manipulations of space. A single mode of perception, or dimensional frame, seems to dominate the conceptual base from which actual buildings were constructed. Winter argues that in this regard, it is most illuminating that there is no word for space per se, in either Sumerian or Akkadian, the languages of ancient Mesopotamia. Rather space is delineated by descriptions of positions from point x to point y. From this one could deduce that the courtyard was seen not as space but as a positive volume which connected the ground plane of human life to the vertical plane of the heavens.

The pre-eminence of the linear measure in Mesopotamian architecture is also visible on the ground, particularly in the orientation of the *cella* or sanctuary of early temples. The shrine consisted of a long room, with its principle entrance on

9.8 **Bird niches in an ancient courtyard house in southern Iraq**

one side, and the cult-focus on the distant short side. For example, in the temple of Anu at Warka, once one has entered, and in order to orient oneself toward the deity, one must make a ninety degree turn to face the altar. This is called the 'bent-axis' approach and occurs in later courtyard houses.

9.9 **A decorative 17th century bird tile**

Winter believes that, however difficult it may be to recover ancient experience as opposed to mere measurements of buildings, there is no evidence that the Mesopotamian worshiper ever encompassed space, as opposed to traversing it. Passage seems quite consistently to follow lines, up the ziggurat via the staircase, across the courtyard, or toward a focal point in a room. In this sense the contained and the axial coexits in both the temple and courtyard house.

## Sacred aspects of the courtyard house

This section explores examples of sacred features that are associated with the courtyard house. Although they are decorative elements they cast light upon the beliefs and rituals of the house. Many of these features have survived as cultural or practical objects, though often modified according to subsequent Islamic and Christian customs.

### Bird decoration

The Sumerian people hold a unique cultural attitude towards animals, particularly birds. This is not the result of the animal's utilitarian value as a source of food but because of inherited religious beliefs which award bird and beast symbolic and sacred status. For example, in many parts of the region today people refrain from killing or harming the pigeon (usually called El-Hussain's Pigeon) due to religious belief or an association with Immam Hussain, the grandson of the Prophet Mohammed. People show their devotion, passion and care for the bird by providing them with accommodation, mainly in the upper parts of courtyard houses or as special structures built into courtyard walls. Here they are left to feed, breed and thrive. Birds also form an important theme of decorative embellishment to household goods.

### Animals

There are numerous historical references to animals being awarded symbolic status, often in association with the home. Kramer (1963) states that the earliest cylinder seals are carefully incised with rows of animals or fairy-tale creatures and monsters. Giedion explains that the role the animal filled in

9.10  **A decorative 13th century jug**

snake brings happiness, wealth and protection to the family. In terms of tradition the snake was offered drink and, being seen as a holy animal, was not to be disturbed. As with birds, the representation of snake is frequently found in iconography from the prehistoric period onwards. When depicted as attributes of deities they are seen associated with both gods and goddesses and often shown in urban contexts. Snakes continued to be portrayed in religious and secular art in later periods as magically protective creatures. The snake gods of ancient Mesopotamia were regarded as protective deities of the temple and provided a protective presence over the surrounding urban areas.

### Tree

The tree that played a dominant role in Sumerian economic life was the date palm, from which a sweet substance known as *lal* or honey was extracted. Kramer states that Sumerian lexicographical lists contain nearly 150 words for the various

the ritual life of prehistory was sacred, but sacred in the sense that where there was no division between spiritual and daily life. Sacredness did not transfer it to a remote celestial or imaginary sphere, for sacred and profane were bound together. As a consequence the animal was simultaneously an object of veneration and food. Though killed, it still possessed power and its spirit lived on, perpetuated by rituals often acted out within the court of the courtyard house. Often the local butcher whispered sacred words to the animal before slaughtering it as part of a ceremony witnessed by the people who would later eat the food produced. Such rituals were generally performed in urban rather than rural contexts.

### Snake

The present population, particularly in some parts of Iraq, accord the snake great respect and care. A snake will often live with the family (usually in hidden places in the roof of their courtyard house). This tradition relates to a belief that the

9.11  **Palm leaf column detail from courtyard house in Homs, Syria**

kinds of palms and their different parts (Kramer 1972), which shows how significant the date palm tree was and indeed still is to the people of the region. Over centuries of natural and cultural transformation, the tree has acquired strong cultural meaning and has therefore been planted in the courtyard house as a symbol of life. The Sumerians commemorated their appreciation of the tree by evolving a motif referred to as 'sacred tree' or 'tree of life'. The literature on this is almost as extensive as the representations of the motif itself. In earlier times the tree was formalised, often made into elaborate geometric patterns, but more recently the trend has been towards greater naturalism.

## Building construction rites

Black and Green (1992, p. 30) state that in ancient Mesopotamia building activities seem generally to have been accompanied by certain construction rites. During the erection of new buildings, there were usually religious ceremonies and magical practices associated with the construction of the edifice. These were intended to aid its purification, dedication and protection from demonic forces. Such traditions are still practised, especially by people who build their own houses. Their belief is that they safeguard themselves and their new home from demons and diseases through invoking and pleasing the mythical aspects of dwelling. They usually deposit a collection of objects such as food and pages with passages from the Holy book of Qu'rān in the foundations. When they finish constructing the foundation they slaughter an animal, usually a sheep, as a sacrifice, believing that this will protect the house from collapse and the residents from death or illness. These traditions, which have Sumerian origins, combine technology and cosmology within a single world view.

## Conclusion

The court of the courtyard house is more than a physical entity, defensive enclosure, climatic moderator or hollow design gesture. It is an ontological phenomenon that condensed human existence and nurtured a longing for eternity and for unification with the world of the cosmos. In the course of its development the courtyard has been drawn into a wider field of social and cultural conceptions. In doing so it established a primordial basis for cultural typology that influenced several millennia and still exists. Unification with heaven was meant to endow the earthly reality with symbolism that is sacred, divine and pervasive. The court was, therefore, the means to engage people with a sense of unity and reverence. It is the architectural leitmotif which ties the existence of ideals and values that are earthly but have acquired heavenly status into the domestic realm. In this sense the courtyard house draws upon the inspiration of the temple in its spatial geometry.

Much of this reality of space and enclosure, its symbolism and decoration, is not the direct expression of a philosophy or epistemology underlying a design ambition. It is the actualisation of forces of nature, transformed through the processes of symbolisation into architecture that celebrates human values whilst acknowledging cosmic ones. It is necessary to draw attention to the distinction that exists between architecture which celebrates existence and that which expresses epistemological philosophies. The study of the courtyard house can enrich architectural theory and can provide insight into present motivations behind growing urban concerns. Understanding the history of the courtyard house in all of its cosmological complexity allows those who wish to revive the typology today to grasp the deeper truths behind this type of domestic design. The courtyard house of Iraq and adjoining countries is the epitome of the type of cultural memory that globalisation too readily sweeps aside. It transcends the physical reality of walls, becoming existential at a spiritual and symbolic level. As we have seen, the roots of this phenomenon are deeply embedded in the harmonisation of geometric and cosmological understandings.

## Bibliography

Black, J. and Green, A. (1992) *God's Demons and symbols of Ancient Mesopotamia*. London, British Museum.

Childe, G. (1964) *What Happened in History*. London, Penguin Books.

Giedion, S. (1981) *The Beginnings of Architecture*. Bollingen Series XXX.6.11, Cambridge, MA, Harvard University Press.

Jeremy, B. and Anthony, G. (1992) *Gods, Demons and Symbols of Ancient Mesopotamia*. London, British Museum Press.

Kramer, S. N. (1963) *The Sumerians*. Chicago, IL, The University of Chicago Press.

Kramer, S. N. (1972) *Sumerian Mythology*. Philadelphia, PA, University of Pennsylvania Press.

Kramer, S. N. (1981) *History Begins At Sumer*. Philadelphia, PA, University of Pennsylvania Press.

Lloyd, S. (1978) *The Archaeology of Mesopotamia*. London, Thames and Hudson.

Morris, A. E. J. (1994) *History of Urban Form, Before the Industrial Revolutions*. Harlow, Essex, Longman Scientific and Technical.

Oates, J. (1986) *Babylon*. London, Thames and Hudson.

Oppenheim, A. L. (1977) *Ancient Mesopotamia, Portrait of a Dead Civilization*. Chicago, IL, The University of Chicago Press.

Popper, K. (1992) *In Search of a Better World*. London, Routledge.

Whitehouse, R. (1977) *The First Cities*. London, Phaidon.

Winter, I. J. (1991) Reading concepts of space from ancient Mesopotamian monuments. In K. Vatsyayan (ed.) *Concepts of Space, Ancient and Modern*. Indira Ghandi National Centre for the Arts, New Delhi, Abhinav Publications.

Woolley, C. L. (1965) *The Sumerians*. Birmingham, W. Norton and Company Ltd.

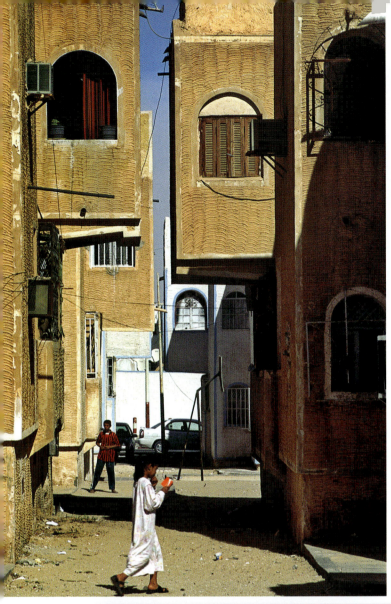

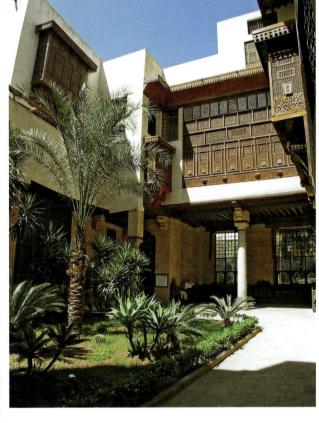

1 (*top left*)   **Public housing project in El Oued, Algeria, which seeks to maintain cultural and environmental references. Notice the use of projecting window bays and timber shutters. Architects: Abdel and Hany El-Miniawy**

2 (*top right*)   **El-Oued public housing project in Algeria based upon surveys of consumer preference for strong regional identity**

3 (*above*)   **Al-Suheime House – eighteenth-century courtyard house in Cairo**

4 (*left*)   **Sitting area in the mashrabiyya at Al-Suheine House – a study in comfort, privacy and filtered light**

5 Residence Andalous in Sousse, Tunisia, by architect Serge Santelli: (*clockwise from top left*)
(a) visual transparency between various courtyards: subtle links using water channels and slight
changes of levels; (b) trees, bougainvillier and water channels; (c) re-interpretation of the traditional
Tunisian courtyard house architecture: use of reflective white surfaces, ceramic tile decoration around
the windows and a covered sitting space facing the water feature; (d) the reception courtyard of the
Andalous residence complex: a truly contemporary Tunisian character

6a Dal al-Gaman Residence – a modern courtyard house
in Khartoum, Sudan, designed by Jack Ishkanes

6b Detail of entrance court at Dal al-Gaman
Residence showing the effect of sun modulation.
Architect: Jack Ishkanes

7   The communal courtyard of the
Ommeyad Mosque in Damascus

8   Al-Azem Palace in Damascus – Iwan
spaces and enclosed courtyard gardens

9 Tourist hotel in the south of Morocco arranged around a central courtyard. The staggered design alludes to the traditional architecture of the region whose ruins are in the foreground

10 NPI housing complex in Mahshahr, Iran, designed by Mandan Consulting Architects. A mixture of courtyard and more orthodox housing layouts of 218 units

11 Courtyard house with passive solar ventilation and wind towers in South Tahrir, Egypt, designed by Samir Hassan Bayoumy Hosni

12 High-density Salwa housing project in Kuwait City, designed in 1992 by Saleh Al-Mutawa. The project contains a number of shared and private courtyards

13    Mud brick courtyard house near Luxor, Egypt, inspired by Hassan Fathy and designed by D. Sims and O. Sednaoui. Built in 1980, this large private house is square in plan with central courtyard and roof terraces

14   Sleeping terrace at Sims and Sednaouri
Residence, Luxor, Egypt

15   Central courtyard. Sims and
Sednaouri Residence, Luxor, Egypt

16　Private courtyard of house in Tinghir
Miners' Township, Quarzazate, Morocco,
designed in 1987 by Taibi Jaafri

17　Entry court at the Villa Anbar,
a courtyard house in Dammam, Saudi
Arabia, designed by N. Al-Turki and
P. Barber

# 10    The deconstructed courtyard: dwellings of central Oman

## SOUMYEN BANDYOPADHYAY

## Unique Oman

Oman is often regarded as a country uniquely distinguished from the rest of peninsular Arabia by geology, topography, history, society, culture and even by the specific sect of Islam practised. Often described as an island, bounded by the Indian Ocean and the Empty Quarters (Rub al-Khali), Oman derives most of the characteristics from her central mountain spine, known as the Oman Mountains. This spine literally severs the country into a landlocked interior and a narrow but long coastal strip. While the coast developed as a seafaring, outward-looking, cosmopolitan entity, the interior (a'Dakhaliya), often described as the 'real' Oman,[1] evolved into an introverted society and culture practising its unique form of Islam, Ibadhism.[2] The settlement pattern carried on the distinction;

while the Batinah coast developed as an almost continuous strip of connected settlements from Shinas to Muscat, the interior was always characterised by isolated oasis settlements like Nizwa, Bahla and Manah (Figure 10.1).

Not unusually, therefore, the dwellings developed their own distinctive characteristics too, with the coastal dwellings exhibiting a spatial organisation based on the courtyard typology. Settlements in the interior of Oman, however, provoke us to question, and what I would argue has long remained, a preconception colouring our understanding of Islamic dwellings. That the traditional Arab-Islamic dwelling universally manifests itself as a spatial entity planned around a courtyard, appears to be untenable in the case of central Omani settlements such as Nizwa, Bahla and Manah. However, as I shall argue in this chapter, these Nizwan or Manhi dwellings reveal a much more complex reality; a reality in which the courtyard is never negated, but is given a subtle articulation through a process of careful deconstruction of its essential functions, allowing the unitary conception of the courtyard to be broken down into discrete, yet interconnected, spatial fragments. In these densely compacted oases, whose settlement histories often go back to the pre-Islamic period, the ground-level courtyard is virtually (or at least largely) absent, giving way to the first floor terrace as its direct spatial equivalent. The programmatic components of the courtyard do not appear to limit it solely to this unique elevated Omani counterpart, as it disaggregates into the ground level light well (*shamsiya*) and the covered women's room (*ka'a julush*) and, wherever appropriate, makes use of an array of semi-enclosed loggias. While light-wells and loggias are common features of Islamic courtyard dwellings (Figure 10.4), the

10.1    **A view of Manah, Oman, showing the importance of roof terraces combined with courtyards**

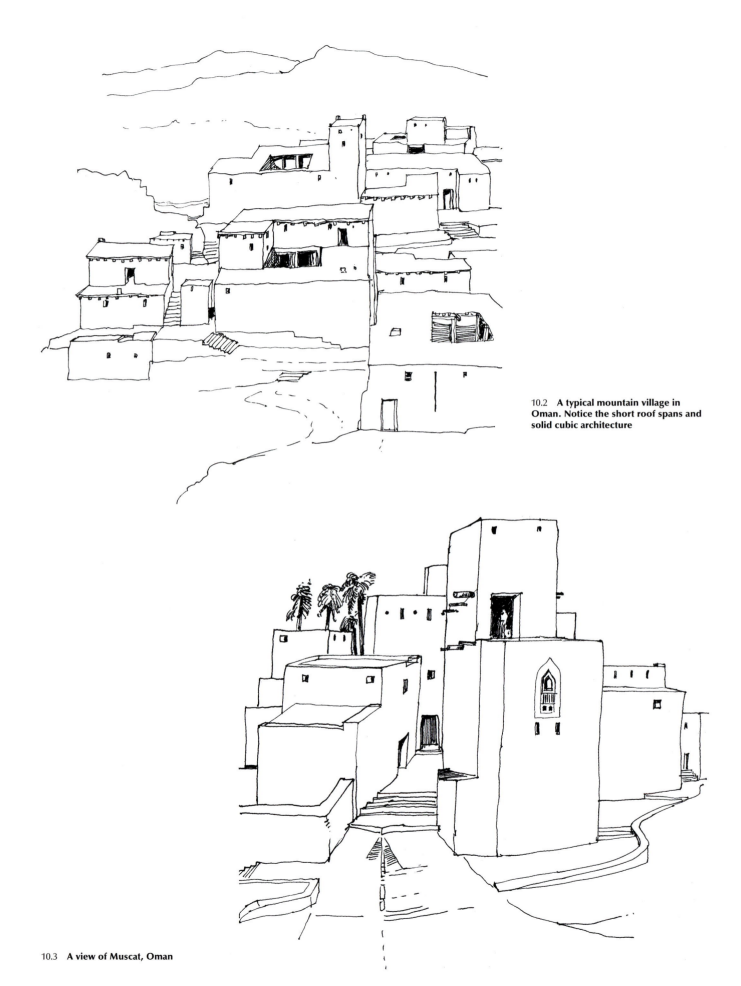

10.2  **A typical mountain village in Oman. Notice the short roof spans and solid cubic architecture**

10.3  **A view of Muscat, Oman**

women's room and terrace disaggregation of the courtyard is unique to central Oman. Like the courtyard, the women's room and the terrace alternate as both the core of this spatial organisation as well as the pivotal functional space during the day and the night (Figure 10.5).

## The Jawf prototype

The 'Jawf-prototype' can be easily distinguished from those found in the coastal areas. Here, possibly due to the extreme climatic conditions, but also probably as a result of a need to conserve scarce arable land, individual dwellings often did not contain any open to sky spaces on the ground level at all. In these houses there seems to be a definite distinction between the activities carried out on the ground floor as opposed to the ones on the upper level. As examples from Manah show (e.g., the Barawina house, Figure 10.4; also the Wurud house, Figure 10.5), the entire lower level was given out to storage cells (*makhzen*) and animal pens of various types and proportions. Water wells and bathing/washing facilities were also part of this organisation. Only larger dwellings made use of small light wells to bring light into the ground floor rooms. The

**10.4 View of a first-floor terrace of Wurud House, Manah with sleeping rooms and toilet (small window). The light well is to the right**

Key
r            room
t (t1, t2)    terrace
k            kitchen
la (la1, la2)    latrine

**10.5 Upper floor plan of Wurud House, Manah**

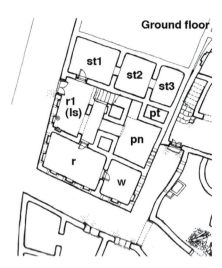
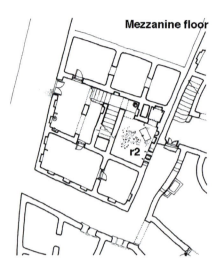
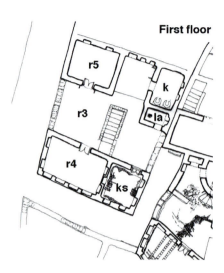

**Ground floor**

**Mezzanine floor**

**First floor**

10.6 **Floor plans of Barawina House, Manah**

employment of larger courtyards (*hawsh*) was more frequent in the form of communal spaces between and amidst dwellings. Such courtyards usually contained the communal water well and washing areas, or the latrine, and acted as the gathering place for women and children of the household and the neighbourhood. Exceptionally, and only in larger dwellings, courtyards sometimes appear as left-over rear yards. The front room in smaller dwellings was used as a multi-purpose space, for carrying out daily chores, including acting as the congregation space for women (*ka'a julush*). This was also the room that generally provided access to the first floor living quarters through a staircase (*darig*; see Figures 10.6 and 10.7).

Barring a very few exceptions, all dwellings in Manah were double-storied. The location, alignment or the design of the staircase was such that the upper level was always hidden from view from the entrance door. The rooms on the upper level were organised around a terrace, which was the roof of the ground floor multi-purpose room. Even in the larger dwellings with one or more shamsiya, the first floor terrace still remained the central focus of the entire organisation with one or more covered galleries (*dihriz*) providing transitory spaces between the room (*hujra/gurfa*) and the terrace. The kitchen (*matbakh*) and the latrine (*hammam*) were also part of this first floor spatial arrangement, but they were located furthest from the main access staircase. A pit underneath the latrine, effectively a sealed cell on the ground floor, collected the night-soil, which was periodically removed for use as manure in the fields. Some dwellings had a store on the first

floor for the purpose of domestic use; one such facility had a grain store (*khalil*) attached to it.[3]

Thus all facilities connected with the activities of domestic life, such as sleeping rooms, kitchens, domestic stores and latrines were located on the first floor around a large terrace.

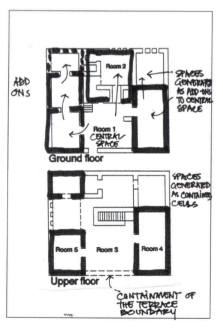

10.7 **Spatial analysis of the ground and first floor plan of Barawina House, Manah**

The location of both the kitchen and latrine on the upper level is unique to Jawf. The lower level, on the other hand, had spaces for storing agricultural produce, animal fodder, and other merchandise, but was used also to keep the goat and other domesticated animals (*ghanam*) at night.[4] The women used the vestibule to perform household chores during the day and to meet other women of the neighbourhood during appointed 'coffee breaks'. The façades of the single-entrance dwellings of Manah are rather solid, with small high-level openings on the ground floor and slightly larger windows on the first.

## The house, patriarchy and the microcosmic fatherland

The house (*bayt*) plays a vital part in the Omani psyche, where its role is often equated with the notions of the 'home' or the 'dwelling' in their most pervasive sense. To perpetuate the societal system, an Omani is almost bound by duty, as it were, to eventually possess a house. Possession of a house brings prestige to the household and helps build the reputation of the family. From this location amidst society, an Omani evokes and expands his sense of 'sociability'.[5] The Omanis see the house first as a refuge, a shelter and a retreat. It protects the inhabitants from 'armed aggression by robbers and from other dangers', and from the harsh climatic conditions of the hot-arid environment. In this context, the house is perceived as the place of rest and quietness for the body and the mind. Second, the house is seen as the 'cradle of the family', where it becomes the centre of procreation and the source of life. It is within the physical framework of the house that conjugal life blossoms and the family is conceived. The image of the house evokes a sense of tenderness, and through its stability allows the inhabitants to kinder a vision of the future. Third, it is seen as the *genius loci* of the fundamental Islamic social unit: the family. The house is the place where the parents and the children meet, generating the sense of family solidarity through reciprocal responsibilities; it is the container that preserves and cultivates customs and traditions faithfully. And finally, the individual house is an important entity within the sociocultural continuum: it replicates the 'fatherland' (Oman) in microcosm and provides a physical fabric for the sustenance of the patriarchal family unit. While many of the conceptions expressed here are not unique to Oman, and closely adhere to the Islamic principles guiding the sacred (*haram*) nature of the house (*bayt*), the specificity of its spatial manifes-

tation is of interest to us. Through such articulation, the central Omani house addresses age-old notions of core and periphery, of purity and of the sacred, born out of highly localised historical, sociocultural, economic and political realities. In this the courtyard and terrace play a pivotal role.

## Two differing concepts of spatial organisation

The clear segregation of activity sets between the two levels was unique to central Oman, and this phenomenon appears even more interesting as we begin to examine the dwelling in a little more detail. I have already mentioned how different the spatial nature of coastal dwellings was from their counterparts in the interior. However, if we analyse their respective morphological evolution, striking similarities emerge. In the case of the predominantly single-storied coastal dwellings, it was the courtyard with a defining high perimeter wall which appeared at the earliest stage of 'dwelling'.[6] Not only was the material manifestation in this early stage of dwelling of a semi-permanent nature, but also the way in which the space within that initial definition was appropriated was very fluid. As increasing functional definition and segregation became necessary, individual, almost autonomous, cells were built against the perimeter wall to cater for that purpose. As a household established itself in a particular location, there was a noticeable shift towards the employment of more permanent building materials. This process was therefore not very different from the speculation, one that has now acquired almost legendary status, on the evolution of the classic Arab courtyard dwelling from its humble beginnings in the flimsy *bedu* tent.[7] Through this process the courtyard retained its primacy in the spatial organisation, as the instituted cells played a modifying rather than a defining role.

Interestingly, this is also the case with the dwellings of the interior. A closer observation reveals that once the lower floor had been established, the terrace was conceptualised and treated in very much the same way as the walled beginnings of a courtyard house; but, instead of a perimeter wall, the raised plane acted here to define the extent of the courtyard. There followed a similar pattern of evolution, where rooms or cells were placed along the perimeter, leaving a section of the terrace open in the middle in a similar a fashion to the single-storied courtyard layouts of the Batinah coast, or its precursor, the *bedu* tent. Like the nomadic establishment on the desert plains, the facilities necessary for living (terrace), sleeping (rooms), cooking (kitchen) and excrement (latrine) were present on the upper floor, organised around a central terrace acting as a spatial core, which gives it a functional autonomy. Absent, however, on the upper level, were the activity spaces through which life was sustained in such a 'core dwelling'. These, the functions related to oasis agriculture and associated animal husbandry, existed on the lower level. In the case of the simpler manifestations, the ground floor organisation revolved around a central space (more often the women's room) not dissimilar to the large 'distribution hall' found in a peculiar Sohari coastal dwelling type which does not conform to the courtyard stereotype. Like the Sohari dwellings, the ones in Manah generate a compact form, with spaces not always set against the perimeter wall in the way the elements of a courtyard organisation are.[8] This organisation is the antithesis of the courtyard type in that the cells are effectively 'add-ons' rather than being 'fill-ins'. However, in Manah and the other interior settlements this add-on typology, centred on the women's room, seems to work in tandem with the fill-in typology generated by the need to remain contained within the property boundary wall.

According to Hillier's 'space syntax theory', the 'central space-to-cell' relationship in the courtyard organisation, as well as in the central Omani house (terrace and women's room) could be said to have a symmetric relationship, while the need to resolve the tension between the add-on and the fill-in resulted in asymmetric relationships around the women's room.[9] In other words, one could suggest that the two levels of a Manhi dwelling represent two differing concepts of spatial organisation at the core of its spatial order, created to cater for two differing activity sets, originating from two opposed views of life: the nomadic (*bedu*) and the sedentary (*hadr*). At the core of this spatial order lies the women's room on the ground level and the terrace on the first floor, mirroring the pivotal role played by the traditional courtyard. What needs to be established, however, is how such a spatial order centred on the women's room/terrace is affirmed by the core activities of the traditional central Omani household.

## Dual spatial order and *bedu* and *hadr* existential images

This differing spatial order not only points in the familiar direction of the *bedu* or semi-nomadic origin of the Omani

population of the interior, but more importantly, it directs us towards understanding how the nomadic nature of the Arab-Omani psyche managed to come to terms with the sedentary realities of a village life that they had fallen heir to. Further, the organisation shows us how the settlers of the desert foreland conceptualised domestic space in terms of an overlay of a nomadic existential image over a spatial agglomeration evolved from the sedentary requirements of an agriculture-based oasis life. A hint of how and why this might have happened is contained in the sedentarisation process of the Arab tribes in lower Jawf.

The first nomadic (*bedu*) Arab migrants from Yemen initially established themselves in the 'western desert borderlands in pre-Sasanid times',[10] where they lived as herdsmen and possibly engaged in some form of trading with the Persianised sedentary (*hadr*) population of the settlements. Through these interactions the Arab tribesmen gradually built a 'genuine rapport' with the lower elements of the Sasanid society, e.g., the *uluj*, the *bayadir* and the *ahl al-bilad*.[11] With the advent of Islam, almost overnight, the Arabs with only an outside knowledge of sedentary life found themselves the master of the land, which had been developed by the Persians over nearly a thousand years through sound investment in land development and irrigation.[12] It is conceivable that the first of these changeovers took place in the desert foreland settlements, around which the Arabs were by then leading a semi-nomadic existence in the way the present day cattle-herding *shawawi* population survive in the lower Jawf.[13] Gradually they took up agriculture, yet retained their tribal organisation; the sedentary and erstwhile non-tribal population on the lower rungs of the Persian feudal social structure were also incorporated into the tribal structure.[14]

> This is what 'Ayyub b. Kirriba … meant when he said that whereas the 'Nabateans' (i.e. sedentary population) of 'Bahrayn' became Arabs (nomads), the Arabs of Oman became Nabateans … the Arabs [in Oman] as they settled introduced their arab (*bedu*) system of social organisation into village life, and assimilated the Nabatean (sedentary) population as equals into it.[15]

Thus the Omani social structure is a complex palimpsest of an organisation brewed in a sedentary state while having a nomadic origin. This peculiar duality had its effects on the Omani attitude towards land, agriculture, irrigation and dwelling architecture. We learn that over the Islamic period the extent of land under cultivation in the major oases settlements had actually shrunk as the Omanis failed to build upon the achievements of the irrigation system once established by the Persians.[16] In fact, as Wilkinson argues, the falaj system never seems to have been entirely assimilated into the Omani life.[17] Similarly, this curious pull of the two opposing forces never deserted the Ibadi ideology, a philosophy born to retain the pure and universal nature of Islam, nurtured in the urban centre of Basra, but eventually adapted to fit the expectations of the tribal population of Oman.[18] The lack of knowledge of sedentary life and of agricultural and irrigational practices[19] led to the perpetuation of the pre-Islamic settlement pattern,[20] which in turn, demanded a significant modification of the tribal organisation.

# Functioning of the dwelling: from an environmental viewpoint

One has to keep in mind that during the high summer many of the dwellings would have been deserted for the palm-reed or mud-brick houses within the cool and humid environment of the shaded and adequately watered oasis. Obviously it is unrealistic to assume a total desertion of the settlement, be it for economic reasons or otherwise: a section of the population would have remained in their two-storied dwellings braving the extreme temperature and an environment of very low humidity. In order to understand how these dwellings worked around the spatial core of the women's room and the terrace, we need to examine it from, first, the environmental and then social viewpoint.

Table 10.1  **Barawina dwelling (Manah): temperature and humidity measurements (August–September 1994)**

| Date/time | RI | RI | R2 | R2 | R3 | R3 | R4 | R4 | R5 | R5 | Out | Out |
|---|---|---|---|---|---|---|---|---|---|---|---|---|
| 29.8.94 | C | % | C | % | C | % | C | % | C | % | C | % |
| 10.00 | 34 | 57 | | 53 | 34 | 43 | | 47 | 34? | 45 | 35 | 35 |
| 12.00 | 37 | 36 | 36 | 32 | 41 | 25 | 36 | 30 | 37 | 30 | 41 | 24 |
| 14.00 | 38 | 30 | 37 | 26 | 41 | 21 | 37 | 25 | 37 | 25 | 42 | 19 |
| 16.00 | 38 | 29 | 37 | 26 | 38 | 22 | 38 | 23 | 38 | 22 | 40 | 21 |
| 30.9.94 | C | % | C | % | C | % | C | % | C | % | C | % |
| 10.00 | 35 | 39 | 35 | 36 | 35 | 34 | 36 | 31 | 36 | 32 | 37 | 31 |
| 12.00 | 38 | 30 | 38 | 30 | 40 | 26 | 39 | 27 | 39 | 29 | 42 | 25 |
| 14.00 | 37 | 31 | 37 | 29 | 42 | 21 | 41 | 22 | 40 | 24 | 44 | 19 |
| 31.8.94 | C | % | C | % | C | % | C | % | C | % | C | % |
| 9.00 | 34 | 41 | 34 | 38 | 35 | 32 | 35 | 33 | 35 | 32 | 34 | 31 |
| 12.00 | 36 | 33 | 36 | 30 | 39 | 21 | 39 | 22 | 39 | 23 | 41 | 21 |
| 15.00 | 37 | 29 | 37 | 26 | 41 | 21 | 38 | 23 | 40 | 22 | 45 | 19 |
| 18.00 | 37 | 31 | 38 | 28 | 38 | 23 | 38 | 25 | 38 | 25 | 39 | 22 |
| 1.9.94 | C | % | C | % | C | % | C | % | C | % | C | % |
| 9.00 | 34 | 38 | 34 | 36 | 35 | 34 | 35 | 33 | 35 | 33 | 34 | 35 |
| 12.00 | 37 | 33 | 37 | 31 | | | | | | | 41 | 24 |
| 3.9.94 | C | % | C | % | C | % | C | % | C | % | C | % |
| 9.00 | 31 | 52 | 31 | 50 | 34 | 41 | 32 | 47 | 32 | 47 | 34 | 39 |
| 12.00 | | 37 | | | | | | | | | 40 | 30 |
| 15.00 | | 37 | | | | | | | | | 38 | 31 |
| 5.9.94 | C | % | C | % | C | % | C | % | C | % | C | % |
| 9.00 | 33 | 41 | 33 | 40 | 34 | 39 | 34 | 39 | 34 | 38 | 34 | 37 |
| 11.00 | 37 | 135 | | | | | | | | | 39 | 31 |

The environment is characterised by high solar incidence, high radiation and glare, high temperatures, exceptionally low humidity levels and feeble air movement. From late summer (August/September) through to winter (January), cloud cover and wind speed increases towards the early evening bringing in rain, which can occasionally be very heavy, causing damage to the traditional mud-dwellings. This usually results in a slight reduction in overnight temperature, but also contributes towards a vital increase in the humidity level. The climatic behaviour of the Barwani dwelling was closely observed between 9.00 a.m. and 6.00 p.m., over a period of eight days in August–September 1994, in relation to the microclimatic conditions within the settlement. The rooms and spaces chosen for the recording of temperature and humidity levels were:

- entrance space on ground level, the women's room (R1)
- mezzanine level room (R2)
- open to sky terrace (R3)
- large room on first floor (R4)
- smaller room on first floor (R5).

The measurements appear in Table 10.1.

The climatic data thus collected results in a set of interesting observations on the way the upper level performed (terrace R3 and rooms R4 and R5) vis à vis the women's room (R1). The evening previous to the commencement of recording there was some rainfall. This had resulted in a slight increase in the morning humidity level on the lane outside (35 per cent), but not a significant reduction in temperature from other days (35°C). However, this had resulted in a dramatic change in the indoor humidity levels: in R1 this was 57 per cent, in R2 53 per cent, in R3 43 per cent, and in R4 and R5 47 per cent and 45 per cent, respectively; there was no significant differences in temperature levels. As the day progressed, the strong solar incidence quickly burnt off the moisture, and by 2.00 p.m. the external humidity was a mere 19 per cent with a temperature of 42°C. Needless to say, the exposed terrace (R3) followed a similar pattern to record 21 per cent with 41°C, while the rooms R4 and R5, which did not have doors, were not far behind. It was R1 on the ground floor that managed to hold the humidity at a comparatively high level as it recorded 30 per cent with 38°C. Thus, as the hours went by, although the upper level spaces closely followed the temperature and humidity patterns of the microclimate outside, so that it became almost impossible to use the upper level during the day, the ground floor kept the

humidity level a good 11 per cent higher and the temperature 4°C lower.

This pattern was unchanged over the next seven days, as while the external temperature varied between 34°C and 45°C (i.e., a total variation of 11°C), the R1 internal temperature fluctuated between 33°C and 38°C (i.e., a total variation of 5°C). The difference between external and internal temperatures at any one time was 0°C (min) and 8°C (max), with the variations between 12 noon and 4.00 p.m. being 2°C (min) and 8°C (max). Between 12 noon and 6.00 p.m., the R1 internal temperatures were held between 36°C and 38°C. These observations are graphically represented in Figure 10.8 and Figure 10.9. In this context, it is interesting to note, Nicol's research on comfort conditions in hot-arid environments of Baghdad and Roorki have shown that there people feel most comfortable at a temperature of 34°C: it is only when the temperature goes beyond 36°C that any signs of discomfort are noticed.[21] The external humidity, on the other hand, varied between 37 per cent and 19 per cent (variation 18 per cent), the R1 internal humidity always remained within the range of 57 per cent and 29 per cent (variation 28 per cent). The increased internal humidity level at any one time was 3 per cent (min) and 22 per cent (max), with the variations between 12 noon and 4.00 p.m. being 6 per cent (min) and 12 per cent (max).

Comfort is a very relative term, even more so in such a hot and hyper-arid condition where the slightest variations in temperature and humidity levels are immediately noticeable. No doubt the lower temperature of R1, compared to both the external lane and the upper level, makes the room comfortable, but it is the significantly higher humidity levels which create the true sense of comfort. The performance of R2 closely followed R1, with a very similar temperature range but a slightly lower humidity level. Both rooms managed to cut down the glare significantly through the employment of small openings; the only difference was that while R1 often had a slight breeze from the lane in front, R2 had very little air movement, which made it comparatively lacking in comfort. Since the rest of the rooms on the ground floor were dark, unhealthy storage spaces, it is conceivable that only R1 and R2 were used as living spaces and for work during the day, while the others remained empty. No doubt, the women of the house had to spend time preparing lunch in the kitchen upstairs, but this was kept short. It is only during the evenings and nights, when the temperature had fallen significantly and the humidity had risen, that the terrace became appropriated.

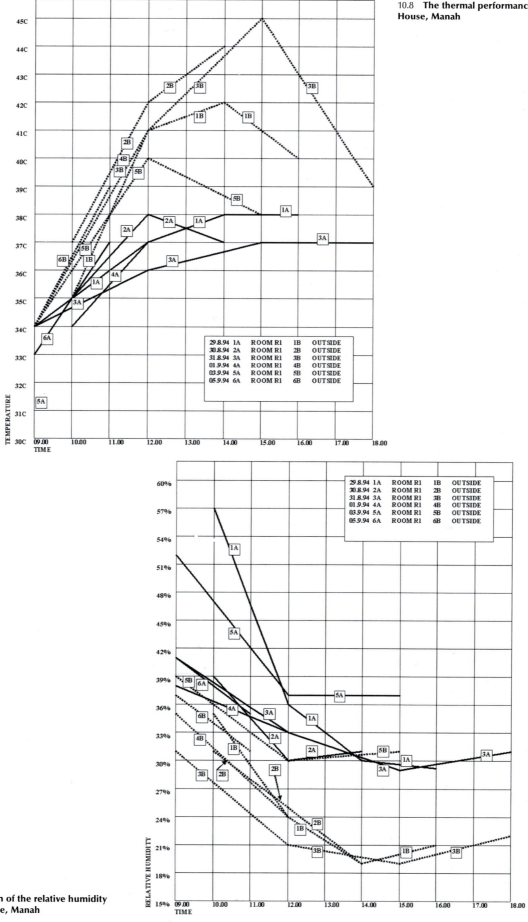

10.8  The thermal performance of Barawina House, Manah

| | | | | |
|---|---|---|---|---|
| 29.8.94 | 1A | ROOM R1 | 1B | OUTSIDE |
| 30.8.94 | 2A | ROOM R1 | 2B | OUTSIDE |
| 31.8.94 | 3A | ROOM R1 | 3B | OUTSIDE |
| 01.9.94 | 4A | ROOM R1 | 4B | OUTSIDE |
| 03.9.94 | 5A | ROOM R1 | 5B | OUTSIDE |
| 05.9.94 | 6A | ROOM R1 | 6B | OUTSIDE |

10.9  Comparison of the relative humidity in Barawina House, Manah

## Functioning of the dwelling: from a social viewpoint

Let us now correlate these observations with the information on 'social time', i.e., the way the Omanis experienced and mapped time, which indirectly resulted in the cyclical and repetitive character of their social reproductionary mechanisms. As al-Harthy notes:

'Social time' in a traditional town in Oman, like most traditional Islamic societies, derives its structure from an integration of the religio-cultural and environmental factors endemic to the five daily prayers (salats), which are organised temporally, according to the daily movement of the sun. This concept of the 'social time' as a temporal framework, which coordinates the daily activities of different social groups by allocating each group to its own 'social space', allows a routinized flow of, on one hand, desirable social interactions ... and on the other, productive economic duties ...[22]

This daily routine of activities, which in effect divides the day into five time zones with the aid of the five daily prayers, could be tabulated as in Table 10.2.[23]

The males are out very early in the morning to attend to the work in the oasis, which keeps them away until lunchtime. If the women are not assisting the males, which they often do, especially during date harvesting season, they are busy in the dwelling looking after the children and attending to other household chores, including tending animals, if necessary. Also, 'they entertain many female guests, either formally or informally. Women are responsible for the smooth running of the household and they seek to ensure their house is known for its hospitality.'[24]

Whereas the males meet in their respective tribal sabla,[25] the informal meetings of the women take place in different

Table 10.2 **Diurnal activities defined by the daily prayers**

| Prayers | Occurring between | Activity of male | Activity of female |
|---|---|---|---|
| 1. Fajr | 4:00–6:00 a.m. | Pray in mosque/home | Pray at home |
| | | | Wake up and prepare children for madrasah |
| | | Work in the fields | Assist male in fields or domestic chore |
| | | | Female meet (dhuhah) at home |
| | | | Cook lunch |
| | | Lunch at home | Lunch at home |
| | | Meet in sablah in winter | |
| 2. Dhuhur (Zuhr) | 12:00–2:00 p.m. | Pray in mosque/home | Pray at home |
| | | Meet in sablah in summer | Work in fields or dwelling |
| | | Go to suq | Female meet (ts'asir) at home |
| | | Meet in sablah, or after paryer | Work in fields or dwelling |
| 3. 'Asr | 3:30–4:30 p.m. | Pray in mosque | Pray at home |
| | | Meet in sablah, or before prayer | Attend to work near dwelling |
| | | Attend to work near dwelling | Attend to work near dwelling/cook |
| 4. Maghrib | 6:00–7:30 p.m. | Pray in mosque | Pray at home |
| | | Dinner at home | Dinner at home |
| | | Meet in sablah | |
| 5. Isha'a | 8:30–9:30 p.m. | Pray in mosque | Pray at home |
| | | Short meet in the sablah (ramshah) | Put children to bed |

houses of the neighbourhood at the same time. Two meetings occur within the day, both when the men are away, one before noon (dhuhah) known by the same name, and the other during the afternoon (asr) and known as the ta'asir.[26] Whoever intends to invite the group into their dwelling for these informal coffee-drinking sessions, goes round the neighbourhood calling the women by their names.[27] These gatherings assume great importance in the life of the women, as these are the opportunities for them to gather information about the life of the settlement, and air their views. Coffee sessions in Oman, even today, are highly ritualised ceremonies, performed with precision, in accordance with the context and importance of the event. Fertility, as Christine Eickelman notes, plays an important role in these coffee sessions, as women avoid gathering in the households of childless women.[28] These 'ritualised' coffee sessions, therefore, act as means of upholding the central role of fertility in Omani society. Through her ability in giving birth to their progeny, the Omani woman acts as the prime instrument in perpetuating the patriarchal system, in recreating the family, and in ensuring a second lease of life after death for the parents.

In its ritualised daily version through the coffee sessions, it seeks to symbolically rejuvenate the bayt (house), the physical fabric for the sustenance of the patriarchal family unit. In the process, it turns the spatial core of the dwelling, the women's room, into the true genius loci of the Omani dwelling, thereby securing for the latter a spatial status paralleling the centrality of the traditional courtyard. Paralleling the sense of sacred unity (tawhid) projected by the open-to-sky courtyard, the lower floor attempts to recreate the Omani fatherland in microcosm, while surreptitiously seeking to establish a female-gendered space. It is the men who are invested with the task of pollinating the date palm, while the women help the men in collecting the harvest and caring for the domesticates. The fruits of such female activities surround the women's room (i.e., the harvest stores and pens); the latter periodically establishes the unity through the 'fertility ritual' of the coffee sessions.

By closely situating spaces representing the role of women in both the oasis (i.e., harvesting) and in the family (procreation through fertility), unity is sought between the two most important components of the fatherland. In doing so, it also clearly proclaims a female-gendered space. This gendered space is at times extended into the evening and spatially out on to the street (sikka or darb). Often the men, after having their lunch, and knowing that the afternoon female gathering is to take place in their dwelling, would not return after the dhuhur prayer and subsequent meeting in the sabla, but instead would depart straight for the suq and return home before dinner. By way of contrast to the women's room, the first floor terrace, like the traditional Arab courtyard, provides unity for the components of the family unit (male, female, children). This distinction between the women's room and the terrace, I hope I have been able to show, is the defining feature of the central Omani dwelling.

The women's gatherings took place in room R1 in the Barwani house in Manah. The infants and toddlers stayed with their mothers, who carried them from one room to another in an Omani version of a crib or Moses basket made of palm fronds and chords. The grown up offspring either helped their father in the zarah or attended the Qurānic school (madrasah).[29] The Madrasat al-Qur'ān was attached to the Masjid al-Bostan, beyond the eastern gate; however, the Sablat al-Falaj Fiqain and the small space attached to the qibla wall of Masjid al-Shara also acted as madrasah from time to time. In this way the women and the young children would spend most of the day at home, and with the upper level virtually unusable after mid-morning, would confine themselves to the ground floor. The women also went out to collect fodder, which they did after the ta'asir meet. In larger dwellings the condition was somewhat more comfortable, as the series of rooms and covered galleries helped to cool down the internal environment even further, while the light well (shamsiya) assisted in some air movement. By the time the men came back from their after-dinner meeting in the sabla, the environment had cooled down sufficiently to enable the full use of the upper level, and to make possible the restoration of the terrace to its primary pragmatic, as well as metaphysical, intentions: as a space for living and as a space to experience the link between heaven and earth. The ground floor is scarcely used during the evenings and nights for any activities other than as a connector between the street and the core dwelling. It is this alternating concentration of activities between the floors, integrally linked to the environmental response pattern of the traditional dwelling, and the internalised understanding of traditional social time, which provides the true picture of the functioning of the Jawf dwelling.

The preceding discussion highlights, amongst other things, the role of woman in the Omani household and her almost continual, powerful, and an all-pervasive presence in the diurnal rituals taking place within the dwelling. This, as could be imagined, has naturally had a very important impact on the spatial organisation of Omani domestic architecture. In the

man's opinion, the wife is the key to happiness and the paradise of this world. She is the chief of the house, the one providing foundation and stability to the house and the home. It is
indeed through the wife that a man attains his particular status
as a husband and as a patriarch. She evokes in a man the notion
of fidelity and stability, as the conjugal nature of their marriage
links the male and female for life. She is the source of love and
tenderness, while her radiating beauty charms the husband.
She also brings prestige for the husband by being their seal of
success. The wife assumes an active role in the education of
her children. She consoles her offspring in the time of suffer-
ings and difficulties, providing rest for the heart.[30] In this the
women's room remained the key that underlined its role as an
extension of the terrace; deconstructed yet diurnally functioning together, the two spaces fulfilled the programmatic, social
and spiritual demands conventionally associated with the Arab
courtyard.

## Notes

1   Today, Oman is divided into seven administrative regions of which
    a'Dakhaliya (Interior) is one. However in olden times the entire non-
    coastal Oman (with the exception of Dhofar which was never *actually*
    part of Omani culture and events) was known as a'Dakhaliya with its
    major regional toponyms of Tu'am, Sirr, Jawf and Sharqiya. Elsewhere I
    have discussed how the Jawf, the 'lower belly', the 'core' interior,
    played an important role from the very dawn of civilization. The
    natural containment and restricted accessibility had emphasised Jawf
    as the 'true' Oman. The discussion also stressed all the major factors
    having a formative influence on the culture and society of the Jawf.

2   Ibadism arose out of the Kharijite division during the first century of
    Islam. For a detailed discussion on the sect see, J. C. Wilkinson, (1972)
    The origins of the Omani State, *Journal of Avid Environments*, **1**, 87–96;
    D. Hopwood (ed.) *The Arabian Peninsula, Society and Politics*, London,
    Allen and Unwin 67–88; also, J. C. Wilkinson (1976) The Ibadi Imama,
    *Bulletin of the School of Oriental and African Studies* **39**: 535–551; and
    J. C. Wilkinson (1987) *The Imamate Tradition of Oman*, Cambridge,
    Cambridge University Press.

3   Such spatial organisation was not unique to Manah, as examples from
    Nizwa attest. Within the still inhabited, dense urban fabric of the
    traditional section of Nizwa, one such dwelling was surveyed. An early
    survey report prepared for the Ministry of Social Affairs contains more
    elaborate examples from Nizwa. Some show the presence of small
    *shamsiya* courtyards, but the basic spatial organisation is similar to that

found in Manah. The larger dwellings in Nizwa, like those from Manah,
had more than one staircase. Renardet-I. C. E., *Popular Housing
Scheme*, Ministry of Social Affairs, Sultanate of Oman, Muscat, August
1974, Vol. II, Appendix: Sociology; Nizwa dwellings in pp. B107–33.

4   They are collectively known as *ghanam* amongst the settled (*hadr*)
    population, and as *dhod* amongst the nomadic people (*bedu*). See J. C.
    Wilkinson, *Water and Tribal Settlement in South-East Arabia, A Study of
    the Aflaj of Oman*, Clarendon Press, Oxford, 1977, p. 72, n. 9.

5   Renardet-I. C. E, *op. cit.*, pp. B12–6. The study collected oral accounts
    of conceptions of the dwelling's role in Omani life.

6   Cain, A., Afshar F. and Norton, J. (1975) Indigenous Building in the
    Third World, *Architectural Design,* 207–24. See the plan of early stages
    of dwelling in the coastal area.

7   For example see Steele, *Hassan Fathy*, Academy, London.

8   Renardet-I. C. E., *op. cit.*, p. B139.

9   Hillier, B. and Hanson, J., *The Social Logic of Space*, Cambridge, 1984
    (paperback edn. 1988), various pp.; for an elemental definition see
    pp. 11–2.

10  Wilkinson, J. C., *op. cit.*, 1977, p. 128.

11  *Ibid.*, p. 133.

12  *Ibid.*

13  *Ibid.*, p. 131.

14  See *ibid.*, pp. 142–3, for discussion on this subject.

15  *Ibid.*, pp. 142–3.

16  *Ibid.*, p. 153, also p. 133. Modern aerial photographic survey has
    established this shrinkage.

17  *Ibid.*, pp. 122–3. The terminology used in *falaj* organization up until the
    present day, as Wilkinson shows, is to a great extent borrowed from
    Persian, and the knowledge and technique of finding water sources and
    digging *falaj* never appears to have been present amongst the Omanis.

18  *Ibid.*, pp. 138–40, but especially p. 140.

19  See J. C. Wilkinson, Islamic water law with special reference to oasis
    settlement, *Journal of Arid Environments*, 1978, Vol. 1, 87–96. Here
    Wilkinson shows how Islamic water laws were restricted in their
    scope, in the area of use of ground water, other than emanating from
    wells. This was because sophisticated underground water accessing
    systems, such as the *qanat* or the *falaj*, were virtually absent from the
    birthplace of Islam (p. 91). As Islam expanded into territories where
    such complex hydrological systems existed, it led to incorporation of
    local practices (*urf*) into Islamic law, or towards a set of ad hoc rulings
    (p. 90). On lack of understanding of agricultural practices see J. C.
    Wilkinson, *op. cit.*, 1977, p. 148.

20  Wilkinson, J. C., *op. cit.*, 1977, pp. 143–4.

21  Nicol, Fergus. *An analysis of some observations of thermal comfort in
    Raukee, India, and Baghdad, Iraq.* Building Research Establishment
    (BRE) Current Paper 4/75, Watford, 1973.

22  Al-Harthy, S. *The Traditional Architecture of Oman: A Critical Perspective*, M.Arch Thesis, University of Arizona, 1992, pp. 62–3.

23  Information compiled from personal observation, and from al-Harthy, Sultan H., *op. cit.*, pp. 62–7. Other sources consulted: Bonnenfant, Paul and Guillemette, & al-Harthi, Salim ibn Hamad ibn Sulayman, *op. cit.*, pp. 115–6, Eickelman, D., Religious knowledge in inner Oman, *JOS*, 1983, Vol. 6, 1, pp. 163–72, and Eickelman, C., Fertility and social change in Oman: women's Perspectives, *Middle East Journal* (MEJ), Autumn 1993, Vol. 47, 4, 652–66.

24  Eickelman, C., *Women and Community in Oman*, New York University Press, New York and London, 1984, p. 43; quoted in al-Harthy, Sultan H., *op. cit.*, p. 66.

25  The *sabla*, a term peculiar to Oman, denotes the tribe-specific male gathering halls. Some *sablas* are shared by two allied clans/tribes. Typically these are long narrow spaces, either entirely enclosed with an access door (e.g., in Manah, central Oman) and windows or arcaded on the street side (e.g., again in Manah). Some *sablas* are fortified to protect the tribe from attacks (e.g., in Mudayrib, eastern Sharqiya region).

26  Al-Harthy, S. H., *op. cit.*, p. 66.

27  Personal observation from Nazwa.

28  Eickelman, C., *op. cit.*, 1993, p. 658, fn. 15.

29  Eickelman, D., *op. cit.*, 1983, p. 65, where he notes, 'A ... significant factor in obtaining an [madrasah] education ... was whether a student's household could afford his absence from agricultural and herding activities.'

30  Renardet-I. C. E., *op. cit.*, pp. B21–2.

# 11 The European perimeter block: the Scottish experience of courtyard housing

## BRIAN EDWARDS

This chapter explores the evolution of the European perimeter block as witnessed by experience in Scotland, especially that of the City of Glasgow in the nineteenth century. In Glasgow the perimeter block was adopted as the model for the reshaping of the historic centre and the expansion of the suburbs. Its dimensions were adjusted to simultaneously serve the Town Council's need for street improvement, effective land utilisation and public health. Access to sunlight and ventilation was a critical factor in the development of the Glasgow perimeter block. In this chapter the Scottish perimeter block is compared with the Middle Eastern pattern of courtyard housing, especially in the context of three key evolutionary forces – climate, privacy and social structure. In each tradition gender zoning existed in building plan and section, and was also a major factor in urban design. The chapter concludes with the identification of parallels which allow the reader to explore possible contemporary revivals of the typology in the context of sustainable development.

The perimeter block of Northern Europe shares certain characteristics with the courtyard house of Middle Eastern origin. The form of both is the result of three critical forces – climate, social structure and the need for privacy. Though they differ in scale and urban ambition, these two housing typologies have evolved subjected to similar determinants. The interior garden or courtyard which defines both did not grow up by accident. It is a designed space whose function and dimensions were carefully considered.

The European perimeter block was formalised in the nineteenth century mostly as a result of public health and town planning legislation. Earlier examples exist back to the Renaissance and beyond that to Imperial Rome. However, it was the growth in city-making as a largely municipal undertaking in the nineteenth century which gave shape to the European perimeter block as we know it today. Until the seventeenth century, city planning was predominantly an unregulated affair. Pockets of enlightened private development did exist, some the result of papal, royal, speculative or philanthropic initiative. These projects, such as the expansion of Bath under John Wood undertaken from 1770 onwards, provided the inspiration for later expansion or reconstruction by local authorities such as the New Town of Edinburgh, begun around 1780 and completed in 1845. The example of Bath and similar grand exercises in civic design in the Bloomsbury area of London and the Millais quarter of Paris, provided the impetus for a range of land-use and spatial controls which found their way into early town planning and public health legislation. The perimeter block as a recognisable element of formal urban design had not yet emerged, and its potential for social and sanitary order remained unexploited.

Courtyard spaces in European urban development have an ancient origin. In the form of cloisters they are one of the characteristic features of monastic planning. The central courtyard is also relatively frequently encountered in Elizabethan country house architecture in the UK and in Renaissance palaces of continental Europe. But their social or functional purpose was rarely related to climatic control, or the search for privacy, or perceptions of public health. These were private, or at least semi-private, spaces within larger development intended to provide natural light to dense interiors. Urban planning, where it existed up to the early eighteenth century, consisted of streets and external squares, not perimeter blocks of regular dimension on all sides with residential units overlooking a shared courtyard to the rear.

One has only to compare the unregulated development of many European cities up to the eighteenth century with the emergence of a planned response to growing insanitary conditions by local councils in the nineteenth century to see the important role played by the perimeter block. Courtyards did occur in medieval and later cities, but these were usually of random shape and increasingly infilled as time passed. As a consequence, the city fabric became devoid of light and ventilation, and access became difficult and at times perilous. By the nineteenth century city administrators had become aware that the loss of urban ventilation space, coupled with unwholesome water supplies, was one of the causes leading to successive epidemics of typhoid, cholera and tuberculosis. They were also aware that the ever-rising density of occupation increased the risk of fire and thwarted its containment. Pressure mounted through the nineteenth century to regulate the construction of urban areas and to deal with the slums which had grown up by clearance and reconstruction based upon a rational disposition of residential units and courtyards.

In many ways the action proposed by Sir Christopher Wren for the rebuilding on London after the Great Fire of 1666 provided a model of the type of comprehensive measures which were needed. Three main actions were suggested by Wren – street widening and straightening, space controls, and new forms of building construction. The idea of street-based improvement linked to dimensional constraint on surrounding property is one of the prerequisites for the emergence of the European perimeter block. Although Wren's ideas were not adopted, they remained a powerful influence over subsequent centuries. Haussmann's rebuilding of Paris around 1850 adopted similar measures, as did the City Improvement Scheme of 1866 in Glasgow. The latter was a comprehensive reconstruction of 21 hectares of slum property (housing around 88,000 people) using a combination of new, widened streets and four-storey perimeter blocks of housing, sometimes with shops and workshops on the ground floor.

## The importance of the street

Street-based urban planning was an important element of city-making into the Industrial Revolution (Morris 1994). The street provided many advantages for the town planner. It regulated visual and spatial form, provided channels for public services, created parcels for profitable land utilisation and, finally, created a hierarchy of public spaces (streets) and private areas (rear courtyards). The street also enhanced the aesthetic landscape, by setting major roads and avenues upon the axes of public buildings such as churches and courthouses. The effect of these measures was to lead to an environment whereby town planning and street construction were complimentary activities. Urban expansion in the eighteenth century provided ample evidence (London, Bath, Bristol and Edinburgh) of the dominant function of street-based estate plans in city making. Those expansion schemes which put the street to the fore also discovered that appearance and prosperity was greatly enhanced (Youngson 1966). In fact, many city plans for urban remodelling and expansion consisted of little more than a layout of streets and service lanes supported by drawings showing the elevations of the principle façades.

The towns created by such measures were largely linear in form and based upon, in Glasgow's case, an open grid which provided socio-spatial ordering (Walker 1999). The dominance of the street with its wide pavements provided processional routes across the town where men could parade on foot or by coach. By the early nineteenth century the street was a world of largely masculine display. Here middle-class men strutting in their frock coats could admire the finely proportioned façades of the long classical terraces which lined the new streets. The world of women was mainly in the kitchens, basements and attics which faced not the street but the service yards and courts to the rear. Under the influence of the planned street two parallel worlds evolved to serve the needs of gender: men to the public front and women to the private rear. Admittedly some women, mainly wives, were to be seen on the wide pavements of the handsome new streets and labouring men in the courtyards behind, but generally men occupied the streets and women the yards and courts. This division existed in the cross section of buildings as well as in estate plans. The public (and hence mainly masculine) rooms faced towards the front overlooking the street, whilst the kitchens, bedrooms and nursery faced the rear.

Architecturally the building façades were also differently treated. The front elevation was ordered, usually to classical lines, with pilasters and string courses establishing a proportional system to which whole street blocks subscribed. The rear elevation, on the other hand, was an ad hoc collection of windows and extensions which responded not to an abstract ideal but to the functional demands of domestic life.

If the street entered the nineteenth century as the basic element of town planning (Markus 1980) it had far-reaching consequences for the role of men and women in city life, and ultimately for the development of the perimeter block. As discussed, the eighteenth century urban legacy was one of terraces lining linear streets which in turn led to public squares or opened onto public parks. John Nash's plan for the Marylebone area of London (1820) was one such survivor into the next century. These were not streets of perimeter blocks but streets of urban terraces. The terrace is a two-dimensional aggregation of two-, three- or four-storey houses, the perimeter block is the same composition arranged in the third dimension to form a hollow cube. The perimeter block required another impetus for its evolution and this came from the twofold effect of the Industrial Revolution – the growth of an urban labouring population and the attendant problem of public health.

## The perimeter block as a model for working class housing

Urban reformers in the nineteenth century faced the problem of housing (or rehousing) the poor. As industry and commerce expanded, labourers were drawn from rural areas to the factories, mills and shipyards of large industrial cities. Much debate surrounded the best type of housing for these people. In England the predominant form was the terraced house but in Scotland, Germany, Holland and much of France, Italy and Spain the perimeter block was the preferred model. The problem with the two-storey terraced house is that of density – only 400 persons per hectare (pph) can be accommodated without loss of privacy, natural light and ventilation. In northern England back-to-back housing offered a refinement which increased density to 560 pph but at the cost of through ventilation. Developers realised that only by building higher could the densities required of the influx of rural people to the cities be achieved. However, flatted accommodation was often outlawed by municipal authorities because of the unscrupulous over-development which took place. Pressure grew to permit tenemental housing (flats constructed within a block) and to regulate its form. After all, the middle classes had long enjoyed apartment living in cities like Edinburgh and

Barcelona, and in London philanthropic developers (such as the Peabody Trust) had begun building working class tenement blocks six or eight storeys high by about 1850. For industrial cities like Liverpool, Newcastle and Glasgow the challenge was how to learn from this experience to create affordable but healthy housing for an expanding working population.

The answer was found in the refinement of the traditional tenement block. In Scotland and much of continental Europe architects (some working for public bodies) developed fresh prototypes of old tenemental forms. Typical was John Carrick, City Architect for Glasgow 1862 to his death in 1891. He was responsible for rehousing the urban poor under the City Improvement Act, 1866; for regulating private development throughout Glasgow via the Dean of Guild Court: for street construction and for the laying out of water mains, sewage pipes and tram systems. Carrick was in the rare position to orchestrate development at various scales, ensuring consistency between town planning, urban design and building construction.

Carrick devoted considerable energy to the refinement of the perimeter block, ensuring its application throughout Glasgow (for working and middle class needs) and beyond. He took the traditional tenement as a model (multi-storey blocks of apartments reached by a common stair), reformed it and arranged it as an enclosing block of repeating units surrounding a central courtyard or garden. It thus became a regular perimeter courtyard, usually four storeys high and arranged to edge a grid of streets of equal dimension. As Glasgow expanded, the city authorities attached the crucial rule upon developers that building was to be 'four square storeys high' with fronts of identical repeating design constructed of sandstone beneath a slate roof (Edwards 1999, p. 85). By the use of this design code, the City of Glasgow became regulated into a visually consistent pattern of perimeter blocks extending outwards from the commercial centre. The term 'four square storeys high' means a perimeter block of four stories on all sides, i.e. extending through the right angle at street corners.

In Glasgow and elsewhere the perimeter block offered four main advantages which ensured its popularity throughout the nineteenth century and into the twentieth. It was economical to build (because of the high level of repeating construction parts), it offered efficient and often profitable land utilisation, it helped create social and sanitary order, and it responded well to climatic imperatives. Such was its robustness that it increasingly met both working and middle class needs, either within the same block or in adjacent units.

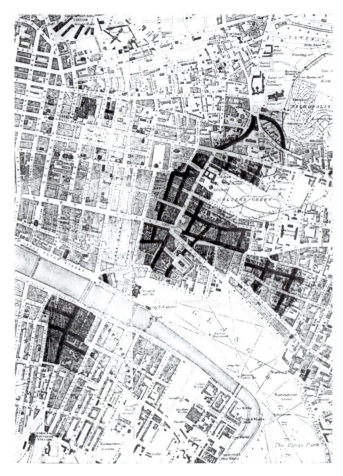

11.1 Outline of widened streets providing for a perimeter block development under the Glasgow Improvement Scheme of 1866

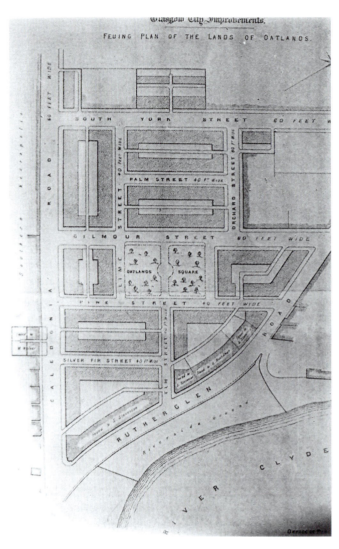

11.2 Housing built by Glasgow Corporation in 1870 showing the emergence of the perimeter block

The perimeter block and the new streets of the nineteenth century had a symbiotic relationship. The needs of each were mutually compatible and their dimensions were adjusted in each party's interest. For example, a common regulation attached to land development by municipal authorities (e.g. Glasgow Police Act 1862) restricted the height of dwellings to the width of the streets. So four storey perimeter blocks required streets to be 40 feet wide, five storey, 50 feet etc. (floor to floor heights were usually 10 feet). As a consequence, a cube of sectional space existed across the street with a 45° line prescribing the cornice level from the opposite pavement edge. The resulting proportional harmony, essentially classical in inspiration, gave dignity and repose to the nineteenth-century city. It also provided housing areas with grids of sunlight and

ventilation which were considered vital for public health. This pattern, though typically Scottish, is also frequently encountered elsewhere in Europe and helps define the perimeter block as a generic type.

The spacing of streets served the dimensional dictates of the perimeter blocks. The size of rear courts was as regulated as the width of streets. Normally (in Glasgow at least) the width of courts had to be one and a half times the height of the enclosing buildings. So with a rear wall of 40 feet, the courtyard was at least 60 feet across. Putting together the minimum width dimensions of the housing block (30 feet) and the courtyard (60 feet) the resulting urban unit was a perimeter block 120 feet wide (2 × 30 feet × 60 feet) or about 38 metres. Allowing for the width of streets, this results in urban parcels of about 50 metres square.

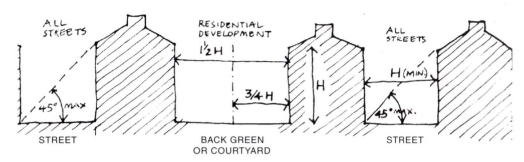

**11.3 A typical cross-section through Glasgow streets showing the planning dimensions imposed by the city authority**

Rarely, however, were the perimeter blocks truly square in plan. Their shape was often adjusted to serve topographical need (as in the west end of Glasgow), to form radiating patterns of streets (as in Amsterdam and Paris), and to maximise the penetration of sunlight into the rear courtyard (as in Berlin). Since a major function of the rear courtyard was that of promoting public health, its aspect and size was manipulated to achieve effective ventilation or to expose as much of its area to sunlight as possible. The latter became increasingly important as the courtyard developed into a winter garden as the nineteenth century progressed (sometimes including large glazed rooms projecting from rear walls). Ventilation and sunlight had two slightly different requirements. Ventilation was served by the axis of the courtyard being placed parallel to prevailing winds (SW in Scotland, S or SE in Germany). A long courtyard could act as a channel to increase urban breezes with benefits (real or imagined) for the rooms facing the courtyard. In an age of airborne disease and faith in fresh air such concerns gave shape to the city. In Glasgow, for instance, many of the new streets opened onto large parks at their ends. Here the streets were seen as avenues for clean healthy air drawn from the parks and driven by prevailing winds along the parallel streets (Edwards 1992).

Sunlight penetration had different dimensional requirements. Here the blocks were ideally built on a north/south axis. This exposed the long east and west façades to equal amounts of sunshine. Only the short north facing inner façade was devoid of sunshine, and here the presence of an outer south elevation was seen as adequate compensation. So the shape and dimensions of the courtyard had to satisfy two contradictory demands:

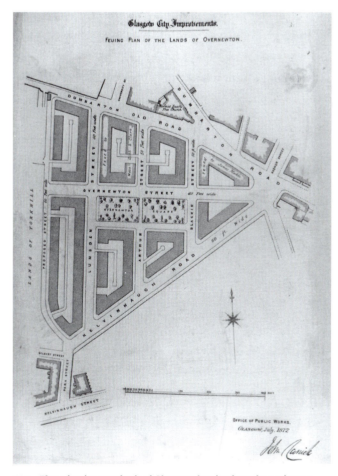

**11.4 Plan of an inner suburb of Glasgow showing how the perimeter block was adjusted to maximize solar penetration**

127

that of the free flow of fresh air and of the health-giving exposure to sunlight. As medical science progressed, local medical officers of health appointed by large city councils had a growing influence upon urban and building design (Edwards 1999a, p. 88). As a consequence, the demands made upon architects varied according to location. In Scotland, where urban ventilation was seen as paramount, the orientation of the interior courtyard tended to favour air flow whilst in continental Europe, and particularly Germany, sunshine was given priority. The latter led in time to the southern unit of the perimeter block being removed altogether or reduced in size. This allowed far more sunshine to reach into the interior of the development, although it compromised privacy.

## Privacy and the needs of women and children

Mention has already been made of the gender zoning of the typical nineteenth-century industrial city. The men occupied the street where it provided the route to work and the promenade for weekend perambulation. The corners of perimeter blocks were often marked (and perceptually at least frequently guarded) by public houses (pubs) which in those days did not admit women. The woman's world was the interior courtyard and the stairwell of the block. In these spaces children played and women met. The zoning had a strong functional basis and was expressed in building design. Clothes

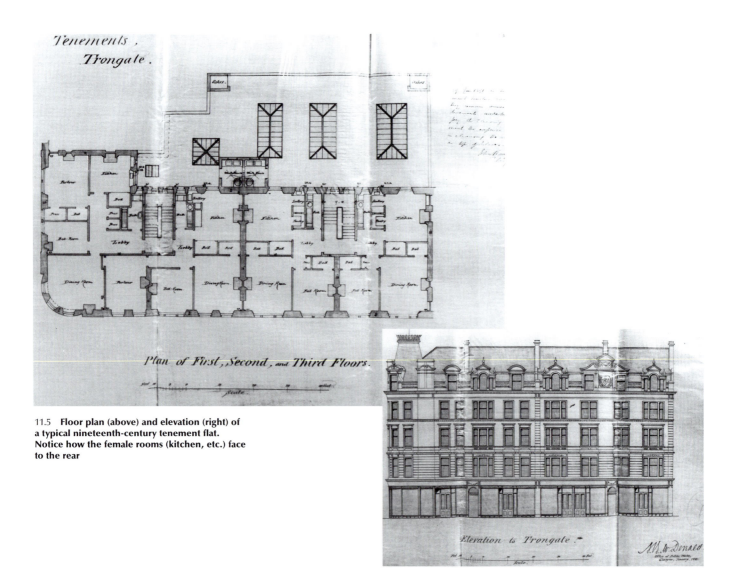

11.5 **Floor plan (above) and elevation (right) of a typical nineteenth-century tenement flat. Notice how the female rooms (kitchen, etc.) face to the rear**

were dried in the rear courtyard and sometimes washed in communal washhouses located near their centre. The courtyard too contained the ash pits and rubbish bins of nineteenth-century domestic life. Often also the courtyard provided space for growing flowers and vegetables. So whilst the womenfolk might use the street for journeys to shops, it was the interior courtyard and stair close which was their principal domain.

The distinction was reflected in the layout of apartments which formed the perimeter blocks. Public rooms such as living rooms faced the street whilst kitchens, bedrooms and bathrooms (where they existed) looked across the rear courtyard. Men could stand in the living room bay window and survey the street whilst simultaneously women stood at the kitchen window watching over the children playing in the courtyard behind. Privacy was further maintained by placing bedrooms to the rear where only other bedrooms faced. To the front, public rooms faced each other across the wide nineteenth-century street. Even in the staircases which provided access to the flats, the windows facing the rear had coloured or obscured glass in order to maintain privacy for the women and children.

The perimeter block provided for the development of high density yet healthy forms of urban living. Through it men could be located close to their place of work, either walking to local factories or taking the tram which was able to exploit the wide straight streets. Density of development and increasing concern for amenity resulted in not only working people but artisans and lower-middle-class families being housed in the block. Here larger flats were provided, sometimes occupying a whole floor with their own front door to the street. But the same rules applied in terms of privacy, order and dimensional dictates, since the middle classes shared an equal interest in avoiding epidemics or social unrest.

As the nineteenth century unfolded, the perimeter block lost its grip on development. There was pressure to relax the orthogonal structure of block and street, and to undertake more picturesque forms of development based upon apartment houses and curving roads. The garden city movement questioned the assumptions made by architects like Carrick, and shifted the emphasis towards suburbs, tree planting and free space. The European city began to lose its urban structure and the perimeter block its supremacy. Part of the erosion was the result of pressure to create more integrated forms of development where housing, industry and shopping occurred within the same block. Although shops and public houses occurred on the ground floor of perimeter blocks from about 1850, by 1890 in Glasgow light industry was permitted to occupy the courtyard behind. This resulted in a significant loss of privacy and undermined the essential gender zoning which was central to earlier success. In some instances, the garden was simply transferred to the roof of the workshops which now filled the courtyard, but in time the inclusion of roof-lights and light wells meant that the private world of the courtyard, became an industrial area of noise and masculinity. Also access lanes were constructed through the enclosing wall of the perimeter block, creating visibility from the street into the courtyard. By 1900 the homogenous structure of block and street was, in Scotland at least, in retreat (Reed 1999, p. 196).

## Alexander 'Greek' Thomson and the glass-roofed courtyard block

In 1870 the architect Alexander 'Greek' Thomson was invited, with three other prominent local architects, to provide competitive proposals for the redevelopment of an area of the Old Town of Glasgow. He was to provide designs for a parcel of land just east of High Street capable of housing, under the City Improvement Scheme, a population of 1,200 people. Thomson proposed a perimeter block about 330 feet square divided by a series of parallel glass-roofed courts and open service yards. Each court was to be semi-enclosed at their

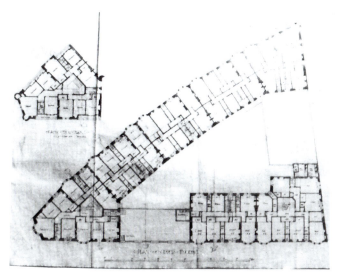

**11.6** **The relaxation of the orthogonal rigour of the perimeter block after 1880, allowing for more picturesque planning**

11.7　CAD reconstruction of an unrealized housing scheme of 1868 by Alexander 'Greek' Thomson for glass-roofed streets containing housing courts to the rear

ends and surrounded on all sides by four-storey tenement housing (in the Greek revival manner). Although the published accounts are open to interpretation (Edwards 1999b, p. 80), Thomson stated that the glazing of the courts at roof level was to provide 'playgrounds for the young' where the warmth which would flow from the method of construction would be 'condusive to the health and comfort of all' (*The Builder*, 1870).

Thomson took the logic of health and ventilation a step further than his contemporaries. He aligned the courts north/south for maximum solar penetration, and rather than leave them open to the Glasgow weather proposed a glazed colonnade or mall. He well realised that the resulting warming of the space would enhance ventilation of the block using what we now call the 'stack-effect'. To fully exploit this he proposed the construction of ventilating ducts which would run through the exterior walls, connecting with the glazed court at low level and open to the roof above. Although nothing came of the proposal, it confirms the interest architects had at the time in using the courtyard to enhance ventilation and health, and to create sheltered play space for children.

## Parallels between the European and Middle Eastern courtyard tradition

Though the scale is different, both the European perimeter block and the courtyard house of the Middle East share certain similarities. Both are largely the result of climatic influence, of social structure and an effective union between land utilisation and wider cultural values. Whereas the climate of the north is cold and damp, and of the Middle East hot and dry, both housing traditions grew up as a response to environmental conditions. In the perimeter block there was the need for ventilation and to adjust dimensions to exploit wind and air currents through the courtyard and surrounding urban area. This too was the case with the courtyard house, especially those in desert regions. Both traditions also adjusted their design to achieve optimum solar conditions – shade in the south and sunshine in the north. In both traditions too, the height of buildings in relation to the size of courts was essential to successful environmental design. Both employed other devices to maximise climatic advantages – water cooling via fountains in the Middle East, glazing of courtyards in the cold north. Added to this both the European perimeter block and the courtyard house adjusted their orientation and design to

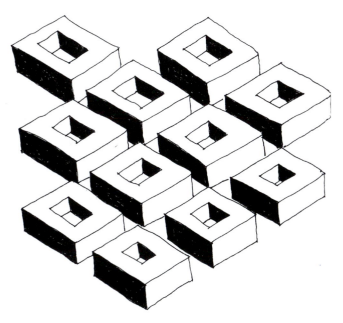

11.8 **Effect on urban form of the spatial controls exercised by the Glasgow Corporation between 1866 and 1892. The result was a cityscape of perimeter blocks which shared certain characteristics with courtyard housing**

balance the benefits of wind and sun. In the hands of Thomson, the concept of alternate glazed and open courtyards was taken to its logical conclusion, acting as an important, though largely unrecognised predecessor to the twentieth-century atrium. In both traditions, therefore, awareness of renewable energy helped shape building design, making them capable of revival today in the interest of sustainable development.

The social structures existing in their respective societies is also reflected in both housing typologies. The perimeter block created a largely separate world for women and children apart from that of men. The courtyard was a protected space within the tough urban grain of the nineteenth-century European city just as the court of the Middle Eastern house was protected from the hostility of desert life. In cities like Glasgow men promenaded along exterior streets whose corners were often marked by the epitome of masculinity – the public house. Within the masculine frame of the perimeter block, women and children were secure within a fortress of architecture and social values. The same is true of the courtyard house, and here the tradition is stronger and the rules of privacy more rigorously upheld. In the Middle East, there is no overlooking of the courtyard except from designated rooms.

Gender division expressed as domestic territory ensured that social and religious norms were upheld.

It is clear that in spite of superficial differences, the European perimeter block and the Middle Eastern courtyard house share common evolutionary forces – climate, the need for privacy, and social organisation which reflects wider cultural values. Whereas the perimeter block houses a community of several hundred, it is fundamentally no different from the courtyard house of an extended family. Both subscribe to a common ideal and are subjected to design constraints which have evolved over centuries. In both examples too, urban design and the details of construction provide a framework which not only served society but expressed wider cultural

11.9 **A shared courtyard in medieval Glasgow as photographed by Thomas Annon in 1868**

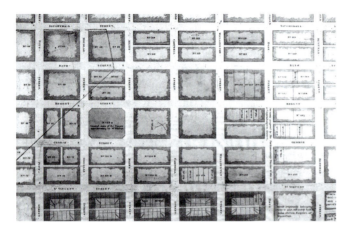

**11.10   Master plan of perimeter block housing in Glasgow's Blythswood area (1822)**

values. Just as the twentieth century threatened and largely destroyed the supremacy of the perimeter block, it too has undermined the authority of the courtyard house in the Middle East. Yet both have survived into the twenty-first century as a record of the past and a possible model for the future. For both could be seen as examples of sustainable development – the integration in built form of environmental and social sustainability.

## Bibliography

*The Builder,* Glasgow improvement scheme, **28**, 26 March 1870.

Bacon, E. (1967) *Design of Cities,* pp. 206–7. London, Thames and Hudson.

Edwards, B. (1992) 'First Architect of the Second City', *RIBA Journal* May 52–6.

Edwards, B. (1999a) Glasgow improvements, 1866–1901. In P. Reed (ed.) *Glasgow: The Forming of a City,* p. 85. Edinburgh, Edinburgh University Press.

Edwards, B. (1999b) Alexander Thomson and glass-roofed streets, *The Architectural Review,* June, 80–2.

Markus, T. A. (1980) *Order in Space and Society,* pp. 70–4. Edinburgh, Mainstream.

Morris, A. E. J. (1994) *History of Urban Form,* pp. 278–91, Longman.

Reed, P. (1999) The post industrial city?. In P. Reed (ed.) *Glasgow: The Forming of a City,* p. 196. Edinburgh, Edinburgh University Press.

Walker, F. (1999) 'Glasgow's New Towns'. In P. Reed (ed.) *Glasgow: The Forming of a City,* p. 32. Edinburgh, 'Edinburgh University Press.

Youngson, A. J. (1966) *The Making of Classical Edinburgh,* pp. 284–5. Edinburgh, Edinburgh University Press.

# Part 3

# Environmental dimensions

# 12 Courtyards: a bioclimatic form?

DANA RAYDAN, CARLO RATTI AND KOEN STEEMERS

## Introduction

Courtyard housing is present in geographically, climatically and culturally disparate regions of the world, and has given rise to an abundant literature in the fields of architecture and urban planning.

Many studies concentrate on courtyards as climatically responsive urban forms. For instance, Fathy (1986) and Bahadori (1978) claim that courtyard introversion fulfilled several functions in hot arid regions: the creation of an open sheltered zone, the adoption of ingenious natural cooling strategies, the protection against wind-blown dust or sand and the mitigation of the effects of solar excess. According to them – and many other scholars – climate appears to be one of the strongest determinants of architectural form, especially the shape of streets and courtyards. Fathy states:

> By simple analysis it becomes quite understandable how such a pattern came to be universally adopted in the Arab world. It is only natural for anybody experiencing the severe climate of the desert to seek shade by narrowing and properly orienting the street, to avoid the hot desert winds by making the streets winding, with closed vistas.

However, opposite claims about the environmental properties of courtyards exist. Mänty (1988), for instance, analyses vernacular architecture throughout Sweden, Norway and Switzerland and praises the use of courtyards in their ability to create 'pockets of solar gain', thus balancing the harshness of cold northern climates.

Is the courtyard therefore a sun protector or sun collector? Broad claims that overlook the particularities of the problem can lead to contradicting observations. Many of the climatic properties of courtyard spaces depend on their proportions, so either of these statements might be acceptable, given the circumstances. The additional problem is that many claims found in the architectural literature remain unsupported, based merely on qualitative observation and common sense. And when they ground themselves on measures or monitoring of existing urban structures, they are generally limited to the proof of the aptness of a given urban geometry in a given climate. But how apt is the courtyard compared with alternative urban forms, such as the isolated high or low-rise box-shaped blocks (that will be referred to as pavilions[1]), that are colonising our contemporary cities? Is it better or worse in terms of response to climate?

This chapter will try to answer some of these questions by calculating a number of well-established environmental variables on simplified vernacular courtyards and two other architectural forms. The analysis is carried out within the hot-arid climatic context, in comparison to the cold Scandinavian northern climatic context. As stated by Oke (1988), there are 'almost infinite combinations of different climatic contexts, urban geometries, climate variables and design objectives. Obviously there is no single solution, i.e. no universally optimum geometry'.

## Related work

Leslie Martin and Lionel March carried out an extensive study of the environmental performance of courtyards at Cambridge University in the late 1960s. In a number of influential papers (1967, 1972) they addressed the question: 'What building forms make the best use of land?' The question of course implies a definition of 'best use'. Martin and March (1972) bound themselves to quantifiable parameters, such as 'built potential' (the ratio of the floor area of the built form to the site area) and 'daylight availability'. They analysed different archetypal built forms, such as pavilions, streets and courtyards. Their findings, based on mathematical analysis, showed that the courtyard was eventually the best performing urban type in terms of efficiency in site coverage:

> The court form is seen to place the same amount of floor space on the same site area with the same condition of building depth and in approximately one-third the height required by the pavilion form.
>
> Martin and March 1972, p. 38

These studies lead eventually to a radical speculation to replace the centre of Manhattan with large courts, thus reducing the height of buildings from an average of 21 storeys to 7. Leslie Martin and his collaborators also designed a number of courtyard-type buildings in the UK, of which a famous example is Harvey Court, a residential development for Gonville and Caius College, Cambridge. Although the beauty of Martin and March's approach owes much to its generality, the answer to the question 'which urban forms make the best use of land?' cannot have an absolute answer, as it ought to take into consideration climatic variables. Even the availability of daylight, one of the basic parameters considered by them, can be negative in climates where protection from solar radiation is required. Moreover when a larger number of comfort variables is taken into account, an optimum geometry will be even more dependent on the climatic conditions.

In this chapter we will extend Martin and March's approach by:

1. Examining different urban forms in the context of the hot-arid climate, which has helped us to identify the environmental variables of interest. These variables include surface to volume ratios, shadow densities, daylight accessibility and view factors from the city to the sky.

They provide key measures related to solar radiation, thermal comfort and urban temperatures, which can be tested against the environmental pressure produced by hot-arid climates. One of these measures, shadow density, which is a climate-dependent measurement, will be further assessed within the cold northern Scandinavian climate, in order to investigate the puzzling dual sun protecting and sun collecting qualities of vernacular courtyards identified above;

2. Reassessing Martin and March's results by repeating their daylight simulations with newly developed image-processing techniques. In fact, Martin and March's mathematical approach was limited by a number of simplified assumptions. Our digital techniques, based on image processing algorithms, allow a better evaluation of lighting parameters;

3. Considering more realistic urban types, which do not have the generality of Martin and March's ones. We start from a simplified courtyard type based on well-documented vernacular examples found in hot-arid regions (as explained below) and subsequently mimic some transformation that might happen – and in many cases have happened – in real cities.

The urban forms, which we will analyse, consist of a courtyard and two shapes of pavilion – as described below.

## Description of the three urban forms

As in Martin and March's (1972) analysis, the governing principle is to take the same built volume and shape it according to different forms, which in turn are then simulated. These forms are described below.

The main case study selected for investigation is taken from a real prototype courtyard house. The specific configuration and dimensions of the courtyard house are adapted from a diagrammatic section of a courtyard urban dwelling as illustrated in Morris (1994) (Figures 12.1 and 12.2). An average number of three floors, each 3 m high, is assumed, as extrapolated from Talib (1984). Although the street network will generally be more irregular, this urban texture seems representative of an Arabic city (Figure 12.3).

The second two case studies are hypothetical yet fairly realistic pavilion types, mimicking potential modern urban

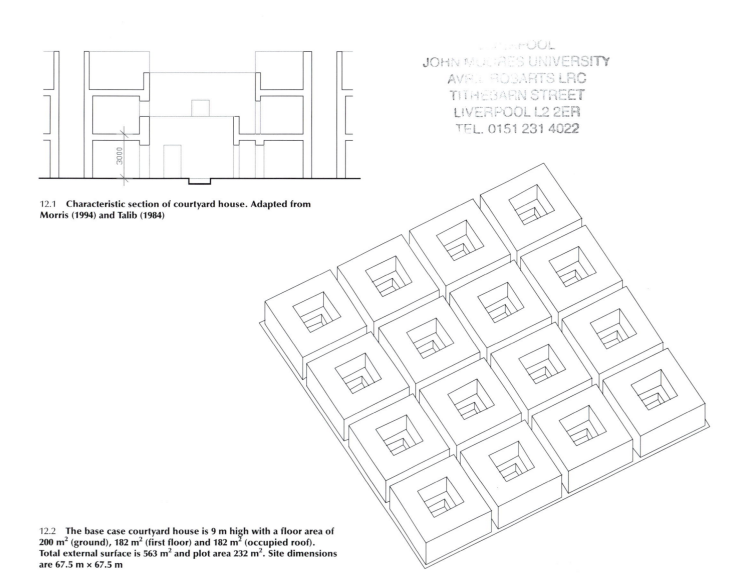

12.1   Characteristic section of courtyard house. Adapted from
Morris (1994) and Talib (1984)

12.2   The base case courtyard house is 9 m high with a floor area of
200 m$^2$ (ground), 182 m$^2$ (first floor) and 182 m$^2$ (occupied roof).
Total external surface is 563 m$^2$ and plot area 232 m$^2$. Site dimensions
are 67.5 m × 67.5 m

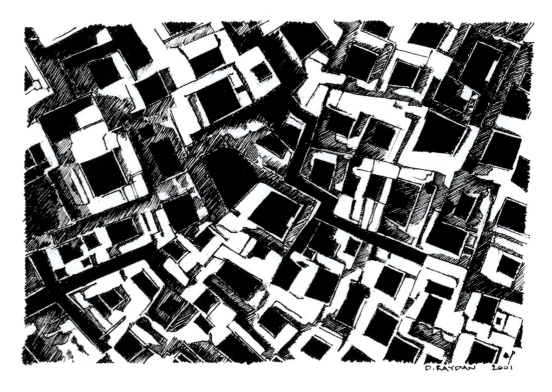

12.3   Courtyard-based urban
fabric of Marrakesh, Morocco,
showing the importance of
courtyard architecture at this
latitude (after Rudofsky 1964)

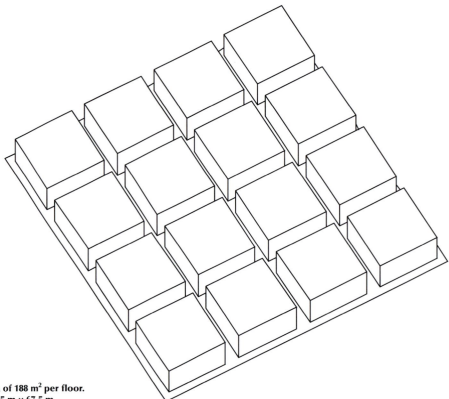

12.4 **Pavilion 1 option is 9 m high with a floor area of 188 m² per floor. Total surface area is 563 m². Site dimensions are 67.5 m × 67.5 m**

transformations that might take place in a vernacular court-yard context. The first variation (pavilion 1) consists of replacing each courtyard with an urban block centrally located in the initial lot, preserving the height of 9 m and obviously preserving the built volume. It is assumed that pavilion 1 option would be a pedestrianised modern urban neighbourhood with no vehicular traffic through the streets (Figure 12.4).

It is interesting to note how this pavilion alternative seems invasive or bulkier as opposed to the courtyard form; the relatively large surface area on the inside of the courtyard is lost to little gain on the periphery of the pavilion. This property was first noted by Raymond Unwin (Martin and March 1972, p. 18), the direct successor of Ebenezer Howard in the garden city tradition. He observed that as population increases around the perimeter of a town, the commuting time (distance from the centre) is increased in less than the direct proportion to this: 'the area of a circle is increased not in the direct proportion to the distance to be travelled from the centre to the circumference, but in proportion to the square of that distance' (quote by Howard from Martin and March 1972).

The same concept on a square geometry is graphically well represented by the Fresnel diagram (Figure 12.5), where surprisingly enough each annulus (including the central square)

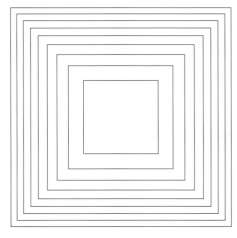

12.5 **Fresnel's diagram of concentric squares which increase at the same rate whilst sharing characteristics with the initial concentric square (after Martin and March 1972)**

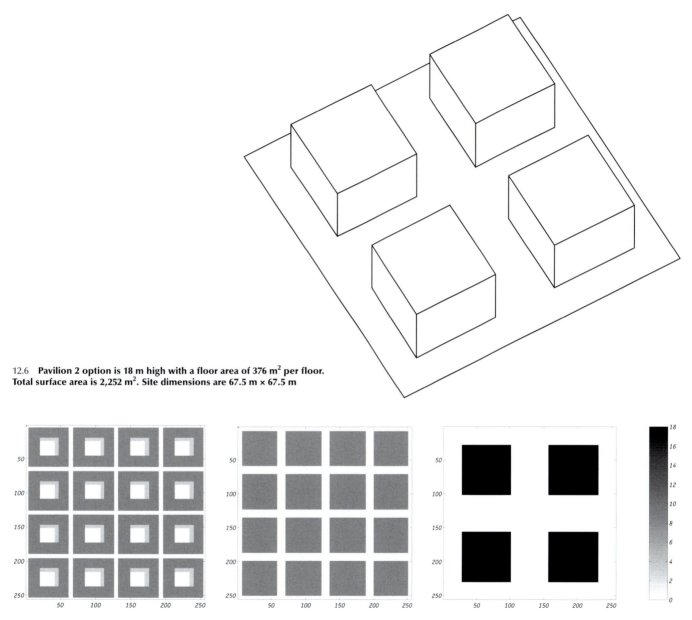

12.6  **Pavilion 2 option is 18 m high with a floor area of 376 m² per floor. Total surface area is 2,252 m². Site dimensions are 67.5 m × 67.5 m**

12.7  **Courtyard's layout and pavilion 1 and pavilion 2 represented as DEM images**

has equal area, i.e. each square ring has the same surface area. This demonstration was extensively adopted by Martin and March (1972) to make their point about the effectiveness of distributing built volume on the perimeter of a site (thus in a courtyard shape) as against building in the centre.

The second variation (pavilion 2) represents an urban composition integrating four courtyards into one urban block that could represent a mixed-use development (residential and

offices). The street width is fixed as to accommodate two-way traffic, parking on the sides and a small sidewalk. Building height was a result of the condition that the built volume needed to be the same as in the previous cases and resulted in a realistic height of six storeys, double of the initial case (Figure 12.6).

Figure 12.7 shows all three case studies as digital elevation models (DEM) – an image where the level of grey is proportional

Table 12.1 **Results from simulations**

| Surface to volume ratio | Total surface m² | Total volume m³ | Surface to volume |
|---|---|---|---|
| Courtyards | 15,797 | 27,030 | 0.584 |
| Pavilions 1 | 10,931 | 27,030 | 0.404 |
| Pavilions 2 | 7168 | 27,030 | 0.265 |

to building heights – the file format required for simulation using the image-processing technique.

## Analysis

Our analysis addressed the following parameters:

- surface to volume ratio
- shadow density
- daylight distribution
- sky view factor.

### Surface to volume ratio

This ratio is obtained by dividing the total surface of buildings (façades plus roofs) by their volume. It has been used in the past to estimate heat loss (Martin and March 1972, p. 57): the higher the ratio the higher the potential for heat loss during the winter season and heat gain during the summer season. More generally, however, it gives an idea of the building envelope surface that is exposed to the outside environment and consequently is a fundamental indicator for implementing environmental strategies. Values are listed in Table 12.1.

### Shadow density

This parameter, the only inherently climate-related measurement, is based on detecting shadows on the ground at hourly intervals on a piece of city for a given day of the year. Then the average number of hours of shadows is calculated at each point. Steemers and Ratti (1999) used this parameter as an environmental indicator to inform bioclimatic urban design. Here, we run a shadowing simulation for a summer

Table 12.2 **Results from simulations for latitutde 31°N**

| Shadow density | Mean shadow density (average number of hours of shadow) on the ground on 21 June for latitude 31°N |
|---|---|
| Courtyards | 10.98 |
| Pavilions 1 | 9.78 |
| Pavilions 2 | 6.10 |

Table 12.3 **Results from simulations for latitutde 60°N**

| Shadow density | Mean shadow density (average number of hours of shadow) on the ground on 21 June for latitude 60°N |
|---|---|
| Courtyards | 12.4 |
| Pavilions 1 | 9.9 |
| Pavilions 2 | 2.8 |

day (21 June) at two different latitudes, 31°N, which corresponds to the latitude of the city of Marrakesh in Morocco and 60°N, which is the average northern latitude of two Scandinavian cities, Oslo and Stockholm. The aim, as stated in the introduction, is to weigh the bioclimatic 'appropriateness' of the simplified vernacular courtyard and the selected pavilion types 1 and 2. Average values are listed in Tables 12.2 and 12.3.

### Daylight distribution

Daylight availability is measured as illuminance values in streets. For this task the selected model of the sky used for simulation is the standard CIE overcast sky, which represents 'ideal' overcast conditions. Although overcast sky conditions are not representative of prevailing sky conditions in hot-arid climates, which are normally clear, the nature of the simulation

Table 12.4  **Results from simulations**

| Daylight distribution | Average normalised illuminance (maximum = 1) at ground level | |
|---|---|---|
| Courtyards | 0.099 in the street | 0.188 in the courtyard |
| Pavilions 1 | 0.296 | |
| Pavilions 2 | 0.530 | |

consists of investigating illuminance distribution only. The zenith is three times brighter than the horizon and the luminance distribution has cylindrical symmetry (i.e. it is solely dependent on the elevation). Values have been normalised (1 represents the illuminance that would fall on an unobstructed surface which sees the whole sky vault, 0 represents nil illuminance). Results are listed in Table 12.4.

### Sky view factor (SVF)

Although the SVF was first introduced in heat transfer literature to model radiative exchange between surfaces, it also offers benefit in terms of urban climatology research. In fact, it represents a good measure of the openness of the urban texture to the sky and has been associated, among other indicators, to the increase in temperature in the urban context compared with the surrounding rural context – the so-called urban heat island phenomenon (Oke 1981). The well-established relation between the SVF and the urban heat island consists of the observation that the smaller the SVF, the higher the temperature of cities (Oke 1981), as will be explained in greater detail below.

Roofs of buildings have a full view of the sky vault and therefore a SVF of 1. Streets exhibit lower values, which are determined by the urban configuration. Street junctions are particularly interesting, as they make evident the linear additive nature of the SVF: their value is approximately the double of streets, as two strips of sky are visible simultaneously.

## Discussion of results

### Surface to volume ratio (Table 12.1)

The benefits of high surface to volume ratios are an increase in the potential for natural ventilation, daylighting, etc. However

the counter-indication to a high surface to volume ratio – as mentioned above – is the increase in heat loss during the winter season and heat gain due to exposure to solar radiation during the summer season.

Results show that the courtyard type has the higher surface to volume ratio (0.584). As for the smaller size pavilions (pavilions 1), their surface to volume ratio is slightly higher than the larger pavilions (pavilions 2) (0.404 for the former compared to 0.265 for the latter). These results suggest that although potentially subjected to a high potential for natural ventilation and daylighting, the courtyard type is also potentially exposed to heat loss during winter and heat gain during summer. Comparing the horizontal and vertical surface areas between the courtyard type and pavilion one for a constant volume reinforces this observation (façades: 802.8 m$^2$ for courtyard type and 493.2 m$^2$ for pavilion 1; roofs: 250.16 m$^2$ for courtyard type and 187.69 m$^2$ for pavilion 1). In the light of the above hypothesis, the courtyard type would not seem to be performing well thermally. However, when the potential heat loss/gain during respectively cold and warm seasons is analysed within the complexity of hot-arid climatic context, results start to indicate more favourable conclusions. In hot-arid climates night-time temperatures are usually lower than daytime temperatures throughout the year, with a diurnal temperature difference between the average daily maximum and minimum ranging between 15 to 19°C for the city of Marrakesh for the hot months of May to August (Pearce and Smith 1993). The winter months, accounting for approximately a quarter of the year, are relatively mild and sunny. Therefore the critical months of the year are the hot months, and mitigating the temperature extremes of this season is a must. The ingenious solution of the courtyard house type in hot-arid climates, such as in Marrakesh, is the use of high thermal mass to store heat through the expansive external surface area during the day in order to benefit from it during the cooler nights. By maximising the surface to volume ratio, the courtyard acts as heat sink and therefore alleviates the extreme temperature stress: it reradiates this heat indoors as well as to the surrounding and to the sky during the cooler nights due to the time lag of the large thermal mass and the cooler air temperature.

In cold climates the tradition is to provide high degrees of thermal insulation – Scandinavian insulation standards are amongst the highest in the world. As a result of this the fabric heat losses are relatively small and ventilation, as well as the potential for solar gains, becomes more significant. The geometry of the building – whether court or pavilion – is less critical in terms of heat loss, whereas improvements through a more sheltered microclimate can provide additional benefits. Increased average temperatures (see sky view factor below) and protection from cold winds (reducing ventilation losses) may offset small disadvantage of the larger surface area.

### Shadow density and daylight distribution (Tables 12.2, 12.3 and 12.4)

Concerning the mean shadow density, high values recorded in the streets are beneficial in hot-arid regions as they provide protection to pedestrians and to the horizontal street surface from solar radiation. Therefore as increased shadow density values can be interpreted as potentially positive, the courtyard type, which has the highest value, seems to be an advantaged configuration (10.98 compared to 9.78 for pavilion 1 and 6.10 for pavilion 2). As expected, high overshadowing also means low illumination values, and the courtyard type, with its narrow streets, ranks dramatically lowest (0.148 mean value for courtyard type compared to 0.296 for pavilion 1 and 0.530 for pavilion 2). However, this observation seems to contradict the daylight benefits suggested through high surface to volume ratios, as explained above. It should be clarified that the shadow density reading in this case is taken in the streets and that the illuminance values are an average of all ground surfaces (streets and courtyard floors). Taken in the courtyard itself, an average illuminance of 0.188 (compared with the low value of 0.099 in the street) proves that daylight is actually benefited from through the courtyard and not through the external façades of the courtyard type. This observation corresponds well with the reality of this introverted house type that interacts with the environment through the courtyard.

However, we note here that our simulation simply takes into account light falling directly from the sky, and not that reflected from the ground and buildings, which in some cases can give a significant daylight contribution. An effective instrument to control daylight availability in cities is manipulating the surface reflectivity of cities; using white paint, for example, increases reflected light and therefore overall illuminance values in the city. In our case, this would probably be enough to bring daylight within the street to an acceptable level, even in the courtyard type. This reasoning is based on an interesting observation made with regard to the external surface colour of courtyard types in north African countries such as Morocco which are generally painted with light colours, with increas-ingly brighter tonalities at northern latitudes in south European contexts, such as in Greece, for example.

Evaluating the shadow density results obtained for latitude 31°N (Marrakesh) against those for latitude 60°N (Oslo-Stockholm), a value of 12.4 hours compares to a lower 10.98 hours for the courtyard type. It should be noted here that the shadow density values obtained must be interpreted relatively to each latitude, whereby the average number of sunshine hours for the latitude 60°N in June is 16 hours compared to 14 hours for latitude 31°N. In terms of the fraction of total sunshine hours, these figures are virtually identical.

Again at first glance, this observation is far from confirming the 'sun-concentrating' quality of courtyards recorded by Mänty (1988) and documented above. Here again, a closer scrutiny is in order. In his assessment of the revival of the vernacular courtyard type of planning, Mänty highlighted climatic key particularities of the vernacular Scandinavian courtyard house-type, such as its predominant south orientation and its ability to act as a buffer against wind. Morris (1994) highlighted the suitability of courtyards for extreme climates due to their climatically buffering and filtering characteristics. The latter, having noted the prevalence of courtyard planning in hot-arid climates, observed the resistance received in implementing it in northerly mild cooler climates when Roman conquerors tried to introduce it in urban planning. This resistance was believed to be a result to the absence of climatic stresses in moderate northern latitudes, which did not necessitate clustering of shelters and introversion around a courtyard to filter the climate.

The sun concentrating character of Scandinavian courtyards is in fact due to the rather low height over width (H/W) ratio of the courtyard as observed by Mänty (1988), which averages 0.6, compared to 1.3 as measured in the selected simplified prototype courtyard adopted for this study and more typical of hot-arid climates. As indicated in the introduction, it is in fact a matter of proportions that confers either the sun-collecting or sun-protecting characteristic to the courtyard.

A further point is that in northerly climates cold winds are a key factor in determining the microclimatic conditions. The greater wind protection offered by courtyards will reinforce the notion of a sun-concentrator due to improved comfort conditions, which are a function of air speed and radiant energy as well as temperature.

Finally, it should be noted that shading on the ground is critical to prevent overheating in hot climates, whereas a key issue for cold climates will be solar radiation received on the

Table 12.5 **Results from simulations**

| Sky view factor | Average sky view factor at ground level | $\Delta T_{\text{max urban–rural}}$ from formula 1 |
|---|---|---|
| Courtyards | 0.127 | 13.51 |
| Pavilions 1 | 0.227 | 12.12 |
| Pavilions 2 | 0.482 | 8.58 |

façades. This will influence the heating energy performance in cold climates. It is likely that a cold climate courtyard will on average receive relatively more solar energy on its façades as a result of the sun path, particularly if the H/W ratio is lower.

## Sky view factor (Table 12.5)

Finally, the interpretation of the sky view factor (SVF) values shows further interesting results. The values for our three forms rank in the following increasing order: courtyard type (0.127), pavilion 1 (0.227) and pavilion 2 (0.482).

A formula was introduced by Oke (1981) to relate the maximum heat island intensity between urban and rural sites and the view factor from the middle of the canyon floor to the sky.

$$\Delta T_{\text{max urban–rural}} = 15.27 - 13.88\psi_{\text{sky}} \qquad \textit{Formula 1}$$

where $\Delta T_{\text{max urban-rural}}$ is the maximum temperature difference and $\psi_{\text{sky}}$ the SVF. The formula was obtained by results from scale models representing rural and urban surfaces, to mimic the passive radiative cooling of these environments following sunset on a calm and cloudless night. It was also verified on a number of cities, such as that shown in Figure 12.3. A preliminary observation would indicate that minimising the urban heat island would therefore suggest sparse and scattered urban developments, with a high view factor, as also suggested through $\Delta T_{\text{max urban-rural}}$ where the lowest temperature difference is noted for the pavilion 2 (8.58 compared to 12.12 for pavilion 1 and 13.51 for courtyard type). In this case, pavilion 2 would be the best urban form and the traditional courtyard type would rank as worse. As in the case of the surface to volume ratio seen above, is this a case of an 'irrational' response to climate (Rapoport 1969, p. 21)? Or could it be justified in urban climatology terms? This dilemma intrigued scholars for a long time.

Let us consider the urban heat island phenomenon in more detail. This is often described using average temperatures; in Givoni's definition (1998) 'on the average the diurnal temperature, in a densely-built urban area, is warmer than the surrounding open (rural) country'. The average however, does not take into account peaks. The urban heat island usually presents two of them: a maximum during the night and a minimum during the day, often described as an 'urban cool island'.

In hot-arid climates night-time temperatures are usually lower than daytime temperatures, as discussed above, and an increase in temperature would probably be welcomed at night if concomitantly extreme temperature stress during the day were alleviated. The existence of this phenomenon can be discerned through a social habit in hot-arid countries (such as Morocco) where, for example, people sleep on building roofs at night, to maximise their radiative losses and also to avoid higher indoor temperature, partly due to time lag re-radiated heat caused by large building thermal mass. As comfort is not only based on temperature, but also on radiative exchange, this is where the benefit of low SVFs comes into play again, especially during day-time hours when people are outdoors in the streets and urban pedestrian comfort is crucial. During daytime hours, low SVFs insure an increase in direct shading and a reduction in reflected radiation.

In cold climates an increased heat island effect in terms of an average increase in temperatures is clearly an advantage as it will reduce heat losses. This suggests courts can provide benefits in cold climates too. However, the benefits of increased temperatures must be compared with potentially reduced solar availability. The balance between these two factors is determined by the H/W ratio, and it would appear that a lower ratio than for hot climates would be the means to optimise this balance.

## Existing quantitative analysis

Quantitative description of these phenomena, which justify the adoption of compact urban structures in hot-arid climates, is given by Pearlmutter et al. (1999), who simulated the energy exchange between a cylindrical body, representing a pedestrian, and the canyon environment. Pearlmutter (1998) further analysed new towns within a hot-arid climate, planned according to the 'garden city' model imported from Europe, concluding that they are climatically inappropriate, as they lack the thermal moderating effect of traditional compact developments.

Similarly, a recent study of the city of Fez (Morocco), based on field measurements, confirms the same results. Rosenlund *et al.* (2000) monitored temperatures in two districts of the city associated with different housing types: a traditional one, based on the compact clustering of buildings using the courtyard structure, and a more recent one, based on modern two- to three-storey houses arranged along wide streets. In the traditional courtyard district temperatures are higher during the night, but during the day a favourable 'cool island' appears. Overall conditions are more stable in the traditional district than in the modernist development, with the tendency for moderating maximum and minimum outdoor air temperatures.

Perez-de-Lama and Cabeza (1998) have also obtained interesting data for courtyard housing in Spain. They examined the environmental performance of patios in Seville using the sky view factor (which they call the configuration factor). They focused on maximum temperatures inside the patios during the day and concluded, 'in all cases but one, maximum temperatures measured in the set of patios have been below the reference temperature considered'. They also suggest that patio cooling performance in summer is proportional to the envelope to plan surface ratio. The smaller the opening to the sky in relation to the general envelope surface (which effectively corresponds to the average SVF), the better the performance is. Again, the climatic advantages of the courtyard form are apparent.

## Conclusions

This chapter demonstrates that the courtyard configuration type shows better response through the calculated environmental variables (surface to volume ratio, shadow density, daylight distribution, sky view factor) than the pavilion types 1 and 2 in the context of hot-arid climates. The potential to improve the environmental performance by adopting court forms in cold climates also exists, although this is largely determined by a lower H/W ratio than in hot-arid regions.

The key aspect in a search for an environmentally optimal urban configuration resides in the possibility and simplicity of carrying out parametric runs that test geometric modifications. The developed technique used for the calculations has proved essential in carrying out comparative analysis between the courtyard type and other urban forms such as urban blocks or pavilions. It can also be used in a flexible way to analyse different archetypal developments (high rise transformations happening in Arab towns and cities) or real developments – by comparing the environmental potential of different development options. The aim of such analysis would be to search comparatively for an 'optimal' configuration, climatically responsive as well as economically feasible. Although the pavilion configurations were environmentally less adequate than the courtyard type, pavilion 1 type still performed better than pavilion 2 type.

The chapter also demonstrates that simulation results always need to be carefully analysed and interpreted within the particularities of the context in order to overcome misleading broad statements. Just as much as a courtyard configuration is climatically suitable in hot-arid climates, it may be – and is – as environmentally adequate in cold climates, with key differences such as proportions and layout, for example as hinted by Mänty (1988). In a search for an environmentally 'optimal' configuration, analysing the subtleties of the case study within its climatic context revealed that there are trade-offs that need to be made based on environmental criticality. In the courtyard case, for example, although low illuminance levels were recorded in the street, better values were seen in the courtyard itself. Pedestrian thermal comfort seems therefore to have been of higher priority than direct daylight availability, which can be compensated for by high surface reflectance. It also suggests that the need of climate-responsible design and the cultural imperative for privacy enjoy a compatible, if not symbiotic, relationship.

We hope that the methodology followed in this chapter will trigger further parametric analysis and investigation of variations on the courtyard type and its environmental potentials in our era, in a search for a modern reinterpretation of this building type.

## Acknowledgements

Aspects of the work in this chapter were carried out within the research project PRECis: 'Assessing the Potential for Renewable Energy in Cities' which was funded by the EU'S JOULE Programme (project no. JOR3–CT97–0192) and is coordinated by Dr Koen Steemers at the Martin Centre, Department of Architecture, University of Cambridge.

# Note

1 Since this work builds on Martin and March's (1972) research as discussed, the term pavilion, which is used by them to indicate rectangular-shaped blocks, will be adopted by us for this purpose.

# Bibliography

Bahadori, M. N. (1978) Passive Cooling Systems in Iranian Architecture. *Scientific American* **2**, 238, 144–52.

Baker, N., Fanchiotti, A. and Steemers, K. (1993) *Daylighting in Architecture – A European Reference Book* Glossary Gl.33. London, James & James Ltd.

Cook, J. (2000) Evolution of American office architecture to 1950 – pollution vs. passive strategies to design the work environment. *Proceedings of PLEA – Passive and Low Energy Architecture*. Cambridge, James & James Ltd.

Fathy, H. (1973) Constancy, transportation and change in the Arab city. In L. Carl Brown (ed.) Princeton, NJ, Darwin Press.

Fathy, H. (1986) *Natural Energy and Vernacular Architecture*. Chicago, IL, The University of Chicago Press.

Givoni, B. (1998) *Climate Considerations in Buildings and Urban Design*. London, John Wiley & Sons.

Hakim, B. S. (1986) *Arabic-Islamic Cities: Building and Planning Principles*. London, KPI.

Mänty, J. (1988) *Cities Designed for Winter*. Helsinki, Norman Pressman, Building Book Ltd.

Martin, L. (1967) Architect's approach to architecture. *RIBA Journal* May, 191–200.

Martin, L. and March, L. (1972) *Urban Space and Structures*. Cambridge, UK, Cambridge University Press.

Morris, A. E. J. (1994) *History of Urban Form before the Industrial Revolutions*. London, Longman Scientific & Technical.

Oke, T. R. (1981) Canyon geometry and the nocturnal urban heat island: comparison of scale model and field observation. *Journal of Climatology* **1**, 237–54.

Oke, T. R. (1988) Street design and urban canopy layer climate. *Energy and Buildings* **11**, 103–13.

Pearce, E. A. and Smith, C. G. (1993) *The World Weather Guide*. Oxford, Helicon.

Pearlmutter, D. (1998) Street canyon geometry and microclimate: designing for urban comfort under arid conditions. *Proceedings of the International Conference on Passive and Low Energy Architecture (PLEA) 1998*. Lisbon, James & James Ltd.

Pearlmutter, D., Bitan, A. and Berliner, P. (1999) Microclimatic analysis of 'compact' urban canyons in an arid zone. *Atmospheric Environment* **33**, 4143–50.

Perez-de-Lama, J. and Cabeza, J. M. (1998) A holistic approach to the Mediterranean patio – extending the new method of configuration factors to semi open spaces. *Proceedings of the International Conference on Passive and Low Energy Architecture (PLEA) 1998*, Lisbon, James & James Ltd.

Rapoport, A. (1969) *House Form and Culture*. Englewood Cliffs, NJ, Prentice-Hall.

Rosenlund, H., Johansson, E., Grundström, K., El-Kortbi, M. and Mraissi, M. (2000) Urban micro-climate in the city of Fez, Morocco. *Proceedings of the International Conference on Passive and Low Energy Architecture (PLEA) 2000*, Cambridge, UK, James & James Ltd.

Rudofsky, B. (1964) *Architecture Without Architects: a short introduction to non-pedigreed architecture*. London, Academy Editions.

Steemers, K., Baker, N., Crowther, D., Dubiel, J. and Nikolopoulou, M. (1997) City texture and microclimate. *Urban Design Studies* **3**, 25–50.

Steemers, K. and Ratti, C. (1999) Informing urban bioclimatic design. *Proceedings of the Architecture and Engineering Conference*, Plymouth European Association for Architectural Education (EAAE), University of Plymouth.

Talib, K. (1984) *Shelter in Saudi Arabia*. London, Academy Editions.

# 13 The courtyard garden in the traditional Arab house

## MAHER LAFFAH

## Introduction

Early courtyard gardens connected layout with religious belief, and their architectural characteristics were acquired as an expression of certain philosophical positions. The concept of 'gardens' in contemporary Arabic life is to:

- provide environmental balance between built and open spaces; between life within enclosed and restricted areas and life in the open air
- make available, for all the family, the possibility of entertainment and creation of a wider social life
- make spiritual contact with nature – gardens and green spaces distributed in the urban tissue provide tranquillity and peace, reflecting aspects of Islamic teaching.

The relationship between 'man' and garden has two dimensions: aesthetic and social. The aesthetic dimension is related to the positive visual image of the garden and its relationship to urban buildings, whilst the social dimension regards gardens as the proper place for fulfilling the needs for family and community interaction. Hence, in the Arab world, the garden is the manifestation of human relationships at the living, cultural and spiritual levels.

This chapter aims to illustrate the essence of this relationship with regard to the interior garden in the traditional courtyard house. Specifically it seeks to:

1   determine the common design characteristics of interior courtyard gardens and the role of the natural elements, such as planting and water

2   provide recommendations for maintaining Arab society's cultural relationship with the courtyard garden by presenting new urban and architectural solutions.

## The garden of the Arabic house and the concept of 'paradise theory'

Traditional architecture in the Arab world was both responsive to the climate of the region and compatible with the local social and cultural traditions. As a consequence, there was a rational philosophical and architectural solution to the whole urban tissue including the design of the individual house. The main characteristics of traditional Arab cities is the existence of the open interior domestic courtyard that provides a pleasant environment for the inhabitants with regard to temperature, humidity and ventilation whilst also meeting the needs of privacy and serenity (Abed 1988). There is also the strong tradition in Arabic cities of enclosing nature as a private interior garden full of trees, shrubs, flowers and fountains. In this sense the Islamic garden is an inner private space. This is in contrast to Western gardens that are public or semi-public spaces.

The main priorities for the design of the courtyard garden were:

- fulfilling the different environmental, climatic and aesthetic functions of different house types
- determining the appropriate dimensions of the courtyard for the specified function of the house
- benefiting both the house and the wider urban fabric.

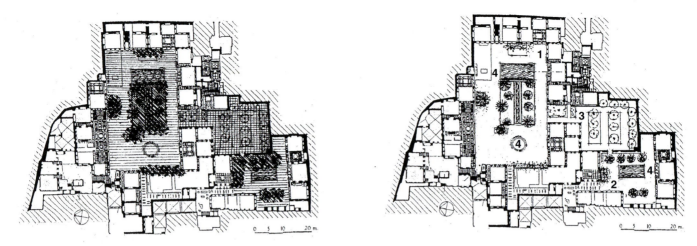

**13.1 Plan of Qasr al-Azem, Damascus: (1) courtyard; (2) courtyard; (3) orchard; (4) fountain. In this house the fully shaded spaces occupy 27 per cent of the area, half-shaded 25 per cent and open spaces 48 per cent (after L. Jones)**

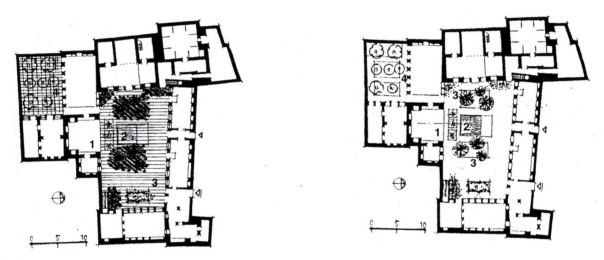

**13.2 Plan of Beit Ghazaleh, Aleppo: (1) liwan; (2) fountain; (3) courtyard; (4) orchard. In this house the fully shaded spaces occupy 20 per cent of the area, half-shaded 28 per cent and open spaces 52 per cent**

In the past, Arab architects were inspired by the Quranic description of paradise, with its tranquility and spiritual pleasures, and attempted to overcome the hard local climatic conditions by creating an earthly paradise. Thus the concept appeared of 'Paradise theory in Islamic architecture' (Waziry 1986). This theory enunciates the aesthetic elements of paradise (plants, water, shaded open benches, calligraphy, fragrances and pleasant sounds), mentioned in many Quranic verses, which were a key inspiration in the design and landscaping of the garden. The idea of an earthly paradise has since the Middle Ages been crystallized mainly through the courtyard garden. It became the catalyst for a functional integration between the elements of the house (*liwan* or *loggia*) and the garden (Saleh 1984). The courtyard garden became the most widespread green form in traditional Arab cities: each one is constructed as a microcosm of paradise and peace. Although there are generic similarities in the design of courtyard gardens after the settlement of the Arab Muslims, in Damascus the gardens had a local stamp with a dis-

tinctive style known as the 'Gardens of Damascus'. Damascus courtyard landscaping has developed over many years and is today found in most old Damascus' houses (e.g. Beit Al-Moseli, Beit Jabri, Beit Al-Sibai, Qasr Al-Azem (Figure 13.1)).

In Aleppo, a slightly different tradition is present and is to be found in interior gardens located in Beit Ghazaleh (Figure 13.2), Beit Ajkhabash, etc. In Cairo, after the advent of Moslems, interior gardens appeared in the houses of Al-Fustat and later developed in the Mamluke and Ottoman eras – with notable examples seen at the gardens of Beit Al-Zahabi and Beit Al-Suheimi (Figure 13.3).

In spite of local differences, many of which are the result of climatic variation across the Islamic world, there is a consistency in the design of courtyard gardens. Those at Quairawan, Tlemcen, Fez and Marrakesh are considered a continuity of the Damascus and Cairo tradition, though with some variations which are discussed in Table 13.1 in the context of a number of case studies.

Table 13.1 **Courtyard gardens – case studies**

| Courtyard garden | Location | Description |
|---|---|---|
| The garden of Qasr Al-Azem (Figure 13.1) | Damascus | The three gardens occupy 38% of the building's overall area |
| | | The main axis for each garden is directed towards an important main hall |
| | | In landscaping these gardens, all kinds of greenery have been used: trees, bushes, flowers, arbours, creepers on walls and galleries and columns |
| The garden of Beit Ghazaleh (Figure 13.2) | Aleppo | The garden dimensions are 12 m × 22 m |
| | | The garden occupies 31% of the building's overall area |
| | | The main axis of the garden is directed from the entrance to the liwan (hall) |
| | | The garden also contains square pools surrounded by trees and basils, in addition to beds of flowers and creepers |
| The garden of Beit Al-Suheimi (Figure 13.3) | Cairo | The garden area is 35.5% of the building's area |
| | | The garden consists of two connected gardens: an interior one which is 10.2 m × 18.8 m, organised along a linear axis passing by a central fountain and ending at the 'Takhtboush' (hall). It contains four parts planted with various bushes. The second garden is of an irregular shape containing vegetables and fruit trees |
| | | One of the distinctive characteristics of the Al-Suheimi garden is the creation of a microclimate that relies on air currents between the shaded and humid interior garden and the sunny open orchard |
| The garden of Beit Radwan (Figure 13.4) | Marrakesh | The garden occupies 25% of the building's overall area |
| | | The main element of the garden is the fountain which is surrounded by fruit trees, bushes and fragrant plants |
| The gardens of Qasr Al-Hambra (Figure 13.5) Al-Mashoka garden (Figure 13.5) | Granada | A square garden of 19.5 m × 19.5 m |
| | | Has a main axis extending from the entrance to 'Al-Mishwar' with a second perpendicular axis ending at the Al-Mashoka tower |
| | | Characterised by the existence of a water pool in its middle, surrounded by a hedge of hierarchical cypress trees |
| The myrtle or basil garden (Figure 13.6) | | A rectangular garden of 36.6 m × 23.4 m |
| | | Has a main axis leading directly to the throne hall |
| | | Consists or a rectangular water pools of 33.4 m × 7.4 m with a depth of 0.5 m |

## The general characteristics of traditional courtyard gardens

The analysis of the plans and characteristics of the courtyard gardens described in Table 13.1 is helpful in determining their main design generators:

### Geometric lines

Interior gardens often have regular geometric shapes mainly rectangular or square. However, the regular geometric shape has affected the garden element forms: linear paths, straight water canals and planted beds of simple geometric shapes predominate. Studying the geometric proportion of these gardens, has shown that the most common proportions of width to length are: 1:1.8 or 1:3.6 (gardens of Qasr Al-Azem, Beit Ghazaleh, Beit Al-Suheimi, Qasr Al-Hambra). These proportions are related to the measuring unit (module) that is used in building design. They also relate to sun path determinants and provide adequate sun exposure while simultaneously affording protection from excessive sun heat in the summer season.

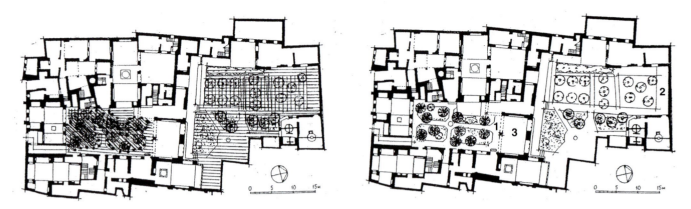

13.3 **Plan of Beit Al-Suheimi, Cairo: (1) courtyard; (2) orchard; (3) takhtboush (hall). In this house the fully shaded spaces occupy 30 per cent of the area, half-shaded 40 per cent and open spaces 50 per cent (after M. Lamei)**

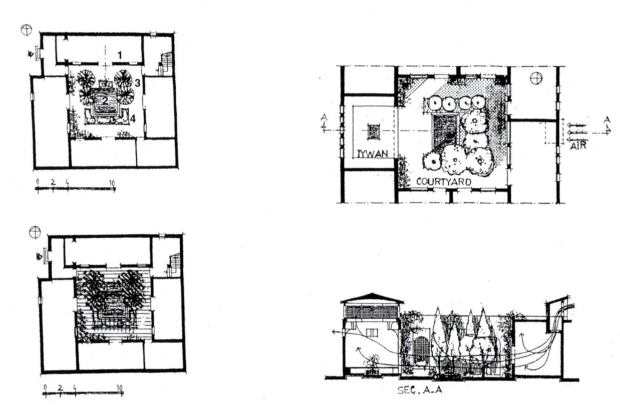

13.4 **Plan of Beit-Radwan, Marrakesh: (1) guest room; (2) fountain; (3) courtyard; (4) shrub garden. In this house the fully shaded spaces occupy 22 per cent of the area, half-shaded 31 per cent and open spaces 47 per cent (after Paccard 1980)**

13.5 **The climatic and environmental function of the courtyard and its planting in relationship to the remander of the house**

## Axial

The main axis of each garden is considered as the structure for the garden design element. It usually ends in the liwan (loggia), a water pool or a pavilion (Qasr Al-Hambra for example). In some types, the main axes were reinforced by water channels and paths. In most cases there is a relationship between the axis of the garden and the layout of the house, thereby providing an aesthetic integration of each part.

## Symmetry and balance

The garden elements are symmetrical with the main axis of the garden, and balanced by architectural features in most examples. The use of different sizes and colours makes a harmony of small architectural forms arranged as a formal composition to give repose to the interior garden.

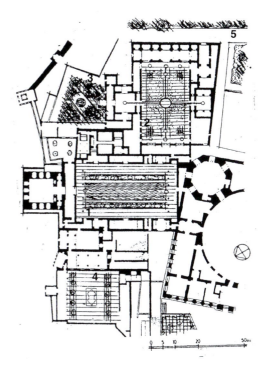
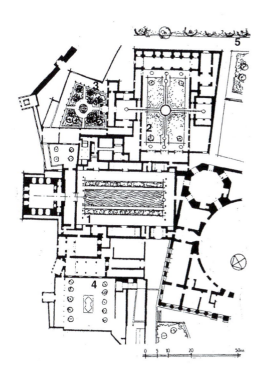

13.6 **Plan of Qasr-Al-Hambra, Granada: (1) basil garden; (2) courtyard garden; (3) Al maashoka; (4) Aeisha garden; (5) Al-portal garden.**
In this house the fully shaded spaces occupy 26 per cent of the area, half-shaded 24 per cent and open spaces 50 per cent (after ICOMOS 1973)

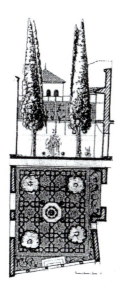

13.7 **The shading and decorative function of trees in courtyard housing (after ICOMOS 1973)**

## Garden size

The courtyard and garden occupies a significant proportion of the overall area of the plot (38 per cent approximately) with the largest proportion of garden area adjacent to the urban edge.

## Water

Water pools and elements occupy different proportions in respect of the garden area and the availability of water provision. In the gardens of Qasr Al-Hambra, for example, water pools occupy about 30 per cent of the garden area and are characterized by their unique style and well–constructed features.

## Overlapping of functions

There are no clear boundaries in the interior gardens for specific functions. As a consequence, activities and usage flow and overlap between areas. Of these activities the main ones that determine the appropriate dimensions of the courtyard are:

- entertaining – gardens are essentially recreational places
- management – gardens and courtyards provide space for housework and practicing agriculture on a small scale
- environmental/climatic – the garden is a moderator influencing the interior climate (Figure 13.6)
- aesthetic – the garden is a reflective space.

## Peculiarity in landscaping methods

By using natural elements such as plants, trees and water, the characteristic of the Arabic courtyard garden can be classified according to its vegetation and horticultural practice:

### Plants

There is variety in the use of plants (trees, bushes, flowers and creepers) according to their fruitful or decorative nature. Decorative trees are planted solitarily, in line or groups. While hardly any interior garden is empty of fruit trees, whole yards or small orchards were specified for this function in some big houses (e.g. Qasr Al-Azem, Beit Ghazaleh, Beit Al-Suheimi, Qasr Al-Hambra).

High walls with climbing plants were used in dividing and separating the gardens into visually connected parts with wall openings, framing specific views. In this kind of landscaping, cypress trees were used as focal points as in the garden of Al-Portal in Qasr Al-Hambra (Maher 1989).

The alternation of enclosed or shaded spaces with open ones increases the aesthetic aspect of courtyard gardens, especially the larger ones. Trees and dense vegetation provided shade in the summer. Other parts of the garden – less used socially – were occupied by fruit bushes and vines, thus forming half-opened spaces. Finally, in addition to the yards and paved paths, open spaces were occupied by pools, fountains and beds of fragrant plants and flowers. The courtyard gardens therefore have well-defined areas with varying degrees of shade (see Table 13.2). These proportions were calculated by the author relying on visits to some of the described gardens and on specialised references for others.

The conclusions drawn from Table 13.2 are that in small interior courtyard gardens, the shaded space is 25 per cent, on average, while it increases to 40 per cent in larger courtyard gardens. This can be explained by the general difficulty of planting trees with thick foliage in small courtyard gardens to provide shade, and also the fact that the surrounding walls usually provide enough shaded areas.

### Water elements

Water is a crucial element in the composition of the Arab courtyard garden. It has a vital cooling role within hot climatic conditions and embodies the purifying ethos of the Islamic religion. The most widespread water elements are fountains, springs and canals of geometric shapes. Such elements are always placed on the main axis of the garden within frames of plants and low walls, often highly decorated. Using water in its two forms – moving and still – has

Table 13.2 **Proportion of spaces with varying degrees of shade in typical courtyard gardens**

| Name of garden | Garden area in hectares | Spaces % | | |
|---|---|---|---|---|
| | | Shaded | Semi-shaded | Open |
| Beit Ghazaleh | 0.038 | 20 | 28.5 | 51.5 |
| Qasr Al-Azem | 0.2 | 27 | 25 | 48 |
| Beit Al-Suheimi | 0.078 | 30 | 40 | 30 |
| Beit Radwan | 0.01 | 26 | 31 | 47 |
| Qasr Al-Hambra | 0.77 | 26 | 24 | 50 |

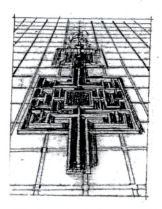

13.8    **Uses of water in courtyard housing. Left, water maze; centre, pool for evaporative cooling and reflection of façade; right irrigation of trees (after Paccard 1980)**

aesthetic qualities and gives many gardens memorable visual and landscape qualities. The most spectacular example of the use of various elements of water is to be found in the gardens of Qasr Al-Hambra (Figure 13.8). Here Arab architects used pools on a linear axis to the building elevation to reflect its image on the water surface, thereby increasing the inte-

gration of architecture and the courtyard garden landscape. Various means were employed to animate water, such as fountains and erupting springs. The aim was to achieve the maximum sensational, audible and visual pleasure of water while using the least possible amount of water and often its recycling.

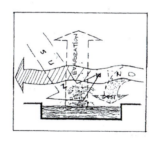

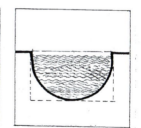

13.9    **Uses of water in courtyard housing. Left, interaction of sun and water to produce evaporative cooling; centre, use of trees to prevent evaporation of scarce water; right, use of deep canals to reduce surface evaporation and rounded shape to discourage stagnant areas (after Paccard 1980)**

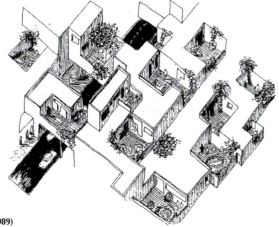

13.10    **An experimental development of raised courtyard garden at Al-hafsieh, Tunisia (after Yaseen 1989)**

The environmental and climatic benefits of water are provided by three main means:

- locating fountains and pools inside garden courtyards and behind high walls, thereby protecting the water from strong sandy winds that often blow in Arab regions
- surrounding pools with plants helps to decrease the level of evaporation (due to the rise of temperatures), thus giving an incremental aesthetic effect through the reflection of plants on the water's surface
- building some elements of water in the shape of narrow canals (approximately 50 cm in depth or in a maze shape like Al-Minshiah in the gardens of Morocco) helps to lower the level of evaporation. Moreover, some water channels were made in a half-oval shape in order to give the impression of more water than there was in reality.

## Conclusion

The Arabic courtyard garden is a good example of the close relationship between man and nature, providing an earthly paradise in the centre of family life. However, the urban design of modern Arab cities pays scant regard to the courtyard, placing the emphasis instead on urban streets and free-standing blocks.

Traditional Arabic courtyard gardens were formed using design methods and elements that are now generally disregarded. Today, few architects and urban designers take into consideration the social, aesthetic and environmental legacy of the Islamic courtyard garden, whether in the private courtyards of houses or the exterior ones surrounding residential building complexes. Few gardens refer back to their use of water, planting or architectural elements in a robust tradition. An attempt should be made to combine originality and modernity with the environmental, climatic, social and cultural legacy of the past.

Today we need to re-activate the relationship between Arab society and the garden. It is increasingly necessary in our global world to find a new urban/architectural solution for the provision of special gardens in the residential quarters of multi-storey buildings in Arab cities. In other words, to providing residential units with elevated or enclosed interior gardens compatible with the conditions and capabilities of modern real-estate development.

## Bibliography

Abed –Al-hamid Abed-Wahed (1988) *Planning and Designing of Green Regions and General Environment Spaces in the Cities*. Cairo.

ICOMOS (1973) *Islamic Gardens*. Spain.

Lehrman, J. (1988) *Earth Paradise: gardens, courtyards in Islam*. London, Thames and Hudson.

Maher, I. (1989) Water in the Islamic Architecture. *AlBeena* **5**.

Paccard, A. (1980) *Traditional Islamic Crafts in Moroccan Architecture*. Paris, France, Editions atelier 74.

Saleh, M. L. (1984) The Islamic character in the designing houses of courtyards. *Alam Albenaa* **49**.

Waziry, H. (1986) The paradise theory in the Islamic architecture. *Alam Albenaa* **68**.

Yaseen, A. (1989) The effect of climate on the form of Arabic architecture. *Alam Albenaa* **1**.

# 14 Climatic aspects and their effect on the dimensions of courtyards in Arab buildings

## HANI WADAH

## Introduction

Mankind has traditionally sought to provide protection from climatic conditions in order to create an appropriate environment for fulfilling his different activities. An understanding of climatic phenomenon, the use of building materials of acknowledged characteristics, and simple methods of construction allowed early desert-dwellers to create the right atmosphere in the interior space. However, even in hot-arid regions, differences in climatic conditions led to a diversity of solutions to domestic architecture.

The harsh environment in the Arab world had a clear effect on the design of houses, leading to the use of the courtyard in its various guises. In Arabic culture, the sky is a place for gods and allows for meditation as well as permitting the entry of sun, wind and rain into the dwelling. The sky with its clearness and sacredness penetrates the house through the interior courtyard, bringing spiritual, functional and climatic benefits to domestic desert life. In this way courtyard housing represents a fusion of secular and ethereal concerns rarely found in other housing types.

## Historical background

Courtyard housing is not unique to the Arab world. Many civilizations have used it as the primary design generator since prehistoric times, e.g. the Assyrians, Persians, Greeks, Romans, Byzantines and more recently in Islamic architecture. Interior courtyards evolved in parallel in different places in the world. However, although courtyard housing formed the main aspect of domestic design in much of the world, there are considerable differences of function and importance attached to the interior courtyard in the Islamic region. Under the influence of the Islamic religion, the importance of the courtyard increased to the point that Arabic architecture became distinctive in plan, in form and in decoration. The courtyard became one of the most essential architectural aspects of Arabic dwellings and gave rise to a range of associated developments: loggias, galleries, high-level openings, oriels and elaborate sun-shade ornamentation.

The existence of the interior courtyard originated in the combination of environmental, climatic and defensive functions. However, under Islam it assumed greater significance for its compatibility with and the physical reflection of religious principles and teaching. The correlation between the functional and the spiritual imperatives formed the bases for the architecture and urbanism of the Arab–Islamic countries. However, the variables that environmental and geographical conditions imposed added a complexity and richness to a tradition which continued to evolve for over 500 years. It is only recently that courtyard architecture has ceased to be the dominant response to the design of a range of building types in desert regions.

## The climatic study

The demands of a hot climate led to a number of design characteristics typical of north Africa and the Middle East. Besides the interior courtyard form adopted for houses, schools, mosques and government buildings, a typical town in the region had narrow streets to shade them from the sun and most houses were reached from cul-de-sacs. As a result there were few open vistas and no opportunity for the hot desert wind to drive right into the heart of settlements. With less than 10 cm of rainfall a year, water was a treasured resource and found pride of place in many courtyards, where it served the valuable function of cooling and humidifying the air.

From a climatic point of view there were three main design factors to consider: insolation, wind and humidity.

## Insolation

There is a proverb in Arabic which says that 'a sunny house will keep a doctor away'. Good sun exposure is essential to the house as long as the dwelling has an appropriate design. Thus the traditional house builder had to take the sun into account from all parts of the house, in all rooms and at different times of the day. Correct orientation required the designer to study the movement of the sun in summer and winter and in relation to plan and sectional arrangement. It was important to ensure that sunshine was a benefit without the harmful effects of excessive temperature and glare. The courtyard house has to perform well under the rotation of the sun, the succession of the seasons, the spring and autumn equinoxes, and the summer and winter solstices. It had to do this without perfect sites and without (for reasons of privacy and security) the opportunity to create openings on the outside.

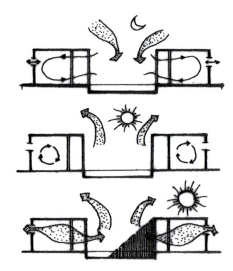

14.2 **Air circulation between the courtyard and adjoining rooms at night (top), midday (centre) and afternoon (bottom)**

Although, in the past, the designer used empirical methods of prediction, the modern architect exploits science to anticipate the impact of the sun on dwellings in hot desert regions. The sun projection angles can be measured in the following ways:

- the sunbeam angle – this is the vertical angle between sunbeam and its horizontal shade
- sun azimuth angle – this is the angular distance extending from the sunbeam shade to the north in a clockwise movement.

Knowing the sun projection angles at different times through the equinox and solstice periods allows the architect to anticipate the degree of solar penetration in the different spaces of the house. Generally speaking it is preferable for the orientation of the interior courtyard to be on the east–west axis, i.e. the longitudinal elevation should be to the north, for the following reasons:

- the sunlight projection should be towards the longitude elevation (i.e. the south)
- the southern elevation takes the largest amount of heat in the cold period and lesser amounts in summer because of the high angle of the sun. Hence it benefits from solar gain in winter and can be shaded effectively in high summer.

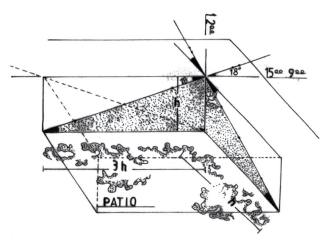

14.1 **Sun penetration in courtyard housing in Syria in winter**

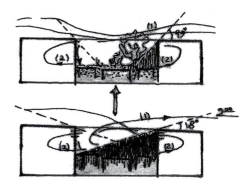

**14.3** **Difference in air circulation betweeen summer (top) and winter (bottom)**

In Syria, the lowest angle of sun projection is at the winter solstice on 21 December. This angle approximates to 18° at nine o'clock and 32.5° at 12 noon in mid-winter and allows for significant solar gain to be achieved through the courtyard with sensible design. In summer when the noon angle is nearly 72°, the altitude allows for effective shading of openings as long as an east–west axis is chosen for the courtyard. By such means orientation can be exploited to reduce the daytime temperature indoors from the outside level of 46°C to something approaching 30°C.

## Wind: air in motion

Wind circulation is the result of the different temperatures caused by the heating of water and earth by the sun. There are both global and local differences which result in seasonal variation in the amount of wind and hence its usefulness in a climatic context. However, the differences of atmospheric pressure which result give rise to wind which can be utilized for the cooling of cities and buildings in hot regions of the world. The global pattern in the differential temperatures between sun and sunless areas is repeated within dwellings which utilize interior courtyards. There are differences in temperature between solid and void elements; those open to the sun and those shaded lead to differences in air density which consequently causes the following air circulation:

- between the interior courtyard and the exterior space at day and night in summer and winter conditions
- between the interior courtyard and the interior space of the building.

As a consequence the wind acts beneficially in reducing ambient temperatures simply because of the nature of the use of courtyard architecture. However, besides moderating temperatures by the gradients created, wind-cooling can reduce daytime surface temperatures which then benefits night-time conditions.

## Humidity

Humidity is the transparent water vapour existing in the air. In northern areas it often forms clouds and fog leading to rain

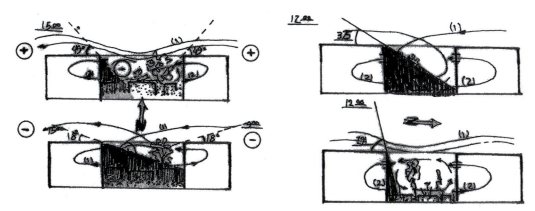

**14.4** **Difference in air circulation at different times of the day (12 noon and 9a.m./3p.m.) between summer and winter**

and dewdrops when the vapour is condensed. For buildings, humidity is important for the comfort of people and the well-being of building materials. In hot dry climates the creation of humidity can reduce wind-blown dust and protect desert towns from sandstorms.

Air that is saturated with water vapour can, however, cause a problem even in hot regions. When it has no ability to absorb any additional amount of humidity, it can cause condensation when the temperature falls. The degree of saturation depends on temperature – the more the air temperature rises, the greater will be its ability to absorb humidity and hence cause problems later.

Humidity is important in reducing the dryness of interior air. Excessively dry air can give a perception of excessive temperature whilst in reality, the same temperature with slightly more humidity may feel more comfortable. Adding moisture to the air (via a fountain or body of still water) can reduce temperature by evaporation as well as adding a welcome increase in general air humidity. So a balance is often struck in courtyard buildings between the shape for maximum temperature control from solar radiation and that which facilitates air currents (wind) and that which provides optimum levels of humidity (via a fountain). Since the water will need the sun to aid evaporation and hence humidify the air, fountains and bodies of water are normally centrally placed in the courtyard because of the vertical midday sun in summer. Also, because air movement is needed at the back of rooms, the wind tower and vents are usually at the perimeter of the building. This has resulted in the distinctive design of courtyard houses with their centrally-placed courts and peripherally-placed wind towers.

## Analytical study

An analytical study of the interior courtyard of two locations of courtyard houses has been undertaken in order to help decide on the best shape, orientation and configuration of the courtyard and its surrounding elevations for different regions. The examples consist of four houses in Old Damascus and two in the ancient city of Aleppo. Although both groups are from Syria the two locations are over 400 kilometres apart – Damascus is at 33.4° north whilst Aleppo is at 36.3°.

The studied houses from Damascus were:

- Beit Romia
- Beit Alshamameet
- Beit Mardam-Biek
- Beit Fakhri AlBaroudi

and from Aleppo:

- Al-Saboun Khan
- Al-Farrarien Khan.

Table 14.1 **Location and characteristics of typical courtyard houses in Damascus and Aleppo**

| Place | Location | Total area m² | Built area m² | Patio area m² | Area built/patio |
|---|---|---|---|---|---|
| Beit Romia | Damascus – south-east of Al-Ammawy mosque estate 243 – Al-Khrab | 450 | 316.67 | 133.33 | 2.37 |
| Beit Alshamameet | Damascus – north-east of Al-Ammawy mosque estate 234 – Al-khymaria | 361 | 264 | 97 | 2.72 |
| Beit Mardam-Biek | Damascus – south-west of Al-Ammawy mosque estate 323 – Al-Haryka | 579 | 404.87 | 173.13 | 2.33 |
| Beit Fakhri AlBaroudi | Southern side of old Damasucs | 945 | 575 | 370 | 1.55 |
| Al-Saboun khan | North-east of the Great Mosque in old Aleppo | 2480 | 1670 | 810 | 2.06 |
| Al-Farrarien Khan | South-east of the Great Mosque in old Aleppo | 2484 | 1706.5 | 777.5 | 2.19 |

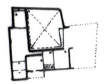

**14.5　Plans and courtyard elevations of Biet Romia house, Damascus**

**14.6　Plans and courtyard elevations of Biet Al Shamameet house, Damascus**

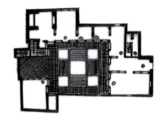

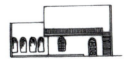

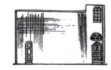

**14.7　Plans and courtyard elevations of Biet Mardam-Beik house, Damascus**

**14.8　Plans and courtyard elevations of Biet Fakhri Al-Baroudi house, Damascus**

159

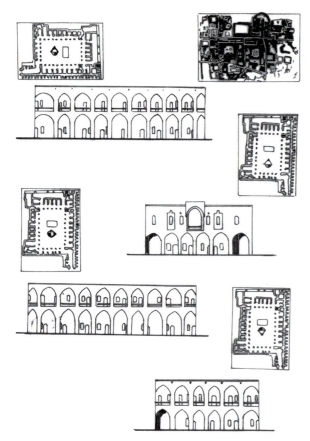

**14.9** Site plan, building plans and courtyard elevations of Al-Saboun Khan house, Aleppo

**14.10** Site plan, building plans and courtyard elevations of Al-Farrarien Khan house, Aleppo

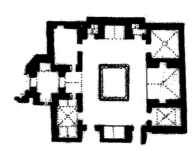

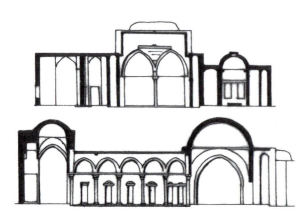

**14.11** Plan and courtyard elevations of Al-Argoni house, Aleppo

**14.12** Plan and north elevation of the courtyard of Al-Nouri house, Damascus

## Results and recommendations for the design of modern courtyard houses at the latitude of Syria

A number of general design guidelines can be gleaned from the study of the climatic conditions and interior environment of the six case-study courtyard houses. They are:

- when designing interior courtyards, the designer should adopt a rectangular shape with its long axis towards east–west
- the length to width proportion of this rectangle should be 1:0.52 with respect to the equator line (33.30) on which Syria lies – this proportion differs according to the geographical location of the region and, consequently, it can be determined by the smallest angle of sunbeam projection in winter
- the height of the southern elevation of the interior courtyard in Syria should not be less than one-third of the width of the courtyard
- the height of the eastern and the western elevations of the interior courtyard in Syria should not be more than 0.64 of its width
- the height of the northern elevation should not be such as to deprive the neighbourhood of sunshine – however, the need to shade streets from the low angled mid-morning and mid-afternoon sun should also be considered
- the built area proportion in relation to the interior courtyard area should not exceed 2.5:3 – beyond this the courtyard becomes too small to be an effective environmental moderator.

## Conclusion

The study suggests that courtyard housing has its own distinctive dimensions from a climatic point of view. Although these vary according to geographical location, the underlying rules do not. There is a consistency in the principles which govern solar radiation, wind-assisted cooling and design for humidification. Although the balances struck are in the hand of the designer, it is the reconciliation of the conflicting climatic pressures, when added to social and cultural pressures, which give character and identity to the buildings of the region.

## Bibliography

Abd AlMasih Ashi (1999) *Designing Criteria of Interior Courtyards in the Arabic Architecture*. Post-graduate thesis.

Alla Al-Deen Lolah (1982) *Theories of Architecture*. Aleppo University Publications.

Alwakeel-Shafik Al-Awadi and Sraj-Mohamad Abdallah (1988) *Climate and Hot Region Architecture*. London and New York, World of Books Publications.

Hani Wadah (1992) *The New Design of School Buildings*. PhD thesis.

Huda Hasan (1999) *Mental Hospitals and their Architectural Aspects*. Graduation thesis.

Kenana Zaher (1994) *Architectural Aspects of Damascus Houses*. Graduation thesis.

Rana Zydan (1994) *Architectural Characteristics of Aleppo Khans*. Graduation thesis.

## Foreign references

Twarowski, M. (1970) *Slonce W Architekturzie*. Warsaw, Urban Planning Institute Publications.

# 15 The thermal performance of the internal courtyard in the hot-dry environment in Saudi Arabia

KHALID A. MEGREN AL-SAUD AND
NASSER A. M. AL-HEMIDDI

This chapter presents the results of research whose aim was to maximize the thermal function of internal courtyard environments in hot dry regions. The empirical work was conducted during the summer season, using a single-family house in Al-Oyynaa, a country town near Riyadh in Saudi Arabia. The main objective of the study was to investigate how the evaporative cooling tower could reduce the internal courtyard air temperature. The courtyard was then utilized as a source for cooling the surrounding house spaces. Three experimental procedures were conducted and analyses carried out. Results indicate that an evaporative cooling tower is effective in cooling both the courtyard and the surrounding rooms. It was found that for the house in question the courtyard and living room maximum air temperatures were reduced by 9.96°C and 6.74°C, respectively. However, when the courtyard and the tower were ventilated by exhaust fans, the courtyard and indoor air temperatures were reduced by 13.5°C and 11.15°C, respectively.

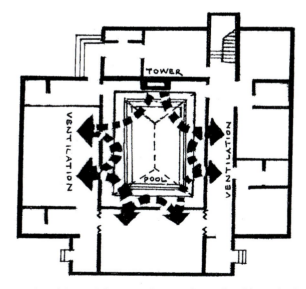

15.1 **Plan of the study house at Al Oyynaa in Saudi Arabia. Notice how the tower to the top of the plan provides ventilation across the central courtyard and swimming pool and into the adjoining rooms. Source: Brian Edwards/ K. A. Al-Saud**

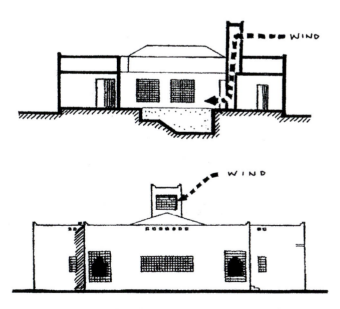

15.2 **Section and elevation of study house at Al Oyynaa showing the role of the tower in ventilating the interior courtyard with its swimming pool. Source: Brian Edwards/ K. A. Al-Saud**

163

## Introduction

Historically, courtyards have been added to buildings for various functions. In the architecture of the Muslim world, most houses contain courtyards and one of the main functions of the courtyard is its positive thermal impact on the surrounding living spaces.

Although electric energy was not available in the past, traditional buildings have survived for long periods of time, providing inhabitants with thermally comfortable shelter. In the Tunisian Sahara specifically the traditional house consists of an open courtyard surrounded by excavated underground rooms. Field measurements showed that the internal temperature was about 27°C when the ambient temperature was 49°C (Cole 1981).

Contemporary planning and design of streets, lots, and setback regulations led to the fragmentation of the urban fabric and, therefore, maximizing exposure to the climatic effects. In addition, the introduction of new construction materials such as concrete, steel and glass, without any consideration of their environmental aspects, has led to the reliance on air conditioning equipment to provide thermal comfort.

## Objectives

The main goal of this study is to explore the thermal role of the courtyard in modern buildings in general, and residential buildings in particular, when cooled by natural evaporative cooling towers. This goal may be stated more specifically as follows:

1   To determine the impact of evaporative cooling towers on the thermal conditions of the courtyard and its surrounding spaces.
2   To suggest applicable design recommendations regarding the use of the internal courtyard as a source of natural cooling for building in a hot dry region.

## Related studies

The technology for harnessing natural phenomena to achieve cooler temperatures inside dwellings has been known since early times (Fathy 1986). Traditional methods of designing and integrating the passive cooling systems within the residential unit (such as storing night coolness in thick walls, underground rooms, creating fountains and ponds and wind towers such as the so-called baud-geer in Iran) were rudimentary, and their efficiency was relatively low. Only recently, with more

15.3   **Exterior sketch of study house at Al Oyynaa showing the main ventilating tower to the left. Source: Brian Edwards/K. A. Al-Saud**

advanced knowledge in physics and architectural design, has interest in those traditional systems of passive cooling emerged. In the hot-dry region of the Middle East, and in Saudi Arabia in particular, this interest is motivated by the need to conserve energy while maintaining a higher thermal comfort inside the residential buildings.

Givoni (1989) has designed an inertial convective/evaporative 'shower' cooling tower to cool an outdoor rest area at the site of EXPO'92 in Seville, Spain. This system consisted of an open vertical shaft at the top of which water is sprayed vertically downward, like a shower. The falling fine drops draw a large volume of air, resulting in an initial air flow. Evaporation of the fine drops cools the air close to the ambient wet bulb temperature (WBT). At the bottom of the shaft, a pond collects the sprayed water and a pump keeps the water circulating upward. This system was tested by Al-Hemiddi and Baruch Givoni to cool outdoor space in the model of a courtyard and a room at UCLA Laboratory (Al-Hemiddi 1991, 1992, 1993). The design of this system was modified by adding a wind catcher measuring 0.6 m × 0.6 m in cross-section and 0.9 m in height with cross vertical barriers to deviate the airflow downward without allowing it to leave through the opposite openings. The performance of this new system was tested in a test cell (4.75 m × 1.2 m and 2.5 m in height) built with plywood and polystyrene panels. The roof of the test cell was 60 per cent open, representing a courtyard or a patio, and was then covered, representing a room.

Cunningham and Thompson (1986) discuss the case where a closed space combines both a system of passive evaporative cooling tower and a solar chimney. In the cooled down-draft chimney, air is cooled evaporatively by using wetted pad 'CELdek' material over the walls of the tower. The cooled air, which is heavier than ambient air, falls down by gravity through the shaft of the tower. The solar chimney is intended to enhance air movement through the roof of the building. The solar chimney did not contribute much to the performance of the cooling tower, and air flow rate is also independent of outdoor wind speed (Fathy 1986). The difference in the temperature between the warm air outside and cool air inside generates the air follow through the pads. This temperature difference is proportional to the WBT depuration (dry-bulb of outdoor temperature – wet-bulb temperature of the exit air from the system: DBTout–WBTexit). Cunningham's system performance was further tested by Givoni (1989) who developed a mathematical model which calculates the tower exit air temperature, the air flow rate, the air speed and the indoor air temperature. For a system similar to Cunningham's, it was found that when the outdoor maximum (DBT) was 40.6°C and the WBT was 21.6°C, the air temperature at the chimney's exit was 23.9°C. The corresponding speed of the exit air at that time was 0.75 m/sec.

These studies describe variations on the fundamental design of passive cooling systems in buildings. Most of the articles referred to are theoretical in their approach and are intended to serve as guidelines for future applications. The present research involves the design and testing of a much simpler system in terms of the methods and materials used. It addresses the passive cooling of indoor spaces using a system that had not been employed previously in Saudi Arabia. The proposed systems will be both functional and aesthetically integrated with the building design, thereby adding to both comfort and design unity.

## Study facility

A single family, one storey, contemporary courtyard house was adopted to conduct the research, Figures 15.1–15.6 show the design of the house and its major components. The house is located in the countryside, 45 km to the north-west of the city of Riyadh. It is constructed using a reinforced concrete skeleton, and 20 cm thick hollow concrete block walls. The walls are plastered and painted using light colours. The roof is 20 cm reinforced concrete slab without thermal insulation. Windows are single glazed without shading, the outside glass area is nearly 8 per cent of the wall area. The courtyard contains a swimming pool and is shaded using a white single-layer translucent tent fabric. Inner house windows overlooking the courtyard are sliding and are 30 per cent of the courtyard wall area.

## Cooling tower

A 2 m by 1 m evaporative cooling tower was constructed in the western side of the courtyard. The height of the tower is 6 m. The tower has two 1 × 1.6 m openings facing east and west. Each opening is blocked with the pad (CELdek). Evaporation occurs naturally by wetting the pad with falling water. Cool air at the top of the tower then falls down, exiting

15.4 Interior view of central courtyard with central swimming pool. The ventilating tower is in the centre. Notice how planting is employed to further modify the internal environment. Source: Brian Edwards/K. A. Al-Saud

15.5 Living room arranged in traditional fashion with full perimeter seating and large central carpet

15.6 Three environmental sensors: (left) temperature gauge in corridor, (middle) data logger, (right) roof-mounted weather station

from the lower opening, and is distributed within the courtyard and surrounding spaces (see Figures 15.1–15.6). Four small fans were installed in the exit opening to assist in increasing the speed of cool air moving through the tower. Other bigger fans were installed within the windows between the surrounding spaces and the courtyard. Cool air is distributed from the tower through the courtyard and into the living spaces.

## Monitoring apparatus

A complete set-up of:

1 local weather station measuring: dry bulb temperature, relative humidity, wind direction, wind speed and solar radiation was mounted on the top of the house (Figure 15.6)
2 a set of thermocouples used to read space temperatures from several locations within the house (Figure 15.6)

3    a data logger connected to the weather station and to the 60 thermocouples recording the measurements from all probes simultaneously every 10 minutes (Figure 15.6)

4    an IBM-compatible PC was used for data storage, processing and analysis. The PC is equipped with the Microsoft spreadsheet program Excel to perform statistical analysis and graphics.

## Monitoring plan

The monitoring period lasted for 25 full days between 1–25 July. This period represents part of the hottest season in Riyadh, where the percentage of time with temperatures above the upper limit of thermal comfort is about 83 per cent (Al-Megern 1987). The monitoring period was divided equally between three phases related to each other.

Phase one represents a base-case (No cooling). In this step, the thermal performance of the courtyard and the house was monitored when the cooling tower is not working. This step is important to work out the improvement in comfort after the operation of the cooling tower.

Phase two represents the thermal performance of the courtyard and the house spaces under the effect of natural cooling when the tower is working (Cooling tower). Step three represents the thermal performance of the courtyard and surrounding rooms under the effect of cooling when the tower is working with the help of auxiliary fans (Cooling tower with fans).

## Data analysis

Analysis concentrated on the data gathered in the three previously mentioned steps. Statistical analysis and graphical presentation were used to present the results. Data recorded from the thermocouples represent more than one week for each step. For the purpose of presentation the temperature readings were reduced to one full representative day. It should be noted that the house during the monitoring period was vacant and all air conditioning units and light fixtures were off.

Four weather elements were monitored during the period of the experiment, as follows:

- Dry bulb temperature – the highest dry bulb temperature recorded during the period of the monitoring was 44.99°C and the lowest was 25.78°C.
- Relative humidity – the highest recorded relative humidity was 30.19 per cent and the lowest 6.42 per cent.
- Wind direction and speed – the day time winds were characterized with higher speed and prevailed from the north-east and north-west. However, they rarely exceeded a speed of 3.5 m/s. The night-time winds were of very low speed and rarely exceeded 1.0 m/s. Night-time winds frequently prevail from the south-east and south-west.
- Solar radiation – the maximum radiation, recorded at 12:00 noon, was 1838 w/m$^2$.

### Phase one – courtyard and house performance before operating the tower (Base case)

Figure 15.7 shows curves representing the air temperatures of the house internal courtyard, the tower exit and the surrounding spaces. The curves are plotted with the curves of the external dry and wet bulb temperatures.

It is noticeable that the average outdoor temperature is about 7°C above the upper limit of the thermal comfort. The outdoor daily temperature is nearly 40°C, which is very high. In contrast, the average courtyard temperature is about 8°C less than the outdoor and the daily temperature range is less: it does not exceed 3°C. The average temperature of the surrounding spaces is higher than the outdoor average, but the daily range is lower. In terms of outdoor wet bulb temperature average, it is relatively low and is below the lower limit of thermal comfort. This proves the dryness of the weather; accordingly the evaporative cooling should be extremely effective.

### Phase two – courtyard and house performance when operating the cooling tower (cooling tower)

Figure 15.8 shows curves representing the air temperatures of the house internal courtyard, the tower exit, and the surrounding spaces while the cooling tower was in operation. In addition, the curves of the external dry and wet bulb temperatures are plotted on the same graph.

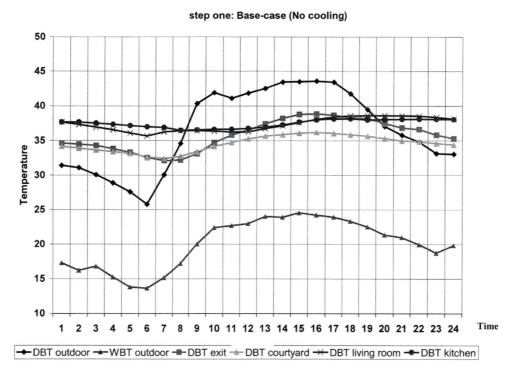

15.7　**Thermal performance of study house without the cooling tower in operation**

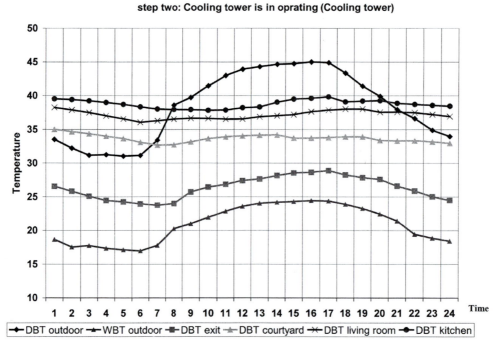

15.8　**Thermal performance of study house with the cooling tower in operation in passive mode**

The tower exit maximum air temperature does not exceed the limit of thermal comfort. The lowest temperature achieved was 24°C, when the wet bulb temperature was 17.5°C. The range of air temperatures exiting from the tower was 4°C.

The difference between the average of outdoor temperature and the upper limit of thermal comfort was 10.01°C. The outdoor daily range was 31.97°C. The average courtyard temperature was 33.36°C: this was lower than the outdoor average by more than two degrees, and the daily range does not exceed 2.5°C. In terms of internal spaces, the average temperature of the living room is 37.15°C, and the daily range is 2.2°C.

It is evident that when the tower was working the thermal conditions improved in terms of maximum, mean, and daily range values for both courtyard and surrounding spaces. However, the courtyard achieved better improvement than the living room.

### Phase three – courtyard and house performance when operating the tower and fans (cooling tower with fans)

Figure 15.9 shows the temperature curves of the courtyard, tower exit and the surrounding spaces when the tower was working with the assistance of fans. It shows also the outdoor dry and wet bulb temperatures.

The tower exit temperature ranges between 22°C and 27°C, while the wet bulb temperature ranges between 17.5°C and 24°C. The tower efficiency improved after the operation of the fans.

As a result of utilizing the fans, the thermal conditions within the courtyard and the surrounding spaces were improved by far more than what was achieved in step two. The average temperature in courtyard and the living room were 29.74°C and 31.31°C respectively compared to 33.36°C and 37.15°C during phase two.

The maximum courtyard and living room temperatures were 30.48°C and 32.84°C respectively, while the outdoor maximum temperature was 43.99°C.

The difference between the maximum outdoor and the maximum courtyard and the living room were 13.51°C and 11.51°C respectively.

### Conclusions

It is evident that the use of an evaporative cooling tower contributed significantly in improving the thermal conditions within

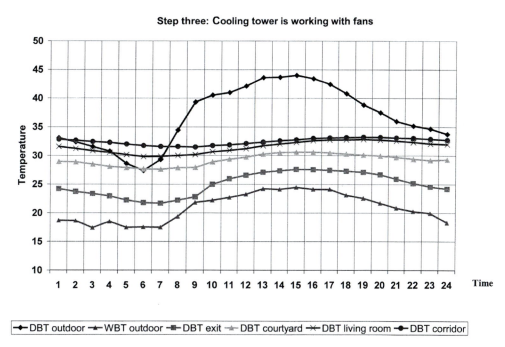

Step three: Cooling tower is working with fans

← DBT outdoor ← WBT outdoor ← DBT exit ← DBT courtyard ← DBT living room ← DBT corridor

15.9  **Thermal performance of study house with cooling tower in operation with fan assistance**

the courtyard and the surrounding living spaces. Furthermore, the use of exhaust fans raised the efficiency of the system.

Integration of the courtyard with the evaporative cooling tower proves to be effective in creating an enclosed space that has unique environmental qualities within a harsh and severe climatic environment. The courtyard becomes a thermal sink that provides coolness to the surrounding rooms with less humidity and a suitable place for tropical plants to grow, creating a pleasant ambiance.

With such environmental qualities the courtyard creates a suitable place for family summer outdoor activities, such as sitting, swimming, playing and relaxing.

## Bibliography

Al-Megern, K. (1987) *Wind towers for passive ventilation cooling in hot-arid regions*. Doctoral dissertation, Ann Arbor, MI, University of Michigan.

Al-Hemiddi, N. (1991) Preliminary investigation of the effect of a passive direct evaporative cooling system on a courtyard at UCLA. In S. Alvarez, J. Asiain, S. Yannas and E. Fernandes (eds), *Proceedings of the 9th International PLEA 1991 Conference*, pp. 643–7, Seville, Spain, Kluwer Academic Publishers.

Al-Hemiddi, N. (1992) A cooling tower for a passive evaporative system in hot-dry climate. In S. Burley and M. E. Arden (eds), *Proceedings of the 17th National Passive Solar Conference*, pp. 151–5, Cocoa Beach, Florida, ASES.

Al-Hemiddi, N. (1993) Passive direct evaporative cooling system in a courtyard at UCLA, In S. Burley and M. E. Arden (eds), *Proceedings of the 18th National Passive Solar Conference*, pp. 151–5, Washington, DC, ASES.

Cole, R. S. (1981) Underground dwelling in South Tunisia. In *Proceedings of The International the Passive and Hybrid Cooling Conference*, pp. 178–179. Miami Beach, FL.

Cunningham, W. A. and Thompson, T. L. (1986) Passive Cooling with Natural Draft Cooling Towers in Combination with Solar Chimneys. PLEA 1986, Pecs, Hungary.

Fathy, H. (1986) *Natural Energy and Vernacular Architecture*. Chicago, IL, The University of Chicago Press.

Givoni, B. (1989) Cooling of outdoor spaces. In *Proceedings, Workshop Interaction between Physics and Architecture in Environment Conscious Design*. Trieste, Italy, International Center for Theoretical Physics.

# Part 4

# The contemporary dimension

# 16  Type as a tool: courtyard housing and the notion of continuity

## KEVIN MITCHELL

The aspects of things that are most important for us are hidden because of their simplicity and familiarity.

Ludwig Wittgenstein

Yet, to the Arab especially, the courtyard is more than just an architectural device for obtaining privacy and protection. It is, like the dome, part of a microcosm that parallels the order of the universe itself.

Hassan Fathy

## Introduction

The rapid economic growth resulting from the discovery of oil in the United Arab Emirates (UAE) has greatly affected the built environment. Unfortunately the tendency has been to either import models of development from elsewhere or to hire architects/engineers who have relied on particular elements or images that they believed best 'represented' the Arabian Gulf. Designers have rarely asked critical questions regarding the appropriateness of form with regard to social, cultural and climatic conditions. Questions regarding the influence of social and cultural factors on built form are complex given the heterogeneous population distribution in the UAE; this inherent complexity imbues these factors with a greater significance and presents a richer challenge to architects. Climate, while an obvious factor to be considered within the Arabian Gulf, has been almost completely ignored, as evidenced by

the extensive use of single-pane glass without regard to solar orientation, the dependence on air conditioning for climate control, and the rejection of traditional courtyard design. A seemingly inexhaustible supply of resources has led to one of the highest rates of energy consumption per capita in the world, and the lack of basic climate-responsive measures in buildings contributes significantly to the excessive use of resources.

The lack of a widespread critical debate on the built environment in the Gulf region has resulted in development practices that cannot be sustained and will have serious long-term consequences. Among those who do engage in a discussion of the issues, no clear agreement on the way forward exists. However, many do agree that the past has a role to play and that a study of previous models of development offers valuable lessons regarding the design and construction of the built environment. Whether Hassan Fathy's claim that the courtyard is 'part of a microcosm that parallels the order of the universe itself' is fully justified, courtyard housing typologies can address the social, cultural and climatic conditions that characterize the region. Unfortunately those responsible for construction in the UAE have abandoned the courtyard dwelling in favor of the typical North American suburban scheme that is characterized by a free-standing house located in the centre of the building plot.

This chapter addresses how the courtyard can be considered within a broader theoretical framework that locates the role of tradition and type in relation to contemporary building practice in the Gulf region. It also discusses how the courtyard approach was employed in the design of a series of new houses for the American University of Sharjah campus in the UAE.

## The courtyard reconsidered

When dealing with the courtyard house it is necessary to address the question of whether adopting the type represents a nostalgic longing for a past that may (or may not) have existed or an appropriate response to factors such as climate and contemporary social and cultural conditions. To discuss the courtyard house in terms of the polarity between 'traditional' and 'modern' is futile. The courtyard model demands consideration in a broader theoretical framework that acknowledges the role of the study of traditional typologies in the process of design. Practitioners must ask whether vernacular architecture is a valid source to be considered during the design process and, if so, then they must critically examine what is meant by tradition and how it can be employed. This chapter argues that a study of the regional tradition is valuable as a learning tool for the designer, especially those operating in the Gulf region. As Amos Rapoport and others have claimed, if traditional architecture is analysed in terms of concepts (e.g. responses to climate, responses to site, spatial distribution as it relates to notions of public and private space, cultural identity, etc.) then lessons can be derived that are applicable to contemporary design.

Questions regarding the role of traditional architecture are bound to notions of regionalism, or the academically acceptable 'critical regionalism'. In a recent essay, Alan Colquhoun (1997) discussed the limitations inherent in the concepts associated with 'critical regionalism'. He argued that the term 'regionalism' is limiting and suggested looking for other ways of conceptualizing the problems to which the notion is supposed to respond. He stated that:

> Regionality is only one among many concepts of architectural representation and that to give it special importance is to follow a well-trodden critical tradition that no longer has the relevance that it may have had in the past. It is true that many interesting contemporary designs refer to local materials, typologies, and morphologies. But in doing so their architects are not trying to express the essence of particular regions, but are using local features as motifs in a compositional

process in order to produce original, unique and context-relevant architectural ideas.

Colquhoun's reference to local typologies and morphologies is especially relevant to discussions of the role of the traditional, specifically in the context of courtyard architecture.

With regard to whether following a type such as courtyard housing demands designing something equal to what has been proposed as a precedent, Micha Bandini has summarized the two answers which are commonly given:

> The first assigns to type an ideal role, that of a mental construct which is not embodied in any specific form but which is adapted and elaborated by the designer, so that invention can coexist with tradition and the authority of precedents. The second sees type as a tool for the composition of schematic objects which might become real architecture if the needs of social and economic production require their particular conformation.
>
> Bandini 1993, p. 387

It would seem that a reconsideration of the role of type as an ideal which has the potential to be adapted and elaborated can present an alternative to the circular nature of the discussions regarding the 'traditional' and the 'modern'.

Considering the application of courtyard types implies examining traditional or vernacular housing models. Determining what constitutes the 'traditional' in the Gulf region is problematic for a number of reasons, which include the variety of building types, the lack of extant examples given the inability of previously employed building technologies to withstand deterioration, and the importation of models from other areas. However, a distinction can be drawn between the dwelling types of the nomadic Bedouin and the settled communities that occupied the coastal zones. The Bedouin relied on easily transportable tents supported by wooden poles or on semi-permanent palm frond and bamboo shelters (a'arish) that were mainly used during the summer near desert oases. The coastal communities inhabited permanent houses constructed of coral stones or mud brick. Arranged in an irregular pattern near the coast, these houses were organized around a central courtyard surrounded by a shaded arcade (liwan) used to connect various rooms. The roof of the house was used for sleeping and as a family gathering area. A number of strategies were employed to deal with the excessive summer heat in the Gulf: thick perimeter walls with minimal

**16.1   Modern courtyard houses on campus at the American University of Sharjah, United Arab Emirates**

openings on the outside; large openings onto the shaded arcade surrounding the courtyard; the use of gypsum on wall surfaces to absorb humidity; and wind towers to promote cross ventilation. While the aforementioned dwelling types are varied in function and technology employed, the spatial distribution in each demonstrates a clear division between public and private space resulting from social, cultural and religious considerations. It is the imperative of these divisions which is the genesis of the courtyard typology.

Courtyard housing from the coastal areas offer a range of lessons for dealing with the challenges facing architects in the UAE. The integration of these lessons in the design process requires that the role of the traditional be reconceptualized to allow designers to move beyond the limitations inherent in the strict categories of traditional, modern and regional. Ernesto Rogers stated that:

> Many of those considered innovators share with the so-called conservators the common flaw that they start from formal prejudices, maintaining that the new and the old are opposed rather than represent the dialectical continuity of the historical process; both are limited, in fact, to the idolatry of certain styles frozen into a few images, and they are incapable of penetrating the essences that are pregnant with inexhaustible energies. To pretend to build in a preconceived 'modern style' is as absurd as to demand respect for the taboo of past styles.
>
> Rogers 1993, p. 201

Consideration of traditional buildings in terms of typologies representative of ongoing historical processes rather than as objects with limited relevance to contemporary design practice transcends the false oppositions of past and present in order to deal with the possibilities inherent in ideas associated with continuity.

As will be discussed in the following section, a re-evaluation of the notion of dialectical continuity can contribute to a practice that considers concepts derived from the study of traditional types and applies them via a process of adaptation and elaboration. The aim is to develop a context-specific architectural response, offering an alternative to the overwhelming trend toward an image-based architecture that characterizes contemporary architectural production in the Gulf region.

## Courtyard houses in Sharjah

The courtyard housing described here is located on the campus of the American University of Sharjah (AUS) in the UAE (See Figure 16.1). Founded in 1996, the AUS campus completes an axis extending through the area known as University City, which contains a number of educational institutions and training facilities. The AUS campus is characterized by a symmetrical arrangement, with the main administration building occupying the central position. All academic buildings measure 40 × 40 metres and are organized around a central open atrium. The buildings are clad in pre-cast decorative panels with motifs derived from a variety of sources (Figure 16.2).

16.2    **Campus at the American University of Sharjah, United Arab Emirates, showing a variety of design influences**

Faculty and senior administrative staff are housed on campus, and housing units range from one-room studios arranged in two-story blocks to free-standing 'villas'.

In 2002, the author was commissioned to provide a proposal for a series of four 350 square metre residences for the Deans of the respective schools at AUS. The challenge of designing housing on the campus was fraught with contradictory requirements: the housing was to be built in an Arab–Islamic context although they may or may not be inhabited by Muslim families in the future; the residences were to fulfil a representative role and serve as a private home for a family; and the buildings were to be designed for an American university campus located in the Arabian Gulf.

Earlier proposals had been made by a consulting architect/engineer. These schemes separated the residences into four individual free-standing buildings to be built on separate plots. Like the majority of buildings in the Gulf, there was no consideration given to solar orientation or other climate-responsive measures. The proposal was based on two residences that were built during the early phases of the university's building efforts and were intended to house senior administrators. They followed the typical model of residential development in the Gulf: a free-standing box-like building at the centre of a large plot. These residences were characterized by large windows on all façades that created problems resulting from glare and excessive heat gain, the lack of private exterior spaces, the lack of a semi-private family living area

and incompatibility between the treatment of the façades and the function of interior spaces (Figure 16.3).

Given the program requirements, the need for a private exterior space that could be used for public functions when necessary, and the climate of the Gulf region, the courtyard type seemed an appropriate model. However, the choice was initially met with resistance by the architect/engineer that served as a consultant to the university. The only argument against the choice was that it was not appropriate for a VIP villa, the implication was that the only appropriate type would be the typical free-standing villa placed in the centre of the building plot. Fortunately the university administration accepted the arguments put forth on behalf of a courtyard scheme (i.e. provision for a private exterior garden, increased privacy within the house, integration of public and semi-private living areas, efficient use of the land area allotted for the houses, and response to climate).

The design strategy relied on a number of lessons from the traditional courtyard houses from the settlements along the coast of the UAE and from other regional courtyard types (Figure 16.4). The attributes informed by traditional architecture include the creation of a microclimate within the courtyard for thermal comfort, the transition between the interior and the courtyard, the treatment of public and private spaces, the use of the roof as an exterior living area, the arrangement of views into and through the house, ordering systems and the treatment of the façade (Figures 16.5 and 16.6).

16.3   Western-style family houses at the American University of Sharjah during the first phase of construction

16.4   An aerial view of a restored courtyard house in the Al Shuwaihiyeen area of Sharjah. Notice the use of roof terraces as private living areas

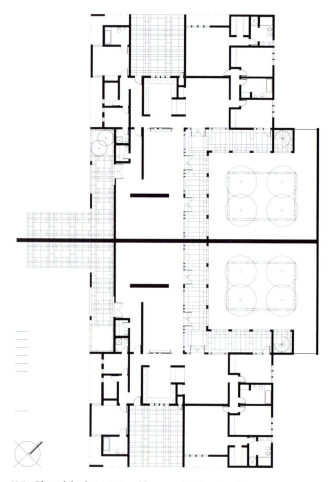

16.5 **Plan of duplex courtyard houses showing transition spaces**

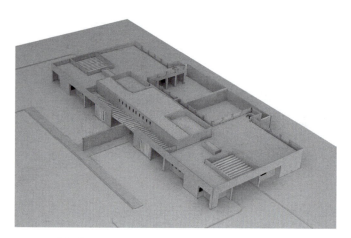

16.6 **Model of duplex courtyard houses**

The public reception areas and the semi-public family living room are arranged around an 11 × 14 metre courtyard, which is oriented toward the north-east. The courtyard is bound on the remaining two sides by a 3 metre high wall. The courtyard is planted with grass and other plants selected by the inhabitants, and the lack of a reflective floor surface greatly reduces glare and heat gain. The intention is to mediate the effects of climate by treating the courtyard as an enclosed garden and ensuring that the majority of the wall surface surrounding the courtyard is in shade for the greater part of the day. As in traditional courtyard houses in the UAE, an arcade provides a transition to the courtyard; the arcade also shades a glass façade that provides light and views from the public areas and the semi-private family living room (Figure 16.5).

The residences are organized as two semi-detached units placed beside each other on the site (Figure 16.6). The primary visitor's entry occurs on the south-west façade and leads to the public areas of the house; a secondary private entry is provided from the covered parking area integrated into the house. The secondary entry provides direct access to a guest suite and service zones. As in traditional dwellings, there is a strict division between public and private space; however, unlike in may traditional houses where the assignment of public and private space was done in an ad hoc manner depending upon need and location of the space, the Dean's housing relies on a formal division and assignment of functions. A wall running the length of the house and expressed on the façade separates the public reception rooms from the family room and private functions. Should more space be required during larger functions, a large sliding door can be opened to allow the family room to be used without compromising the privacy of the sleeping areas (Figure 16.7). Stefano Bianca has noted that in traditional architecture of the Arab world:

> The domestic reception room was always perfectly integrated into the envelope of the house, for the functional differentiation did not take place by segregating the respective architectural volumes, but by accommodating the internal circulation network in such ways as to achieve the desired levels of accessibility. Each major component of the house had its own centrality and needed to be linked with, as well as separated from, the remaining parts of the building and the main entrance. This implied a rather complex system of interior corri-

16.7    **Large sliding doors provide functional flexibility without compromising the privacy of living areas**

dors, thresholds, doors and buffer spaces within the house. In the case of normal family use, the internal circulation network was totally permeable, whereas with the arrival of external male visitors the various sluices, barriers and sub-divisions were put into use. As a result, there are clear similarities between the internal circulation structure of the house and that of the residential cluster: the position of the reception room with regard to the surrounding house corresponds to the relation between the house as a whole and the encompassing residential structures. The internal corridor of the house replicates, as it were, the function of the alleyways within the residential district.

Bianca 2000, p.78

Although the families occupying the Dean's housing may or may not be Muslim, the Arab–Islamic concern for privacy remained an important consideration, as the house was required to serve both a public representational role and a private residential function. In order to ensure varying levels of privacy, the internal circulation and the entry sequence were planned accordingly. As in traditional courtyard house typologies, the street façade offers no opportunities for views into the house and the mode of entry is not direct. On approach, visitors are required to make a series of 90° turns before entering the main reception areas (Figure 16.8). Upon entering the vestibule, visitors are afforded a narrow framed view into the courtyard before seeing the entire courtyard upon making their way into the main reception room. This corresponds to Dariush Zandi's observations that the main doors of traditional houses in the Gulf region rarely gave a direct view to the courtyard within (Zandi 1997). Once inside the public area of the house, visitors do not have direct visual access to private areas; they must again make a further series of 90° turns in order to enter the private areas. The entry sequence and the internal circulation paths also set up a series of views through the house intended to give hints of what lies beyond while ensuring privacy (Figure 16.9).

While the use of geometry as a basis for design was usually reserved for religious and public structures in the Arab–Islamic world, the design strategy for the houses relied on two geometrical ordering systems: one derived from a study of decorative patterns found in various Islamic traditions and another derived from the golden section (Figure 16.10). The reliance on geometry as a basis for ordering the houses was carried out as an investigation into the potential that geometry possesses as a tool for design. The fact that geometry plays a central role in the conception of space and form in architecture throughout the Islamic world also makes its use particularly relevant, although the author does not make the claim that employing geometry would necessarily result in a 'regional' building or in an appropriate context-specific response. The ordering systems were employed to establish proportional relationships between the various parts of the building and to relate the plan, sections and elevations. And, when exercised with rigor, carefully chosen ordering systems can result in specific visual and experiential qualities which evoke context-specific associations.

The façade system of the houses is based on the adaptation and elaboration of the façade treatment of traditional

16.9 **Note how the entrance hall does not provide views into the courtyard**

180

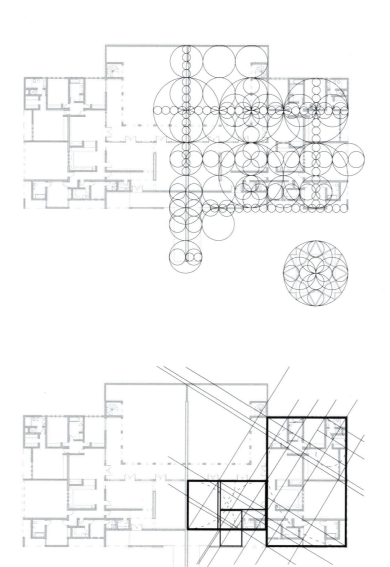

**16.10** **Plan showing the ordering system based on Islamic patterns**

courtyard houses in the Gulf, which is characterized by volumetric expression, articulation of the massive wall surface using niches and deep openings, and the subdued expression of the entry (Figure 16.11). The façade of the Dean's housing consists of three integrated elements: an outer blank wall surrounding the house that is opened to allow light, views and circulation; a recessed stone-faced wall defining the private spaces; and a stoned-faced volume containing spaces for public functions and extending above the datum established by the outermost wall (Figure 16.12). Reinterpreting the sequence of entry in the traditional courtyard houses in the Gulf, the space between the outermost blank wall and the volume housing public functions provides a shaded transition area that mediates between the harsh glare of the exterior and controlled natural light in the interior. The space between the outer wall and the wall defining the private spaces also allows for protected windows used for light and ventilation in the guest bedroom.

While traditional courtyard housing models use thermal mass to mediate the climate, the Dean's housing relies on staggered wall surfaces on the south-east and south-west façades to reduce the exposed area and provide shade; openings in these façades are recessed and kept small. Light wells prohibit direct light from entering the clerestory windows in the volume containing public functions (Figure 16.13). The outer façades surrounding the courtyard are opened to form an arcade, and the inner façades are glazed to allow abundant north light and views into the courtyard. The glass wall can also be opened to allow for circulation and ventilation (Figure 16.14). A large clerestory window allows additional north light and a view of the sky for the main reception area. With an annual mean of 9.7 hours of sunshine per day, the control of light is of primary importance in the UAE. When the challenges associated with the effects of the sun are considered as they have been in traditional courtyard typologies, there can

16.11   **The subdued entrance to a traditional courtyard house at Bait Al Serkal**

16.12  **The external façade to a modern courtyard house in the United Arab Emirates**

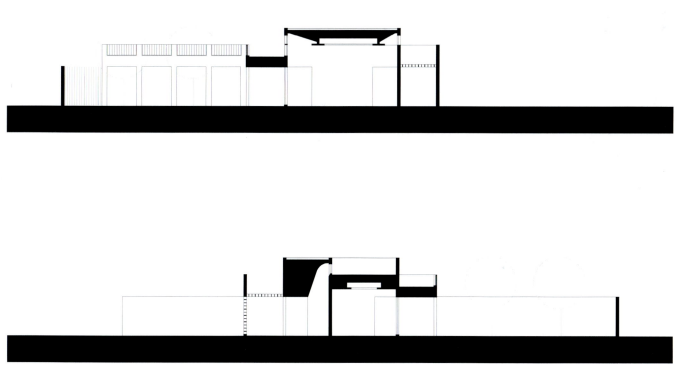

16.13  **Section showing controlled use of sunlight**

16.14 **Internal courtyard elevation showing internal arrangement of openings**

be a significant increase in physical comfort and a reduction in the excessive consumption of resources.

## Conclusion

While a study of types should not result in immutable models to be emulated, a critical re-evaluation of traditional courtyard typologies can result in appropriate contemporary responses to factors such as climate, social and cultural conditions. With regard to the role of the traditional, William Curtis has written:

Most vernaculars are in fact hybrids of indigenous and imported types and these types also change and adapt. To pretend that a peasant culture contains some immutable essences has an obvious romantic appeal and has actually been used in support of myths of national identity. The authentic regionalist acknowledges that conditions alter drastically and that the present world is one of increasing inter-change and interdependence.

Curtis 2001, p. 74

The claim that most vernaculars are hybrids of indigenous and imported types certainly holds true in the UAE. Also the commentary on the notion of the romantic appeal of the vernacular and its role in establishing a national identity is relevant to discussions regarding the use of the courtyard model in the Emirates. Fortunately preservation policies have led to the reconstruction of a number of courtyard houses from the coastal areas in the UAE; however, by presenting them as prime examples of 'heritage', courtyard houses have taken on unintended associations with a past characterized by a lack of progress.

Analysis of courtyard typologies of the region in terms of concepts offers the potential for adaptation and elaboration. Discussions of the courtyard model must move beyond the superficial distinctions of traditional and modern. The notion of a dialectical continuity between past and present is valuable because it demands a consideration of the past, not as a frozen image but as representative of ongoing historical processes that remain incomplete. This approach privileges neither past nor present, but recognizes that both must be considered for the future of the built environment. In this balance of past and present, 'type' plays a pivotal role in the development of context-specific responses that are often lacking in contemporary architectural practice.

## Bibliography

Bandini, M. (1993) Typological theories in architectural design. In B. Farmer and H. Louw (eds) *Companion to Contemporary Architectural Thought*, p. 387. London, Routledge.

Bianca, S. (2000) *Urban form in the Arab World.* Zürich, ETH/ORL Institut.

Colquhoun, A. (1997) The concept of regionalism. In G. B. Nalbontoglu and W. C. Thai (eds) *Postcolonial space(s)*, Princeton, NJ, Princeton Architectural Press.

Curtis, W. (2001) Regionalism in Architecture. In *Regionalism in Architecture*, p. 47. Geneva, The Aga Khan Award for Architecture.

Rogers, E. N. (1993) Preexisting conditions and issues of contemporary building practice. In J. Ockman (ed.) *Architecture Culture: 1943–1968*, p. 201. New York, Rizzoli.

Zandi, D. (1997) Qatar. In P. Oliver (ed.) *Encyclopedia of Vernacular Architecture of the World.* Cambridge, Cambridge University Press.

## Acknowledgements

A number of people contributed to the development of the ideas and the project presented in this chapter. His Highness Sheikh Dr Sultan bin Mohammed Al Qassimi, Founder and President of the American University of Sharjah, is acknowledged for creating an intellectual environment which allows for the discussion of the issues addressed in this chapter. Dr Roderick French, former Chancellor of AUS, supported the project and contributed significantly to its realization. Dr Martin Giesen, Dean of the School of Architecture and Design, and his wife Leslie were instrumental as enlightened clients and critics. AUS Campus Architect Mark Kirchner made invaluable suggestions for improvement of the project and was responsible for the construction of the project on behalf of the university. Construction manager Jamil Assaf and intern architecture student Amr El Shiwy also made valuable contributions. The insightful criticism and support of Professor Jay Randle and Prof. Dr Frederich Ragette continue to inform my thinking on the built environment.

# 17 The geometry of single and multi-family courtyard housing

MOHAMAD HAKMI

This chapter does not merely romanticize traditional architecture or advocate the accepting of all its principles. It is an attempt to bring to life again those principles which proved their effectiveness with regard to climatic and social aspects that characterize local residential environments, such as the existence of the courtyard as an essential architectural element within each housing unit. The assumption is 'that true identity is the result of a living culture and that the imposition of external values leads only to the loss of identity with unsustainable results' (Lycett 1996, p. 46). In this the courtyard is seen as the simple defining element.

The chapter proposes architectural and urban design models for future residential development based upon the adaptation of courtyard housing to meet modern social, climatic and economic needs. It seeks in particular to:

- develop housing types which respond to local residential needs
- evolve urban concepts that suit modern needs but incorporate courtyard housing as the primary element
- define a set of generic design principles and indicators to guide developers (public and private)
- re-engage modern development with the traditions of Arab architecture and urban form
- question the extent to which the current urban norms and architectural standards respond to local climatic and social requirements.

## The research methodology

Different methods are used to carry out each phase of the research discussed in this chapter. The first part is concerned with gathering information about several residential projects that introduce examples of contemporary Arabic residential architecture.

In the second part, an analytical method is used to examine critically the performance of single and multi-family dwellings at both urban and architectural levels. This helps in defining the shortcomings, difficulties and the potential of future design development.

The third part, the experimental part of the research, forms the final part of the chapter and tests many possible configurations against social, climatic, privacy and daylighting considerations.

In this part, a large number of possible concepts and alternatives are examined in an experimental manner. The use of computer simulation provides the ability to test different compositions of housing units together with their open and covered spaces. This allows for the assessment and selection of a number of basic architectural types and design alternatives capable of being formed into urban structures which take into consideration the climatic nature and social aspects of local environments.

# Analytical study

## *Arabic residential architecture and modern architecture*

Besides the advantages that successive scientific and techno-logical developments have brought as a result of the Western cultural antecedence, there is a growing gap between global international culture and local priorities. In the second part of the twentieth century, architecture has had to face a number of problems such as the loss of vernacular architecture solutions particularly in the developing countries (Hakmi 1995, p. 266). These changes revealed themselves with particular starkness in Arab residential environments. The negative effects can be summarized in the following points:

- Lack of a clear understanding of the relationship between buildings and the wider urban fabric. Modern architects tend to deal only with individual urban units following the 'modernistic practice – the free standing, functionalist monument' (Jencks 1978, p. 108). In addition, the impor-tance of the traditional dense urban fabric as a tempera-ture moderator of individual buildings has been ignored.
- As a result of changes in the nature of transport modes, pedestrian movement and road connections, urban design has suffered.
- The adoption of European architectural standards and planning has had enormous consequences at both urban and architectural levels.
- The pretext of using of modern building materials and construction technology has led to the abandonment of local cultural traditions, instead of subjugating them to serve local architectural thought and environmental cir-cumstances. This can be attributed to the popular under-standing that using modern materials leads to a radical change in architectural principles. As a result the lan-guage of architectural form is invariably the logical result of using new construction materials and modern tech-niques of structural assembly.
- The loss of local urban and architectural character which stems from the use of a repeating language of simple urban form (e.g. courtyard house).

## *Single-family dwelling types commonly used in Arab cities*

There is lack of statistical studies assessing the success of dif-ferent housing types (both single and multi-storey) in meeting housing needs at local levels. However, looking at new hous-ing districts it is evident that the application of multi-storey dwelling types constitutes the major part of contemporary housing development in urban areas.

In new housing areas there is an almost complete absence of single-family housing types but a few developments do exist. For instance, in Damascus, examples occur in the Al-Assad suburb and in Al Mazza new district, as well as the work-ers's suburban housing project at Adra. In Homs, the third largest city in Syria, examples are to be found in Al-Inshaa't dis-trict; in the New Homs housing area and in Al-Waleed suburb. They are also to be found in Tichreen suburb in Latakia and Abi Al-Fidaa' suburb in Hama. These examples were constructed

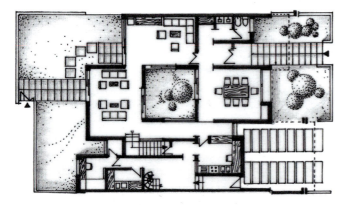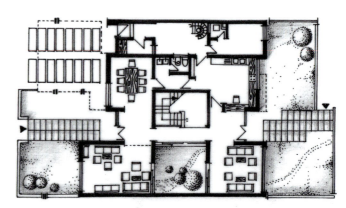

**17.1   Modern two-storey courtyard houses with (left) central and (right) side courtyard. These examples are from the Khitan project, Kuwait, built in 1983**

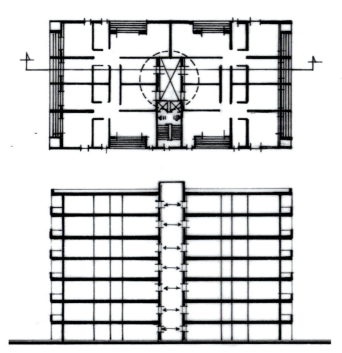

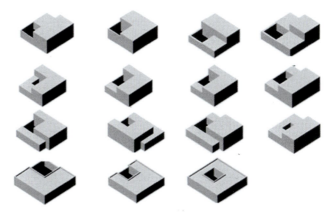

17.3  **Different possible layouts for a single family courtyard of one or two storeys**

17.2  **The use of a central light well for ventilation in multi-storey housing in the Middle East**

either by the General Housing Foundation or by cooperative housing groups. Other rare examples of single-family housing developments have been built by the Military Housing Foundation in various Syrian cities.

The predominance of multi-storey dwellings is mainly attributed to economic reasons, such as the expense of carrying out infrastructure and landscape works. However, it is

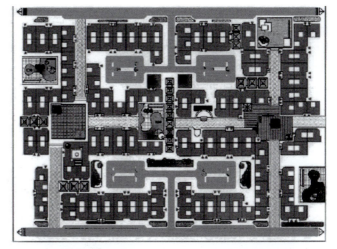

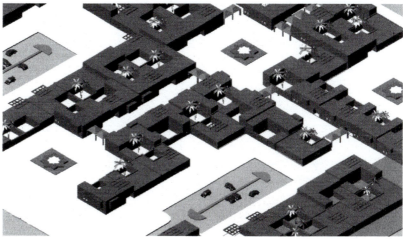

17.4  **An urban form of single family courtyard housing. Notice in the plan (above right) and the bird's-eye view (right) how there are both domestic courtyards and larger community ones**

worth mentioning that there may be other reasons and motivations behind the predominance of multi-storey dwellings, such as Western construction practices and the speed of erection of new communities. The consequences of this phenomenon in terms of urban design, cultural continuity and social cohesion deserve more attention.

An examination of recent residential architecture in Arab cities shows the influence of European urban concepts and architectural types without any serious attempt to adapt them to local social and environmental demands. Thus, most single-family dwellings are based on row and detached house types. In the few cases where Arabic traditional houses are adopted (i.e. courtyard houses), the majority of these are based on row houses or detached houses and in most cases plots have front and rear setbacks, as in normal row housing. As a consequence, the size of the courtyard is less than expected, transforming its role to that of a light well rather than a living space (Hakmi 1997, p. 61).

### Multi-family dwelling types commonly used in Arab cities

Multi-storey housing in Arab cities differs very little from what usually exists in other geographic areas (Figure 17.2). In Syria and other Arab countries, the staircase access system predominates over other housing types. Dwellings with this system, usually organized in three to five storey blocks, constitute the major part of the local housing stock. Next comes the high rise blocks. Tables 17.1 and 17.2 illustrate the frequency of applications of these two housing types in the housing areas of New Homs and in the Dummar Housing Project in Damascus. The high frequency of terrace-housing in the Dummar Project is due to the topography and the geographical features of the site in the project area.

In some housing areas, buildings combine features of more than one housing type. In this case, dwelling blocks adopt the staircase access system and are adjacent to each other, having the same front and rear setbacks like single family row houses type. Examples of this case are found in Al-Inshaat and Al-Qousour districts in Homs and in many other Syrian cities.

## The need for housing alternatives

Restoring the balance between tradition and modernity requires the development of new architectural prototypes for hot-arid regions. The strength of the Arab environmental residential tradition needs to inform design at both urban and architectural levels. This is further justified by the following critique of much contemporary housing in Arab cities:

Table 17.1   **Multi-storey dwellings application in the housing area of New Homs, Syria**

| Types of multi-storey dwellings | No. of buildings | No. of stories | No. of units in a single floor | Total no. of units of this type | Total no. of units in the project | Percentage |
|---|---|---|---|---|---|---|
| Multi-storey dwelling with staircase access system with or without setbacks | 624 | 4 | 2–4 | 5886 | 6750 | 87.2 |
| High-rise block | 24 | 9 | 4 | 864 | 6750 | 12.8 |

Table 17.2   **Multi-storey dwellings application at the Dummar Project, Damascus, Syria**

| Types of multi-storey dwellings | No. of stories | No. of units | Total no. of units in the project | Percentage |
|---|---|---|---|---|
| Multi-storey dwelling with staircase access system | 4 | 2300 | 5300 | 43.4 |
| High-rise block | 12 | 2000 | 5300 | 37.7 |
| Terrace housing | 2 | 1000 | 5300 | 18.9 |

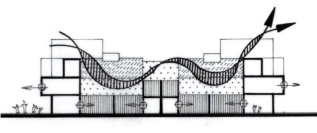

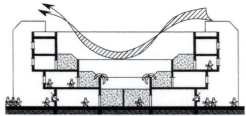

**17.5   Possible re-arrangement of cross-section to provide compact courtyard housing**

- No serious attempts have been made to adapt the dimensions and forms of housing to local needs, requirements and specific climatic conditions.
- The difference in the area of dwelling units required in local residential practice from that in common European housing standards results in spatial stress of residential building in Arab cities. This in turn has created design difficulties related to natural light and ventilation of the building core. These difficulties are often solved by providing small light-shafts in common areas which rise as high as the building. The disadvantages of this solution include loss of privacy and non-conformity to building regulations.
- Duplicating the European concept of a balcony in multistorey dwelling units fails to conform with local needs for privacy and climatic requirements.
- The mechanical distribution of large windows is not supported by technical studies into local natural lighting and ventilation requirements. The required building setbacks also fail to be justified environmentally.

## Experimental study

As mentioned earlier, this part discusses possible alternatives at both architectural and urban levels. The former suggests a number of design modifications to common housing types

while in the latter the potential for putting the alternative layouts into urban design and planning concepts is explored.

### Design types and alternatives for single family housing

The experimental architectural study suggests three basic models. The design concept is based on the existence of a courtyard as an essential element in the compositional structure of each type. Basic dimensions of the three models studied are: 12 × 12 m; 12.80 × 13.50 m; 14 × 14 m. Additionally, several possible alternatives were derived from these basic models. The derivations allow for the existence of courtyard types at a single or double level, or modified by place or the area of the courtyard within the suggested type. The purpose of the model is to add flexibility in the resulting urban concepts. The area of these possible alternatives ranges from 100 m$^2$ to 250 m$^2$, allowing for larger house units than what is usually available in most urban housing in the region.

The experimental design models have the following advantages:

- The courtyard has an important compositional and functional role and constitutes between 16–30 per cent of the ground floor plan.
- In addition to its social and decorative role, the courtyard is essential for the lighting of central elements of the house.
- The two zones of the house (namely day and night) are functionally separated through the suggested treatments for the models.
- Movement among different elements of the house takes place through the covered areas. This is different from the design pattern in traditional Arabic house, which depends on the courtyard as a basic linking element for parts of the house in both summer and winter.
- The suggested design alternatives allow the reinterpretation of some important architectural elements from vernacular architecture while providing benefits derived from modern house planning.

### Urban design consequences

An elementary urban design concept based on clusters of dwellings is developed in the experimental study in an attempt to reach an urban form and at the same time conform with the following conditions:

- An urban layout which follows the pattern of traditional urban texture in Arab cities.
- An urban unit which provides security and privacy in semi-public and semi-private spaces.
- An urban layout which incorporates green space, children's play areas and general landscape for shade.
- A layout which provides car accessibility to all housing units, with necessary car parking nearby without conflicts between vehicular movement and pedestrian routes.

## The courtyard house as a basic unit of multi-storey dwelling

This part of the study seeks to insert a courtyard within each of the dwelling units that compose a multi-storey residential building. It also seeks to test the proposition that the integration of courtyards can provide conditions of good lighting and ventilation at the building and urban levels whilst overcoming some potential design difficulties.

## Design difficulties

The design difficulties encountered were related to the following points:

- Ensuring complete privacy for each courtyard at different levels of the residential building.
- Ensuring sufficient natural lighting and ventilation to each courtyard at all levels of the building and to the covered spaces that directly overlook the courtyard in each dwelling unit.
- Compensating for the areas occupied by the courtyards which increase proportionately with the increase in the number of storeys.
- Minimizing noise transmission which can result from the extensive use of neighbouring courtyards.

## Overcoming design difficulties

Through the systematic exploration of alternative design solutions, using computer-aided design methods, the following conclusions were drawn:

- Courtyards located at different levels should be grouped together and arranged so that they adjoin each other. This is to avoid the courtyard from functioning merely as a narrow shaft on the lower floors, i.e. the ground and first floor.
- Assembling four back-to-back units that constitute the residential building makes it possible to arrange the courtyards of four dwellings in a fashion where they adjoin each other both vertically and horizontally.
- The stepped design of the courtyards helps deal with issues of natural lighting and ventilation. The resulting amphitheatric form (Figure 17.5) achieves optimum resolution of privacy, energy efficiency and construction cost.
- The use of cantilever projections allows extra floor areas to be gained for the individual apartments both to compensate areas occupied by courtyards and to create duplex housing units in the last two floors.
- The provision of small one-meter deep stores in the walls separating courtyards can reduce noise transmission between adjacent courtyards.

# Suggested alternatives to current practice based on the experimental study

The residential type with staircase access system and that with gallery or balcony access system formed the base for the suggested architectural concepts. The staircase access system is the most common multi-family dwelling type in Syria and internationally (Hakmi 1998, p. 71). The gallery access system, which is rarely used in Syria and other parts of the Arab world, makes it possible to have a greater level of flexibility in the entry points of different dwelling units whose designs may differ from one level to another as a result of the way the courtyard exists at different levels of the building. If this system was adopted, the privacy of the spaces that overlook the gallery can be protected by a combination of:

- reducing the length of the corridor (gallery) leading to the flats so that the gallery accesses a smaller number of units

- making the level of the gallery slightly lower than the level of the floor of the flats – this is to provide more privacy for any windows located on the gallery
- adapting some special treatments of the windows over looking the gallery such as the use of Mashrabiyya and shutters.

The suggested architectural concepts (Figures 17.6–17.10) contain five basic types which are not related to any specific context but merely constitute starting points. Applying these types in certain Arab countries requires further study to take into account climatic features of the region. Such detailed analysis will define the precise shape and dimensions of the courtyards and the appropriate methods for gathering them into urban configurations. The five types are presented here as generic models suited to the modern Islamic world in order to help generate housing with appropriate climatic, social and cultural characteristics. They are based upon two access types–gallery and staircase.

## Experimental type A

Adopted design type: multi-storey block with gallery access system

- Dwelling unit major dimensions: 13.20 × 13.20 m
- No. of floors: 3 + 1
- No. of dwelling units: 30 units
- No. of probable types: 12
- Most of the units (flats) are of one level, a few of them are double-leveled.

## Experimental type B

Adopted design type: multi-storey block with gallery access system

- Dwelling unit major dimensions: 13.20 × 13.20 m
- No. of floors: 4
- No. of dwelling units: 38
- No. of probable types: 16
- The majority of the units are on a single level, the remainder on two.

## Experimental type C

Adopted design type: multi-storey block with gallery access system

- Dwelling unit major dimensions: 13.20 × 13.20 m
- No. of floors: 4
- No. of dwelling units: 38
- No. of probable types: 17
- Most of the types are of one level; only a few are of two levels.

## Experimental type D

Adopted design type : multi-storey block with staircase access system

- Dwelling unit major dimensions: 13.20 × 13.20 m
- No. of floors: 4
- No. of dwelling units: 64
- No. of probable types: 19
- All the flats are of a single level.

## Experimental type E

Adopted design type: multi-storey block with staircase access system

- Dwelling unit major dimensions 12.00 × 12.00 m
- No. of floors: 4 + 1
- No. of dwelling units: 20
- No. of probable types: 7
- All the flats are of double-level.
- Each of the ground flour flats has setbacks.

It is clear that there is considerable design variation which can meet different conditions (see Table 17.3). This variation is based upon:

- the adopted type of multi-family dwellings
- the dimensions of the basic unit
- the spreading of the dwelling unit over one or two levels
- the dimension and location of courtyards in different types, their relation to each other and the methods of arranging them both horizontally and vertically
- the area that is allocated for a single unit, the extent of the courtyard at different levels, and the relation between covered and uncovered spaces.

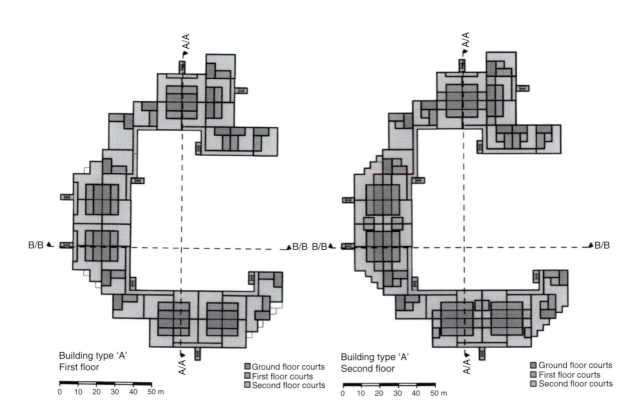

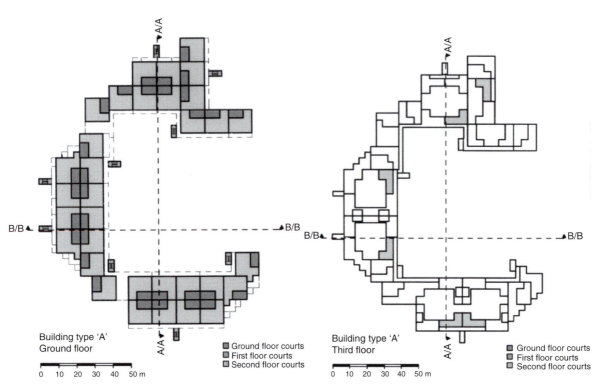

Building type 'A'
First floor

☐ Ground floor courts
☐ First floor courts
☐ Second floor courts

0   10   20   30   40   50 m

Building type 'A'
Second floor

☐ Ground floor courts
☐ First floor courts
☐ Second floor courts

0   10   20   30   40   50 m

Building type 'A'
Ground floor

☐ Ground floor courts
☐ First floor courts
☐ Second floor courts

0   10   20   30   40   50 m

Building type 'A'
Third floor

☐ Ground floor courts
☐ First floor courts
☐ Second floor courts

0   10   20   30   40   50 m

**17.6   Courtyard housing type A. Plans at ground, first, second and third floors**

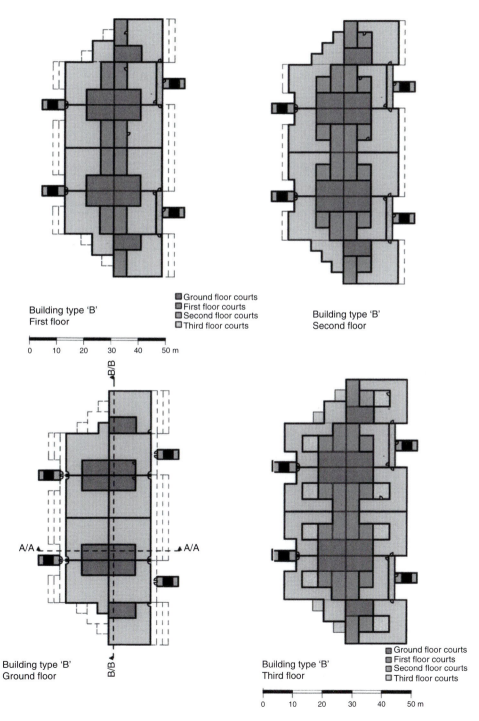

Building type 'B'
First floor

0   10   20   30   40   50 m

■ Ground floor courts
■ First floor courts
■ Second floor courts
□ Third floor courts

Building type 'B'
Second floor

Building type 'B'
Ground floor

Building type 'B'
Third floor

■ Ground floor courts
■ First floor courts
■ Second floor courts
□ Third floor courts

0   10   20   30   40   50 m

**17.7   Courtyard housing type B. Plans at ground, first, second and third floors**

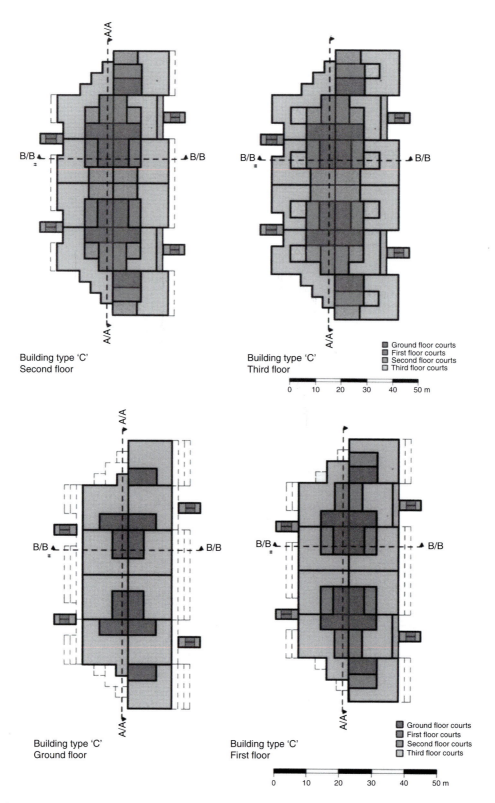

Building type 'C'
Second floor

Building type 'C'
Third floor

■ Ground floor courts
□ First floor courts
□ Second floor courts
□ Third floor courts

0   10   20   30   40   50 m

Building type 'C'
Ground floor

Building type 'C'
First floor

■ Ground floor courts
■ First floor courts
□ Second floor courts
□ Third floor courts

0   10   20   30   40   50 m

**17.8   Courtyard housing type C. Plans at ground, first, second and third floors**

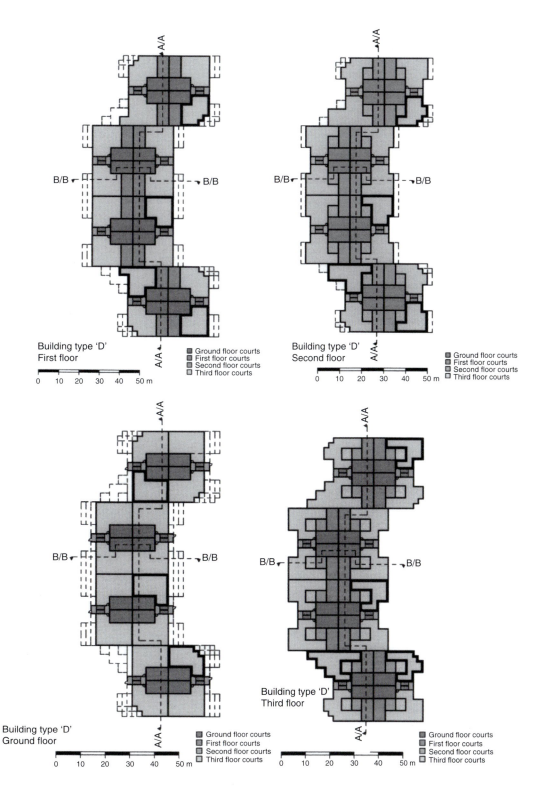

Building type 'D'
First floor

■ Ground floor courts
■ First floor courts
□ Second floor courts
□ Third floor courts

Building type 'D'
Second floor

■ Ground floor courts
■ First floor courts
□ Second floor courts
□ Third floor courts

Building type 'D'
Ground floor

■ Ground floor courts
■ First floor courts
□ Second floor courts
□ Third floor courts

Building type 'D'
Third floor

■ Ground floor courts
■ First floor courts
□ Second floor courts
□ Third floor courts

**17.9 Courtyard housing type D. Plans at ground, first, second and third floors**

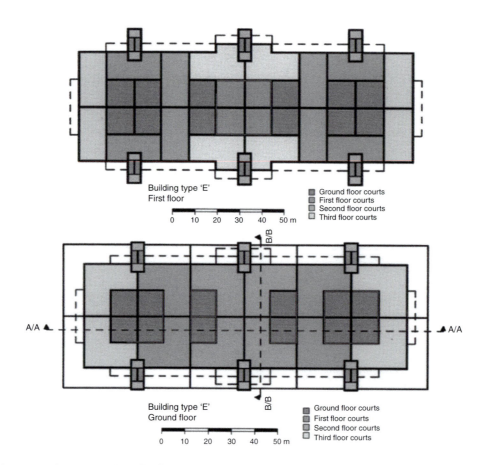

Building type 'E'
First floor

■ Ground floor courts
■ First floor courts
■ Second floor courts
□ Third floor courts

0    10   20   30   40   50 m

Building type 'E'
Ground floor

■ Ground floor courts
■ First floor courts
■ Second floor courts
□ Third floor courts

0    10   20   30   40   50 m

**17.10   Courtyard housing type E. Plans at ground and first floor**

Table 17.3   **Characteristics of experimental types A–E**

| Area (m²) | | Presence of setbacks ground floor | No. of levels of dwelling unit | No. of probable types | No. of dwelling units | No. of floors in block | Adopted design type | Basic dimensions of dwelling units (m) | Type |
|---|---|---|---|---|---|---|---|---|---|
| Covered | Open | | | | | | | | |
| 80–167 | 20–40 | Without setbacks | One and two | 12 | 30 | 3 + 1 | Gallery access system | 13.2 × 13.2 m | A |
| 130–205 | 20–40 | Without setbacks | One and two | 16 | 38 | 4 | Gallery access system | 13.2 × 13.2 m | B |
| 130–200 | 20–40 | Without setbacks | One and two | 17 | 38 | 4 | Gallery access system | 13.2 × 13.2 m | C |
| 110–135 | 20–40 | Without setbacks | One | 19 | 64 | 4 | Staircase access system | 13.2 × 13.2 m | D |
| 145–195 | 20–40 | With setbacks | Two | 7 | 28 | 4 + 1 | Staircase access system | 12 × 12 m | E |

17.11 **Bird's-eye view of courtyard housing type A**

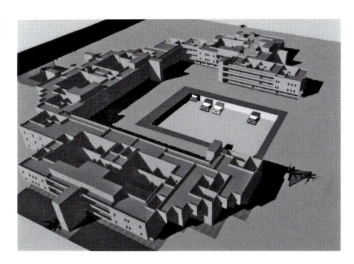

17.12 **Perspective views of courtyard housing type A: (left) central area; and (right) perimeter**

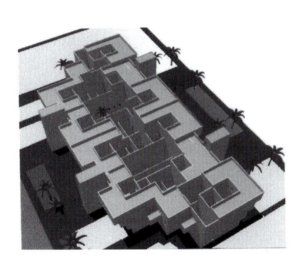

17.13 **Bird's-eye view of courtyard housing type B**

17.14 **Perspective view of courtyard housing type B**

## The common characteristics of the five experimental types

- The courtyard plays a vital compositional and amenity role for each dwelling. It provides residents with the opportunity to enjoy a private open space with green elements for a period of more than eight months per year in any Arab country.
- The role of the courtyard is not limited to decorative and recreational purposes: it is essential to the supply of lighting and ventilation of the house, thereby reducing energy consumption over non-courtyard typologies.
- The suggested alternatives help to maintain a distinctive local architectural character.
- The variety in covered as well as opened areas of the suggested types helps in meeting the residential needs of families of different sizes.
- The use of cantilever-like projections along the elevations helps in shading the surfaces of the building elevations and in enriching the building form. This also has energy advantages in reducing the cooling load.

## Urban design experimental study

The planning and urban design part of the study suggests a defined area at neighbourhood level. The urban concepts are built upon the forms and basic dimension of the suggested experimental architectural types discussed earlier. The urban design difficulties which resulted from the quadruple gathering of the different types were:

- The need for accessibility (vehicles and pedestrian) from both sides brings about considerable difficulties in site arrangement and landscaping, and in the provision of car parking areas near access points.
- The need to provide full privacy to courtyards that adjoin each other limits the height of adjoining buildings.

However, the advantages of the new urban configuration discussed outweighs the difficulties. These are as follows:

- The proposed urban concept achieves a tightly knit urban fabric that responds to climatic and environmental aspects.

17.15   **Perspective view of courtyard housing type C**

17.16   **Perspective view of courtyard housing type D. Notice the self-shading layout**

- The compact urban composition with a limited number of storeys helps in defining open space and ensuring privacy to semi-public and semi-private areas. In addition, it creates conditions where landscaping flourishes under climatic conditions similar to those of arid residential regions.
- The non-existence of intersection between pedestrian and vehicle movement is possible as long as accessibility of vehicles to parking lots is near the building in small groups related to the residential units shared by the single stair or gallery system.

## Residential density issue

Although the number of floors does not normally exceed four storeys, the gross density of the suggested urban concepts is expected to reach 275 pph (persons per hectare). This is higher than the gross density of the two Syrian case studies of the New Homs and Dummar Project where it is 150 pph and 250 pph respectively. This comparison clearly indicates that it is possible to reach a desired residential density with medium height buildings incorporating courtyards within each dwelling unit instead of building ten to twelve storey dwelling blocks. Thus, these concepts can be used effectively in areas requiring medium to high densities. This in turn has social, environmental and climatic advantages. It is also possible to use such courtyard concepts for low-density areas through further modification of the typologies discussed earlier.

## Main conclusions and recommendations

- It is possible to generate innovative architectural types and urban alternatives which combine certain features of modern residential architecture whilst still enjoying the advantages of traditional housing, as long as the courtyard form is adopted.

- European urban systems for single family dwelling (detached houses and row houses), which incorporate the presence of setbacks, does not constitute a proper basis for the courtyard housing type. This type requires an appropriate urban system derived from the nature and spirit of the compact city textures found in the Middle East.

- Plots with dimension of 12 × 12 m to 14 × 14 m facilitate the optimum size for the adoption of the courtyard housing type in single family dwellings.

- The presence of a central courtyard within each dwelling surrounded by closed spaces on at least three sides allows the effective use of the courtyard for lighting and ventilation, thereby saving energy.

- This study has also shown that the dwelling units of dimension ranging from 12 × 12 m up to 14 × 14 m also make possible the adoption of courtyards within the structure of each unit of the multi-family and multi-storey dwellings. This becomes possible as long as quadripartite dwelling units with their amphitheatric courtyards forms are followed, in accordance with the illustrated architectural study.

- This study suggests that urban blocks of three to four floors followed in accordance with the experimental architectural and urban concepts can be adopted instead of high buildings (e.g. multi-storey dwellings with staircase access system and point block), and are particularly suitable to the context of Arab societies.

- This study questions the suitability of the European type of multi-storey dwelling. The aim of conforming them to the specific conditions and requirements of local residential environments suggests a fundamental redesign of the type based on the recommendations in this chapter.

- This chapter highlights the necessity of modifying the planning rules and building standards adopted in Arab cities. Current regulations pay little regard to lighting, ventilation and shading needs or to Arab urban traditions.

- The analysis of existing types and their shortcomings in this chapter should encourage further research aimed at a practical outcome that will address the needs of urban development.

## Bibliography

*Alam Al-Binaa* (Magazine) (1985) Housing or kernel house, December, 64, 9.

Brolin, B. C. (1976) *The Failure of Modern Architecture*. London, Studio Vista.

Hakmi, M. (1995) *Theory of Architecture*, vol. 2. Homs, Syria, Al-Baath University Edition.

Hakmi, M. (1997) Traditional Arabic house and main dwelling types, *Bassel Al-Assad Journal for Engineering Sciences*, **8**, November, 57–82.

Hakmi, M. (1998) *Theory of Architecture*, vol. 1. Homs, Syria, Al-Baath University Edition.

Jencks, C. (1978) *The Language of Post-Modern Architecture*. London, Academy editions.

*Khitan Project* (1983) Project report published by the General Housing Establishment, Kuwait, February 1983, pp. 28–29.

Laberie, I. and Ruomi, M. (1982) Dummar, Cite Satellite de Damas, les Conditions d'une Realisation Contemporaine, *Les Cahiers de la Recherche Architecturale*, 10/11, Espaces et formes de l'orient, 140–9.

Lycett, W. (1996) Cultural identity and development. In *International Development & Practice: Bridging the Gap*. Proceedings of the 13th Inter-Schools Conference on Development, 26–27 March, edited by Dr Magda Behloul, Huddersfield, University of Huddersfield.

# 18 Courtyard housing in Saudi Arabia: in search of a contemporary typology

## TAREK ABDELSALAM

## Introduction

Studying courtyard housing in Saudi Arabia allows the distinctive nature of tradition to be reinterpreted in the context of the contemporary era. Although most Saudi people link the courtyard house with the traditional Saudi lifestyle, an increasing number are keen to see the courtyard typology adapted for modern needs. The question is, how is this to be achieved, what design principles should be followed, and what are the likely urban consequences?

Saudi Arabia is one of few countries in the world where most people still adhere to a strictly traditional way of life whilst at the same time having the wealth to possess advanced

18.1 **View of the old city of Riyadh, Saudi Arabia showing the predominance of courtyards**

means of technology. However, like many other traditional societies, Saudi society has been subject to a great many changes due to the phenomenon of globalization and this has resulted in a conflict between the authentic and the occidental, the local and the global, the traditional and Western models.[1] Many people in Saudi Arabia continue to believe that the courtyard house is a manifestation of the local tradition linked, essentially, to a poor past. They have doubts regarding the appropriateness of the courtyard house to the contemporary needs of Saudi society, especially in the area of climate moderation and gender privacy. This notion could be ascribed to a number of factors:

- a misunderstanding of the different values implicit in the courtyard concept
- a lack of appropriate contemporary models of the courtyard house that fulfil the needs and aspirations of contemporary Saudi society.

Majjdi Hariri[2] has classified the types of courtyard in the traditional Saudi houses into:

1  family courtyard, which represents the heart of the house
2  guests' courtyard
3  kitchen courtyard – cooking court
4  animals court, which is used in some cases as a playing court for children (Hariri 1991).

This chapter will discuss in particular type 1, the family courtyard, as it embraces the essential social and cultural

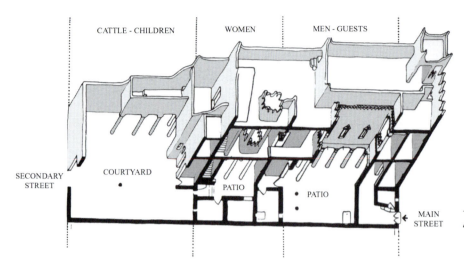

18.2 **Axonometric view of a traditional Saudi Arabian courtyard house**

18.3 **Decorative elements used to enhance energy efficiency by promoting air movement in a courtyard house in Najdi**

implications of the courtyard house as a general concept and one applicable to the contemporary condition.

The specific functions of the traditional family courtyard as identified by Hariri are:

- an appropriate place for family gathering as a living and dining area
- a comfortable and calm place for sleeping during the hot summer nights

- a safe area for children to play under their mother's supervision
- a source for daylight and natural ventilation for the surrounding rooms
- an internal environment with a pleasant microclimate
- the circulation hub of the house linking all the spaces in a controlled fashion.

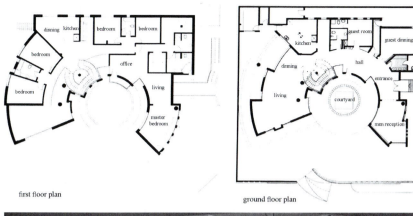

first floor plan

ground floor plan

18.4  **Plan and views of modern circular courtyard house in Riyadh**

# A 'modern' courtyard house in Riyadh

This modern house was built in Riyadh in 2001 with a total area of 1300 sq m. It embraces a basement and two floors. The basement includes an entertainment zone with a swimming pool, a squash court, and an activity hall. The ground floor consists of a guest area with bedrooms, a guests' reception and dining area, and a guest kitchen. The first floor includes the family bedrooms, living area, and an office. As such the first floor is private, the ground floor semi-private and the basement semi-public.

In this project, the architect has attempted to integrate the concept of the courtyard typology into a Western-oriented design where the spaces are arranged in an open and free plan layout.[3] Such a house organization will be perceived by some people as an ideal model for the combination of the local and the global, for preserving the concept of a courtyard spatial organization while adopting the open plan approach and modern building materials of the West. Others will perceive it as occidental and alien because of the inconsistency with which the traditional and modern ways of life are resolved.

To discuss the appropriateness to modern needs of this contemporary courtyard house in Saudi Arabia, we need to examine it from different perspectives. The emphasis in the analysis will be on the spatial organization around the courtyard in the context of contemporary social and cultural values.

From the cultural point of view, the courtyard in this house does not ensure total privacy for women at two levels. First, as the courtyard is open to the main façade and exposed to the neighbouring buildings, it cannot be considered as a private enclosure. Second, the entrance lobby and men's reception hall partly overlook this court. This may hinder the women's free movement and use of this space when receiving guests in the men's reception hall.

The original role of the courtyard as a thermal modifier inside the house is questionable in this design. The open circular form of this courtyard minimizes the shaded façades and maximizes the exposure to the sun heat. With an open court to an adjacent garden and using thermally conductive materials such as steel and glass in its façades, this architectural design has provided a debatable environmental scenario, depriving the courtyard of its traditional climatic justification.

It could be argued that the court in this design is better considered as part of the garden rather than an internal courtyard of the house. Hence, the functions and activities that can take place in this court are complementary to those that are acted out in the adjacent garden. This suggests that this courtyard design has failed both to attain the full range of cultural and climatic advantages or to maintain the functional benefits of the courtyard typology. If we look at the aesthetic aspects in this courtyard, we find the variety of surface materials and treatments affects the required calm atmosphere for the courtyard. The extent of glazing and metallic panelling adds an alien dimension to the scene, and highlights the difficulty of balancing traditional and contemporary design.

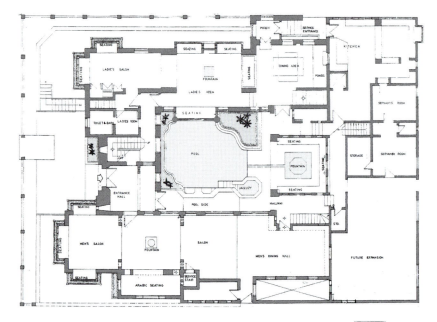

18.5 **Ground floor plan (top) and upper floor (bottom) of Almakkiyah House, Jeddah**

## A neo-traditional traditional courtyard house in Jeddah

The Almakkiyah House was constructed in a modern neighbourhood in Jeddah, where the streets are a separator rather than an integrator of people. With the implementation of the 'setback' regulation, the adjacent buildings are detached and divorced from each other resulting in a western urban character. In this project, the designer adopted the traditional model of Hijazi architecture in Makkah.[4] The two-storey villa is built around a central courtyard. On the ground floor, a guest wing for men on the right side, and another for women on the left are articulated around the swimming pool in the centre of the courtyard. Adjacent to the pool there is a seating area, which is connected to the kitchen. The first floor includes the bedrooms, family living room, and the library room.

The adoption of the traditional model in this project should not be seen as a rejection of contemporary design and means, but rather as a solution to some of the problems imposed by climate and the inappropriate use elsewhere of modern building materials and construction techniques. The central courtyard with a pool serves both practical and aesthetic purposes. The pool functions as a climate modifier since it cools and humidifies the air before it reaches the surrounding spaces. By orienting the villa to the prevailing breeze and utilizing the circulation of air through the courtyard, the architect has succeeded in obviating the need for air conditioning in the surrounding spaces for 6–8 months of the year.

Privacy for women in the Almakkiyah House is ensured by using the concept of the courtyard correctly. The courtyard presents a private enclosure where women can move and sit freely without being overlooked by neighbours or guests. The project demonstrates that the adoption of the traditional model of courtyard can help in providing the cultural and religious values of the community, compared to the Western-oriented courtyard of the previous example.

From the functional point of view, the courtyard of the Almakkiyah House is utilized on all three levels. First, it functions as a circulation hub for the house, connecting the different parts and spaces of the ground floor. Second, the swimming pool and green area in the centre represent an ideal focal point for the house when viewed from the first floor. Third, in the Eastern side of the courtyard, adjacent to the pool, there is a seating area with a fountain in the middle, which serves as a place for private family gathering.[5] The maximum utilization of the courtyard spaces emphasizes the functional advantages of the courtyard space in the house. Many

18.6 **Two views of the courtyard of Almakkiyah House**

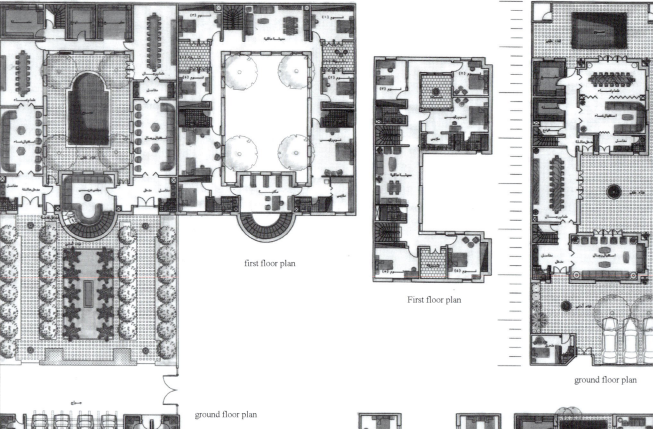

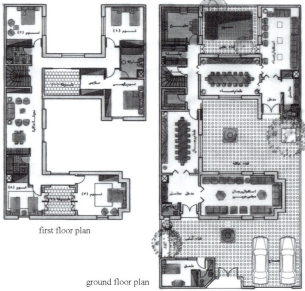

first floor plan

ground floor plan

First floor plan

ground floor plan

first floor plan

ground floor plan

**18.7  Examples of contemporary middle-income courtyard housing in Saudi Arabia: type 1 (above), type 2 (top right), type 3 (right) (Architects: Beeah Architects)**

aesthetic values inspired from Islamic architecture are reflected in the treatment of surfaces in the courtyard such as the crafted wooden screens and the use of mosaic and ceramic tiles with geometric patterns and calligraphy.

This design represents an ideal solution for the element of courtyard at the cultural, functional and climatic levels. However, the aesthetic aspects of this courtyard, which are based on the craftsmanship and detailing of Islamic architecture, are difficult to employ in contemporary projects due to the rarity of artisans and the high cost of construction. As such the house offers useful pointers but is not universally applicable.

## The revival of the courtyard concept in a contemporary housing project: Al-Nakheel district in Riyadh

This project was designed by Beeah Planners, Architects and Engineers in Riyadh, in 2002. It aims to develop an ideal and

safe new residential environment within affordable cost limits. The site is located in the Al-Nakheel district of Riyadh and occupies an area of 452,000 sq m. The project houses 500 residential units with a range of different sizes and designs, all based on the concept of courtyard housing. Each unit consists of ground and first floors within plot areas which vary from 176 sq m to 1475 sq m. In addition to the residential units, the project comprises the necessary community facilities (schools, social centre, mosques, open areas and gardens, and commercial facilities) some of which also feature courtyard designs.

The design concept of the master plan of the Al-Nakheel housing project is based on:[6]

- encouraging social interaction by dividing residents into homogeneous groups
- encouraging pedestrian movement by providing safe and pleasant walkways
- providing an efficient and safe network of streets
- providing a pleasant and comfortable atmosphere for residents around a series of linked green spaces.

The project contains four main parts. The first consists of the main public park, which includes playgrounds, schools, a social centre, mosque, recreation facilities, and restaurants. This part, in the heart of the district, is entirely for pedestrians. The second part of the development consists of a network of narrow streets which connect the residential area with the surrounding public streets. The third part consists of residential clusters organized around courts. These include children's playgrounds, small gardens and car parking facilities. The fourth part of the development is the commercial area, located adjacent to the outer streets on the borders of the district.

The residential units are classified into six types according to their design concepts. This chapter focuses on three of them to explain the different approaches that the designer explored in the project as a whole. In type 1, the designer adopted the conventional courtyard in the centre of the house surrounded by the other residential elements. In this design,

18.8 **Urban grain resulting from the use of contemporary courtyard housing**

all of the dwelling spaces are articulated around this courtyard and overlooking it. Reception and dining areas for both males and females share the same courtyard, which affects the level of privacy negatively in this layout. In terms of utilizing the courtyard space, the swimming pool in the middle hinders the use of the courtyard as a place for family gathering and activities. In addition, it ceases to function as a play area for children although the pool provides useful climate moderation.

In type 2, the designer employed three connected courtyards with three different levels of privacy. The front courtyard serves as an entrance court for the dwelling and can be used by both the residents and guests. The male reception and dinning areas are articulated around another courtyard, which is connected to the front courtyard. This approach ensures a

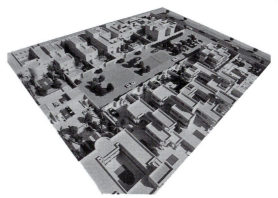

18.9 **Views of the new urban quarter in Al-Nakheel, Saudi Arabia**

proper segregation between male and female spaces, which is one of the most important considerations in Saudi culture. To the rear of the dwelling there is a third courtyard, which is adjacent to the female area. This courtyard helps in ensuring an appropriate level of privacy for women and provokes physical segregation between male and female guests. However, as this courtyard is partly open to view on three sides to the surrounding external areas, there is a potential loss of privacy.

The third type of residential unit has a similar approach to the second type with some significant differences. The most important is that in type 3 the back courtyard provides for women a higher level of privacy than in type 2, as the courtyard in type 3 is enclosed by rooms on three sides.

outs and methods of construction. The retraining of the workforce and of professional advisors who tend to follow Western patterns would also be required. If, however, the middle course is followed based upon planning and material choices made so as to maximize the cultural and climatic benefits of courtyard architecture, then there will be benefits for the community at large. The middle course offers urban design solutions which re-establish the dense pattern of streets and sheltering parkland of traditional Saudi cities. Into this a variety of modern courtyard house types can be designed to coexist, providing a degree of authenticity and social harmony without compromising the values of contemporary architecture.[8] What the examples examined show is that as a typology the courtyard form generally offers advantages over imported Western models.

## Conclusion

In conclusion three perspectives can be drawn. First, that a token use of the courtyard typology, now increasingly commonplace in Saudi Arabia, fails to satisfy either the climatic and cultural benefits of the courtyard type or the advantages of the free-plan Western house. The hybridization of typologies requires thought at a deeper level than usually occurs in contemporary housing projects in the region. There is a need to consider both the requirements of architecture as a discipline, and of identity as a cultural imperative, if the design response is to address both social and technological change.[7]

Second, the application of traditional courtyard solutions brought up to date technically can be expensive to build and is constrained by lack of skilled craftsmen. However, should society adopt such a model for future housing, there will be a need to exploit economies of scale by standardizing plan lay-

## Notes

1   Abdelsalam, T. (2002) The Arab Architectural Identity Dilemma: a Conflict between the Authentic and the Occidental. *Architecture+*, **1**, pp. 12–15.

2   Hariri, M. (1991) 'The Courtyard House' Hariri, Makkah.

3   *Albena* (2003), Issue No. 157.

4   Archive of the Amar Centre, Jeddah.

5   Abdelsalam, T. (2002) 'Unity in architectural composition and language' *Architecture+*, **2**, pp. 66–70.

6   Archive of Beeah Planners, Architects and Engineers, Riyadh.

7   Abel, C. (2000) *Architecture and Identity: responses to cultural and technological change*. Oxford, Architectural Press.

8   Abdelsalam, T. (2003) Visual Complications of Cultural Attributes. *Architecture+*, **3**, pp. 42–45.

# 19   New design thinking for contemporary courtyard housing

## YASSINE BADA

## Introduction

The courtyard, as the basic organizing element of the traditional Arabic house, is an enclosure that offers environmental advantages and privacy as required by Arab culture. The courtyard constitutes the outdoor living space, favoured by local climatic conditions and family life. The courtyard house offers an equilibrium between internal and external lifestyles and spaces. Despite all these advantages, the courtyard house has been neglected and ignored in the development of contemporary housing projects in the Arab world.

This chapter discusses the chronological growth of the courtyard as an organizing element in the development of the town of Touggourt in the south of Algeria. It focuses on the wider spatial organization, use and transformations that the courtyard house has undergone. Attention is focused on courtyard design in order to identify the real causes of change.

Touggourt is a town of about a hundred thousand inhabitants located in the north-eastern part of southern Algeria. It is an oasis settlement, situated at 650 km from the Mediterranean Sea, and is known for its hot climate during summer and a pleasant climate in winter.

The urban texture of the town is composed of four different structures that chronologically represent the major phases of growth of the town (Figure 19.1). The first sector (a), which is the oldest (1200 onwards) and occupies the centre of the town, is half-moon in shape and is a closely built organic structure with partially covered narrow streets organized around a mosque. The second sector (b) is the first extension of the town, during the colonial period (1870), for the Arab population. This structure is less dense, with larger streets, and surrounds the first one. The third sector (c), built around 1900, is laid out on a regular grid pattern with large streets defining square blocks of residential occupation (European population, during the colonial period). The last sector (d) is a series of sporadic developments including auto-constructed houses and mass housing sectors and dates mainly from 1950 to the present day.

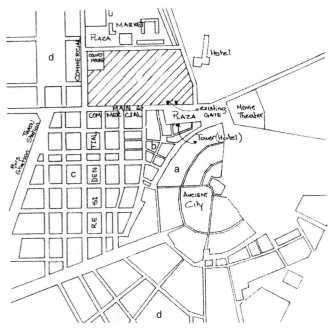

**19.1   Plan of Touggourt, Algeria showing the four zones studied**

This chapter will examine house design in each sector using a comparative approach, addressing space, society, environment and construction. The case studies will be examined according to the chronological growth of the different areas, in order to see how people have adjusted and altered the organization of their houses to respond to new needs and constraints, and how new housing developments have been designed in the expanding urban areas.

The study will examine the typology of the houses in relation to the urban organization of each sector and its evolution. In doing so, the courtyard will be the underlying theme which allows for the different house forms to be assessed and compared.

## House typology in the first urban sector (the historic urban core)

Nearly all houses in the historic core of the city of Touggourt are organized around a central courtyard. All rooms and spaces within each house have multi-purpose uses that vary on a daily and/or seasonal basis. So rooms have no specialized uses in that their function alters according to season, time of day, or as family circumstances change.

The major components of these courtyard houses are:

- *El hosh* (courtyard): an open-to-sky space that is the only source of light and air to the entire house. It is an outdoor living room where family life goes on.
- *Es sabat* (as the iwan in oriental houses): a covered space whose structure articulates the rooms and the hosh – an extension for these spaces. It permits, for instance, the

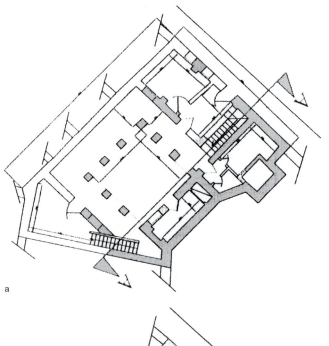

a

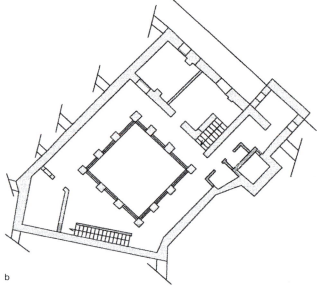

b

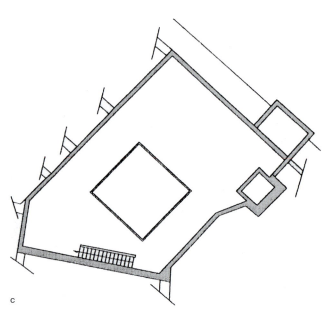

c

19.2  **(a) Ground floor, (b) first floor and (c) roof terrace of Spanioli House, a traditional courtyard house in Touggourt**

enjoyment of outdoor activities such as eating outside in a shady space on a hot summer day.

- *Es sguifa*: the intermediary space between the public realm and the private realm of the house. It is also the space giving access to the guest room without intruding upon house privacy.
- *Es stah*: the terrace roof, used as a private outdoor sleeping space during the hot season.

This traditional inward-looking house reveals a response to climatic and sociocultural contexts. Most of the major elements and principles of the Arab house design are present. The courtyard, as the basic organizing space, is the result of enclosure that offers environmental advantages and privacy for family life that must be screened from outside. It is a sacred requirement in Arab culture and results in the spatial arrangement whereby the guests' room is close to the entrance. Also, access by the *sguifa*, whose space configuration avoids direct views into the interior of the house, enhances the sense of privacy. There is no specialization of spaces; therefore activities happen according to many circumstances such as season, time of the day, climate, festivities and so on. It is a form of interior

nomadism with few permanent functional references such as room names or room-specific furniture.

Some of the houses selected for this study (for example, Figure 19.2) remain in their initial state because they house poor families whose lifestyle shows no major differences to the old way of living despite the introduction of modern conveniences such as a television, refrigerator and so on. Their houses have, therefore, seen no structural transformation.

The houses of the old sector are generally of irregular shape, and are one or two stories high with no major external façades as most external walls are shared with other houses (Figure 19.3). The shape of the courtyard is usually square or rectangular, and the irregularity of each house urban plot is absorbed by the secondary spaces. The presence of stairs in the courtyard makes the movement between the exterior spaces (terrace and courtyard) efficient – one being an extension of the other. The inner envelope of the courtyard house presents no other openings than the room doors and the arcades of the saba. The courtyard house, therefore, is windowless to the exterior realm and open, often with an arcade around the interior realm: the courtyard (Figure 19.4).

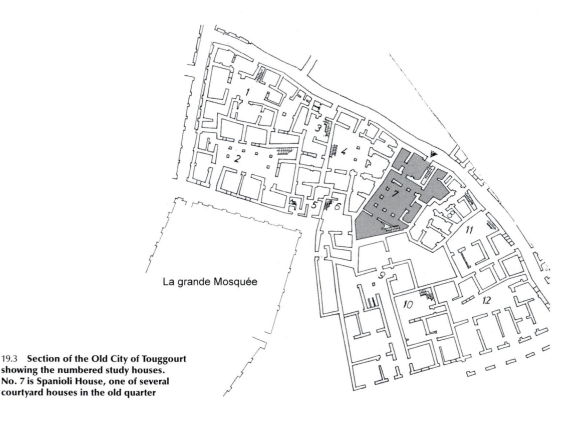

19.3 **Section of the Old City of Touggourt showing the numbered study houses. No. 7 is Spanioli House, one of several courtyard houses in the old quarter**

La grande Mosquée

**19.4 Section of Spanioli House, a courtyard house from the early twentieth century**

## Typology of houses in the second urban sector

Pressure for space due to population growth and the deterioration of some old houses meant that new houses were needed. The houses of the second sector were built in the late 1940s during the French colonization. The houses present the same courtyard organization as the older ones but with significant structural changes. These changes affected the dimensions of the internal spaces. The use of steel beams (I-beam shape) as a new material in roof construction instead of palm trees trunks, with the use of the same roofing materials as before (gypsiferous rocks and mud), enabled builders to have longer spans and consequently larger spaces. There is also the emergence of an exterior façade with no significant openings except for the entrance door, which by its details marks the start of the individual expression of the house on the public realm (Figure 19.5). We can conclude that the organization principles of the old houses were maintained in the houses of the second sector despite significant changes in floor areas and façade treatment.

Conveniences such as refrigerators and televisions have affected the way of life and psyche of people and have led to the specialization of function in the rooms in these courtyard houses. Two types of transformations have occurred as a consequence.

In the first type of transformation, the courtyard and the *sabat* are the prime victims. These open spaces are used to build an extra room such as a bathroom or a kitchen, or covered totally to create an internal hall. This has led to a total transformation of the original house organization (by subdivision or addition) to accommodate the new desire for specialized rooms favoured by the adoption of Western lifestyles. There is also the appearance of the new internal linear distribution space: the corridor.

The second type of transformation is more sensitive as it responds to modern needs without altering the character of the houses. In the Senoussi House (Figure 19.6), for example, which is organized around two courts, the proprietor has respected the courtyards by using a movable device that protects the space during the cold season in a way that maintains the internal relationship. The family can move from space to space comfortably without crossing an open external space. The *sguifa* is no longer a space to separate the exterior (the street) and the courtyard by screening views from outside, it is now just a transition space. The introduction of landscaping into the courtyard space has enhanced its esthetical qualities and improved its microclimates conditions. The courtyard is maintained as a circulation as well as a flexible space used for different functions such as entertaining guests and family gatherings throughout the year.

These transformations (Figure 19.7) are the start of the disappearance of the courtyard as the core organizing space of the house. Instead, the internal corridor becomes an organizing element of internal spaces. The truncated courtyard is maintained and is still used for family gatherings and other activities despite its spatial inadequacy. There is, however, a divorce between the internal spaces and the external ones. Whereas in the traditional courtyard house they both formed an extension of each other, this vital connection has been lost in modern transformation. It seems that the need for an internal circulation space is strongly expressed in both transformations, by either covering the courtyard by a movable device or annexing it to internal spaces. This illustrates the need for a new organization of the house, which does not necessarily mean the complete disappearance of the courtyard. In fact, the courtyard is not eliminated, but rather changed, or reduced.

**19.5 Traditional elements of courtyard architecture surviving into the twentieth century. Notice the expression of the doorway**

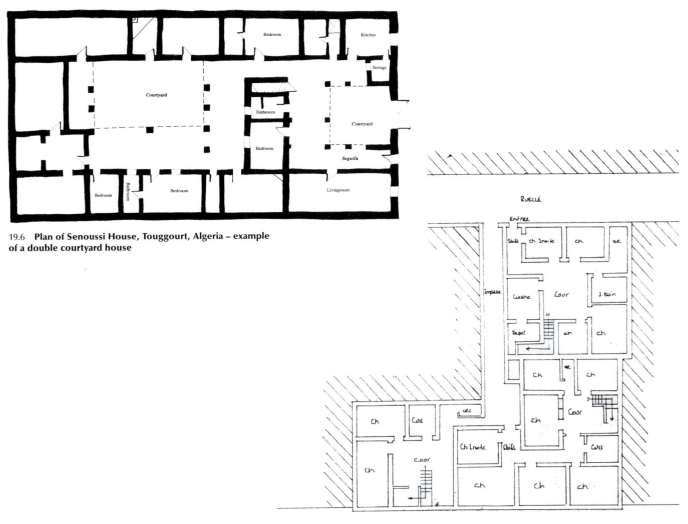

**19.6 Plan of Senoussi House, Touggourt, Algeria – example of a double courtyard house**

**19.7 Plan of three modified courtyard houses of mid-twentieth century showing the survival of traditional elements**

In both types of transformations windows appear on the external façades, which were originally windowless. These windows are not only used for their prime role of lighting and ventilation, but are also a medium for people to appear on the social scene as modern and progressive. Windows are often the first sign of the beginning of individualization and reorientation of the house to the public space, and a symbol of rejection of deep-rooted cultural/religious imperatives. It is also the result of a new urban organization where the houses are not clustered in the traditional way.

## Typology of contemporary houses

Houses being built today have turned away from the principles that have guided house organization for generations. This is particularly marked in the total disappearance of the courtyard. Where this has happened, women are the ones who suffered the most from these transformations, since they are deprived of space or contact with nature or the outside realm. Houses are now reoriented to the street. Consequently, outwardness substitutes inwardness, giving more importance to external façades. This is favoured by inhabitants and architects who have become object-oriented. Hence houses have become more a medium of expression of the inhabitants' social status, instead of a place to offer comfort, privacy and joy – a total reconversion from content to container. Thus the courtyard, that was once a response to a particular cultural and climatic context, has been eliminated from house design and replaced by long corridors and internal halls. This covered central space, around which different spaces are organized, is multifunctional in use. It is a place for family gathering, eating, entertaining and so on – it is a family living-room with a ceiling.

Exterior spaces are reduced to small verandas and balconies that are seldom used because they offer neither privacy (exposed to public spaces) nor functional space (dimensions and relationship with other spaces are frequently inadequate).

Thus, their role is to express modernity, or façade modulation rather than use. Although some designs attempt to re-interpret the courtyard principle in housing, the results are often unsatisfactory for many reasons. The exterior space created is relegated to either the corner or rear of the house plot and does not constitute the centre of the plan. Moreover, its poor spatial quality and inefficient relationship to other spaces makes it a deserted and useless space for the inhabitants. Hence, it lacks the courtyard characteristics of the traditional house and is neither a functional nor a symbolic space. In spite of creating an external covered space (analogous to the *sabat*) as an extension of the interior spaces and large scale landscaping work, including the forming of a small oasis, this space does not have genuine courtyard characteristics because there is no sense of enclosure. Its character is that of a modern garden rather than that of a traditional courtyard.

The case study analysis of Touggourt presents a picture that is similar to many parts of the Arab world. Adaptation to the new sociocultural context has been difficult and has caused, in architecture, a loss of continuity and identity. By simple observation of the urban environment we notice the chaos caused by the values of present-day architecture and urbanism. Almost all Arab countries share the same history and have undergone similar changes in the social and cultural domain and subsequently in architecture. It is the loss of the courtyard house which is central to the crisis faced in Arab cities.

To respond to modern housing needs and commercial growth, town planners have replaced the traditional pattern of Arab cities with layouts based upon staggered housing blocks and amorphous urban spaces. The latter are not treated as areas for communal living whilst streets have become merely means of transportation inspired by functionalism urban concepts. This has affected not only the image and typology of Arab cities and the associated cultural and social patterns of people, but has damaged the quality of the environment.

The international style of the housing blocks has dominated the urban environment and disfigured the local context. The courtyard, which was considered the sacred space for privacy and comfort, formed the basic organising element of the traditional towns, whilst the streets were the places for communal life. These have been substituted by free standing blocks in broken-up urban spaces that inhabit human contact and undermine quality of life. The modern way of urban planning has also caused serious environmental problems. The large and unplanted spaces surrounding housing blocks are a source of discomfort, energy waste and pollution (air, visual), whilst the large areas at the periphery of housing estates are a source of climatic stress, pollution from cars and urban rubbish.

## Impact of sociocultural changes

The new social context is shaped by the sociocultural changes within Arab society itself, and by the effects of the importation of Western ideas and technologies. Arab old towns were created in accordance with community values (social, cultural, and religious), with the urban design principles which shaped urbanisation in harmony with those values. Today the pattern of values which favoured communal life has changed to that of greater individualization. Modern urban design is the material expression of these changes.

Architecture is strongly influenced by the world of technology, an influence which touched even the house, as evidenced by Le Corbusier's '*machine à habiter*'. Western exportations range from goods – cars and construction materials – to concepts of ways of living. This is helped by means of communication via television, the Internet and so on. As a result the local way of life and the psyche of Arab people has been steadily undermined, leading to consequential changes in housing requirements. By following modern trends and international agendas, local architects have encouraged the disappearance of traditional identity.

Discussing housing design requires a profound understanding of many contexts – social, cultural, economic, psychological and so on. To respond correctly to the genuine needs of the people, spatial configuration must be the result of the manipulation of these different domains. It is not an easy task to strike a balance between so many interacting contexts. The context of architecture itself contains several trends and visions which impact upon housing layout. There are two groups of designers in the Arab world: those who believe that vernacular architecture is the most appropriate to the Arab world, despite their own reticence with regard to this kind of architecture, and those who believe that modern architecture should adapt to local contexts. Neither of these two groups has succeeded in ensuring harmony or continuity with the architectural heritage without compromising the need for change or the evolution of people's way of life. 'Muslims like other people want to be contemporary. They do not want to live in medieval environments.' (Professor Dogan Kuban).[1]

This leads us to ask some difficult questions: what should be preserved from the architectural heritage of Algeria and what should be left to evolve in order to ensure both continuity (identity) and a contemporary spirit?

This question is difficult to answer with regard to housing design, because housing is the main component of the urban structure and prime representative of the sociocultural context. In a world where Islamic values are still upheld in spite of globalization, the relationship between housing form and society cannot be addressed devoid of the religious and cultural dimension.

## Reasons for the disappearance of the courtyard house in modern Algeria

The reasons for the disappearance of courtyard house can be summarized as follows:

- The family structure has changed from a multi-family to a single one.
- Housing policy has imposed small plots, making the introduction of courtyard space a difficult task.
- The reorientation of the house to the street has created a social need to expose the inhabitants' social status to the wider world. Urban planning regulations have encouraged this effect.
- The individualization of rooms has undermined the collective life of the family and made the need for a shared internal space largely unnecessary.

People are more concerned about the image of the house than ever before. It is the medium by which they appear on the public scene: the very thing that the traditional house with its blind wall and door rejected. There is a strong psychological need in this matter. People prefer their house to express their status and, as a medium of relation with others, the reorientation of the house to the street has made the inversion from content to the container. In this way the courtyard becomes less useful as a symbol of status. In addition, the individualization of rooms (as a modern way of living) undermined the need for an internal space for family collective life. In terms of comfort, people refuse to cross the open space (the courtyard) in order to move from one place to another, preferring the sheltered, air-conditioned, volumes of modern houses.

## The courtyard as centre(s)

The concept of the centre is strongly present in courtyard architecture and traditional Arabic urban design. The centre is both functional and symbolic. It is advocated today by many architects. '*Every whole must to be a center in itself and must produce a system of centers around it.*' (Alexander 1976). Contemporary Arab architecture should reappropriate the concept of centre, thereby reviving the courtyard. There should be two centres: an external one (the courtyard); and an internal one (living space for the family). These two centres need to be organized in such a way as to create a whole, which builds upon tradition, but is modern in spirit. Thus the spatial relationship between these two volumes should be fluid to ensure a functional continuity. Emphasis should be focused on the visual relationship between these different spaces in order to give the sense of spatial connectivity and openness. In this way, the collective family could move from one space to another according to climate or other circumstances, with the benefits of contemporary amenities and the advantages of the traditional courtyard way of life.

## Sense of enclosure

The courtyard, by its enclosure, has two principal roles – to create a microclimate and to provide privacy. This is the essence of the traditional Arab house. However, air-conditioning undermines the first and globalization values of the second. Reviving the principles of the traditional house for contemporary life should entail more than reusing the same spatial configuration or repeating the same architectural elements and decoration. A compromise is needed by the introduction of contemporary know-how in old spatial compositions and architectural form. Enclosure, as achieved in the traditional house, presents a paradoxical situation: certainly privacy and microclimate are well concretized; however, a sensation of being 'closed up' is present, which is counter to the opening up of Arab society. Furthermore, the inner envelope of the courtyard, which is usually handled with a certain rigidity, deprives the house of its spatial diversity and richness. Architects could usefully redefine aspects of the courtyard, such as the degree of enclosure, spatial configuration, façade proportions, architectural details, materials and so on, in order to modernize the typology. For instance the inner envelope of the traditional house could be broken down and treated as a dynamic façade using techniques

Yassine Bada

such as environmental layering, recesses, texture and so on. Instead of simple symmetry and the closed form, the traditional house courtyard could become a dynamic, asymmetrical balance of interacting walls and spaces.

## Courtyard landscaping

Landscaping could play a major role in improving the aesthetic and spatial quality of the courtyard. Greenery and water do not just enhance the microclimate created by the courtyard but also create healthier and more enjoyable environments. Thus the courtyard could fulfil its real function as a family space in contact with nature: an exterior living room, since the weather is conducive to exterior life. Nature, peace and generosity are Islamic values communicated through the courtyard design. As discussed earlier, the courtyard is a representation of earthly paradise. These qualities are achievable only by a symbiotic composition of architectural, artistic and landscaping elements. The stereotyped courtyard with a fountain at the centre gives emphasis to the centrality of the plan but at same time makes the space static and functions rigid. Vegetation and water, if manipulated in a modern way, could enliven the space and make it more dynamic while still meeting the contemporary needs of Arab families.

## Conclusion

The courtyard house remains an appropriate built form, not only for the climatic conditions of hot-arid regions but also for Arab culture. It could still fulfill the requirements of contemporary lifestyles, if redefined and considered in the light of technological and socio-economic changes. The reproduction of traditional models, however, has failed to convince most clients. Architects need to avoid romanticizing the past, accept the reality of today and seek to built a better future. Thus the way they solve local problems can also contribute to the wider architectural and social discourse in the modern Arab world (Davidson and Serageldin 1995). What is required is a contemporary revival of the courtyard typology based upon a fusion of past and present values. This will lead to the design of more responsive urban forms in the rapidly growing Arab cities of the Middle East.

## Note

1 Aga Khan Award of Architecture (1990) *Expressions of Islam in Buildings. Proceedings of an International Seminar held at Jakarta and Yogyakarta, Indonesia*, Powell, R. (ed.). Geneva, Aga Khan Award of Architecture, p. 208.

## Bibliography

Aga Khan Award for Architecture (1990) *Expressions of Islam in Buildings. Proceedings of an International Seminar held at Jakarta and Yogyakarta, Indonesia*, Powell, R. (ed.). Geneva, Aga Khzan Award of Architecture.

Aga Khan Award for Architecture (1990) *The Architecture of Housing. Proceedings of an International Seminar held in Zanzibar, The United Republic of Tanzania*. Geneva, Aga Khan Award of Architecture.

Alexander, C. (1976) *A Pattern Language*. Cambridge, MA, MIT Press.

Antoniades, A. C. (1990) *Poetics of Architecture. Theory of Design*. New York, Van Nostrand Reinhold.

CARDO (Center for Architectural Research and Development Overseas) (1984) *The Arab House. Proceedings of The Colloquium*, A D C. Hyland and A. Al-Shabi (eds) Newcastle, The University of Newcastle upon Tyne.

Curtis, W. J. (1982) *Modern Architecture since 1900*. London, Phaidon.

Davidson, C. C. and Serageldin, I. (1995) *Architecture Beyond Architecture*. London, Academy Editions.

Norberg-Schulz, C. (1984) *Genius Loci: Towards A Phenomenology of Architecture*. New York, Rizzoli.

Ravereau, A. (1981) *Le M'Zab, Une Leçon D'architecture*. Cairo, Sindbad.

Steele, J. (1994) *Architecture For Islamic Societies Today*. London, Academy Editions.

Tanghe, J., Vlaeminck, S. and Berghoef, J. (1984) *Living Cities*. London, Pergamon Press.

# 20   Conclusions

The courtyard house highlights an important principle concerning the relationship between urban density and building form. High land occupation does not entail the inevitable construction of high-rise blocks; on the contrary, enclosed courtyards arranged as a strict or approximate urban grid achieves much higher densities.[1] Of the common housing types – tower block, linear high-rise block, two-storey terrace, detached and semi-detached villas, and courtyard dwellings – it is the latter which uses land most efficiently. Such efficiency carries with it two further advantages. By covering the land surface with a relatively even spacing of buildings and open areas, the internal environment of the dwellings is moderated to the advantage of the occupants. Furthermore, the external streets and lanes are also sheltered from the sun, wind and rain. The second main advantage concerns the social control and interaction in the external environment. By enclosing the courtyard and overlooking the street (the two types of space), a high level of surveillance and security can be engineered by architectural means alone.

As the examples in this book demonstrate, the courtyard house displays its own indigenous means of environmental and social control. Through generations of application an approach to environmental design and community well-being has evolved quite naturally. Its roots lie in the vernacular traditions of desert architecture, whether town or country, where an understanding of how people react to heat, light and sound is the result not only of building physics but the trials and errors of countless builders. The environmental systems and associated cultural practices led to little imported resources drawn from outside the region.

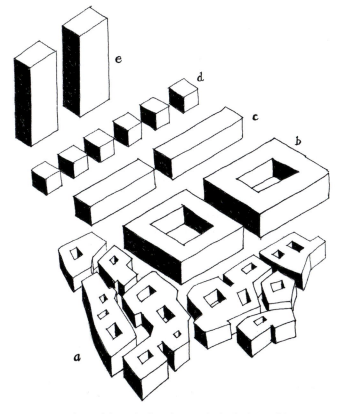

20.1   **Comparison of the major housing typologies in the world (a) court-yard housing, (b) European perimeter block, (c) terraced or row houses, (d) detached or villa housing, (e) high-rise blocks**

20.2 **The traditional courtyard house created streets which were a contained and controlled space. Doors were placed to achieve strategic advantage with windows positioned high for surveillance without loss of privacy. An example is from Hama in Syria**

As such the traditional courtyard house is truly vernacular in spirit and form.

Although the courtyard house is associated with Islam, its origins extend far deeper into housing practices in the region. The scarcity of resources in many desert or arid areas resulted in two types of housing response – the tented structures of nomadic tribes and the courtyard house intended for more permanent occupation. Only the latter concerns us here, but it could be observed that the nomadic tent is itself a form of courtyard housing. Here life is acted out beneath a fabric shelter with sleeping quarters arranged around the edge in a fashion which closely parallels that in the courtyard house.

Earlier chapters suggest that the courtyard house is the indigenous and perhaps inevitable solution to the design of housing in regions with a hostile climate. It also offers the advantage of a plan which mirrors the structure of single or extended patterns of family life. Kinship practices help reinforce the role of the courtyard, complementing the climatic imperatives. The analysis of individual courtyard dwellings in this book establishes the close relationship between environmental and social factors in the development of the courtyard typology. Family life has been shaped by the geometry and spatial configurations of the courtyard house just as the plan of the courtyard house has itself had to adapt to changing domestic needs. The symbiotic relationship between climate and social patterns is more marked in the courtyard house than any other common building type. In this sense the loss of the courtyard housing tradition in many regions of the world, but particularly the Middle East, is a loss of global proportions and an attack on the concept of sustainability. The layout of cities and the design of dwellings, have been undermined by a conspiracy of factors benign in themselves but disastrous when taken as a whole. A tradition whose roots extend backwards for at least 5,000 years has practically disappeared in a couple of generations.

The essays collected together in this book are the result of scholarship by academics based mainly in various parts of the Middle East or North Africa. They have been produced for various reasons – to provide a commentary on the significance of the environmental or social dimension of courtyard domestic architecture; to set the courtyard typology into a global context of building types; to highlight themes which though rooted in history may still be relevant today; and finally, to seek to influence governments and organisations responsible for housing in the regions discussed. But there is one bigger

20.3 **The courtyard house represents the fusion of social and environmental factors. This example from Algiers is exceptional for the richness of the tilework**

20.4 **Old Damascus showing the importance to urban character of the courtyard house**

221

20.5 **An aerial view of Tripoli in Libya showing the Old Town alongside Western-inspired development**

motive which lurks beneath the surface. In a world of increasingly global values and methods of building and city-making, how can individual local solutions be protected to provide a model for the future? Many of the examples in this book are of large prosperous courtyard houses from the past – the dwellings of merchants and local princes. What is needed is a recognition that the everyday courtyard architecture of places like Fez, Tripoli and Damascus provides valid examples for the fast growing urban settlements of the Middle East. Such validity resides in the area of sustainable development, in the integration of environmental, social, economic and cultural themes. There is some hope that a surviving current exists away from the big cities. In Chapter 4 the argument is made that the courtyard house continues to be the primary choice for the self- builders of the sub-Sahara in southern Algeria.

What is evident is that much of the contemporary landscape of cities with their detached building blocks, large areas of neglected open space, roads and car parks, is the very opposite to the principles which are at the foundation of the concept of sustainable development. In highlighting the integration of environmental, cultural and social factors through

the examples in this book, the authors have presented an alternative pattern of building for the future. A sustainability audit of building types would confirm the central proposition of this book, namely, that the courtyard house is a model of low-energy design, of built form which supports rather than destroys family and community life, and is a unit which creates the essential building blocks for the making of sustainable cities.

The reader will have noticed that the chapters are arranged into groups which follow a structure aimed at shedding light upon sustainable development. The first part brings together a series of chapters on the history and theory of the courtyard house. The approach is typological as well as historical, in the hope of understanding the special geometry of the type and how it has evolved over centuries and in different regions. The second part explores social and cultural dimensions. Here both theoretical and critical reviews of individual buildings are combined to bring insights to bear upon contemporary issues such as gender, the design and control of space, security, privacy and functional change. To be sustainable, the courtyard house needs to serve a changing society as well as a static one. What the authors suggest is the surprising level of flexibility and social diversity within the armature of the traditional courtyard form.

The third major theme concerns environmental and climatic factors. Here a series of chapters, both theoretical and case study-based, are grouped together to explore the relationship between building design, landscape and climatic control. Central to part three of the book is a discussion of

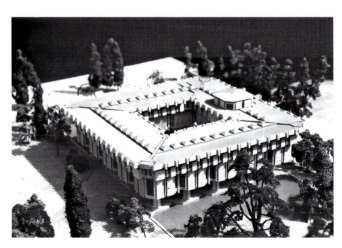

20.6 **The UK architect Basil Spence adopted the courtyard form in his design for the British Embassy in Rome, designed in 1960**

energy use and the employment of layouts in both plan and section aimed at reducing daytime temperatures whilst also exploiting night-time cooling. An understanding of the technical and constructional methods employed in traditional building can point the way towards future solutions for mass housing based upon the refinement of older technologies. In the post-fossil fuel age, such technologies may have to be revived if the desert regions of the world are to be occupied.

What is of note here is the way the traditional courtyard house wrapped itself around an inner space whose environment could be controlled to the benefit of the whole family. Unlike the western house with its external aspects, the courtyard house has a contained world open only to the sky. The sense of climate mastery through plan layout and construction is an enduring feature of the type. Not only were the harsh conditions kept at bay but the family could conduct its business with remarkable privacy. Hence social life and climate co-existed in a symbiotic kind of way. It is a lesson the West could usefully learn.

This part of the book has particular relevance for a world facing the prospect of global warming. As climates change and deserts expand, the need to understand vernacular practices increase. Technologies which once had relevance in arid and semi-arid regions now find use across areas once considered temperate. In countries around the Mediterranean, in Latin and Central America, housing (and other building types) which are cooled naturally using shade and wind will become increasingly necessary. One can see examples in the UK where wind-towers are used for cooling and earth construction is exploited for its thermal properties. One interesting example from 1960 is the design of the British Embassy in Rome by the UK architect Basil Spence, who employed a central courtyard and pool, and stepped section to reduce the air conditioning load. Such transferring of building practices from vernacular to commercial buildings, and from desert regions to those parts of the world witnessing climate change, will become increasingly necessary. This part of the book seeks to provide examples of vernacular practice for others to follow in a more high-tech context.

The chapters confirm Reyner Banham's hypothesis that historic buildings use ambient energy sources in creating comfortable domestic environments supplemented only where necessary by imported energy sources.[2] In more recent times, however, imported energy (wood fuel, coal and more recently oil) has supplemented the control and manipulation of the environment by natural means, undermining tried and tested vernacular courtyard practices. Earlier chapters also confirm Banham's other proposition regarding the similarities between the environmental/social interface and the human/animal interface. The latter point is worth underlining since the courtyard formula evolved because of its benefits to both human and animal comfort. The inter-dependent relationship between family life and family animals (both as pets and food source) resulted in close physical proximity of livestock and people. This pattern, evident in the case studies (see for instance Chapter 9) had both a spiritual and climatic function. The book confirms the proposition that the courtyard house has a more complex form and an enclosing envelope of greater responsiveness to ambient energy sources than

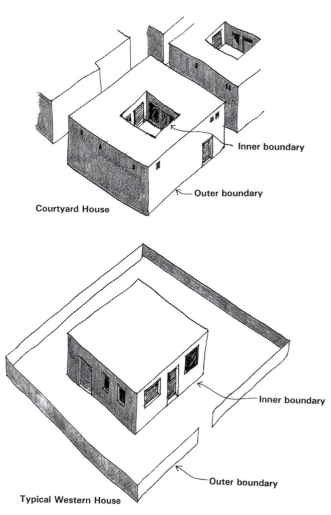

20.7 **The different boundary relationships between Courtyard and Western housing**

20.8 **The rural landscapes of the Middle East often depend upon courtyard towns for their cultural identity. This example is from Syria**

modern Western-style homes. This allows a distinction to be drawn between the courtyard house which is 'selective' in its response to climate and the modern house which is 'exclusive'. Mechanical systems are relatively rare in the courtyard house (other than electrical wiring for lights) because of the effectiveness of natural means of heating and, particularly, cooling. However, one trend in the design of new courtyard housing and to a lesser extent in the modification of older buildings is the roofing over of the central courtyard. Sometimes it is glazed over for additional shelter, at other times roofed in more substantial material (Chapter 19). In both cases there is an additional energy burden in terms of imported energy (mainly for cooling). The historical examples examined show the fine balances struck between the connection of the inside to the outside – a balance which varies according to region but which retains remarkable consistency of approach.

The distinction between 'selective' and 'exclusive' design is confirmed by the comparison of historic courtyard houses and their modern equivalents. The contemporary dwelling for most in the Middle East is an apartment in a multi-storey block or, for the wealthy, a detached villa. In both cases the environment is mainly controlled by mechanical means (air-conditioning, etc.) with the inevitable consequence of isolating the interior world from the exterior. This is what is called the 'exclusive' model because the form of the building and the nature of the envelope encourages isolation. Modern buildings are self-contained

blocks surrounded by free space.[3] In such buildings people are isolated from their surroundings, becoming physically and socially separate. Cheap energy sustains such practice but, as the lens of history shows, it is a form of urbanism far removed from the carrying capacity of local resources and local customs.

History has other lessons as well. The traditional courtyard house depended upon a sophisticated level of environmental control by users. They manipulated blinds, vents, window openings and moved their own position in the house according to weather and season. As such, there was a complex relationship between the building interior and the exterior environment. Social life in the courtyard house was influenced by climate, with the internal climate modified by design and the subtle controls in the house. Hence, the courtyard house brought building design, social patterns and environmental manipulation into a harmonious whole.

Karl Popper's theory of 'objective knowledge' applies with particular force in the Middle East. History is expressed through cities, artefacts and crafts rather than in written texts. The evolutionary narrative of common elements like the courtyard house and courtyard towns is the bedrock of historic evidence. Such evidence becomes objective knowledge when the subjective is removed by familiarity. Hence in describing a number of surviving examples of courtyard architecture, we arrive at a kind of cultural memory which transcends the physical reality. According to Popper[4] the objective

20.9 **Traditional courtyard architecture employs a number of local terms to describe various elements such as liwan – the open colonnade surrounding the courtyard – tarma – high level veranda, and majlis – the men's reception room. This example is Farfouh House, Homs, Syria, showing (top) main view and (right) detail**

knowledge of historic examples reinforces cultural identity. In this sense the courtyard house is both a reality and an icon of a civilisation. Inevitably it survives best where contemporary currents flow less strongly.

In discussing the courtyard house from three different perspectives – social, environmental and historical – various authors have come across the problem of language. There are few words in English which mirror accurately the subtle meanings of Arabic terms. Hence, local names are used for common day elements set alongside an approximate translation. Hence, too, this book is provided with a glossary of terms. Even in different parts of the Middle East and North Africa, different words are used according to local custom. Language is therefore an aid to understanding both the specific circumstance and, in general terms, in strengthening the cultural properties which lie beneath the surface. Hence Popper's proposition exists in both built reality and the cultural memory of local words used to describe aspects of the courtyard house.

20.10  **Early courtyard houses were partly defensive in nature. This example, with a central tower, is from near Baniyas in Syria**

If design is itself a form of social narrative influenced by religious, technological and gender issues, it is one where the indigenous builder plays an important role. The concept of a house with a central open space able to exploit the natural buoyancy of warmed air grew up over millennia. The compaction of such houses into dense urban settlements again was the result of subtle evolutionary pressures. If climate and defence were key ingredients, so too were external factors. The architect of such cities balanced practical experience with theoretical perspectives. As various chapter authors have noted, the teachings of Islam and the older religions of the region influenced the layout of houses, sometimes their orientation,

20.11  **The courtyard house demonstrates the ingenuity displayed by architects faced with hostile climates. Al-Adhem Palace in Hama, Syria**

their decoration, and their relationships to the internal garden and the wider city. Building design as a discipline is in perpetual dialogue with history, theory, technology and practice. How theory influenced the architecture of courtyard houses is discussed by several authors, and how practice can be used to enhance our understanding of the social science of buildings is explored by others.

An analogy can be drawn between the sheltering aspect of the traditional courtyard house and the costumes worn by their occupants. In both cases the emphasis is upon shade and layers. Protection from the sun means that openings are small and only necessary for movement or ventilation. The sharing of design principles between clothes, courtyard houses and other building types (such as the mosque) is a further aspect of the unification of cultural identity through objective knowledge.

20.12 **The courtyard is a positive void in towns. Note the two types of courtyard: city and house**

20.13 **The skilful placing of windows creates a mixture of types of light and ventilation**

20.14 **Desert architecture relies upon mass to moderate temperatures. These pigeon houses near Isfahan employ similar principles to courtyard houses**

227

The courtyard house is a potent model of the complex relationships between function and symbol. A central theme of this book is the importance of a vernacular housing type to cultural identity. Such identity is not the result of frivolous engagement with building methods or community need but the consequence of deep thought and sound practice over perhaps fifty centuries. Arguably, the courtyard house is the oldest form of domestic architecture. The tap-root of the type extends across continents to find its late flowering in the Middle East. Although the genetic code of the type is modified by geography and climate countless examples exist in much of Asia, America, Africa and also in parts of Europe. This book, however, concentrates on courtyard housing in the Middle East where human history is more bound up in this type of dwelling than any other. By concentrating here it is possible to assert that the courtyard house is an indelible symbol of human evolution – of the ability of our species to adapt and survive even in the most hostile territory.

The type of research described in this book allows only abstract statements of a general nature to be drawn from the analysis of specified types. Case study research does not permit the drawing together of explicit guidance for today's architects and housing managers. Only general principles can be extracted, but these all the same have validity in a world where globalization threatens to destroy local culture. A key finding concerns the need to question 'technological determinism'. The celebration of the machinery of environmental control threatens the inheritance of sound environmental practice found in vernacular building. The courtyard house modified climate by design, not engineering or posturing technology. All elements of the courtyard house subscribed to the same set of principles – the building, its details, activities and the dress of occupants. The holistic nature of courtyard life strengthened the family and community and ultimately of cultural identity. Coherence is found in these cities, not fragmentation or alienation. In this the courtyard house was a significant factor, as were the courtyard towns in which they existed.

There is the sense that the courtyard is a positive void in the community and architecture of the Arabic house. In cosmological terms the courtyard was not open to the sky but roofed by the sky and at night by the stars. The engagement through the dark desert nights with the cycle of moon and planets opened the courtyard house to meanings and beliefs beyond the earthly plane. Whereas the Western house opens onto a landscape which is fenced and controlled, the Arabic–Islamic house engages upwards with the heavenly realm. This signifi-

20.15 **Internal window shutters allow the environment of rooms to be adjusted. Notice the hard tiled surfaces to further reduce temperatures**

cance is worthy of particular note. Within the spiritual frame described by the circumference of the courtyard exist meanings suppressed by modern-day functional analysis and discarded by contemporary building regulations.

Architecturally, a few lessons can be drawn. First, that shape is important. In hot regions it is important that there is minimum interaction between the exterior and interior environments. This means a simple cube with windows restricted in area but balanced by a large central opening. The role of the central opening (or courtyard) is to exploit the buoyancy of the heated air to force ventilation through the smaller strategically-placed windows. Such space necessarily assumes a social function where the addition of a pool can add further climatic modification. Towers placed at the corners can trap or redirect the wind, aiding natural ventilation.

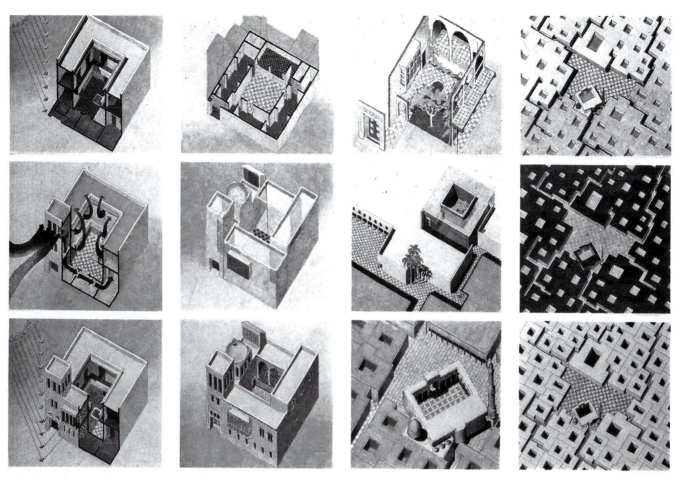

20.16  **The influence of traditional courtyard architecture on the design of the modern Helwan University in Saudi Arabia (architects Skidmore, Owings and Merrill)**

20.17  **Master plan of Helwan University showing adaptation of the courtyard style to faculty building (top part) and student housing (bottom part) (architects Skidmore, Owings and Merrill)**

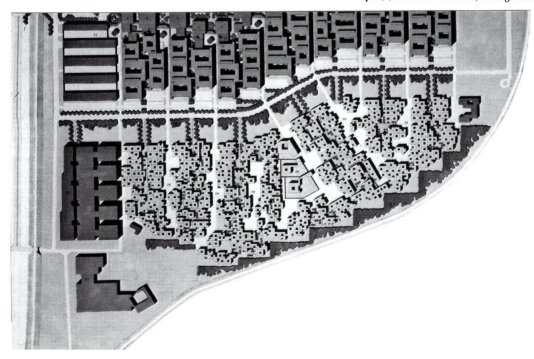

20.18 **Perspective sketch of experimental high-density multi-storey courtyard housing in Syria (architect Professor Mohamad Hakmi)**

Orientation in the Middle East is relatively unimportant, since the midday sun is mainly directly overhead. Shade and shelter, however, are needed from both the morning and afternoon sun but this is normally provided by timber shutters and fruit trees. In the examples discussed, orientation is more the result of wind or street alignment than sun angle. The midday sun poses a particular problem solved often by fabric awnings or lattice screens, designed to provide light and ventilation into the house without the disadvantage of direct sunlight.

Energy use is a combination of ambient sources and generated. The amount varies throughout the year but generally lighting is the main user of externally generated energy. Hence, if window openings are small to avoid overheating, they have a crucial role in providing daylight to the interior. As Louis Kahn noted a 'room is not a room without daylight'. In any contemporary application of courtyard housing, window area and solar control have to be considered jointly.

20.19 **Traditional crafts are kept alive by maintaining courtyard housing**

20.20 **Traditional techniques of shading used at the Intercontinental Hotel, Makkah (architects Beeah Architects)**

Finally, the control of the domestic environment should be by manual means with occupants able to vary conditions according to need. This requires systems of environmental control which are understood, accessible and easily maintained. Where automatic methods are employed, such as air-conditioning, natural systems should take priority and be employed first.

In these general characteristics it is important that the architectural features complement and reinforce social patterns. The traditional courtyard house was a well-balanced organism where socialcultural factors integrated with architectural/environmental ones. Family life was acted out in a finely tuned architectural framework where the culture of the house and the culture of the people were unified. An aspect of this culture, common to all Islamic archecture, was the interchangeability of room function. Within the limits of privacy, rooms were spaces which were used for different purposes at different times of the day and at different seasons of the year (see Chapters 4 and 5). Functional flexibility suited well the limited resources available and the needs of domestic architecture to respond to wider social values. Recent developments in many Middle Eastern cities suggest the dislocation of this principle. In writing this book the authors seek to share a particular aspect of humankind's domestic inheritance in the hope that a greater understanding of the courtyard housing tradition will provide a firmer platform for development in the future. The courtyard is afterall a tradition which over the past century has come under three great threats – war, earthquake and globalisation – yet remains vibrant and relevant.

## Notes

1   Dean Hawkes, *The Environmental Tradition: studies in the architecture of environment*, London, E & F N Spon, 1996, p. 7.

2   Reyner Banham, *The Architecture of the Well-Tempered Environment*, London, Architectural Press, 1969, pp. 11–15

3   Hawkes, *op cit*. p. 15.

4   Karl Popper, *Objective Knowledge: an Evolutionary Approach*, Oxford, University Press, 1972.

# 21 Courtyard housing: an 'afterthought'

PETER LAND

## Introduction

This book is a unique set of contributions on the subject of the courtyard house mainly in the Arab Muslim world. It examines in considerable detail the characteristics, evolution and variation of this house type in the different cultures of the region. It also includes some material on contemporary issues such as climate control. The content of this book is not only scholarly but it is also interesting reading about a subject which is at a heart of urban life and settlements in the Arab Muslim world. It is of importance for future urban and regional development, practices and policies, and it will promote better understanding of Arab Muslim urban culture outside the region. The chapters show great variety in both the richness of courtyard houses in history and in living vernacular traditions. However, it should not be viewed as only research. The real challenge is to use this information to develop a new generation of modern courtyard houses for contemporary needs and evolving Arab Muslim life styles. If this is not done, the type will remain anchored to the historical past and Western concepts of housing will fill the vacuum in growing Arab Muslim urbanization.

Any discussion of the courtyard house in the Arab Muslim world must keep in mind the accelerating social, economic and political dynamics of this important region which is apparent to any visitor to the towns in the area. This is revealed, to some extent, in the contributions in the book. Changing life styles and economic progress impact upon the traditional larger home for the extended family and probably foster the smaller house for the nuclear family. Expanding urban development around cities in the region show a growth in apartment house structures on one hand and on the other a proliferation of spontaneous settlements with few examples of planned neighbourhoods.

This author was invited to prepare an 'afterthought' or reflective essay on some of the contents of the book with possibly some fresh perspectives on the subject. His own experience extends over several years on the subject of courtyard housing and the concept of high-density, low-rise, energy efficient urban planning. He was United Nations chief architect and planner of the 'Experimental Housing Project' (PREVI) in Lima, Peru – a new neighbourhood of 450 mostly courtyard houses completed in 1974. The shortage of basic data on the subject of the high-density, low-rise concept in general and the courtyard houses in particular, prompted the author to initiate a research base design development program which extended over several years after the completion of PREVI. This program generated a range of fresh data and ideas on lot size and shape, house size and form, clustering patterns, pedestrian and automobile access, densities, passive solar design and energy planning, etc. These experiences have convinced the author of the merit of the courtyard house and its suitability globally for modern use, coordinated with other house types.

## The courtyard: features and functions

The courtyard house possesses several very important and attractive features which are inherent in its concept and shape. The surrounding wall provides security, particularly when built of masonry. The inward looking spatial concept, in contrast to the outward looking Western house, offers family privacy. The enclosed house effectively excludes the noise, dust and urban clamour of the street. The middle court(s) is a space which offers the opportunity for the family surrounding it to create a quiet private area uniquely identified with the family and its culture through architectural design and detailed treatment. The courtyard by its shape, dimensions and environmental systems can positively modify a range of hostile climates to make a space with comfortable optimum conditions. These inherent features and advantages render the courtyard house attractive and adaptable to changing social need.

The courtyard house concept makes it the most common domestic type in Islamic culture. The emphasis on security and privacy, thereby protecting the sanctity of the family unit, is combined with the historical concept of paradise as represented by the walled garden. The unique affinity with these features and tenets of Islam is possibly the central reason why it achieved such an advanced level of development and refinement in the Arab Muslim world. As Islam expanded, the tradition of the courtyard house followed and developed accordingly with the subtle variations that this book describes.

The inner space of the house is essentially screened off from hot or cold winds and thus becomes a climatic 'tabula rasa' to be modulated according to the human and cultural needs and demands of the exterior climate of the locale. Over generations, unique strategies, solutions and devices have evolved; the principles of some of them are summarized as follows. Solar zoning dictates a house layout so that rooms looking into the middle court and surrounding spaces are cool in summer and warm in winter. One tradition is to have a series of rooms and loggias around the court, which enable living functions to move to the most appropriate side according to the solar season. In summer, living would be on the south side, looking north during the hottest months, thus avoiding the high temperature summer sun, in the northern hemisphere. In winter, living functions are relocated to the north side thus receiving full solar exposure for warming in winter. Solar planning principles are modified by wind patterns, social and cultural traditions, which will also influence seasonal movement of family components around the court.

One of the unique features of many courtyard houses is the Iwan. This is a spacious covered setback space, closed on three sides and generally extending up through two storeys.

The Iwan is really a large semi-outside room facing and opening into the middle courtyard. It may be entirely open, partly or completely glazed. Various living functions extend into the Iwan itself from rooms on its two or three closed sides. Generous Islamic courtyard houses may have three, or possibly four Iwans, one on each side of the main courtyard, each with its respective solar orientation. One Iwan is used during a specific solar season of the year. Thus an optimum solar orientation is established for the winter and summer solstices and the equinoxes by the use of a different Iwan. This is a simple and elegant spatial solution which is sometimes ingeniously related to building technology, particularly in large structures. In practice, the design of Iwans according to the solar season is modified by the exploitation of prevailing winds.

Living on different sides of the court according to season (to exclude or receive the sun) is one way of avoiding excessive summer heat gain whilst also being warmed by the sun in winter. Others modifications include interior roof overhangs and wall setbacks, which are just sufficient to exclude the summer sun but not enough to prevent winter sun from accessing spaces and rooms behind. In this practice the overhangs vary on the sides according to orientation. Instead of moving horizontally according to season, in some house types families move to cool semi-basements. This space avoids direct solar radiation and takes advantage of the berming effect of the surrounding earth for the near constant temperature phenomena. Both of these passive solar ideas could be incorporated in modern courtyard house design.

Temperature control by airflow through the rooms of a house, and in some cases combined with evaporative cooling, is highly developed in certain courtyard houses. The main feature in these types is the wind tower. This device intercepts wind currents above roof level, diverting airflow downward through shafts and then horizontally into rooms and spaces at different levels. In some examples, and where relative humidity permits, large unglazed ceramic, water-filled jars are placed within the shaft where air is discharged into a room. Air flowing over the wet surface of the jar drops the air temperature significantly by evaporative cooling as it enters the room, also accelerating the movement of air downwards within the shaft.

This airflow concept varies in configuration from region to region, depending upon climatic factors including humidity, prevailing wind flow patterns and also building materials. Wind interceptors may be at roof level or as towers above the roof. They can take the form of scoops where there is a prevailing wind direction during the summer when cooling is most needed. Where the wind direction varies seasonally or diurnally, some wind towers are ingeniously built to scoop and/or exit wind flow according to the time of day or season from any direction. Towers may have one, two or four shafts according to wind direction and performance required. They are generally constructed of brick or stone but are also found in timber. Masonry towers or scoops have the special advantage of thermal storage. Their walls warm-up during the day from solar radiation, and by warm air descending the tower shaft(s). At night outside temperatures drop but the relative temperature of the shaft masonry remains comparatively high.

Depending upon the number and configuration of shafts in a tower, airflow may thus be reversed and become upward by 'stack effect' thereby purging heat from the spaces and structure in the house below. Several airflow patterns operate in wind towers and scoops. In towers with front and rear shafts, air may be scooped in at the front shaft, descend and enter the house below. Then simultaneously the air can exit the rear shaft by top 'venturi' effect exhausting the air from the rooms of the house below at the same time. The airflow pattern is thus cyclical. It also may combine 'stack effect' and 'venturi', together with scooping action, which depends upon diurnal and seasonal wind patterns. Cyclical airflow pattern may operate during the day or night depending upon solar orientation of masonry wind towers and thermal flywheel effects, scoops and wind patterns.

## Courtyard treatment of the courtyard garden

Screening out or allowing solar radiation access according to season or microclimate modification, especially temperature control, is an important function of the courtyard garden. The climate modifying action and airflow pattern of the classic courtyard house such as the examples in Spain is as follows. Outside air over a house descends and is drawn down by the cool air within the courtyard. Tree shade, and evaporative cooling from water ponds and fountains, cool the new air. Cool air within the volume of the courtyard then moves horizontally into the loggias and rooms surrounding and opening into the courtyard. This basic concept with its many adjustments in dimension and treatment steadily evolved to a peak of considerable perfection and refinement in many cultures, and in particular in the centres of Arabic Muslim culture in Spain.

In addition to its climate-modifying role, the courtyard garden appeals to the senses and its design and plant materials are often based upon philosophical and historically evolved principles as evidenced in courtyard gardens of China and other cultures. Citrus and other fruit trees provide fragrance in courtyard gardens, flowers give scent and bouquet, both give colour and form, and water invites contemplation.

The earlier Persian tradition specifies the parts for a garden. The 'bustan', a garden of fragrances; an orchard of fruit trees and shade with herbs and vegetables. The 'gulistan', a garden of roses and flowers, colour and scent for pleasure. And the 'riyadh', which is the paved area for music and celebration. The courtyard garden may contain fragments of these four components or may possess predominately the character of one.

In some Islamic regions the garden is an important aspect of the courtyard. It can be beautiful and elegant in the simplest and most humble of houses or in the grandest. These gardens have profoundly influenced Western garden tradition. Their influence reached the West initially through first-hand contact with gardens in the Middle East and during the Christian crusades and through the monasteries.

## Distribution and adaptability

The courtyard house is possibly the most enduring and widespread housing type in history. It is found in antiquity and in modern times, in most world regions, in different climates and cultures, and in a range of different building materials. It is found in simple peasant communities, and in highly sophisticated palaces. The courtyard house concept has independently appeared in some regions and in others it has evolved with ideas and typologies migrating with trade, conquest and expansion. It is commonplace in the Mediterranean, but is also found in cold regions such as in Roman towns in north England and continental Europe as well as in Spain.

The special feature of the courtyard house is its adaptability, particularly for different climates and cultures. This is a major reason for its diffusion and migration often over great distances. The most dramatic example is its appearance in the New World, via Iberia. The courtyard house arrived in Spain with the first wave of Arab Muslim conquest from North Africa in about 750 AD. The concept took root and its development began. Later influxes of skilled artisans from Islamic cultural centres added to the progress in Iberia itself. By the end of the thirteenth century the courtyard house had reached a high level of refinement and ingenuity in its environmental adaptation in the main cities of Islamic culture, such as Cordova, Granada, Seville, Toledo and others.

Spanish conquest in the Americas was followed by settlements patterned after Iberian models influenced by Arab Muslim culture. Not well known is that entire new towns were laid out and built in the Americas by the colonisers in virgin territories in various climates. The basic house type of the new towns and cities was the courtyard house. Also, the courtyard form was used extensively for public building complexes, universities, etc. New cities were laid-out according to modified Hippodamus plans, with courtyard houses in the blocks formed by the plan. As South America urbanized, entire new cities with courtyard houses were established. In the wave of colonisation after the conquest, artisans, engineers and architects brought skills and traditions from Spain. From workshops and experience in the New World emerged new generations of builders who made adjustments to the original Iberian model of the courtyard house. In these new vast territories a few outstanding examples are at Popayan and Tunja, Colombia; Lima, Peru; Quito, Ecuador; and La Paz, Bolivia.

The rich tradition of courtyard houses based upon the Iberian model exists in most of the colonial cities of Latin America. Some are in the high altitude cold climate regions of the Altiplano; some are in hot desert and tropical regions. They are built using a range of materials including stone, brick or adobe. These houses reveal their Arabic and Iberian origins in their morphology, gardens, details and ceramic decoration. It should be noted, however, that compact towns of irregular semi-courtyard houses existed earlier in Pre-Columbian civilizations. Equally important is that Peru and Mexico had highly developed courtyard rectilinear planning traditions in their ceremonial and urban centre complexes. An outstanding example is the pre-Inca city of Chan-Chan in north Peru. The existence of such a widespread tradition confirms the universality of the courtyard form up to the twentieth century.

From a historical perspective, the concept of the courtyard house has tended to develop in two ways. The basic form gradually evolved in stationary urban centres and regions, or, it migrated with conquest and expansion, sometimes over great distances. In both cases the form is differentiated by climate and culture. Where the courtyard house tradition has migrated, it often did so in an advanced stage of development with the features of its originating culture.

Strong localized vernacular traditions in form, spatial organization and building methods have produced some of the most varied, unique and interesting courtyard houses and urban complexes. Another important and ancient influence on the evolution of the courtyard house is the idea of paradise as a walled garden. The English word 'paradise' is a simply a transliteration of the ancient Persian word 'pairidaeza', which means a walled garden. The concept and word was encountered by Xenophon, the Greek soldier and historian, when he was in Persia fighting with Greek mercenaries in 401 BC. Paradise is a sophisticated concept and had wide influence. Later it became an integral part of the Islamic house, was brought to a high level of refinement in centres of Islamic culture and ultimately influenced Europe through the monasteries and other contacts. The affinity between the courtyard concept and Islam is not, therefore, unique. It is also highly developed in other civilisations such as Buddhist China. As in some Islamic houses, the Chinese courtyard house places great emphasis on the garden. However, the spatial concept and treatment is different. The Chinese garden is contemplative and 'ordered', with nature arranged to follow strict rules.

## Modern issues, research and projects

Little contemporary design and neighbourhood planning has been done in the Arab Muslim world using the courtyard type. A top priority should be given to systematic research based design development programmes to create prototypes and plans for modern courtyard houses and neighbourhoods. In view of the wide distribution of the courtyard house in history, it would be wise to examine the experience of modern Western architects and planners and their projects in other counties. Plan forms are entirely different for Muslim social needs but the Western experience of modern courtyard housing and planning is still relevant to any review aimed at formulating policy for the contemporary Arab world. A study of the various projects would offer useful information, which is important for courtyard projects in any world region. Of particular interest would be lot size and corresponding built form, pedestrian and vehicular circulation patterns, house layout and clustering, solar orientation and energy planning. These issues have some universality, largely independent of cultural differences.

Though different to historical models, the courtyard house had a special place in the development of modern architecture because of its unique spatial concept. Courtyard houses were designed and some built by well-known architects of the modern movement in the West, and a few were conceived to aggregate into neighbourhoods. A few large-scale urban projects were planned with courtyard houses in the immediate post WWII years but were not realized. Shortly afterwards a number of neighbourhood projects were planned and built in Europe, in new towns in the UK and Denmark, and in the USA. One well-known project of 2,000 houses, built in two stages, is the Seidlung Puchenau in Linz, Austria (1970). A more recent project is the United Nations Experimental Housing Project, PREVI, in Lima, Peru (1974). This new neighbourhood, with facilities of 450 mostly courtyard houses, was sponsored by the Government of Peru and the United Nations. It was planned and built to demonstrate economic and improved new house designs, clustering and building methods. It also demonstrated that the low-rise concept with courtyard houses and compact gardens can achieve high densities and produce a human-scale built environment superior for family life compared with apartments in high-rise structures. Social, economic, planning and technical research was initially carried out in Lima to obtain realistic data on which the design of these houses and neighbourhood was based.

It is recognized that apartments in high-rise structures, large houses and other types will continue to be built, and there is no single solution for housing form or policy. However, a major thrust should be concentrated on a residential and neighbourhood approach which recognizes the merit of the courtyard concept at both the building and urban design level. This means a low-rise, high-density urbanism with off-street parking and houses designed to fully utilize the climate for warming in winter and cooling in summer.

In view of the merit of the courtyard house in history and its potential for contemporary housing and planning in the Arab Muslim world, the scarcity of basic information about the concept should be rectified. Research and design development programmes could be initiated in schools of architecture and planning to produce much needed information with generic studies of plans and clustering suitable for Arab Muslim towns and climates. Up-to-date information would enable local and national authorities to properly integrate this unique concept in a modern form in the national development plans for the built environment.

Development work for the courtyard house should initially focus on plans for a variety of unit forms (as discussed in Chapters 16–19). Different lot sizes and shapes, one, two and three storeys, with and without garages, arranged around north–south and east–west streets should be investigated. Plans must accommodate social customs in a compact way and be based upon passive solar design and self-cooling ventilation principles. Clustering studies should then be done to bring together the different courtyard house types, as well as other housing forms, in an ordered way recognizing the modern and historical solar and ventilation principles of design and planning.

A review of current patterns of contemporary housing shows three types in and around cities in the Arab region: 1) apartment houses; 2) informal settlements; 3) traditional houses for extended families, generally of a modified courtyard house type. These trends appear to be prevalent in provincial areas and larger cities to different degrees. It is difficult, though possible, to insert the traditional features of the courtyard house, such as the compact courtyard and garden, in a multi-level apartment structure (Chapter 17). The difficulties for family life, particularly low-income families, and raising children in apartments disconnected from the ground in tall structures, are well known, especially in the Western experience. Other features, such as automobile parking, solar orientation, through ventilation, environmental quality and human scale, in general present difficulties for the apartment and the high-rise formula. The apartment structure is also energy intensive and generally dependent upon air-conditioning. These features must be considered in the long-term development policies for the region for a time when energy will no longer be cheap. The next generation will certainly live to see the beginning of the end of the petroleum age and cheap energy. An energy efficient urban infrastructure should be put in place now for that eventuality, rather than burden future society with a costly energy inefficient habitat infrastructure.

The courtyard house offers a superior solution on these points but only if high densities are planned for. Low densities in urban development with low- or high-rise will lead to spread-out cities with more automobiles and escalating pollution. A central policy must be to plan compact cities integrated with public transportation systems, as well as bicycling in order to avoid the mistakes of Western urban experience that is evident in the evolution of its cities. Current trends indicate an accelerating expansion of settlements in the region. Urban public transportation favours linear patterns and high-densities, which must be planned for at the outset. In this way automobile use and congestion and pollution can be minimized for the future. Settlements on these lines should be planned in dense neighbourhoods so that residents can conveniently access public transportation for the daily journey to work. It is well known that a major source of pollution in urban areas is from the automobile. To ensure a healthy urban environment, public transportation conveniently accessing neighbourhoods should be a priority.

The problems posed by the special social and climatic requirements of the modern Arab Muslim world could, through design innovation, lead to modern courtyard configurations useful for the future. Such work would then help to formulate housing and planning policies also affecting such areas as density, transportation and energy conservation. In general, the courtyard house permits high densities as the historical examples discussed elsewhere in this book clearly demonstrate. However, courtyard houses in the past were mostly for extended families and many have quite large plots.

In contrast, the nuclear family on one plot permits higher densities, particularly with contemporary design and urbanism. It is therefore important to fully understand current social trends, i.e. family types, extended or nuclear, in order to plan house types and densities for the future. Extended families in small courtyard houses are feasible with careful planning, as is the case with urban courtyard houses in cities like Kyoto in Japan. However, Japanese culture does not possess such strict rules for privacy as in Muslim societies. In South America, traditions often prefer two courtyards, one for the family and one smaller one for service. Visitors entering the house might not pass directly to the family quarters but would be shown into a small room off the entrance, called 'estar'. Undoubtedly this, like much else we take for granted today, has its root in the traditions of the Arabic courtyard house.

# Bibliography

Abdulac, Samir (1982) Traditional housing design in the Arab countries. In M. B. Sevcenko (ed.) *Urban Housing*. Cambridge, MA, Aga Khan Program for Islamic Architecture.

Bagneid, Amr (1989) Indiginous residential courtyards: typology, morphology and Bioclimatics. In *The Courtyard as Dwelling*, Traditional Dwellings and Settlements Working Paper Series, Volume 6, IASTE WP06-89. Berkeley: Center For Environmental Design Research, University of California.

Bianca, S. (2000) *Urban Form in the Arab World, Past and Present*. London, Thames & Hudson.

Blazer, Werner (1985) *Atrium: Five Thousand Years of Open Courtyards*, translated by D. Q. Stephenson. Basel, Wepf & Co.

Brown, G. Z. and DeKay, M. (2001) *Sun, Wind and Light*. New York, John Wiley & Sons.

Clement, Pierre (1982) Courtyard Houses. In *Mimar 3: Architecture in Development*. Singapore, Concept Media Ltd.

Fathy, Hassan (1973) *Architecture for the poor: An experiment in rural Egypt*. Chicago, University of Chicago Press.

Fathy, Hassan (1986) *Natural Energy and Vernacular Architecture*. Chicago, University of Chicago Press.

Gianni, Scudo (1988) Climatic design in the Arab courtyard house. In *Environmental Design: Journal of the Islamic Environmental Design Research Centre*, 1–2; 82–91.

Hanna, R. and Simpson, P. (1996) *The Climate and the Social Climate of a Design Stereotype: The Courtyard Paradigme*. In Traditional Dwellings and Settlements Working Paper Series, Volume 88. Berkeley: Center for Environmental Design Research, University of California.

Hinrichs, Craig (1989) The Courtyard Housing Form as Traditional Dwelling. In *The Courtyard as Dwelling*, Traditional Dwellings and Settlements Working Paper Series, Volume 6, IASTE WP06-89. Berkeley: Center for Environmental Design Research, University of California.

Honold, Renata and Rastorfer, Darl (1983) *Courtyard Houses in Architecture and Community*. New York, Aperture.

Lehrman, J. B. (1980) *Earthly Paradise: Garden and Courtyard in Islam*. London, Thames and Hudson.

Martin, L. and March, L. (1972) *Urban Space and Structures*. Cambridge, Cambridge University Press.

Morris, A. E. G. (1994) *History of Urban Form*. London, Longman Scientific and Technical.

Noor, M. (1986) The function and form of the courtyard house. *Proceedings of the Colloquium held in the University of Newcastle upon Tyne on the Arab House*. University of Newcastle upon Tyne.

Reynolds, J. S. (2002) *Courtyards: Aesthetic, Social, and Thermal Delight*. New York, John Wiley & Sons.

Polyzoides, Stefano, Sherwood, Roger and Tice, James (1992) *Courtyard Housing in Los Angeles*, 2nd ed. Princeton, NJ, Princeton Architectural Press.

Schoenauer, N. (1981) *6000 years of Housing, Volume 2: The Oriental Urban House*. New York, Garland STPM Press.

Talib, K. (1984) *Shelter in Saudi Arabia*. London, Academy Editions.

Warren, John and Fethi, Ihsan (1982) *Traditional Houses in Baghdad*. Horsham, England: Coach Publishing House Ltd.

# Glossary

| | |
|---|---|
| **al-Ablaq** | Layers of white and black stones used in the façades of the courtyard houses of Syria |
| **al-Haramlek** | The women's section in the courtyard house |
| **al-Salamlek** | The guest's section in the courtyard house |
| **Badghir or Badgir** | Wind-catcher |
| **Beyt** | A house |
| **Bedu** | The bedouins |
| **Bidonvilles** | Shanty towns or squatter settlements |
| **Beyt diaf** | Guests' reception room |
| **Bortal** | A covered open space facing the fountain in the Moroccan courtyard house |
| **Dar** | House |
| **Darb** | Alleyway |
| **Darig** | Staircase |
| **Dehliz** | Entrance hall |
| **Dihriz** | Covered gallery on roof space |
| **Diwaniya** | Men's reception area |
| **Driba** | Small alleyway |

| | |
|---|---|
| **Dwiriya** | A small courtyard house annexed to a main house |
| **El Hosh** | The courtyard |
| **Es Sabat** | A volume bridging a street or an alleyway and connecting two houses on both sides of the street |
| **Es Sguifa** | The bent entrance space of the courtyard house |
| **Es Stah** | The accessible flat roof space of a courtyard house |
| **Gurfa** | A room |
| **Halqa** | The courtyard opening at roof space level |
| **Hammam** | An Islamic public bath |
| **Haramlek** | The women's section of the courtyard house |
| **Hawsh** | The courtyard |
| **Hejab** | The Muslim woman's veil |
| **Hoash al-Diwaniyya** | The courtyard of the men's reception area |
| **Hoash al-Matbakh** | The kitchen's courtyard |
| **Hosh** | Courtyard |
| **Hujra** | A room |

| | |
|---|---|
| **Ivan or Iwan** | A covered sitting area that opens onto the courtyard |
| **Kbu** | The central area of the T-shaped room in the courtyard house of Tunis or Algiers (referred to locally as Kbu) |
| **Ksar** | A desert fortress |
| **Ksour** | Plural of Ksar |
| **Liwan** | The covered gallery around the courtyard |
| **Mashrabiyya** | A wooden lattice screen used on widows to provide privacy and reduce glare |
| **Masriya** | A small independent annexe of the courtyard house in Morocco used for guests' overnight stays and usually organised around a small light well |
| **Matbakh** | A kitchen |
| **Medina** | The Islamic city |
| **Mejaz** | A passageway |
| **Mushrabiya** | See Mashrabiyya |
| **Qa'a** | A room |
| **Qibla** | Orientation towards Mecca |
| **Riyadh** | An enclosed garden |
| **Sabat** | See Es Sabat |
| **Salamlik** | Same as al-Salamlek |
| **Sardab** | Basement level in the Iranian or Iraqi courtyard houses |
| **Sguifa** | See Es Sguifa |
| **Shanashil** | Protruding sections from the first floor rooms |
| **Sirdab** | Same as Sardab |
| **Skiffa** | Same as Es Sguifa |
| **Sqifa** | Same as Es Sguifa |
| **Suq** | Market |
| **Taddart** | House |
| **Takhatabush or Takhtboush** | A raised ground floor room in the Iraqi courtyard house |
| **Talar** | A covered sitting space open onto the courtyard |
| **Tarma** | A balcony overlooking the courtyard |
| **Ursi** | The largest room in the Iraqi courtyard house |
| **Wast ad-dar** | The centre of the house, meaning the courtyard |
| **Wast-ed-dar** | Same as Wast ad-dar |
| **Wast dar** | Same as Wast ad-dar |
| **Zellidge** | Ceramic floor tiling in the Moroccan courtyard houses |

# Index

Abed, Al-hamid Abed-Wahed 147
Abu Helal house 10
Achaemenid dynasty 21
Africa see north Africa
Aga Khan Award for Architecture 61
agora 7
al-Ablaq 241
Al-Adhem Palace (Syria) 226
Al-Argoni (Aleppo) 160
al-Azzawi, S. 25, 26, 27
Al-Bukari 80
Al-Farrarien Khan (Aleppo) 158, 160
Al-Fustat (Cairo) 50, 148
al-Haramiek 241
Al-Harthy, S. 118
Al-Hemiddi, N. 165
Al-Mashoka (Granada) 149, 150
Al-Megern, K. 167
Al-Minshiah (Morocco) 154
Al-Nakheel (Ryadh) 208–10
Al-Nouri (Damascus) 160
Al-Oyynaa (Saudi Arabia) 163–70
Al-Saboun Khan (Aleppo) 158, 160
al-salamlek 67, 241
Al-Shahi, A. 65
Aleppo 13, 16, 31, 148
Algeria 58
   Touggourt development 211–16
   see also southern Algerian houses
Algiers 14, 18, 51–3
Almakkiyah House (Jeddah) 206, 207–8
American University of Sharjah see Sharjah campus
Amsterdam 127
Andalusia 5
anderooni 26, 27, 29
apartment buildings 7–8, 58, 59–60, 237
Arab houses see Iranian-Arab houses

Arab-Islamic city 5
architecture
   global/local gap 188
   Hijazi 207
   lessons learned 228
   and loss of the vernacular 188
   and regionalism 174, 184
   and religion 99
   traditional/modern polarity 174, 184, 190–1
Arts and Humanities Research Board (AHRB)
      (UK) 59
Asia Minor 4
Asur Palace (Parthian period) 21
atrium 4
Ayyubid palace 17
Azzawi, S. 65

badghir 24, 26, 88, 241
Baghdad 14, 27
Bahadori, M.N. 135
Bahla 109
Bandini, M. 174
Barwani 116, 119
Bath 123, 124
Bayt al-Badr 86
Bayt al-Ghanim 86
bayt (byt) 9–11, 49–50, 113
Bazzana, Andre 4, 5
Bedouin 174
bedu (nomadic) 113, 114, 241
Beeah Planners, Architects and Engineers 208
Behloul, M. 60
Beit Ajkhabash (Aleppo) 148
Beit Al Shamemeet (Damascus) 158, 159
Beit al-Ghanim 27
Beit Al-Moseli (Damascus) 148
Beit Al-Sibai (Damascus) 148

Beit Al-Suheimi (Cairo) 148, 149, 150, 152
Beit Fakhri Al-Baroudi (Damascus) 158, 159
Beit Ghazaleh (Aleppo) 148, 149, 152
Beit Jabri (Damascus) 148
Beit Mardam-Biek (Damascus) 158, 159
Beit Radwan (Marrakesh) 149, 150
Beit Romia (Damascus) 158, 159
Berlin 127
beyt 241
beyt diaf 241
bhu 55
Bianca, S. 178–9
bidonvilles 58
bioclimatic form
   analysis 140–4
   case studies 136, 138–40
   daylight distribution 140–1, 142–3
   quantitative studies 143–4
   shadow density 140, 142–3
   sky view factor (SVF) 141, 143
   studies on 136
   surface to volume ratio 140, 141–2
   variables 136
   see also climate
birooni 26, 27, 29
Biskra (southern Algeria)
   climate 43–7
   colonial stage 42
   courtyard area 42
   courtyard house design 42
   creation of microclimates 41
   French courtyard 42
   Ksour settlements 40–1
   post-colonial stage 43
   pre-colonial stage 40–1
   self-constructed courtyard 43
   town of 40

Black, J. and Green, A. 106
Blida 14
Bloomsbury (London) 123
Bodiansky, Vladimir 58
Bonta, J.P. 78
*bortal* 57, 241
Bristol 124
Bronze Age 4
Buti, G. 3
Byzantium 13

Cairo 14, 16, 18, 148
Candilis, Georges 58
Caniggia, Gianfranco 14
Carrick, John 125
Casablanca 13, 58
Childe, Gordon 96, 97–8, 100
Chogha Zanbil 21
climate 23–6, 40, 43–7, 78, 130, 205–6, 228,
    230
  case study 158
  creation of microclimates 41
  design factors/guidelines 89, 155–6, 161
  effect on courtyards 135, 136, 155–61
  humidity 157–8
  insolation 156–7
  in Oman 116
  wind/air in motion 57
  *see also* bioclimatic form
coastal house 174–5
colonial developments
  north Africa 58
  southern Algeria 42–3
  Touggourt 214–15
Colquhoun, A. 174
commercial buildings 6–7, 18
cosmology *see* Sumerian, cosmology
courtyard
  access to inner 81
  bioclimatic form 135–44
  as central feature 50, 56
  deconstructed 109–20
  and environmental/social control 219
  as evocation of Garden of Eden 3
  functions of 22
  importance of 3
  openings to inner 81
  as poduct of cultural polygenesis 3–4
  as private space 42
  and role of landscaping 218
  size of 126, 127–8
  solutions to 78
  traditional 220
  types of 203
  urban density/building form link 219
  and ventilation/sunlight 127

courtyard house
  as act of enclosure/construction 3
  adaptation for future development 187
  alternatives to current practice 192–3
  appeal of the vernacular 184–5
  background 233
  as best performing urban type 136
  as centre 217
  and climate/social life symbiosis 13, 220–1,
      222–3
  commercialization of residential space 6–7
  common characteristics of experimental types 200
  and control of domestic environment 231
  cosmological genesis of 95–106, 228
  and cultural identity 225, 228
  and culture 14
  density issues 200–1, 238
  depth of 4
  development of 49
  differences in 4
  dispersal of 12
  distribution/adaptability 235–6
  energy use 230
  environmental/social interface 223–4
  experimental types 193–9
  exterior/attached 4–5
  and family life 4, 220
  features/functions 233–5
  function/symbol relationship 228
  generic similarity 4
  historical background 155
  holistic element 228
  interior/block-like 4–5
  internal/external link 211, 214–16
  inward looking spatial concept 234
  lack of external openings 4
  language problem 225
  light-source 4
  metamorphosis of 13–14
  misconceptions concerning 5
  modern issues, research, projects 236–8
  Muslim influence 13
  and notion of continuity 173–85
  reasons for disappearance of 217
  recommendations 201
  and reinforcement of social patterns 231
  and sense of enclosure 217–18
  serial/organic 17–18
  spatial organization of 65
  sub-division of 8–9
  as sustainable 222
  traditional model 174–5, 207
  transformation of 214–15
  as universal archetype 12–17
  validity of 222–3
  as vibrant/relevant 231

Cresswell, K.A.C. 17
cultural dimension *see* sociocultural dimension
Cunningham, W.A. and Thompson, T.L. 165
Curtis, W. 184

Damascus 14, 148, 158, 188
*dar* 17, 56, 241
*Dar El Msafer* 59
*Dar Sfar* 50
darb 241
Dardir palace 17
*darig* (staircase) 112, 241
David, J.C. 16
Davidson, C.C. and Serageldin, I. 218
*dehliz* 29, 241
design/decoration
  behavioural issues 77
  building materials 89–90
  and climate 89
  effect of privacy on 77
  selective/exclusive distinction 224
  and sharing of principles 227
  tiles 53, 55, 56, 208
  twisted columns 53
  water 57
*dihriz* (covered galleres) 112, 241
*diwaniya* 85, 90, 241
*dolan* 67
*domus* 4, 9, 13, 15, 17, 18
*dra* 10
*driba* 51, 241
Drieu, J. 58
*dwiriya* 55, 241

Edinburgh 123, 124
Edwards, B. 125, 127
Egyptian house 16–17
Egyptian-Sumerian civilization 4
Eickelman, Christie 119
El Hajja (Rabat, Morocco) 60
*El hosh* (courtyard) 212, 241
El-Habous (Casablanca) 58
Eldem, Sadat 16
*Es sabat* (covered space) 212–13, 241
*Es Sguifa* (bent entrance) 51, 213, 241
*Es stah* (terrace roof) 213, 241
Ettadhamen (Tunis) 60

family 4, 80–1, 82, 178–9, 220
  multi-family dwellings 190, 192
  single-family dwellings 188–92
fasha 17
Fathy, H. 13, 135, 164, 173
Fatimid-era houses 16
Fez 4, 9, 14, 53–6, 59, 148
Firuz Abad Fire Place 21

forum 7
Fustat 13, 16

Gabriel, A. 16
*ga'iza* 11
garden city model 129, 143–4
gardens 206, 218, 227
  aesthetic/social relationship 147
  axial 150
  case studies 149
  Chinese 236
  concept of 147
  general characteristics 149–54
  geometric lines 149
  overlapping of functions 152
  and paradise theory 147–8, 234
  peculiarity in landscaping methods 152–4
  plants 152
  size 151
  symmetry/balance 150
  treatment of 235
  water 151, 152–4
gender 26–7, 65
  accessibility/movement 72–3
  benefits of double courtyard 85
  control of space 74–5
  importance of women in domestic sphere
    119–20
  integrated/segregated areas 69–71
  and Islamic teaching 79
  in Omani house 109, 114, 118–19
  and patriarchy 8, 13
  and perimeter blocks 123
  privacy issues/needs 65, 79, 87, 90, 128–9, 131,
    205, 207
  and relationship between spaces 73–5
  and ritualised living 119
  and space configuration 67–8
  and urban zoning 124, 128
General Housing Foundation (Syria) 189
*ghanam* (domesticated animals) 113
Ghazvin region 21
Ghodar, A. 21
Giannini, Alessandro 7
Giedion, S. 96, 99, 102, 103
Givoni, B. 165
Glasgow 124, 125–30
Golvin, L. 51
Gottlieb, L.D. 78–9
Gregotti, Vittorio 3
gurfa 241

Hadith 91, 92
*hadr* (sedentary) 114
Hafsia (Tunis) 61
Hakmi, M. 188, 190

*halqa* 11, 241
*hammam* (latrine) 112, 241
Hanson, J. 65
*haram* (the sacred) 113
*Haramlek* 34–5, 241
  architectural elements 35–6
  building materials/construction techniques
    37–8
  climatic factors 36
  courtyard organization 36
  economic factors 36–7
  social factors 38
Hariri, M. 204
Harvey Court (Cambridge university) 136
*hashti* 29
Haussmann, G.E. 124
*hawsh* 17, 112, 241
*hejab* 79, 241
Helwan University (Saudi Arabia) 229
Hillier, B.
  *et al.* 65, 71
  and Hanson, J. 65
hoash 241
*Hoash al-Diwan-Khana* 27
*Hoash al-Diwaniyya* 26–7, 241
*Hoash al-Haram* 27
*Hoash al-Matbakh* 27, 241
*Hoash al-Tola* 27
Homs 188
house-cum-mosque 83
Howard, Ebenezer 138
hujra 241

Ibadhism 109, 120(n2)
Iberian model 235–6
Indus Valley 4
*insula* 7–8, 15, 18
Intercontinental Hotel (Makkah) 230
Iranian-Arab houses
  access 28–9
  access to 22
  architectural-climatic patterns 23–6
  background 21–3
  basements 25–6
  bent entrances 28–9
  boundaries in 22
  circulation/cooling in 22
  cultural-religious patterns 26–8
  functions of courtyard 22
  gender segregation/privacy 26–7
  organization of 22–3
  similarities in terminology 21
Iraq 22, 24
Istanbul 14
Italica (Spain) 4
ivan (iwan) 242

*iwan* 15–16, 33–4, 67
*iwanchas* 67

Jami Fahraj Mosque 21
Japan 238
Jawf prototype 111–13, 119
Jeddah 207–8
Jencks, C. 188
Jilin (China) 4

*ka'a julush* (covered women's room) 109
*kabishkans* 68, 70
*kafshakan* 67
Kahn, L. 230
*kama* 10
Kasbah (Algiers) 51–3
*Kasbet* 41
*kbu* 50, 242
*khalil* (grain store) 112
Khan Madresseh (Shiraz) 21
Khitan project (Kuwait) 188
Koleini, M. 26
Kramer, S.N. 96, 100–1, 104, 105
*ksar* 40–1, 242
*ksour* settlements 40–1, 242
Kuwait 24, 27
Kuwait houses
  background 83
  building materials 89–90
  characteristics of 84–9
  and climate 89
  common features 88–9
  design influences 89–92
  double-courtyard 85–6
  gender issues 85, 87
  neighbour issues 91–2
  plan of 84
  privacy issues 87, 90–1
  seafront 86–8
  single-storey norm 87–8
  size of 84
  town 88
  water features 84–5
Kyriakopoulos, J. 58

Laoust, E. 14
Laprade, Albert 58
Latakia 188
Le Corbusier 58, 216
Lebanese house 15–16
Lebanon 14, 18
Levant 14
Lewcock, R. 89
  and Freeth, Z. 27
*liwan* 15–16, 84, 174, 242
London 123, 124, 125

low-income informal houses 60
Lycett, W. 187

Madrasat al-Qu'ran 119
*madrash* (Quranic school) 119
the Maghreb 5, 8, 13, 14
Maher, I. 152
*majlis* 27, 29
*makhzen* (storage cells) 111
Malek-i Shahmirzadi 21
Mamluk dar 17
Manah 109, 111, 114
Manhattan 136
Mänty, J. 135, 142, 144
Manzil Zaynab hatun 17
maq'ad 17
Mare Nostrum 14
Maretto, Paolo 14
Markus, T.A. 125
Marrakesh 140, 148
Martin, L. and March, L. 136, 138–9, 140
Marylebone (London) 125
mashrabiyya 17, 242
Masjid al-Bostan 119
*masriya* 55, 242
*matbakh* (kitchen) 112, 242
Mecca 24
Medea 14
medinas 242
   comparisons 56–8
   development of 49
   Fez 53–6
   Kasbah of Algiers 51–3
   Tunis 49–50
Mediterranean 4, 13, 14
*mejaz* 67, 70, 242
mercantile house 15
Mesopotamia 95
Middle Ages 7
Milan 13
Military Housing Foundation (Syria) 189
monofamilial buildings 5–8
Morocco 154
Morris, A.E.J. 102, 136
multi-family dwellings 190
   courtyard house as basic unit of 192
   design difficulties 192
   solutions 192
Muratori, Saverio 14
mushrabiya 242
*Mushrabiya* 35

na-mahram 26
Nash, John 125
neighbours 91–2
Nizwa 109

nomadic tent 220
Noor, M. 61, 65, 89
North Africa 13
   comparison of houses in 56–8
   French colonisation/protectorate 58
   in historic centres 58–60
   low-income informal 60
   medinas 49–58
   persistence of traditional space use patterns 60
   present trends 61
Nuo Mosque (Shiraz) 21

*oda* 16
Oke, T.R. 135, 141
Olgyay, V. 24
Oman
   administrative regions 109, 120(n1)
   and *bedu/hadr* 114–15
   coastal dwellings 109, 113
   dual spatial order in 114–15
   environmental viewpoint 115–16
   functioning of the dwelling 115–16, 118–20
   gender issues 109, 114, 118–19
   house as vital aspect of 113
   and idea of fatherland 113
   importance of women in 119–20
   irrigation in 115, 120(n17, n19)
   Jawf prototype 111–13
   and location of kitchen/latrines 112–13, 114
   and patriarchy 113
   rituals in 119
   social viewpoint 118–20
   spatial organisation in 109, 113–14, 120(n3)
   as unique 109, 111
*osk* 16
Oslo 140
Ostia Antica (Rome) 7
*otagh orsi* 24, 25
Ottoman Empire 14, 17, 148

Padania (Po Valley) 13
Paris 124, 127
*pastas* house 4
*pastoo* 24
pavilions 135, 136, 138–40
   analysis of 140–4
Peabody Trust 125
Pearlmutter, D. 143
Perez-de-Lama, J. and Cabeza, J.M. 144
perimeter block
   advantages of 125
   based on tenements 125
   dimensional dictates of 125–7
   evolution of 123–4
   formalisation of 123
   gender needs 131

and glass-roofed courtyard block 129–30
   importance of the street 124–5
   Middle Eastern/European parallels 123, 130–2
   and needs of women/children 128–9
   privacy issues 128–9
   and public health/town planning imperatives 124
   room-layout 129
   ventilation, sunlight, health issues 126–8
   as working class housing 125–8
Peru 237
Petherbridge, Guy 4, 5
Plan de Constantine 58
Popper, Karl 96, 224–5
*portego* 15
privacy 26, 42, 215, 231, 238
   and access to courtyard 81, 82
   architectural identity 78
   background 77
   behavioural factors 78, 82
   and climate 82
   concern for 65
   family 80–1, 82
   gender issues 26–7, 65, 79, 87, 90, 205, 207
   and guests 91
   guidelines 90–1
   influence on design 77
   and layout 81
   openings to inner courtyard 81
   in Saudi architecture 77, 78–9

qa'a 17, 242
Qasr Al-Azem (Damascus) 148, 149, 152
Qasr Al-Hambra (Granada) 149, 150, 151, 152
Qavam-al-Molk 25
qibla 242
Quairawan 148
*qufi* 11
Qu'ran 26, 36, 79, 80, 90, 91, 92, 106, 148

*rab* 17
Ragette, F. 15
Rapoport, A. 143, 174
Rawda Island 17
Reed, P. 129
religion 26–8, 97, 226–7
   and architecture 99
   and writing 99
Revault, Jacques 53, 55
*Riyadh* 56, 242
Rogers, E. 175
Roman Empire 13
Rosenlund, H. *et al* 144
row-house 4, 13, 18
*rozna* 43
rural buildings

insula process 7–8
orientation/access 5
residence/annexes 5
*taberna* process 6–7
transitions/transformations 5–9
Ryadh 205–6

*sabat* 9, 242
Safavid period 27
salamlik *see* al-salamlek
Saleh, M.L. 148
Samarra 16
Santelli, S. 60
*sardab* (*sirdab*) 25, 26, 242
Sarvistan Palace 21
Sasanid society 114
Saudi Arabia 22, 24, 77, 78–9, 81
   and continued appropriateness of courtyard
      203–4
   modern courtyard house in Ryadh 205–6
   neo-traditional in Jeddah 207–8
   revival of courtyard in contemporary project
      208–10
   traditional way of life in 203
   types of courtyard 203
Sayyidat al-Mulik palace 16
Scanlon, G.T. 16
Schoenauer, N. 67
Seidlung Puchenau (Linz, Austria) 237
self-built housing 43
Semper, Gottfried 3
Senoussi House (Algeria) 214
*sguifa see Es Sguifa* (intermediary space)
*shamsiya* (light well) 109
shanashil 242
Shannon, C. and Weaver, W. 67
Sharjah campus (UAE) 174
   climate considerations 181, 184
   courtyard houses in 175–84
   design strategy 176, 180
   dimensions 175–6
   façades 180–1
   public reception areas 178
   residential/familial areas 178–9
   and use of geometry 180
   use of pre-cast decorative panels 175
*shenashil* 67
Shiraz 24, 25, 27
single-family dwellings 188–90
   design types/alternatives for 191
   urban design consequences 191–2
*sirdab see sardab* (*sirdab*)
*skiffa see Es Sguifa*
sociocultural dimension 14, 18, 40, 77
   adaptation to new 216
   behavioural factors 78

impact of changes 216–17
and objective knowledge 224–5, 227
and sharing of design principles 227
southern Algeria 39
and transformation of courtyard use 214–15
and Western lifestyles 214
Sohari 114
southern Algerian houses
   background 39
   Biskra 40–6
   climatic factors 40
   colonial stage 42
   cultural factors 40
   post-colonial stage 43
   social factors 39
space syntax 65–7
   accessibility/movement 72–3
   analysis/findings 69–75
   case studies 67–8
   configuration 66
   consistency 67
   functions of space 70–2
   genotype 66, 67
   integration 66–7
   justified graph 66
   location of specific areas 73–4
   social logic 67
   techniques 66
   theory of 66
Spain 14, 235–6
Spanioli House (Algeria) 214
Spence, Basil 223
*sqifa see Es Sguifa* (intermediary space)
*squero* 15
Steemers, K. and Ratti, C. 140
structural organization
   access 28–9, 42, 56
   and airflow concept 234–5
   balconies 10
   basement 25–6, 31–2
   bent entrance 65, 67
   ceiling 11
   combination house-warehouse 15
   door 10
   gallery on pillars/columns 10, 11–12
   gender segregation 9, 26–7
   house/garden relationship 56
   light 10
   loggias 109
   masonry-timber-masonry construction 9, 10, 12
   modular rooms 9
   orientation of building 24–5, 41, 55, 230
   patio 9–10
   peripheral cells 10
   portico (*portego*) 15
   secondary rooms 9

and solar zoning 234, 237
stairs 9
terrace 9
territorial zoning 27
tripartite layout 15, 16
two-storey with patio 9
and use of plaster of lime/sand 10
use of roof space 53, 57, 58
width/functionality 10
Sukhte building (Tepe Hesar, Damghan) 21
Sumerians 95
   and animals 104–5
   and architecture 99
   bird decoration 104
   building construction rites 106
   cosmology of 96, 100–2, 106
   houses of 102–3
   inventions of 98
   real/spiritual link 978
   religion of 99
   sacred aspects of courtyard house 104–6
   and snakes 105
   and space conception 103–4
   and system of writing 98, 99
   temples of 102
   and trees 105–6
suq 242
Susa palace (Dario) 21
Syria 18, 161, 189
Syrian houses
   access 32
   background 31
   façades of internal courtyard 32
   *Haramlek* 34–5
   inside/outside transition 32
   *iwan* 33–4
   landscaping 32
   organization of 31–2

*taberna* 6–7, 18
*taddart* 14, 242
*tahal* 9
*takhatabush* 67, 242
*talar* 23, 24, 26, 67, 242
Talib, K. 136
tarma 242
*tarma* 24, 67
*tej* 12
temples 102, 103–4
thermal performance
   at Al-Oyynaa 163–70
   background 164
   cooling tower 165–6
   data analysis 167–9
   monitoring apparatus 166–7
   monitoring plan 167

thermal performance (*continued*)
  objectives 164
  related studies 164–5
  research study 163
  study facility 165
Thomson, Alexander 'Greek' 129–30
Tipasa 14
Tlemcen 148
Touggourt
  background 211–12
  contemporary houses 215–16
  French colonization era 214–15
  historic urban core 212–13
  sociocultural effects 214, 216–17
  transformation of space in 214–15
Tripoli 14
Tunis 49–50
*turi* 11
Turkey 14, 18
Turkish house 16

Umayyads 13

United Arab Emirates (UAE) 173
United Nations Experimental Housing Project
  (PREVI) (Lima, Peru) 237
Unwin, Raymond 138
urban planning 123–4, 200, 222
  environmentally optimal configuration 144
  and front/rear building facades 124–5
  and gendering of space 124, 128
  remodelling/expansion of 124
  streets 124–5, 136, 215
  tenement blocks 125
  and terraced buildings 125
*ursi* 67, 68, 69–71, 72, 74, 242

Venetian house 15
Venice 14, 18

Walker, F. 124
*waqf* 16
Warren, J. and Fethi, I. 65, 67, 70
*wast ad-dar* 10, 13, 242
*wast dar* 43, 242

*wast ed dar* 50, 242
water 207, 218
  in gardens 151, 152–4
Waziry, H. 148
Westin, A.F. 78
Wilkinson, J.C. 115
Winter, I.J. 103, 104
Wood, John 123
Woods, Shadrach 58
Woolley, Sir Leonard 96, 102
Wren, Sir Christopher 124

Xenophon 236

Yazd 25–6, 27
Youngson, A.J. 124

Zandi, D. 179
Zehrfuss, B.H. 58
*zellidge* 55, 242
ziggurats 103